THE ATLAS OF HOLY PLACES & SACRED SITES

THE ATLAS OF HOLY PLACES & SACRED SITES

COLIN WILSON

A DK PUBLISHING BOOK

PROJECT EDITOR
PETER JONES

ART EDITOR
MARK JOHNSON DAVIES

ASSISTANT EDITOR
DAVID WILLIAMS

US EDITOR
CONSTANCE M. ROBINSON

DESIGN ASSISTANT
JO LONG

DTP DESIGNER
ZIRRINIA AUSTIN

MANAGING ART EDITOR
TRACY TIMSON

MANAGING EDITOR
GWEN EDMONDS

DEPUTY ART DIRECTOR
TINA VAUGHAN

SENIOR MANAGING EDITOR
SEAN MOORE

CARTOGRAPHERS
JOHN PLUMER, DAVID ROBERTS,
DALE BUCKTON

PRODUCTION
SARAH COLTMAN

PICTURE RESEARCH
CHRISTINE RISTA

First American Edition, 1996
2 4 6 8 10 9 7 5 3 1

Published in the United States by
DK Publishing, Inc.,
95 Madison Avenue,
New York, New York 10016

First published in 1996 by Dorling Kindersley Limited,
9 Henrietta Street, London WC2E 8PS

Library of Congress Cataloging-in-Publication Data

Wilson, Colin, 1931-
The atlas of sacred sites and holy places / by Colin Wilson. -- 1st American ed.
p.   cm.
Includes index.
ISBN 0-7894-1051-6
1. Sacred space--Guidebooks. 2. Shrines--Guidebooks. I. Title.
BL580.W55 1996   96-5632
291.3'5'09--dc20   CIP

Reproduced in Singapore by Colourscan.
Printed in Italy by Mondadori.

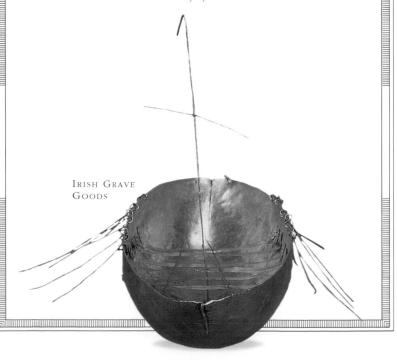

IRISH GRAVE
GOODS

CONTENTS

INTRODUCTION 6-9

MECCA AT NIGHT

JAPANESE INCENSE BURNER

NORTH AMERICAN
GRAVE FIGURE

INTRODUCTION

HUMANS DIFFER FROM all other animals in one peculiar respect: for some reason no one has ever been able to explain, they have always been religious animals. Materialist philosophers of the 19th century tried to explain away this religious urge as superstition: they claimed that early humans did not understand the thunder and lightning so they decided that they were gods. But anyone who takes a long look at the religions and belief systems of the world – as I have done during the year that I have been compiling this book – will soon come to recognize that there has to

VENUS FIGURINE

be more to it than that. Most animals are perfectly content if they find food, drink, and shelter. Humans are the only animals who are driven by an obscure need to *change themselves*. Too much "happiness" makes them rather bored.

Dr. Johnson wrote a novel called *Rasselas*, about a group of people who live in a Happy Valley where nature provides them with everything they need. Yet the young Prince Rasselas is fretful and dissatisfied, and muses: "Surely there is some sixth sense, or some faculty apart from sense that must be satisfied before we can become happy." This sixth sense, this desire to change and evolve, seems to be fundamental to all human beings, regardless of intelligence. It has all the urgency of a biological compulsion, like the caterpillar's biological need to change into a chrysalis, before its final transformation into a butterfly.

And as far back as we are able to look into history, human beings seem to have worshipped nature, and connected it to a higher spiritual reality, which they call God or the Divine. Study of "nature religions" like Shinto make it clear that this is not because they were afraid of natural foes, but because they felt a deep kinship with the earth. The earliest religion of which we can find traces in history is a cult of the Mother Goddess.

THE GREAT CHALLENGE

What is the alternative to the materialist view of religion as the "great illusion"? Humans have been on earth for at least three and a half million years – the estimated age of the human remains known as "Lucy," found at Hadar in Ethiopia. Yet a mere half a million years ago, the human brain doubled its size at such a rate that scientists call it "the brain explosion." No one knows why. According to Darwin, there should have been some great

MOUNT FUJI

challenge that forced our ancestors to make a huge effort, or some marvelous stimulus, like the invention of tools. Neither of these seems to have occurred. In 1929, in a cave at Choukoutien, near Peking, paleontologists discovered bones of a remote human ancestor, Peking Man, who used fire and enjoyed roasting venison. But they also found 40 human skulls that had been opened to extract the brain. Modern cannibals believe that eating the brains of an enemy endows a warrior with an enemy's strength and intelligence. If Peking Man indulged in ritual cannibalism, then he had some form of religion. And it is impossible to imagine religious ritual without some kind of verbal communication. I would suggest that "the brain explosion" was due to the development of language. And language would seem to be deeply involved with the human religious sense. One hundred thousand years ago, Neanderthals buried their dead with religious rituals involving flowers; they also carved round, flat stones suggesting sun worship. They mined red ocher, carefully resealing the mine, to propitiate its spirits. Clearly this apelike creature believed in life after death as much as the modern humans who built Newgrange in Ireland 5,000 years ago.

THE BOND WITH THE EARTH

I would suggest that the belief in life after death and in the world of spirits is the common denominator of all religions. And the priest or shaman is the person who, by passing through a series of ordeals, has succeeded in becoming an intermediary between the material and spirit worlds. The first actual evidence of shamanism comes from the cave paintings of our immediate ancestors, Cro-Magnon Man, who appeared on earth about 50,000 years ago. It was at first believed that these were the product of an artistic impulse, but it gradually became clear that their purpose was "magical" – to bring success to the hunters of bison and reindeer. Anyone inclined to dismiss this as quaint superstition should first read the account of the "calling of the porpoises" in Sir Arthur Grimble's classic autobiography *Pattern of Islands*, or of the hunting rituals of the Amahuaca people of Brazil in Bruce Lamb's *Wizard of the*

Upper Amazon. Grimble's "porpoise caller" of the Gilbert Islands entered a dream state that somehow caused dozens of porpoises to swim ashore and beach themselves. Such works make us aware that in many senses civilized human beings have lost that close bond with nature that still exists among more primitive peoples. Anthropologists like Joseph Campbell and Mircia Eliade have expressed astonishment at the fact that shamanistic beliefs and practices all over the world are virtually identical, among people who cannot possibly have had any cultural contact with one another.

AN EARLIER CIVILIZATION

Where the ancient religions of Central and South America are concerned there seems to be a more disturbing common denominator. When the Spaniards landed in Mexico in 1519, they were appalled at the tradition of human sacrifice – the Aztecs sacrificed hundreds, sometimes thousands, of prisoners. These sacrifices were intended as messengers to the spirit world, to persuade the gods not to involve the earth in some awful geological cataclysm. For the ancient Americans believed that humanity had been wiped out on previous occasions. This legend of cataclysm can be discovered all over Central and South America, as can another legend about a tall, bearded white god, sometimes called Viracocha, sometimes Quetzalcoatl, sometimes Kon Tiki, Votan,

PERUVIAN KNIFE

or Kukulcan, who came after the last great catastrophe and taught the arts of civilization. Professor Alexander Tollman of the University of Vienna has suggested that this catastrophe may be explained by evidence of the impact of a comet, whose fragments struck the earth 12,000 years ago and caused tremendous floods and earthquakes. In the 1930s, a maverick Egyptologist, Schwaller de Lubicz, asserted that the Sphinx was several thousand years older than originally had been thought, a view recently echoed by Boston geologist Robert Schloch (see pp.14-15).

ANCIENT ORIGINS

All of which raises the possibility that civilization may be far, far older than we assume. And this controversial conclusion would, in fact, fit in with the theme of this introduction, which is that the religious sense has played a vital part in human evolution. Modern humans have a sense of separateness; an individual can feel totally alone in a city with a million inhabitants. Yet there is good reason to assume that primitive people possessed a kind of "collective consciousness" of the kind that allows a flock of birds to wheel and change direction simultaneously. This assumption is supported by the existence of human telepathic skills and the ability of some preliterate people to sense the unseen – for example, the presence of underground water beneath their feet. According to Darwin, evolution is basically

"accidental," depending on how well a creature can adapt to its environment. Civilization consists of a lot of individuals coming together for both security and convenience. Certain individuals stumble on important discoveries – the steam engine, the telephone – and the rest of us benefit from the "accident." We cannot conceive of a society in which, in spite of differences between individuals, there is not a kind of basic unity, so they are like owners of a family business, each of whom contributes something. We can see that a closely knit family can "evolve" in a way that is impossible for a family whose members each go their own way. I would suggest that societies of early humans were more like a family business than modern society, and that there should therefore be nothing intrinsically surprising in the notion that a reasonably organized civilization may have developed 10,000 or so years earlier than we – with our Darwinian model – assume.

It was Auguste Comte who, in the early 19th century, suggested that religion is a prescientific attempt to understand the universe. This is simply a failure to grasp something basic about the human relationship to nature; that when the Chinese or Japanese describe a mountain as sacred, they are not simply projecting superstitions onto it, but are aware of it as a living being, embodying a "telluric force." The Chinese believe that lines of sacred force – called *feng shui* – run across the countryside. In Europe, *feng shui* has been revived in the concept of "ley lines," sacred paths, known to Stone Age humans. Ancient sacred sites often remain sacred; for example, many Christian churches have been built on the site of pagan temples.

Over 40 years ago, my first book, *The Outsider*, and its sequel, *Religion and the Rebel*, were devoted to the proposition that there is a profound truth in the religious view of the human being as an imperfect and incomplete creature struggling for "salvation" and completion. All my work since has been a development of this idea. As I wrote this book, studying every kind of religious site from barrows and sacred groves to cathedrals and mosques, again and again I have experienced the conviction that religion expresses a basic truth about humans and the universe. I have never ceased to believe that people are on the point of an evolutionary leap to a higher stage, and that this leap will involve the faculty that we call imagination, but which is actually a kind of "reality function" – an attempt to reach out and touch the reality of other times and places – of "other realities." For me, every cathedral and mosque, every temple and sacred mountain, has come to symbolize this possibility.

Colin Wilson

COLIN WILSON

THE SACRED ROCK, JERUSALEM

PART ONE

THE HOLY PLACES & SACRED SITES

THE WORLD'S GREATEST RELIGIOUS sites have one thing in common: they inspire awe in those who look upon them. Humanity's first religions seem to have involved worship of nature, particularly mountains, and when man began to create religious buildings – like the pyramids of Giza or Mexico – they often resembled mountains. Ggantija, one of the earliest temples on Malta, was originally called Gigantija. Later temples contain blocks of stone so gigantic that we have no idea how they were lifted. Religion has inspired some of the most breathtaking art and architecture. It has also inspired some of the greatest human effort. Let anyone who feels they lack the religious faculty try to imagine the labor that went into the building of Stonehenge or Angkor Wat, and they will feel something akin to religious awe.

THE POTALA PALACE, LHASA

Traditional home of the Dalai Lama, the majestic Potala Palace (left) dominates the religious center of Lhasa in Tibet. In the foreground are prayer flags, on which the faithful write their troubles. They believe that as the wind blows the flags, so their problems are blown away. The practice originated in Chinese and Indian folklore, and has become common among Tibetan Buddhists.

AFRICA & THE MIDDLE EAST

AFRICA AND THE MIDDLE EAST have both been great centers of human religious development. Two major forms of religion now dominate Africa: the world religions of Islam and Christianity and the indigenous religions of the African people themselves. The former are seen in the mosque at Jenne, and in the Christian churches at Lalibela in Ethiopia. Christianity exists in many forms, from the Coptic Church of Egypt to the various congregations of South Africa. Indigenous forms of worship also vary enormously, from animism – worship of nature and natural objects – to ancestor worship. When misfortunes occur, devotees turn to a priest or religious specialist to find out if they have offended the ancestor spirit. Yet they would feel that there is something incongruous in building a church or temple to spirits, for nature itself is such a temple – in this sense, the whole of Africa is a religious site. This may also explain why there are relatively few religious buildings in Africa.

While the indigenous belief systems of Africa have only recently begun to be known outside the continent, the development of religion in the Middle East has been amply documented. When the worship of the gods and god-kings came to Egypt and the Middle East, religion entered its second great phase; monuments of this period – such as Luxor and Palmyra – are still among the most impressive in the world. Monotheism, in the forms of Judaism, Christianity, and Islam, has come to dominate the history of the Middle East and, from there, the history of the African peoples as well.

ALGER

COPTIC WALL-HANGING
The name Coptic means Egyptian in Arabic; it describes a sect of early Egyptian Christians. This was one of the earliest Christian communities in the world; its art was based on Graeco-Roman styles.

MAURITANIA   NIGER

MALI

⑭ BANDIAGARA
⑮

⑮ JENNE
The largest mud-brick building in the world, the Friday Mosque at Jenne was built in an age when Mali was as legendary for its wealth as El Dorado.

EGYPTIAN HARP
This Egyptian five-stringed harp was intended to provide the dead with music in the underworld, where Egyptians expected life to go on much as usual, with feasting and merrymaking. The head of the pharaoh on the harp indicates that it was used at court. Such harps could vary in size, some being as tall as the player – often a girl, who held it against her body as she played.

N

ATLANTIC OCEAN

BLACK SEA

TURKMENISTAN

①① SANTA SOPHIA
Built by the Roman emperor Justinian, Santa Sophia was once the largest church in the world.

③ NINEVEH
A city whose name caused terror in the ancient world, Nineveh became a synonym for barbaric splendor.

② EPHESUS   **④ PALMYRA**   **③**

AFGHANISTAN

MEDITERRANEAN SEA

⑦ JERUSALEM
The city of Jerusalem is sacred to Jews, Muslims, and Christians.

⑤ BABYLON
Home of the famous Hanging Gardens, Babylon was once the center of a vast empire.

⑤

PAKISTAN

NILE FAN

⑦

⑨

⑧⑧ PETRA
Petra was once one of the most powerful cities in the Middle East.

⑥⑥ UR
The reputed birthplace of Abraham and capital of Sumer, Ur was one of the earliest religious centers in the world.

⑨ GIZA
The famous pyramids at Giza, near modern Cairo, were allegedly positioned according to astronomical alignments.

⑩⑩ LUXOR & DENDERA
These southern Egyptian sites show the diversity of Egyptian culture.

RIVER NILE

EGYPT

SAUDI ARABIA

ARABIAN SEA

OSIRIS
The Egyptian god of the dead and fertility was chief of the nine gods. His royal crook and flail scepter show that he was also lord of the underworld.

⑪

⑪ MECCA
Built around the sacred Black Stone, Mecca is a center of the Islamic faith and the greatest pilgrimage site in the world.

⑫ AXUM

GULF OF ADEN

⑬

AFRICA

⑬ LALIBELA
No one knows how the eleven Christian churches of Lalibela in Ethiopia were hewn out of solid rock.

DEAD SEA SCROLLS JAR
Discovered in 1947 in a cave at Qumra'n, the scrolls were apparently the work of the Essenes, a monastic Jewish sect. The scrolls contain startling parallels with New Testament Gospels.

LAKE TURKANA

LAKE MAPUTO

KENYA

LAKE EDWARD

LAKE KIVU

LAKE VICTORIA

ZAIRE

LAKE TANGANYIKA

ZAMBIA

ZIMBABWE

⑯⑯ GREAT ZIMBABWE
The ruined citadel of Great Zimbabwe was once believed to be the Queen of Sheba's gold mine.

INDIAN OCEAN

MADAGASCAR

THE ORIGINS OF THE SPHINX

Archaeologists believe that the Sphinx was built in about 2500 B.C. by the pharaoh Khafra, son (or brother) of the Fourth-Dynasty pharaoh Khufu. But when geologist Robert Schoch and the Egyptologist John Anthony West examined it in 1990, Schloch concluded it had been weathered by rainfall, not by wind and sand. If rain had worn the rock, the date might be closer to 7000 B.C.

GIZA
THE PYRAMIDS & THE SPHINX

——— GAZETTEER P.133 - SITES NOS.7 & 9 ———

THE LARGEST SINGLE building ever constructed, the Great Pyramid at Giza was built during the era known as the Old Period (c. 2575– 2130 B.C.). The Greek historian Herodotus visited Giza in about 450 B.C. and was told by priests that the Great Pyramid had been built by the Fourth-Dynasty pharaoh Khufu (Cheops). They said it took 400,000 men 20 years to build, working in three-month shifts of 100,000 men each. It weighs six million tons, the weight of all Europe's cathedrals put together. Its foundation was a hill made of rock. According to Herodotus, the base was laid, then the great blocks – each weighing on average seven tons – were levered into place, a step at a time up all 203 steps. In fact it cannot be done, as the Japanese found when they tried to build a duplicate of the Great Pyramid in the 1980s.

THE MYSTERY OF THE SPHINX

The Sphinx was originally no more than a piece of hard rock that stuck up above the surrounding limestone plateau. At some point, a head, possibly a lion's, was carved into it. Later, when it was decided to carve the lion's body, the limestone was cut from around the Sphinx in 200-ton blocks – we know this because the blocks were then used to build the temple in front of the Sphinx. But we do not know why the builders chose such heavy and enormous blocks when they could have cut them down to a reasonable size. Nor do we know how they moved them. When the maverick Egyptologist R. A. Schwaller de Lubicz

visited Giza in the 1930s, he immediately declared that the Sphinx had been weathered by water, not by wind. Schwaller proposed that the Sphinx had been worn by seawater and that its origins lay in the ocean. He also suggested that the Sphinx was far older than its accepted date of about 2500 B.C.

The current date for the beginnings of Egyptian civilization – about 3000 B.C. – means that the Egyptians developed their sophisticated science, mathematics, and building skills in a mere 500 years, while Europe took three times as long to learn to build its cathedrals. He proposed that Egyptian knowledge was not a new development, but a legacy from a far older civilization, possibly Plato's "Atlantis."

GLOBAL PROPORTIONS OF THE PYRAMIDS

The Greek grammarian Agatharchides was told that the total length of the Great Pyramid's base was a precise fraction of the earth's circumference, and that the ratio of the pyramid's height to its base perimeter was the same as that of the earth's radius to its circumference.

Pyramid of Menkaura (Mycerinus)

The smaller pyramids were the burial place of royal courtiers

THE PYRAMIDS

Among the most fascinating features at Giza are the four vents in the north and south faces of the King's Chamber of the Great Pyramid, and the two vents in the Queen's Chamber beneath it. Belgian engineer Robert Bauval calculated that in 2500 B.C., the southern "air vent" of the King's Chamber would have pointed directly at Orion. When he found that the southern shaft of the Queen's Chamber would have pointed directly at the star Sirius – the star sacred to Osiris's consort Isis – it confirmed his belief that the pyramids were astronomically aligned.

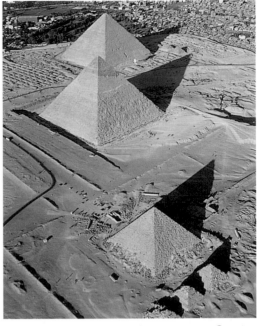

THE BELT OF ORION

The constellation of Orion was sacred to the ancient Egyptians as the home of Osiris – they even thought the hourglass shape of Orion looked like the god. When Robert Bauval noticed that the odd arrangement of the three pyramids of Giza was exactly the same as that of the three stars of the Belt of Orion, he theorized that Giza was intended as Osiris's home on earth, and the Nile a "reflection" of the Milky Way.

THE BELT OF ORION

AERIAL VIEW OF THE PYRAMIDS AT GIZA

THE STEP PYRAMID
The earliest pyramid – the Step Pyramid at Saqqara – was built in about 2650 B.C. by the pharaoh Snofru. Its architect Imhotep, later deified, was identified with the Greek god of medicine Asclepius.

HEAVENLY PROJECTILE

Bauval theorized that the airshaft of the King's Chamber was intended as a channel to direct the dead pharaoh's soul to Orion, where he would become a god. In other words, the ritual ceremony to release the pharaoh's soul from his body would take place when the shaft was targeted on Orion like a gun barrel, and the pharaoh's soul would fly there like a fired missile.

If the pyramids reflected the stars of Orion's Belt, then they must have all been planned at the same time. But when? A phenomenon called "precession of the equinoxes," due to the slight "wobble" on the earth's axis, means that over the course of thousands of years (almost 26 millennia), the stars in the sky appear to go up and then down again. Since the constellation moves as if it were attached to the hourhand of a clock (so its angle changes), it follows that the pyramids on the ground will not normally mirror the stars in Orion's Belt. The only time it did so exactly was in 10,500 B.C., and Bauval suggests this as the date when the pyramids were planned and the Sphinx was built.

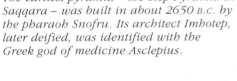

Pyramid of Khafra (Chefren)

The pyramids were once covered with white limestone

The Great Pyramid of Khufu (Cheops)

LUXOR
THE GREAT TEMPLE OF AMUN
GAZETTEER P.133 · SITE NO.20

THE TEMPLE OF LUXOR, like the nearby Temple of Karnak, lies in the town of Thebes in southern Egypt. In about 2160 B.C., as the Egyptians conquered surrounding territories, such as Nubia, Ethiopia, and Libya, Thebes replaced Memphis as the capital of the empire. Vast temples and palaces were erected on a colossal scale to impress the conquered peoples. What remains of the Temple of Luxor today has been called one of the world's greatest open-air museums. The temple was dedicated to Amun, a fertility deity who later became king of the gods. It was built mainly by two pharaohs, Amenhotep III (1391–53 B.C.) and Rameses II (1290–24 B.C.), although Tutankhamen and Alexander the Great later added to it. It is 853 ft (260 m) long and fronted by no fewer than six huge statues of Rameses II. The temple is regarded by many as the most important site in Egypt; it is certainly among the most beautiful.

RITUALS THROUGH TIME
Luxor has always been a site of religious activity. The Abu el-Haggag Mosque in the courtyard was built on the site of what may have been a Byzantine church. The ritual boat procession held during the annual Islamic feast here echoes Amun's yearly journey from Karnak to Luxor.

ENTRANCE TO THE TEMPLE
Flanking the entrance, the (79-ft-) (24-m-) high pylons (the flanking walls of the temple gates) show scenes of Rameses II defeating Hittites and nomadic Bedouins during the Battle of Kadesh in Syria. The colossus on the right was cracked in an earthquake.

This obelisk was one of a pair; the other is in Paris

These huge statues of the pharaoh Rameses II flank the entrance

EGYPTIAN TEMPLES

Egyptian temples were not places of worship for all; apart from the priests, few people were admitted to the inner sanctum. The temples were sites of sacred mysteries, where pharaohs and priests established contact with the gods. At Thebes, it has been suggested that the mysteries were mainly sexual in nature, for the Egyptian creation myth stated that the universe was created by an act of masturbation. The temple was dedicated to Amun in his form as a fertility god, depicted with an erect sexual organ.

During the annual Nile flood, the statue of Amun would be taken by boat up the Nile from Karnak to Luxor in a ritual celebration of the union with his wife Mut, the divine mother. The two temples were connected by a ceremonial walkway of sphinxes. Only the last 656 ft (200 m) remain, the rest covered by the modern town.

Beyond the entrance lies the court of Rameses II, which has a striding statue of the pharaoh in its northeast corner. The Grand Colonnade leads to the Forecourt of Amenhotep III that lies in front of the main temple; here the pharaoh performed his secret ritual in its innermost sanctuary. One of the temple's halls was later reused for a Roman cult.

The Temple of Luxor is, in many ways, the most mysterious of Egyptian sites. For centuries, no one could explain why it was built in a curve, as if the plan had been changed halfway through construction. When hermetic scholar René Schwaller de Lubicz visited Luxor in 1937, the beauty and harmony of the temple convinced him that its shape was no accident; he concluded that it was built on no fewer than three axes based on the plan of the human body – a "Temple of Man." Its very intricate mathematics reveal how the Egyptians used a science of proportion to recreate the body of Amun so as literally to worship from within it.

THE FORECOURT OF AMENHOTEP III
An open court surrounded by columns, the forecourt corresponds to the human trunk, from chest to genitals. The 32 columns of the adjoining Hypostyle Hall represent the lungs. Temples based on the human body are found all over the world.

ABYDOS
THE TEMPLE OF SETY I & THE OSIREION
GAZETTEER P.133 · SITE NO.16

THE SACRED CITY of Abydos is Egypt's greatest funerary site, in use as early as 3100 B.C. Dedicated to Osiris, god of the underworld, the temple of the 19th-Dynasty pharaoh Sety I (1305–1290 B.C.) is one of the best preserved temples in Egypt. His son Rameses II, who built a temple here, is believed by many to be the pharaoh mentioned in the Bible who drove the Israelites into the desert.

Just as remarkable is the strange temple called the Osireion – once thought of as the tomb of Osiris, who was much revered here. There had been rumors of another temple near that of Sety I, but it was not until the end of the 19th century that Margaret Murray cleared the sand to discover a temple below. It was excavated in 1912 by Professor Naville. Built of huge "Cyclopean blocks," it was similar to the temple in front of the Sphinx at Giza (see pp.14-15). Naville was certain that it dated from the same period – at the time, the Sphinx was thought to be older than the pyramids – and that it could be the oldest building in Egypt.

However, the next excavator, Henri Frankfort, found Sety's name, as well as an outside passage constructed by the pharaoh. He thought Sety I built the entire temple. Others think it is a cenotaph, or honorary mortuary.

John Anthony West argues that the Sphinx could have been built as early as 10,500 B.C. The "Cyclopean blocks" of the Sphinx Temple and the Osireion do seem to hint that the builders belonged to a different – and perhaps far earlier – culture. It cannot be ruled out that Sety I found the Osireion buried under the sand, and added to it – a practice by no means unknown to the later pharaohs.

Most of the underground temple is closed due to flooding. When excavated, it proved to be below the watertable, rather apt for a temple dedicated to the god of the underworld.

THE TABLE OF ABYDOS
At the heart of the Temple of Sety I, reliefs show the pharaoh and his son making offerings to their 76 predecessors. With its ideas of a divine monarchy, the cult of Osiris ensured the stability and continuity of the dynasties.

OSIRIS, KING OF THE DEAD
Abydos became an important pilgrimage site: to be buried near the tomb of Osiris increased chances of immortality. This god was also the giver of life from the underworld, causing vegetation to sprout during the Nile floods.

DENDERA
THE TEMPLE OF THE GODDESS HATHOR
GAZETTEER P.133 · SITE NO.17

THE END OF AN ERA
Dendera is a remarkable picture gallery. The priests of this decadent age tried to preserve their ancient knowledge. Many figures and rituals are found in relief: pictures of Roman emperors can be found alongside pharaohs and Egyptian deities.

BUILT UNDER ROMAN OCCUPATION, the impressive Temple of Hathor at Dendera is of a late date – 30 B.C. to A.D. 14 – and has been the subject of heated discussion. Dedicated to Hathor, the sky and fertility goddess, wife of the god Horus, it stands alone on the edge of the desert between Luxor and Abydos. Archaeological evidence reveals that it was built on the site of a former temple whose date has caused controversy. One of the chapels on the roof of the temple dedicated to Osiris contains a sundial and a circular zodiac that consists of two circles of constellations roughly superimposed. One is centered on the geographical north pole, the other on the true north pole. The zodiac, now a copy (the original is in the Louvre), has an axis passing through Pisces, showing that it was built, as we know, in the age of Pisces just over 2,000 years ago. But two hieroglyphs on the edge of the zodiac suggest that another axis passed through the beginning of the age of

Taurus, over 4,000 years earlier, and 1,000 years before the advent of dynastic Egypt. It raises the possibility that the original temple may have been built in the bleak, colossal style of the Osireion at Abydos. The huge blocks of stone spanning the architraves suggest that the Temple of Hathor may indeed have followed the style of the earlier building. The temple, with its mysteries, certainly evokes the style of earlier dynastic tombs.

THE SISTRUM OF HATHOR
This rattle was used by priestesses during rituals. Its stem depicts the head of the goddess Hathor, who was also the goddess of love, beauty, and healing. Recent research has revealed that Dendera was once a healing center, an ancient Egyptian equivalent of Lourdes.

LALIBELA
ROCK-CUT CHURCHES & THE STELAE OF AXUM
GAZETTEER P.132 · SITES NOS. 39 & 41

ALTHOUGH ETHIOPIA lacks the romantic associations of ancient Egypt, it can trace its history almost as far back into antiquity. In fact, the Pharaonic Egyptians believed that some of their gods had come from Ethiopia, which they knew as "the land of Punt." But since the fourth century A.D., the religious history of Ethiopia has been bound up with Christianity. Knowledge of Christianity spread into Ethiopia from different directions: on contact with the Egyptian Coptic Church, and from Syria and Palestine through trade with the Axumite Empire. Ethiopia became Christian at about the same time as the Roman Empire, but for a long time its development remained almost entirely separate. Missionaries later "rediscovered" Ethiopian Christianity in the 19th century, and were amazed by different local interpretations of the faith. The strength of this faith is nowhere more clearly shown than in the 11 churches of Lalibela cut from the solid rock of the landscape. The vast scale of these projects reveals that their belief was as all-absorbing as the faith that led to the building of the Sphinx and the pyramids.

SIDE VIEW OF ST. GEORGE'S
A casual glance at this red rock cruciform church fails to convey to the viewer just how amazing it is – more than 40 ft (12 m) high, it is carved from a single piece of rock.

THE AXUMITE EMPIRE

Ethiopia remains one of the world's Christian strongholds. The town of Axum was once the capital of a large empire. By the sixth century it was the most important power between the Roman Empire and Persia.

Christianity came to Axum around A.D. 320, when two Syrians, Frumentius and Aedesius, were seized by pirates and taken to Axum. Its ruler, King Ella Amida, made one his treasurer and the other cupbearer. When the king died, they stayed on to help the queen, who acted as regent for her son. Frumentius did his best to convert Ethiopia to Christianity, and succeeded in converting its new king Ezana, who declared the rest of the country Christian. Frumentius was created First Bishop by the Coptic patriarch Athanasius of Alexandria in A.D. 331.

Ezana pushed the boundaries of his country west, into what is now Sudan, and east across the Red Sea into modern Saudi Arabia and Yemen. It continued to flourish until Persians invaded in A.D. 582 and the Arabs 30 or so years later, taking the eastern part of the empire. Although Axum declined, it remained the most powerful Christian enclave in north Africa.

THE CHURCH OF ST. GEORGE, LALIBELA
The building of the Church of St. George dates to the 13th–14th century A.D., several hundred years after Christianity first reached Ethiopia. This remarkable structure is still a place of active worship for Ethiopian Christians.

THE ROCK-CUT CHURCHES

The small town of Lalibela now forms one of Africa's most potent pilgrimage sites. The town – originally called Roha – was renamed after the 12th-century king credited with the construction of the town's 11 extraordinary rock-hewn churches. These churches are cut into the rock-face, almost like caves, and their passages wind back into the hills themselves. The most remarkable examples, however, are the four free-standing churches carved below

CHURCH OF ST. GABRIEL
St. Gabriel's Church or Beit Gabriel, surrounded by a 36-ft (11-m) trench, is one of four churches cut into the same hill. Mostly hidden from view, the churches burrow deep into the rock-face, connected by an elaborate system of passages and tunnels leading to secret crypts and grottoes.

ground level. In each case a single block of granite would have had to be isolated within a steep-sided courtyard cut into the ground. Features of the interior and exterior were hewn from the solid rock. The churches can be seen as both great works of religious sculpture and architecture. The carving of the nave, for example, is an astonishing work of craftsmanship.

Even builders armed with modern pneumatic drills would find the creation of these churches an overwhelming task, so it is difficult to conceive how 12th-century masons armed with hammers and chisels succeeded. Ethiopian legend declares that they were built by angels; historians speculate that Indians or Egyptian Copts may have been hired; the truth is that they were probably created by Christian monks. Writer Graham Hancock relates how inside the Church of St. Mary's he was shown a rock-hewn pillar at the entrance to the Holy of Holies, wrapped in a spiral of very old cloth, and told by the priest that Lalibela himself had engraved on it the secret of how the churches were made. The priest was horrified when Hancock asked to see it, declaring that this would be sacrilege.

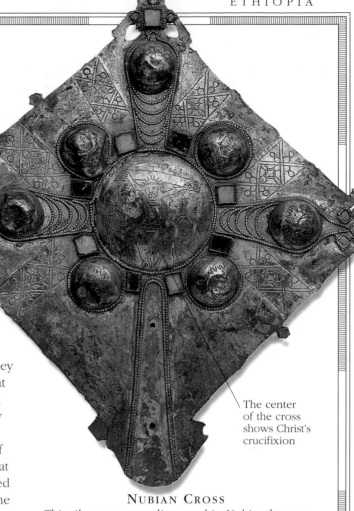

The center of the cross shows Christ's crucifixion

NUBIAN CROSS
This silver cross was discovered in Nubia, the area that covered parts of Egypt and modern Sudan. The profusion of Christian artifacts in northeast Africa shows how the whole area became Christian through influences from across the Mediterranean.

THE STELAE OF AXUM

Axum is famous for its giant stelae, often wrongly called obelisks. The tallest now standing upright is 70 ft (21 m) high, and its granite faces were carved to represent cross beams, floor levels, and doors and windows. The features of the stelae are characteristic of a type of "timber and mud" architecture still seen in some villages in the Tigre Highlands. Obviously, this and some of the other "obelisks" are supposed to represent buildings – virtually skyscrapers. The largest stela lies shattered across the ground. The stelae probably predate the Christian era in Axum, and their significance may be associated with an earlier religion. Some writers have speculated that they represent funerary monuments. The town of Axum has existed since the first millennium B.C. and was a major early center for traders in ivory and incense; this is how the kingdom absorbed many of its later Christian influences. The second largest of the stelae was taken by the Italians during Mussolini's occupation and removed to Rome where it now stands near the Arch of Constantine.

THE TRAIL OF THE LOST ARK

Ethiopia's greatest Christian mystery concerns the ancient Hebrew Tabot, the Ark of the Covenant. Guardian monks believe that it lies in the cathedral at Axum erected by Emperor Haile Selassie in the early 1960s. Ethiopian Christians claim that the Ark enabled earlier kings to raise the great stelae at Axum.

In 1982, Graham Hancock set out to establish how the Ark of the Covenant had travelled from Jerusalem, 1,200 mi (1,930 km) to the north, to the southern end of the Red Sea. Biblical sources convinced him that the Ark vanished from Jerusalem between 687 and 642 B.C. Learning that there had been a Jewish temple on the island of Elephantine in the upper Nile, he discovered that the temple (now destroyed) had been in the exact form of Solomon's Temple, convincing him that he had found the Ark's first major staging post. The Jews had left Elephantine due to a clash with the Egyptians, who worshipped a ram-headed deity, and objected to the Hebrew sacrifice of rams. From there, Hancock traced the route of the Ark to the island of Tana Kirkos in Lake Tana, and from there to Axum.

GREAT ZIMBABWE
THE "VENERATED HOUSES" OF SOUTHERN AFRICA

THE HILL RUIN
Lying a quarter of a mile (400 m) to the north of the Great Enclosure, the Hill Ruin belongs to the oldest phase of Great Zimbabwe's history. It contains the Eastern Enclosure. This was the chief sanctuary where circular stone platforms held monoliths, some surmounted by stone birds.

THE ANCIENT RUINS OF ZIMBABWE are without doubt the most impressive ancient structure in southern and central Africa. Indeed, when the site was "rediscovered" in the 19th century, European explorers assumed that the walls had been built by Greeks or Phoenicians, so skillful was their construction. They were convinced that Africans would be incapable of building such an impressive structure. The earliest settlement here dates to the fourth century, but the chief period of occupation was between the tenth and 15th centuries, when the site became both a major religious and trade center. It went into decline after the mid-15th century, when the chief moved north toward the Zambezi River. The major feature of the site is the elliptical Great Enclosure, a massive structure with walls over 20 ft (6 m) thick. Since the chief who reigned here was a semidivine ruler, the building served as both the royal palace and Great Zimbabwe's temple. Among all the southern kingdoms of Africa the ancestral spirits of chiefs were believed to give legitimacy to the leaders who followed, and at Great Zimbabwe the chief himself would intercede with these most powerful of spirits.

WHAT WAS ZIMBABWE?

Great Zimbabwe probably always served as a religious center. The traditions of local peoples emphasize the religious nature played by the founders of their tribes, and Great Zimbabwe plays a central role in almost all these traditions. But Great Zimbabwe was also a great trade center for the surrounding area. Much of the architecture at Great Zimbabwe, however, suggests a religious purpose; the stone towers, monoliths, altars, and the concentration of soapstone figures in the Eastern Enclosure of the Hill Ruin (see left, above) all point to this end. It is difficult for modern archaeologists to establish for certain what form this religion took, and to what extent Great Zimbabwe's importance depended on its role as a trade center and what on its role as a spiritual center, for local traditions have mythologized much of its original function and practice. During Great Zimbabwe's decline as a trading center, the site seems to have been increasingly identified with *Mwari*, the chief god of the region, and the ancestors of the surrounding peoples.

THE MAIN COMPLEX
In the foreground (left) stand the remains of stone enclosures; these surrounded mud buildings where the majority of Great Zimbabwe's population lived. Behind, to the right, stands the Great Enclosure, where the paramount chief lived and where the later religious center was probably located.

THE EERIE CORRIDOR
The walls of Great Zimbabwe with their close-fitting granite blocks were built without foundations or cement. The outer wall of the Great Enclosure contains about 182,000 cu ft (5,154 cu m) of stone, the largest prehistoric structure in sub-Saharan Africa.

ZIMBABWEAN SOCIETY

There are many other ruined enclosures scattered over the modern state of Zimbabwe – more than 150 of them in all. The site of Great Zimbabwe has played an important symbolic role in the formation of the new nation, as is shown by the adoption of the name in the modern state. It is proof of a rich historical tradition distinct from foreign involvement. The Shona word "zimbabwe" means stone houses, but can also refer to "venerated houses."

The area covered by the "zimbabwe" developed into a huge trading empire covering over 1,000 sq mi (2,500 sq km). There is evidence at Great Zimbabwe of extensive trade with distant civilizations. Pieces of Ming Dynasty (1368–1644) pottery from China have been found at the site. Copper, bronze, and gold were also mined here, and it is this material wealth that may have led to the site's eventual destruction. After its discovery in the 1870s, European adventurers continued to exploit Great Zimbabwe, pouring in like the '49ers in California. Richard Hall, a Bulawayo journalist who explored the site and wrote *Great Zimbabwe* (1905), made money from "treasure," such as gold wire and beads. The graves on Zimbabwe Hill, many of them containing gold objects, had mostly been looted before the 20th century.

RELIGIOUS TRADITIONS

Great Zimbabwe remained a ritual site into the 19th century; indeed, as its political and economic importance declined, it returned to its original function as a religious center. In the tradition of the Shona people, the site seems to have been connected with rainmaking, propitiating the gods to ensure plentiful rain and abundant crops. The chief god of the religion was *Mwari*, the creator. The Mbire, an early group of the Shona people, are believed to have introduced worship of *Mwari* and the cults of *mhondoro*, spirits associated with the ruling dynasties. The Torwa people, who ruled the area around Great Zimbabwe, are said to have supported flourishing *mhondoro* cults. The Eastern Enclosure was closely associated with the cult of Chamunika, one of the most important *mhondoro* spirits.

Mbire tradition tells how a shortage of salt led the leader of the Mbire to conquer peoples in the surrounding area. As a result of his success, the chief was called Mwene Mutapa, or "Master Pillager." This chief and his successor established a large kingdom. In theory, the Mwene Mutapa held absolute power, though his actions were limited by the traditions of his people. He was regarded as semidivine and the welfare of the group was seen to depend on his health. His religious importance lay in his role as an intermediary between his people and *Mwari* and the *mhondoros*. The kingdom of Mwene Mutapa gave way to the Rozwi kingdom, which maintained the reverence of the ruler, who acted as an intermediary with *Mwari*. The Rozwi seem to have continued to regard Great Zimbabwe as a site of ritual importance.

THE MYSTERY OF THE CONICAL TOWER
One of the major mysteries of Great Zimbabwe is the 33-ft- (10-m-) high conical tower (above). No one has succeeded in getting inside it, and it is believed by many to be solid. The tower is approached through a long dark corridor between high walls (see right, above).

RITUAL FIGURES
Sacred birds and anthropomorphic figures, perhaps symbols of dead chiefs or representing clans, were found carved in soapstone at Great Zimbabwe. They stand on top of columns about 3¼ ft (1 m) high. They were mostly found in the Eastern Enclosure (see opposite), and the concentration of these figures in one place has led most commentators to suppose that the Eastern Enclosure was a kind of temple, and that the figures may have had some religious purpose. They may have represented the dead, for part of Shona ritual involves appeasing the spirits of ancestors to ensure prosperity.

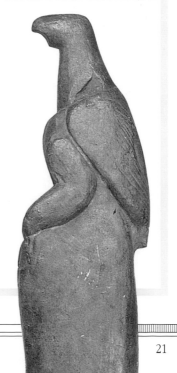

BANDIAGARA
SITES OF THE DOGON

GAZETTEER P.132 - SITE NO.28

DOGON "PO" GRANARY
The Dogon eat a grain that they call po. *It is stored in "holy" granaries and they say the grain represents a tiny star, called* po tolo (tolo *means star), which is important to their rituals.*

THE DOGON PEOPLE of the highlands and mountains of southern Mali live by agriculture. A population of a quarter of a million people inhabit 700 villages built in pairs along the 124-mi (200-km) Bandiagara Plateau. Most of the villages are an extended family unit. Each district has a spiritual leader known as the *Hogon*, and the *Hogon* of Arou is the spiritual head of the whole country. The climax of Dogon religious life comes every 60 years in a ceremony called the *Sigui*, a ritualized version of the creation myth; this is approximately the same as both the average human lifespan and the orbital cycle of the companion star of Sirius. Incredibly, the Dogon have been aware for centuries that Sirius has an invisible companion. However, the existence of this double star system did not become known to Western astronomers until 1862.

KNOWLEDGE OF THE DOGON

In 1931, two French anthropologists, Marcel Griaule and Germaine Dieterlen, went to Mali to study the Dogon people. By 1946, the Dogon trusted them sufficiently to agree to initiate Griaule into the secrets of the *Sigui*. This is a spectacular ceremony that takes place every 60 years and explains the creation of the world and human beings by one god, Amma. It is celebrated over a period of eight years, representing the eight ancestors who the Dogon believe descended from the sky.

The Dogon knew that the star Sirius has an invisible companion that moves in an elliptical orbit around Sirius every 50 years (which is correct); they call it *po tolo*, naming it after the seed that forms the staple part of their diet (botanically *Digitaria*). When they drew the elliptical orbit of Sirius for Griaule, they showed it off-center, not in the middle. Their knowledge of the solar system was also remarkable; they told the anthropologists that the Moon was dry and dead, knew the planets revolved around the Sun, drew Saturn with a ring around it, and were aware of the moons of Jupiter.

They also declared that *po tolo* is made of matter far heavier than the earth. In fact, Sirius B is a white dwarf – a very dense collapsed star. It was only in 1928, three years before Griaule and Dieterlen arrived in Mali, that Sir Arthur Eddington had postulated the theory of white dwarfs. The Dogon people's extraordinary knowledge of astronomy still remains difficult to explain.

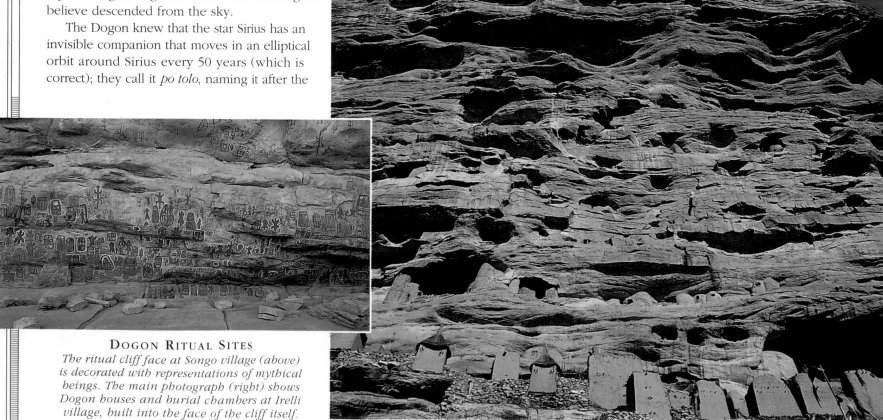

DOGON RITUAL SITES
The ritual cliff face at Songo village (above) is decorated with representations of mythical beings. The main photograph (right) shows Dogon houses and burial chambers at Irelli village, built into the face of the cliff itself.

JENNE MOSQUE
THE LARGEST DRIED-EARTH BUILDING IN THE WORLD

GAZETTEER P.132 - SITE NO.27

TOWERS OF THE MOSQUE

At the top of each of the mosque's 36-ft (11-m) towers is an ostrich egg, a symbol of creation and life. Eggs are often found in Africa in mosques, temples, and some churches.

EARTH BUILDING

The name Mali was once a synonym for wealth. The country lies between the jungles of the south and the deserts of the north, and was on one of the main caravan routes that transported gum, ivory, ostrich feathers, gold, and slaves. The original town of Jenne, Old Jenne or Jenne-Jeno, lies about 1 mi (1.5 km) upstream from the current town. This settlement had flourished since 250 B.C.; around A.D. 1400, the site was abandoned in favor of the new city. The reason for this move is not clear, although it is believed that it came about because its Muslim rulers felt that it was a center for paganism, and decided to move. (For some time, the two belief systems of local religions and Islam existed in parallel.) The building of the first Friday Mosque at Jenne was one consequence of this move.

The two great cultural centers of Jenne and Timbuktu became famous throughout the civilized world through a pilgrimage to Mecca undertaken by the emperor Mansa Musa (died around A.D. 1332) in the 17th year of his reign. The procession that carried him there was so magnificent that it is probably the most famous in Africa's history. The fame of Mali's wealth – spread abroad by Musa's pilgrimage – led others to look at the center with greedy eyes. In the 1460s, the powerful King Sonni 'Ali of Songhay, who came from lands to the east of Mali, plundered Timbuktu, then spent seven years besieging Jenne, which fell in 1467. As sea routes eventually replaced the caravan routes, landlocked Mali began its long decline.

JENNE (DJENNE) IS A LEGEND; to walk through its streets, with their mud-brick houses, is virtually to travel back in time to the days of trans-Saharan caravans from Morocco and Algeria to Ghana. Now a relatively minor agricultural trade center, Jenne, together with Timbuktu, once formed one of the greatest centers of trade, learning, and religion in West Africa. The caravans that traveled south across the Sahara also brought Islam, and in about 1300, the kings of Mali became Muslims. Friday is the day Muslims pray together, and so the mosque at Jenne is known as the Friday Mosque. Originally constructed some time in the early 14th century, the mosque is still the largest mud-brick building in the world. The structure was rebuilt in the 20th century. Jenne Mosque is a perfect example of how a site can remain sacred despite changes in the buildings that stand upon it.

THE FRIDAY MOSQUE

The ruins of the Friday Mosque dominated the city for many years. First built in the 14th century, it was destroyed and rebuilt by Shayki Ahmadu in the 1830s. The present building was built in 1905. The ancient Songhay royal palace is said to have stood on the same site.

The mosques of West Africa, like that at Jenne and the Friday Mosque at Mopti, are built with the only local material available in quantity, mud. The wooden beams that stick out of the side walls act as reinforcement to the mud bricks. Each year, heavy rains wash away part of the structure and during the dry season the mosque is rebuilt. It is a remarkable achievement then, that Jenne's Friday Mosque is the largest dried-mud building in the world.

THE CHURCH OF THE HOLY SEPULCHRE
It was Emperor Constantine's mother, Helena, who allegedly discovered the tomb of Christ on the site of a Roman temple to Aphrodite. Her son built the Church of the Holy Sepulchre over the tomb, today Christianity's most sacred spot.

JERUSALEM
THE HOLY CITY

GAZETTEER P.134 · SITE NO.13

FOR ONE AND A HALF THOUSAND bloody years Jerusalem, the "Holy City," has been the scene of murderous struggles as three religions – Judaism, Christianity, and Islam – have battled for possession. The city has been captured 11 times and destroyed on five occasions. Anyone who wanted to see the old Jerusalem would have to dig down through about 69 ft (21 m) of the debris of history. For Jews, the city is the location of their most holy site and the ancient capital of the Jewish state. Christians revere Jerusalem as the site of Christ's crucifixion and triumphant resurrection. For Muslims, it is the site of Muhammad's "night journey" and the third most sacred shrine of Islam. Jerusalem probably has more shrines than any other city in the world. Some have indisputable provenance, such as the Monastery of the Cross. Others, such as the Church of St. Anne, built on the site of the house of the parents of the Virgin Mary, are a matter of pious hope rather than historical evidence.

CHRISTIAN HOLY SITES

Since the time of Christ's crucifixion, Jerusalem has expanded, so that the Mount of Olives, the Hill of Golgotha, and the Holy Sepulchre all now lie within the city. The Holy Sepulchre is the rock cave where, according to tradition, Christ was buried and rose from the dead. The crusaders built a larger church and complex of buildings covering nearby holy sites, including what was believed to be Golgotha, the site of the crucifixion. The "Angel's Chapel" under the dome in the Church of the Holy Sepulchre contains the stone that the angel is said to have rolled away from the entrance to the tomb.

The route along which Jesus carried his cross has moved position several times (the actual street is now deep underground). The present Via Dolorosa, a narrow alley with overhead arches that looks like a market, has signs indicating the 14 stations of the cross.

As the most holy Christian site, Jerusalem is a center for many different denominations (the Church of the Holy Sepulchre is controlled by no fewer than six). The Garden of Gethsemane, at the foot of the Mount of Olives, the place of Christ's prayers before his crucifixion, is kept – by order of the Pope – by Franciscan monks.

VIEW FROM THE MOUNT OF OLIVES
The Old City of Jerusalem: in the foreground is the Russian Orthodox Convent Church of St. Mary Magdalene, built in 1885 near the Garden of Gethsemane, site of Christ's Agony before his arrest. In the midground stands the Dome of the Rock, third most holy site in Islam.

THE TEMPLE MOUNT

King David captured Jerusalem in about 1000 B.C., uniting the northern tribes of Israel and the southern tribe of Judah and making the city the capital of this united kingdom of the 12 tribes of Israel. The First Temple was built on the Temple Mount, the natural acropolis outside the city, by David's son and successor, Solomon. The Temple contained the Ark of the Covenant (God's contract with man) and formed a part of a larger administrative complex. After Solomon's death, the tribes of Israel split again and Jerusalem returned to being the capital for the tribe of Judah. When the Assyrians destroyed the northern kingdom 200 years later, it became a center for northern refugees and once again the chief center for Israelite religious life. Jerusalem escaped the Assyrian threat, but the Temple was destroyed by the Babylonians in 598 B.C.

The Temple was rebuilt by Herod, himself a member of the Jewish faith, who was appointed King of Judea by the Romans in 31 B.C. During the following 36 years he rebuilt the city of Jerusalem. A part of the supporting wall of the Temple Mount from Herod's Second Temple today forms Judaism's most sacred shrine. The Western or Wailing Wall was officially recognized by the state as a sacred Jewish site at the beginning of the Ottoman period (16th century A.D.).

Today the Temple Mount is dominated by the Dome of the Rock, the shrine containing the rock that is sacred to both Jewish and Muslim faiths (see below). According to one Jewish tradition, this is where the world was first created, while, according to another, it is where Abraham was asked to sacrifice his son.

THE WAILING WALL

The Wailing Wall was the only section of the Temple left standing by the Roman Titus, who destroyed Jerusalem in A.D. 70. Here, Orthodox Jews mourn the downfall of the Temple. Modern pilgrims place written prayers in the crevices of the wall.

THE SACRED ROCK

Muslim tradition claims that the Prophet Muhammad ascended from the rock into heaven. The hole that runs through the rock may first have served to drain off blood from sacrifices, which suggests that it was probably used as an altar.

THE DOME OF THE ROCK

Built between A.D. 688 and 691 by the caliph 'Abd al-Malikbn Marwan, the magnificent Dome of the Rock is the third holiest place in Islam after Mecca and Medina (see pp.28-29).

According to Muslim tradition, the Prophet Muhammad ascended from the rock into heaven during his "night journey." The Archangel Gabriel appeared one night and presented him with a strange flying beast called al-Buraq (Lightning), on which he was carried from Mecca to Jerusalem. There, he prayed with Abraham, Moses, Jesus, and other prophets at the sacred rock, and then ascended to heaven on his steed, where Allah instructed him about prayer. He returned to Mecca before morning.

A shrine inside the Dome of the Rock (on the upper left in the image above) contains a hair alleged to be from the head of the Prophet. Devout Muslims believe that on the Day of Judgment a horsehair will be stretched from the Dome of the Rock to the Mount of Olives all the dead will have to walk across it, and sinners will fall off into perdition.

THE JEWISH REVOLT AT MASADA

The Jews rebelled many times against Roman occupation. Four years before the downfall of Jerusalem in A.D. 70, 960 Jewish partisans secured themselves in Herod's mountain stronghold of Masada (above) by the Dead Sea. They were besieged by Roman troops. Realizing they had no hope, the Jews committed mass suicide by cutting their throats. The last man set fire to the stronghold before dying on his sword.

COINS MARKING THE END OF THE JEWISH REVOLT

PETRA

"ROSE RED CITY HALF AS OLD AS TIME"

GAZETTEER P.134 - SITE NO.35

IN THE EARLY 19TH CENTURY, the outside world knew nothing about the "lost city" of Petra, which the local people kept secret. Then, in 1812, a Swiss named Johann Burckhardt heard of the fantastic ruins hidden in a valley behind the Wadi Musa (Valley of Moses). He persuaded a local guide to take him through it by claiming that he had to sacrifice a goat at the tomb of Aron (Harun) at the end of the valley. He was awestruck by the "Treasury" with its magnificent frontage carved out of the pink sandstone. The road that winds down the valley beyond the Treasury leads to a series of magnificent sacred buildings. These include three impressive royal tombs, one of which, the Urn Tomb, was used as a church in Byzantine times. There were also three places of worship: the Temple of Dhu-Shara, the Temple of the Winged Lions, and the "Monastery."

FIRST SIGHT

Petra is approached through a narrow gorge called the Siq. At the end of it stands a magnificent red building known as the Khazneh or Treasury (there was a story that pirates hid treasure there). It is actually an unfinished tomb.

El-Deir is the largest of the rock-cut buildings at Petra

EL-DEIR, THE MONASTERY

El-Deir was known as the Monastery because of a belief that it served as a church for monks in the Byzantine period (when Petra had a bishop). In fact, it was almost certainly a temple or a tomb. Behind the impressive frontage is a large chamber.

THE LOST CITY

In spite of its isolation, Petra – one of the most spectacular sites in the Middle East – was once the most powerful city in the area. The earliest evidence of occupation suggests that there was a Neolithic community here around 7000 B.C., which places it among the oldest farming sites in the world. In the Iron Age (around 1200 B.C. in this area), it was the home of the Edomites of the Old Testament.

The valley was taken over by a western tribe called the Nabataeans in the sixth century B.C. They became rich by robbing merchants passing through the territory and by exacting tolls from the caravans on the Silk Route that crisscrossed the area. The Nabataeans expanded their lands until they were the most powerful force in what is now southern Jordan, even occupying Damascus. But their power began to wane when the Roman general Pompey conquered areas of their kingdom in 63 B.C. By A.D. 106, the Romans controlled Petra itself. Much of the ruined city in its present form is Roman. The Muslims came in the seventh century, and the crusaders five centuries later. Although by this point Petra had ceased to be on a major trade route, and in succeeding years its beautiful monuments were forgotten.

AERIAL VIEW OF PETRA

The holy place of the Nabataeans is reached by steps cut into the mountainside. A large platform covered in marble was used here for sacrifices. Below, the "Treasury" lies nestled in the rock-face.

THE FRAGILE TOMBS

Most of the tombs and temples that have survived at Petra are cut into the rock-face from top to bottom. There are literally hundreds of them. In places, the different layers of stone give the appearance of silk. Although they look so magnificent, the buildings at Petra are carved out of soft sandstone – so soft that chips can easily be knocked out of the rocks and crumbled in the hand. Fortunately, Jordan has virtually no rain, otherwise the monuments would have crumbled long ago.

PALMYRA
TEMPLES OF THE DESERT CITY

GAZETTEER P.134 · SITE NO.7

PALMYRA, IN NORTHERN SYRIA, was the great trading center in the Middle East that prospered from Petra's demise. Its name is Greek and means "city of palms." The second-century city grew up around a remote oasis on the Silk Road from China and India to the Mediterranean. Like Petra, it was a city that prospered by heavily taxing trading caravans. Its wealth attracted the attention of the Roman Empire, which invaded in the first century A.D. However, it maintained a sort of independence: the Romans built the magnificent streets and temples, but the emperor Hadrian declared it a vassal city, with rights equal to those of Rome. The most impressive of the Roman structures stands at the end of the Grand Colonnade. The Temple of Bel, with its Corinthian columns, is a vast space surrounded by a 49-ft- (15-m-) high wall; it contains an inner shrine with a sacrificial altar.

VIEW OF THE TEMPLE
The Temple of Bel was dedicated to the cosmic god Bel, who was associated with the sun and moon gods Yarhibol and Aglibol, and later identified with the Greek god Zeus. He may also be connected with the Babylonian god Bel-Marduk who, as chief among the gods, controlled the destinies of men.

THE ANCIENT TEMPLES

Like most of the other remains at Palmyra, the Temple of Bel (A.D. 32 onward) is Roman in style. It was dedicated to the Syrian god whom the Bible calls Baal, suggesting a link with the Phoenician god of the same name. There is evidence that animals were sacrificed to him: a passage is still visible in the wall of the temple where animals were brought for ritual slaughter. The people who lived in the deserts around Palmyra were the Aramaeans – who spoke a similar language to that spoken by Christ – and it is their gods who were worshipped here. There are several other temples and shrines at Palmyra – a first-century A.D. temple to Nabu, son of the Babylonian god Bel-Marduk, a shrine to Bel-Shamin, god of storms, others to Allah and Bel-Hammon – but none so magnificent or in such good repair as the Temple of Bel.

At the outskirts of Palmyra are the rock-cut tombs of Palmyra's more illustrious citizens, dating to the third century. One of the site's most striking ruins is the more recent Arab Castle (see below) that stands high above the city; it dates to the 17th century A.D.

Some of the granite columns are probably of Egyptian origin

Of the 375 original columns, about 150 remain either in fragments or whole

Third-century funerary temple with reconstructed portico

THE GRAND COLONNADE
This, the main artery of the town, shown leading away from the Temple of Bel, was one of the great thoroughfares of the ancient world, with its baths, theater, and huge agora.

MECCA
THE HOLIEST CITY OF ISLAM

GAZETTEER P.135 · SITE NO.1

FROM TIME IMMEMORIAL, Mecca has been a stopping place for travelers, maybe because of the well of Zamzam, which provided water in the mountainous desert landscape of western Arabia. At some time, a cube-shaped temple was built near the well. Muslim traditions connect its construction with Adam, and relate that Abraham and his son Ishmael rebuilt it. This is the Ka'ba, the holiest shrine of Islam. Mecca attracted both worshippers and traders, and its position on a main trading route meant it enjoyed considerable prosperity. Until the seventh century A.D., Arabs worshipped many gods – one creator of the universe and a host of minor deities. This changed with the advent of Islam, when the Prophet Muhammad transformed Mecca into one of the greatest pilgrimage centers in the world.

THE HAJJ
The hajj *is the world's largest annual pilgrimage, and one of the five pillars or duties of Islam. It centers on the Ka'ba and other sites near Mecca. Circumambulations of the covered black shrine usually mark the beginning and end of the observances. The* hajj *is the spiritual climax of many Muslims' lives.*

THE PROPHET

Muhammad, the founder of Islam, born in about A.D. 570 was raised by his uncle Abu Talib. He may have had early contact with Christianity on a trading journey to Syria. Married at 25 to Khadijah, a wealthy woman 15 years his senior, he led a pious life. Later, in his forties, during a period devoted to meditation, he retreated alone to a cave on Mount Hira and spent time in prayer and fasting. Here, in a vision, an angel – whom he believed to be Gabriel – gave him the first verses of the Qur'an, the holy book of Islam. He was told to carry a message to the world that there was only one God, no others.

For three years, he spoke of his beliefs only in private. During this time, he is said to have received the verses of the Qur'an. Once he began to preach, Mecca became very hostile. In 622, Muhammad left for Yathrib (later Medina), narrowly avoiding death; this migration, or *hijra*, was the turning point in his life. Received with zeal, the number of his followers swelled.

In 629, Muhammad approached Mecca with 10,000 men, but met little resistance. His Muslim forces entered the city, casting out the idols that had been previously worshipped and initiating worship of the one God, Allah. The Prophet died in Medina in 632.

THE HOLY PILGRIMAGE
On arrival in the Holy City, male pilgrims must put on two seamless white sheets that symbolize purity. Pilgrims first make the ritual procession – the tawaf *– seven times in a counterclockwise direction around the Ka'ba and if possible kiss the Black Stone in the southeastern corner.*

METEORITE

THE BLACK STONE
Some modern writers claim the holy Black Stone of the Ka'ba is a meteorite. Islamic tradition relates that it was sent down to Adam, who used it as a seat. During Muhammad's life, the Stone caused much dissension. When the Ka'ba was damaged by a flood, there were quarrels over who should lift the Stone until Muhammad put it into place raised on a cloth (see above).

CENTER OF THE FAITH

All over the world, around 900 million Muslims bow down to face Mecca at five different points during the day – at dawn, midday, afternoon, evening, and night. In mosques, its direction is indicated by niches called *mihrabs*. Every year, in the month of *Dhu'l-Hijja* (the 12th month of the Muslim calendar), pilgrims converge on Mecca from all parts of the world for the *hajj*, the great pilgrimage. All Muslims who possess the means must perform the pilgrimage to Mecca at least once in a lifetime. The city and its surrounding area is considered so sacred that non-Muslims are not admitted. With travel now much easier than in the past, over two million Muslims are able to make the pilgrimage to Mecca each year.

BABYLON
GLORIOUS CAPITAL OF NEBUCHADNEZZAR
GAZETTEER P.135 - SITE NO.13

FOR 70 GLORIOUS YEARS, mostly under the reign of Nebuchadnezzar II (died 562 B.C.) Babylon, with its Hanging Gardens and reputed 1,179 temples, was the largest city in the world. A provincial capital during Ur's dominance, Babylon became the most important city in Mesopotamia during the reign of Hammurabi (1792–1750 B.C.). Sacked in 1595 B.C. by Hittites and taken over by Kassites in 1570 B.C., it became a center of worship of the god Marduk for four centuries. Between 1200 and 900 B.C. the Middle East was plunged into a violent dark age. It was not until the reign of the Assyrian Esarhaddon, who rebuilt the holy city under fear of divine retribution, that Babylon regained its former glory. With the help of their allies, Babylonians regained the city in A.D. 612.

The most important center of worship was the Esagila, the temple dedicated to Marduk, impressively rebuilt by Nebuchadnezzar. An 11-day new year festival – "Akitu" – honored Marduk with sacrifices and the recital of an epic poem that related his creation of the world and triumph over the forces of chaos. Once a year, on the fifth day of the festival, the king would visit the Akitu Temple outside the city. This was the holiest of places, where a fertility rite took place and the king would ask for Marduk's blessing. On the final day, the king and a statue of Marduk were carried down the sacred Processional Way in a great ceremony.

Near the Esagila, the Ziggurat of Etemenanki reached a height of 300 ft (91 m). It is believed by some to be the legendary Tower of Babel. Babylon's glory did not last and the city was raided by the Persians in 539 B.C.

THE HANGING GARDENS
The fabled gardens were actually terraces hung with greenery and were built on an artificial hill. No exact location has yet been found, and their very existence is still disputed.

BABYLONIAN BOUNDARY MARKER

NINEVEH
THE GREAT SHRINE OF ISHTAR
GAZETTEER P.135 - SITE NO.15

THE MOUND OF KUYUNJIK had been inhabited since the sixth millennium B.C., but it was the site's later name, Nineveh, that created a reputation for terror. It was chosen as the Assyrian capital by Sennacherib around 700 B.C. He was killed while praying in the Temple of Ishtar by his son Assurbanipal, whose brutality exceeded that of his father. The son reconquered Babylon and destroyed the city of Elam, which had assisted his campaign. However, victory was achieved at the cost of provoking the hatred of neighboring states and after his death in about 627 B.C., the Medes finally conquered and destroyed Nineveh in 612 B.C.

Though nearby Assur was the Assyrian religious center, the Temple of Ishtar, named after the revered goddess of war, was one of the great shrines of Mesopotamia. Assurbanipal also restored a temple to Nabu, the god of writing. Divination was popular with the Assyrians and the main god Assur is found on many reliefs hovering above the king (hence the name of the king *Assur*banipal), other reliefs show the king being sprinkled with holy water.

ISHTAR THE WAR GODDESS

THE NERGAL GATE
The gate was part of the huge stone fortress wall that surrounded the city, behind which stood another higher mud-brick wall. Sennacherib called it "the wall that terrifies the enemy." Though mostly rebuilt, the two winged bulls on either side are original.

Ur

SACRED CENTER OF ANCIENT SUMERIA

GAZETTEER P.135 - SITE NO.14

ACCORDING TO THE BIBLE, "Ur of the Chaldees" was the birthplace of Abraham. Situated on the east bank of the Euphrates, the city reached its peak around 2100 B.C. during the reign of Ur-Nammu. The heart of the city was its walled, sacred precinct dominated by a large ziggurat where the majority of its temples were dedicated to the moon god Nanna and his wife Ningal. In the 1920s, the excavation of Ur by the archaeologist Sir Leonard Woolley unearthed an impressive royal cemetery (c. 2600–2300 B.C.); it included around 1,500 tombs, lavishly filled with precious goods, that showed the opulence of Sumerian civilization. Suggestions that an inundation of the site around 3200 B.C. was the biblical flood have never been entirely disproved.

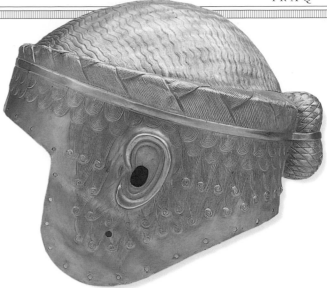

GOLD HELMET OF MESKALAMDUG
This magnificent helmet made of electrum (an alloy of gold and silver) was found in the tomb of the Sumerian king Meskalamdug; it was still wrapped around the skull. Most of the goods found were in the grave called the Great Death Pit.

CITY OF THE MOON GOD

Mesopotamia, the land of the two rivers – the Tigris and the Euphrates – is often called the "cradle of history." Around 10,000 B.C. farming began, man discovered the art of weaving, and began to domesticate animals. Settlements here were made of mudbrick, so that as the houses were built over, mounds rose out of the plains, preserving the history of thousands of years.

Occupied as early as the fourth millennium B.C., the site of Ur became the royal capital of the Sumerian kingdom during the 25th century B.C. The contents of hundreds of graves leave no doubt as to the city's great prosperity. There is evidence, too, of human sacrifice, with bodies of women wearing gold headdresses and lapis lazuli. A lack of signs of struggle probably meant that victims were drugged and then killed, intended as servants in the afterlife.

Although Sumerians had an extensive pantheon, each city had its own patron god; Ur's was the moon god Nanna. The Temple of Enunmakh was dedicated to both Nanna and his wife Ningal, the latter having her own temple and priestess. The rulers were also deified and Ur-Nammu was no exception; he built most of the temples and created an impressive empire. Yet his successors were unable to continue the grandeur and Ur was conquered by Elamites in 2006 B.C., who allowed the city to fall into ruin.

ZIGGURAT OF NANNA
Ur was dominated by its great ziggurat. Here, a monumental stairway leads to Ur's holiest place, the House of Nanna. It is believed that the ziggurat represented the cosmic mountain of Sumerian mythology, symbolizing life-giving force.

"THE RAM IN THE THICKET"
The graves at Ur were filled with elaborate objects, both functional and decorative. Woolley found two small statues showing goats on their hind legs before a golden plant. The goat was one of the first domesticated animals in Mesopotamia.

EPHESUS
SANCTUM OF THE MOON GODDESS
GAZETTEER P.136 - SITE NO.35

EPHESUS WAS ONCE RENOWNED as a center of magic and the occult arts, and was one of the great trading areas of the classical world. Its temple to the moon goddess Artemis (the Roman Diana) was the greatest of the Seven Wonders of the World. Even in ruins, Ephesus is magnificent, covering 26 sq mi (67 sq km). This was the fifth and last of the temples to Diana on the site. Ephesus later became known as a Christian center – St. John allegedly died here, and this town is where the clash between early Christianity and Greco-Roman paganism reached its peak. Paul's criticism of makers of silver idols during his early ministry led to a near riot and resulted in his expulsion from Ephesus. As the Roman world accepted Christianity, the eviction of St. Paul by worshippers of the goddess was revenged by Christians and the Temple of Artemis was totally destroyed.

HOUSE OF THE VIRGIN MARY
St. John is said to have brought the Virgin Mary to Ephesus, where she spent the remainder of her days. Her house, a little south of Ephesus, has been a shrine for pilgrims for many centuries.

SITE OF THE GODDESSES

Legend has it that the site of Ephesus – settled by Greeks following a prophecy of the Delphic oracle – was once occupied by the mythical Amazons. A shrine, dedicated to an Asiatic mother goddess and built at a spot where a meteorite had fallen, was soon identified with the Greek moon goddess Artemis. This, and two successive wooden temples, were burned down by invaders. Then the Lydian king Croesos invaded and contributed generously to a new temple of wood and marble that took 120 years to complete. Its magnificence was noted by the Greek historian Herodotus in 450 B.C. But it was burnt down in 356 B.C. by a fanatic, Herostratos, who explained that he destroyed it to make his name immortal. The temple that replaced it was listed by the scientist and engineer Philon of Byzantium as the greatest of the Seven Wonders of the World. Its vast statue of Diana had three rows of seven breasts, probably symbolizing ripe dates, grapes, or other fruits of the earth. The emperor Julian (A.D. 361–363) tried to restore the cult of the goddess in an attempt to revive paganism in the Christian empire, but he was murdered. A Christian zealot destroyed the statue of Diana in A.D. 400, describing it as "the demon Artemis." Later, the site became a pilgrimage destination for another female holy figure – the mother of Christ, the Virgin Mary.

THE ARCADIAN WAY
This marble-paved avenue is over 1,968 ft (600 m) long. Named after the Roman emperor Arcadius (A.D. 377–408), inscriptions declare that it was lit at night by lanterns. The street runs from the ancient theater down to the port.

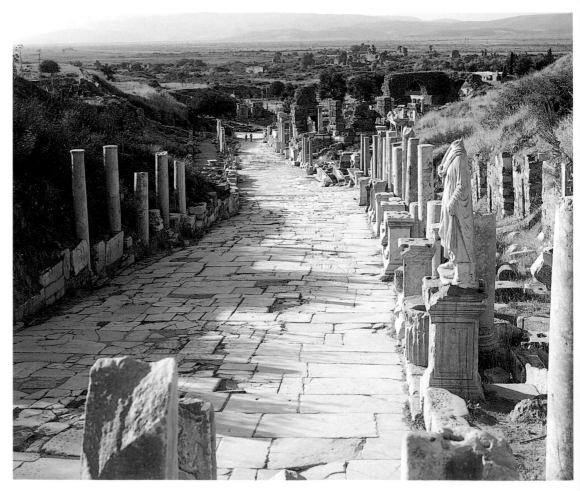

BYZANTINE MOSAIC
This mosaic from the interior of the church is typical of Byzantine depictions of Christ. Many of the mosaics of Christ and the Virgin at Santa Sophia are accompanied by figures of the emperors Constantine and Justinian and their wives.

THE HISTORY OF THE CHURCH

When he made it the capital of the Roman Empire in A.D. 330, the Emperor Constantine changed Byzantium – the Greek name for the city founded in 667 B.C. – to Constantinople. He was wise to move; in its remaining years, ancient Rome was pillaged repeatedly by barbarian invaders, before finally collapsing in A.D. 476. But Constantinople survived. The Emperor Justinian ordered the building of Santa Sophia (Sophia in Greek means wisdom) in A.D. 527. Immense quantities of red porphyry, white and yellow marble, and green serpentine were brought in shiploads, and the church – the third on the site – was built in six years, starting in 532. But Santa Sophia is in an earthquake zone, and a mere 21 years later, most of the dome collapsed and took five years to rebuild. It lasted another four centuries before further earthquakes required another rebuilding. In 1204, crusaders captured the city and sacked Santa Sophia. The dome collapsed once again in 1346. With the capture of Constantinople by the Turks in 1453, Santa Sophia was converted into a mosque. Four minarets were built that now seem an essential part of the design. The building was reopened as a museum in 1935.

AWE-INSPIRING INTERIOR
The mosaic of the Virgin and Child in the apse are flanked by two Ottoman roundels, bearing the names Allah and Muhammad in Arabic. In 1964, restoration work revealed mosaics that had been plastered over in the building's days as a mosque.

SANTA SOPHIA
"HOLY WISDOM"

GAZETTEER P.137 · SITE NO.31

ISTANBUL'S SANTA SOPHIA (*Aya Sofia* in modern Turkish) was once the greatest church in Christendom, and had a good claim to be the Eighth Wonder of the World. The dome and ceiling were covered in gold mosaic, which was mirrored throughout the church's polished surfaces. The marble columns were in such subtle and beautiful hues that the historian Procopius compared them to flowers blooming in a meadow. Probably few buildings have been created to be so overwhelming in their sheer beauty. In 987, the envoys of Prince Vladimir of Kiev declared: "We knew not whether we were in heaven or on earth." Even today, when the gold has tarnished and the building is a museum, it is still one of the wonders of world religion.

CENTER OF EASTERN ORTHODOXY
Santa Sophia (Holy Wisdom) was for centuries the center of Eastern Orthodox Christianity and the most magnificent religious building in the Christian world. The vast dome is breathtaking; it is said that when Justinian first walked under it, he exclaimed: "Solomon, I have triumphed over you."

GREECE & THE MEDITERRANEAN

OF THE GEOGRAPHICAL AREAS in this book, the Mediterranean has exercised one of the greatest influences on human culture. Its religious sites also cover a vast time span, from the tombs and temples of Malta (about 4000 B.C.) to the Temple of Apollo at Delphi (in use until the fourth century A.D.). We now know a little of the Neolithic civilization that built the ancient temples on Malta long before the pyramids of Egypt. We know something of the first Greeks from about 2000 B.C.; of the Mediterranean's first great civilization, the Minoans; of the "heroic age" of Achilles and Agamemnon that came to an end soon after the fall of Troy in about 1250 B.C.; and of the "Dark Ages" of Greece that preceded its flowering into the civilization of Plato (428–348 B.C.) and Aristotle (384–322 B.C.). Sites like the Rock of Aphrodite in Cyprus and the Cave of Zeus in Crete also remind us of the origins of the Greek gods, who would be carried throughout the Roman Empire as Jupiter and Venus before being suppressed by Christianity. It should not be forgotten that in first-century Rome, the cult of the bull god Mithras was more popular than Christianity. Archaeology has uncovered many secrets of the past, and revealed something of the truth about the Cretan labyrinth, the fall of Troy, and the collapse of Mycenae. However, the truth behind many puzzles – such as what rituals took place in the Ggantija temples of Malta or during the mysteries of Aphrodite in Cyprus – still eludes us.

① DELPHI
On the slopes of Parnassus, the Delphic Oracle had important religious and political roles.

② OLYMPIA
The temple here was sacred to Zeus, and it was in his honor that the first Olympic Games were held in 776 B.C.

IONIAN SEA

MEDITERRANEAN SEA

ALGERIA

LIBYA

N

GOZO GGANTIJA ⑦

MEDITERRANEAN SEA

MALTA

N

5 KILOMETRES
0
5 MILES

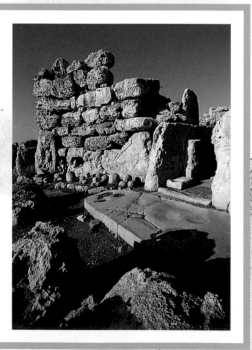

GGANTIJA TEMPLE, MALTA

Ggantija (right), on the island of Gozo, was built by Stone Age farmers about 3000 B.C. as a sanctuary of an Earth goddess. Deep "cart tracks" worn in the stone still puzzle archaeologists, although recent finds have provided more information about worship here.

SAMOTHRAKI

LIMNOS

THRACIAN SEA

LESBOS

TURKEY

SAMOS

TAURUS MOUNTAINS

BAY OF
ANTALYA

PAROS NAXOS

AEGEAN SEA

CRETE

CYPRUS

NILE FAN

NILE DELTA

EGYPT

WINE JAR
This wine jar, called a *chous*, shows two youths. It would have been given to a youth at the time of the festival of Dionysus, god of wine.

③ **MYCENAE**
The story of King Agamemnon of Troy was given new life when "golden Mycenae" revealed its secrets.

④ **KNOSSOS**
The buried palace of King Minos in Crete revealed the possible origins for the myth of the labyrinth.

⑤ **CAVE OF ZEUS**
Zeus was the father of the Greek gods. A cave on a mountainside in Crete has strong claims to be his legendary birthplace. In the votive offering on the right, Zeus is shown with his chariot and horses.

GREEK COINS
Money was invented in Asia Minor at the beginning of the seventh century B.C., and these coins, from the Greek city of Aegina, are among the earliest known. The owl was later the symbol of Athena, the goddess of Athens.

⑥ **ROCK OF APHRODITE**
The island of Cyprus includes the site where Aphrodite, the goddess of love, was allegedly born from the sea.

KNOSSOS

& THE LABYRINTH OF THE MINOTAUR

GAZETTEER P.136 - SITES NOS. 26

THE CRETAN LABYRINTH
To early visitors, the complexity of the palace at Knossos suggested the word "labyrinth." According to legend, Pasiphae, wife of King Minos, fell in love with a beautiful bull, and gave birth to a monster, half-man half-bull, the Minotaur. Minos had the labyrinth built in order to contain the monster.

IN 1883, AN ENGLISH ARCHAEOLOGIST named Arthur Evans bought part of a site near Iráklion in Crete, believing it to be associated with the legendary King Minos. It proved to be all he had hoped for. In 1900, within weeks of beginning to dig, he began to uncover the remains of a huge building. It turned out to be the ruins of a palace covering over five and a half acres (two hectares), dating to between 2000 and 1400 B.C. The west wing of this palace was clearly a center for religious activity, mainly centering around a cult of the bull. The splendor of the palace suggested that it had been part of a great culture 1,000 years before the heyday of Athens. Evans was convinced that this was the palace of King Minos that had once been virtually the center of Mediterranean culture.

THE MYTHS OF CRETE

Every nine years, in revenge for the murder of his son by King Aegeus of Athens, King Minos is said to have demanded a tribute of seven young men and seven young women to be sacrificed to the Minotaur. Theseus, son of King Aegeus, volunteered to go as one of the third group of hostages. Minos' daughter Ariadne fell in love with Theseus, and gave him a ball of wool to guide him out of the labyrinth. Theseus fled with Ariadne, but deserted her on the island of Naxos. As he sailed into Athens, he forgot to hoist a white sail on his ship – which he had promised his father as a sign that he was alive – and Aegeus committed suicide, throwing himself into the sea.

Just visible is an original fresco of a bull

This building is partly a reconstruction

THE MAIN PALACE BUILDINGS
What puzzled excavators about this magnificent 800-room palace that had once been full of treasure and luxury was that it had no external walls or fortifications. They eventually realized that Crete's navy had been so powerful that invaders would never have been allowed to land.

36

THE CAVE OF ZEUS

The leader of the gods, Zeus was allegedly born in Crete. His father Cronos had been warned that one of his children would overthrow him, so he swallowed them at birth. Zeus was hidden by his mother in a cave. When he grew up, a great war ensued, in which he deposed his father as chief among the gods. Two caves on Crete vie for the honor as his birthplace, one on Mount Ida (above), the other on Mount Dikte. Excavations revealed that both caves were full of votive offerings. The Ida cave (Idaion Antron), situated on the plateau of Nida, was used for worship long before it was associated with Zeus – probably devoted to a cult of the Mother Goddess.

BULL JUMPING

In one of the main rooms of the palace there was an extraordinary fresco that showed a charging bull, with one youth grabbing it by the horns as if preparing to vault. Another is shown upside down as he vaults over the bull's back, while a figure at the other end waits to catch the vaulters. Clearly, this was an extremely dangerous form of exercise, for which no record has survived. But since other pictures of bulls make it clear that the Minoans regarded the bull as sacred, this has naturally given rise to speculation that there is some truth in the story of Theseus and the Minotaur, and that the king of Crete may have exacted a tribute of young men and young women, who were sacrificed in some religious ritual involving bulls.

Many mysteries about the Minoan civilization remain, among them, why it came to an abrupt end around 1400 B.C. when it was apparently at the height of its power. Could it have been destroyed by an earthquake that left it shattered and defenseless? Or is it possible that the tremendous eruption of the volcanic island of Thera (ancient Santorini) – 70 mi (113 km) to the north of Crete – around 1450 B.C. had something to do with its downfall? The Thera eruption is estimated as three times as great as that of Krakatoa, near Java, in 1883, which was heard as far away as

Africa and Europe. It produced a tidal wave 130 ft (40 m) high, washing a warship half a mile (800 m) inland, so the explosion of Thera must have devastated the Mediterranean, and Iráklion may have been virtually washed away. However, this theory has been questioned, and war is thought to be a more likely cause of the Minoan downfall. Whatever happened, the power of the Minoans was permanently broken. The prosperity that had grown since 2800 B.C. disappeared, and the Greek mainland became the cultural center.

SACRED HORNS
These sacred horns on the roof of the Palace of Minos, looking southward over Crete, were obviously the royal symbol, and seem to imply that all these lands were the property of the king. During the period of its greatest power (about 2000–1450 B.C.), Crete certainly had no rivals.

THE CRETAN SCRIPT

Evans found clay tablets in and around the Palace of Knossos, some dating to 3000 B.C. He divided scripts on the tablets into four types, calling the most recent Linear A and Linear B. Convinced that the Minoans had conquered mainland Greece, Evans was confirmed in his belief when more Linear B script was found on mainland Greece at Pylos and Mycenae. His opponents believed that the Greeks had conquered Knossos (which was the only site on Crete where Linear B was found).

At a talk given by Evans in 1936, a boy named Michael Ventris was captivated by the mystery and determined to solve it. By 1952, new Linear B material offered further clues, and Ventris reached the remarkable conclusion that Linear B was an early form of Greek. His discovery suggested that Achean Greeks had conquered Crete – possibly about 1450 B.C. – and that, after all, the downfall of Knossos had been brought about by enemies from the sea.

A GREEK VASE DEPICTING THE MINOTAUR

THE AGE OF THE BULL
Were the Minoans bull worshippers? It has been disputed because they were also known to sacrifice bulls; but this is also true of the ancient Egyptians. The clue may lie in astrology: the age of Taurus was roughly 4000 to 2000 B.C. and Minoan civilization began to flourish during this period. Bull worship may be another sign of ancient humans' obsession with the stars.

RELIGIOUS SITES OF MALTA

The temple (foreground) is in alignment with the church at Xewkija, with its vast dome, and the Ta'Cenc megalithic complex on the south coast, which contains dolmens and a ruined temple.

THE MYSTERY OF THE TOMBS

The first Maltese were Stone Age farmers, who arrived around 5000 B.C. About 1,000 years later came immigrants from Sicily, and it was they who began building tombs and temples. These were carefully planned: small models of them have been unearthed at the sites.

The temple builders were totally isolated – there is no evidence of any kind of contact with the rest of the ancient world. And then, quite suddenly, they disappeared. We do not even know the precise date – one writer gives 2000 B.C., another 2500 B.C. Did invaders pour in and carry them all off as slaves? Or did the farmers move elsewhere?

BURIAL FIGURES

It has been suggested that these seated human figures are representations of the mother goddess believed to have been worshipped in Malta. The figure on the left holds a cup, while that on the right holds a smaller figure, possibly a baby.

GGANTIJA
THE MEGALITHIC TEMPLES

GAZETTEER P.136 - SITE NO.1

THE GREATEST AND MOST IMPRESSIVE array of Stone Age temples in Europe is to be found in the Maltese Islands. One of the finest is Ggantija, near Xaghra, on the island of Gozo. It is believed to date from about 3000 B.C. Ggantija is often spelled Gigantija, meaning "giant's tower." The temple (or temples – there are two of these prehistoric structures side by side) certainly deserve the name; they are as impressive in their way as Stonehenge, which dates from roughly the same period. The two Ggantija temples, one smaller than the other, are both shaped like a kind of five-leaf clover, and are surrounded by an outer wall composed of huge slabs stood on end. Some of the stones weigh 50 tons. It has been suggested that the shape might represent a woman – or a mother goddess – with large breasts and hips. An 18th-century antiquarian claimed that he had discovered a labyrinth of tombs below the temple, but this has never been located.

NEW FINDS AT XAGHRA

In the 1980s, a remarkable discovery at Xaghra near Ggantija suddenly enlarged our knowledge of the ancient Maltese. A 19th-century painter named Charles Brochtorff had made paintings of an impressive-looking site that had been lost. A building application galvanized archaeologists to start digging. The result was the discovery of many human bones from as early as 4000 B.C., and remarkable models and sculptures. Many of the statuettes are corpulent, leading to the belief that they represent a mother goddess.

HOME OF THE FERTILITY GODDESS

The Maltese believe Gozo is the island of Calypso, the goddess with whom Homer's Ulysses spent eight years after being shipwrecked. Calypso may be a version of the fertility goddess to whom the temples of Ggantija (above) may be dedicated.

A cache of thinner figurines, probably male, was also found. Their purpose seems to be religious, and associated with burial. The Maltese divided the bones into groups, so there were groups of skulls, long bones, or smaller parts of the skeleton. These were clearly interred with funerary rites in many stages.

APHRODITE'S ROCK

BIRTHPLACE OF A GODDESS

GAZETTEER P.137 · SITE NO.50

THE GODDESS OF LOVE
This mirror case shows Aphrodite playing a game of knucklebones with Pan, the shepherd god who has goat's legs and ears. Hovering behind her is her son Eros (the Roman Cupid). The bird at the bottom is a goose, often associated with Aphrodite.

ALTHOUGH CYPRUS LIES NEARLY 500 mi (800 km) from mainland Greece, and only 60 mi (96 km) from Turkey, its culture has been Greek since settlers arrived from the Peloponnese in about 1200 B.C. It is the alleged birthplace of the Greek goddess of love, Aphrodite. We are now almost certain that Aphrodite was in fact a nature (and earth) goddess. In early depictions she has a robust figure – like a Neolithic "Venus" – and it was only later that artists preferred to see her as slim and more shapely. Neither was she originally the goddess of "higher love" (as opposed to lust) – sacred prostitution was part of her cult. *Hetairai* (temple prostitutes) believed they were performing a service to the goddess by giving their bodies to men. But the mysteries of Aphrodite involved days of ritual preparation, culminating in a ceremony in the "bedchamber of Aphrodite" designed to raise the initiates to a state of ecstasy.

THE BIRTH OF APHRODITE

According to legend, Aphrodite was born from the sea. Her father Uranus was the tyrannical sky god, who refused to allow his children to see the light of day, confining them to the underworld. Their mother Gaia, the earth goddess, prompted them to rebellion. Her son Cronos sliced off his father's genitals while Uranus was making love to her, and threw them in the sea. As they floated, sea foam gathered around them, which became fertilized with sperm. When Aphrodite stepped ashore at Paphos on Cyprus, she was quite literally "seaborn." Zeus made her the goddess of beauty.

When Hephaestus, the god of fire, was allowed to pick a wife, he chose Aphrodite. Although her husband was the greatest of all smiths, he was lame and ugly, and Aphrodite was often unfaithful. On learning of her affair with Ares (the Roman Mars), the god of war, Hephaestus devised a cunning trap – a net so fine it could not be seen, arranged over her bed. He announced he was going away for a few days and the lovers hastened to bed, but were soon caught in the net. Unable to move, they had to remain in this humiliating position while other gods were summoned to laugh at them.

THE CULT OF APHRODITE
Cyprus was the center of the cult of Aphrodite, goddess of love, whom the Romans called Venus. The Rock of Aphrodite, near Old Paphos on the southwest coast of Cyprus, is the legendary site of her birth. Even the Greeks accepted this, and Homer refers to her as "the Cyprian." The result is that Cyprus contains many temples to Aphrodite.

MYCENAE
CITADEL OF THE GOLDEN TOMBS

GAZETTEER P.136 · SITE NO.18

THE LION GATE
*When first built – in about 1250 B.C., perhaps
by Agamemnon – the Lion Gate, the main
entrance to the citadel of Mycenae, must have
looked magnificent with its lionesses' heads.
They were originally covered in bronze.*

MADE FAMOUS IN HOMER'S epic poem the *Iliad*, in 1876 Mycenae became the focus of the work of German archaeologist Heinrich Schliemann. Five years earlier he had excavated a hill at Hissarlik on the coast of Turkey and, using the works of Homer as a guide, discovered the remains of the fabled city of Troy. He was convinced that by using similar methods he could find the royal tombs of Mycenae, especially that of the warrior king Agamemnon, murdered by his wife Clytemnestra on his return from war with Troy. To a point, his work proved successful; he found tombs filled with many golden burial objects. On discovering a golden funerary mask, he was sure that it represented Agamemnon. Schliemann sent the king of Greece a telegram announcing "with extraordinary pleasure" that he had found Agamemnon's tomb. He was proved wrong, having instead found graves from four centuries earlier (c. 1650 B.C.). Excavations inside and outside the citadel have uncovered other sacred burial areas, many with rich burial goods, leaving no doubt as to why the ancient Greeks spoke of "Golden Mycenae."

EXCAVATION OF THE CITY

Heinrich Schliemann was fascinated by the work of Homer. In the *Iliad,* Homer had spoken of Mycenae as home of the hero Agamemnon, who had led the expedition to Troy to rescue his sister Helen from the Trojan prince, Paris. On his return, along with his prophetic Trojan slave, Cassandra, he was killed by his wife Clytemnestra, who had become enamoured with Aegisthus, Agamemnon's cousin. Agamemnon's death was later avenged by his son Orestes, who killed both the lovers.

Ignoring the opinion of experts, who based their views on Greek geographer Pausanius (who stated that the graves lay outside the citadel), Schliemann began to dig inside the city walls, moving hundreds of tons of rubble from around the Lion Gate. He soon uncovered a circular structure that at first he thought to be the *agora*, or public meeting place. But on unearthing vases, terra-cotta idols, and skeletons covered with gold and jewels he realized they were shaft graves that, he felt certain, included those of Agamemnon and his father Atreus. Although he was later proved wrong, his work had uncovered an unusually rich burial site.

HILL OF BURIAL
Most of the nine tholos *or beehive tombs at
Mycenae are found outside the walls of the
citadel, here seen from the east. The Treasury
of Atreus can be found to the south, with the
tombs of Clytemnestra and Aegistus to the west.*

MYCENAEAN RELIGION

Excavations have uncovered evidence of settlement at Mycenae as far back as 2000 B.C. The goods of early graves (c. 1600 B.C.) show engraved cult scenes. They depict dances and rituals performed before a female divinity, though it cannot be proven that such scenes were an integral part of early Mycenaean life.

Yet it is from the more famous later period that we learn most about their culture. Votive statuettes, bead offerings, and models of coiled snakes found in the graves outside the citadel probably served a protective purpose. These later Mycenaeans also spoke an early form of Greek, as Michael Ventris discovered by deciphering the Linear B tablets (see p.39). From these we know they were a polytheistic society. Among the gods mentioned are Zeus, Hera, and Poseidon, and from these it is clear that the religion of classical Greece was already developing as early as the 13th century B.C.

CIRCLE GRAVE A – SACRED BURIAL AREA
Like the earlier Circle Grave B, this area was continually used as a burial ground. Yet the fact that it was incorporated within the citadel, and surrounded by a double stone circle, suggests that it was particularly revered by Mycenaeans.

THE ANCIENT CITY OF GOLD

The original "robber barons" of Mycenae spent vast fortunes to have themselves buried in shaft graves. Dating from around 1600 B.C., the graves were thief-proof, undisturbed for nearly 3,500 years until Schliemann found their treasures. But the "great age" of Mycenaean civilization actually followed about 300 years later, when their even-richer descendants – like Atreus, father of Agamemnon – built *tholos* tombs so huge that the tops often became uncovered, and thieves plundered the contents.

The Mycenaeans profited from the downfall of the Minoans (see pp.36-37). When the volcano on the island of Thera (Santorini) erupted in about 1500 B.C., Crete was devastated by a tidal wave, and the Mycenaeans took over the Cretan role in the Mediterranean. Trade with the rest of this area brought immense wealth and by 1250 B.C. – around the time of the Trojan war – Mycenae had become the dominant power. The structure of the citadel, with its "Cyclopean blocks," is a testament to its power. But 50 years later, Mycenae collapsed. Continual war had exhausted its people, while a tremendous earthquake in 1190 B.C. completed the city's eventual decline.

THE TREASURY OF ATREUS
The wrongly-named Treasury of Atreus was at first thought to be a huge bakery oven. In fact, it is neither oven nor treasury, but a tomb, and, at 43 ft (15 m) high, the largest on the Greek mainland. No body or burial goods were found.

"AGAMEMNON'S MASK"
King Agamemnon was murdered by his wife Clytemnestra and her lover Aegisthus on his return from Troy; eight years later, his son Orestes took revenge by killing them both. Schliemann believed that this golden mask found in the tombs at Mycenae represented Agamemnon, but it is almost certainly of an earlier date.

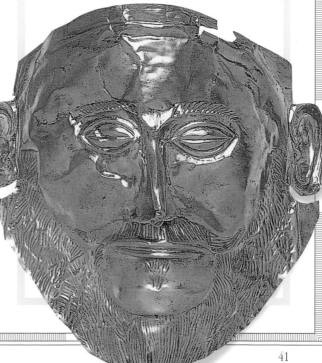

DELPHI
APOLLO'S TEMPLE & THE SACRED ORACLE

GAZETTEER P.136 - SITE NO.9

THE TEMPLE AREA
The area around the Temple of Apollo was the site of various other shrines. The existence of a stadium confirms that Delphi, like Olympia, was a center for games. The Pythian games, celebrating Apollo's slaying of Python, were held every four years.

ON THE SLOPES OF MOUNT PARNASSUS, legendary home of the Muses, stands Delphi, rugged and austere. For the ancient Greeks, it was the omphalos, or navel, of the world. Zeus was said to have released two eagles from opposite ends of the world who met here – the spot marked by the omphalos stone. This great temple sanctuary was dedicated to Apollo, and the oracle was his mouthpiece. Previously it had been the sanctuary of the earth goddess Gaia. In the ancient world, anyone who had some weighty problem made the pilgrimage to Delphi. A priestess sat above a gulf from which vapors rose; she went into a trance and gave her verdict in obscure utterances, which were then "translated" into verse by a priest.

THE ORACLE

Greek legend tells of a great flood submerging everything on earth. After this, a great snake named Python, daughter of the earth goddess Gaia, lived in a cave on Mount Parnassus, eating human beings from nearby villages. Then Apollo the sun god came to Pytho – as Delphi was then called – and killed the snake, flinging the huge corpse into a cleft in the earth, from which a stench of decay arose. The name of the place was changed to Delphi, Apollo's homeland, and Gaia was banished. The temple to Apollo was built and a priestess called the Pythia was regularly possessed by the god and answered questions.

THE TEMPLE OF APOLLO
Little now remains of the Temple of Apollo except the foundations, but that little is very impressive. Construction began in 370 B.C. and took 30 years to finish. The chief Greek cities were anxious to contribute, each wishing to have influence there.

FACT OR FRAUD?

It would be too simplistic to assume that the oracle was a fraud. Many people possess "psychic" powers, and the fumes from the gulf undoubtedly induced a trancelike state and vision. The priests who ran the temple may be more questionable. They were aware of their influence on political affairs throughout Greece, and were opportunistic and skilled in stagecraft and intrigue. In ancient times, the Sacred Way at Delphi must have been overwhelming, lined with statues and treasures given by grateful city states for what they believed to be the wisdom of the god Apollo himself.

THE CASTALIAN SPRING
Steps lead up to the Castalian Spring, which according to legend was created by the hooves of Bellerophon's horse Pegasus. It is where the nymph Castalia committed suicide to escape Apollo. Pilgrims cleansed themselves here before consulting the oracle. It was probably the center for the earlier cult of the goddess Gaia.

THE OMPHALOS STONE
The marking on this stone found at Delphi may be geomantic, perhaps a form of longitude and latitude.

OLYMPIA
"MOTHER OF THE GAMES"
——— GAZETTEER P.136 · SITE NO.15 ———

AS DELPHI IS THE SANCTUARY of Apollo, so Olympia is the sanctuary of Zeus, chief among the Greek gods. The Olympic Games were an event of great religious significance. Holy sacrifices and sacred oaths formed an integral part of the festival, and winning athletes were elevated to the status of demigods. The original Olympics took place 292 times. Then, in A.D. 394, the Christian emperor Theodosius I banned the games because of their pagan connotations. Unlike Delphi, Olympia disappeared so completely that in the 18th century no one even knew where it was. Rivers covered the ruins with layers of mud. Major excavations started at Olympia in 1875; 20 years later, the games began again in Athens.

THE OLYMPIADS

Unlike Delphi, Olympia is peaceful and pleasant rather than magnificent. In the first millennium B.C., it was a sanctuary of the goddess Rhea, mother of the gods. Later, as the age of matriarchy passed away, it was dedicated to her son Zeus. A small festival was held as early as 1100 B.C., but the Olympiad – the Olympic Games – began in 776 B.C. For a three-month period, all the states of Greece were bound by an *ekeheiria*, or "sacred truce" and anyone who broke it was heavily fined. The Olympic Games lasted five days, around the time of the first full moon in August. They were held in honor of Zeus, who was credited with being their founder. Events included footracing, horseracing, wrestling, discus and javelin throwing, the long jump, and boxing. Only Greek males were allowed; women were not even admitted to the sanctuary – any who tried to enter by stealth were thrown off a nearby rock. In addition to this, poets and prose writers read their works aloud to vast audiences.

The original Olympic stadium had a track over 650 ft (200 m) long and could seat 30,000. Little now remains except the starting and finishing lines and the judges' seats. Nearby in the hippodrome, horseracing took place.

Greece became a Roman province in 146 B.C., but the Romans were eager to preserve Greek society, and the Olympic Games continued under Roman rule – now with Romans also allowed to compete. The Roman emperor Nero himself took part in a chariot race in A.D. 69. In spite of cheating (by entering ten horses when the other competitors were only allowed four), he still managed to fall out of his chariot and lose the race. The judges saved the day, and probably themselves, by awarding the race to him anyway.

SACRED SPORTS

The sports events at Olympia were interspersed with regular sacrifices to the god Zeus. These began with the slaying of white oxen at the opening of the five-day event. Athletes would often call on the gods for help in winning the contests themselves. Exoidas, the owner of the discus below, won a contest with it in the sixth century B.C. He dedicated his winning discus to Castor and Pollux, the twin sons of Zeus, the god in whose honor the Olympic Games were held. Pollux was a champion discus thrower.

BRONZE DISCUS

THE PALAESTRA
Athletes prepared for races and fights in the palaestra; its columns surround an open area (seen left in the photo above). Here, they trained and oiled their bodies for wrestling matches. All athletes ran naked, a practice reputedly begun after a runner's shorts came off in a race in 720 B.C.

OLYMPIAN BOXER
This Roman copy of a statue from Olympia is of a young boxer called Kyniskos. The original was a bronze by the famous Greek sculptor Polykleitos.

EUROPE & RUSSIA

ICELAND

① **THINGVELLIR**
Unique among the world's sacred sites, Thingvellir is situated in a long ravine in a field of volcanic lava.

NORWEGIAN SEA

ALTHOUGH IT SEEMS NATURAL to link them together geographically, Europe and European Russia have developed two different religious traditions. With the conversion of Constantine, Christianity became the religion of the Roman state, and in Europe never lost that association of state authority, even where a separate Protestant tradition developed. As often as not, religion in Russia has been opposed to that authority – for example, between 1672 and 1691, 20,000 "Old Believers" burned themselves to death in mass immolations rather than accept the new liturgical texts advocated by the Patriarch Nikon, and supported by the czar Alexis. It is fitting that one of Russia's greatest monasteries, the Solovyetsky, should have a long association with dissenters and political imprisonment. Such rebellions were unknown in Europe until the Reformation, with its rejection of Rome and the creation of the Protestant denominations, but even then the new Protestant religion was strongly identified with the state. Once the center of the greatest pagan empire, Rome had become the home of the papacy and, as such, one of the most powerful religious centers the world has ever known. But the earliest sacred sites in Europe, such as the megaliths at Carnac in France and Almendras in Portugal, probably predate Rome as a religious center by more than 2,000 years; while in the caves beneath Lascaux lies one of the oldest sanctuaries known to man.

② **NORTHERN LIGHTS**
Sacred to the Norsemen, regarded with superstition by those farther south, the aurora borealis is seen in many locations in the northern hemisphere.

N

NORTH SEA

REPUBLIC OF IRELAND

UNITED KINGDOM

④ CHARTR[...]

⑤ **CARNAC**
The purpose of these long rows of stones still baffle antiquarians.

⑤

RIVER LOIRE

FRANCE

VIKING CARGO SHIP
Boats played an important part in Viking religion. Viking warriors were allegedly carried to the afterlife in a magical vessel. This cargo ship is from Roskilde Fjord in Denmark. The prow is a copy; the original was elegantly carved.

BAY OF BISCAY

⑥ **LASCAUX**
Cave paintings here date back to 15,000 B.C.

⑥

⑦ SANTIAGO DE COMPOSTELA

⑧ **MONTSERRAT**
The famous Black Virgin was said to be carved by St. Luke.

⑧

SPAIN

ATLANTIC OCEAN

PORTUGAL

⑨ **ALMENDRAS**
Portugal's largest stone circle may have been created as a temple to the stars.

③ **GOTLAND**
The stone ships of Gotland were designed to carry the souls of dead Norse sailors to the afterworld.

⑲ **SOLOVYETSKY MONASTERY**
One of Russia's most northerly monasteries, it has for centuries been a refuge for holy ascetics and a prison for political dissenters.

⑳ **ST. BASIL'S CATHEDRAL**
The cathedral was built to commemorate a victory of Ivan the Terrible.

⑱ **TRINITY MONASTERY**
Two holy ascetics, who were also brothers, founded Russia's most historic monastery.

⑩ **EXTERNSTEINE**
Sacred in pagan times, these rocks were later Christianized and, more recently, were a center for German nationalism.

⑪ **AACHEN**

⑰ **IPATEYEV MONASTERY**
The monastery lies in one of the "golden ring" towns that encircle Moscow.

⑯ **SUCEVITA MONASTERY**
This massive Romanian monastery-fortress was founded by a murderess.

⑭ **STECCI STONES**
These remarkable Bosnian tombstones are the product of the surplus wealth of prosperous merchants.

⑫ **CERVETERI**
The Etruscans vanished from history more than 2,000 years ago. Fortunately their painted tombs survive.

⑮ **RILA MONASTERY**

⑬ **ST. PETER'S**
Founded nearly 3,000 years ago, Rome became a religious center due to its status as the hub of an empire.

ICON OF CHRIST
The Eastern Orthodox faith favors icons (painted images – from the Greek *eikon*, image) over the religious statues of the West. Byzantine and Russian icon painters were principally concerned with the portrayal of mystical states.

ST. SERGIUS
MONASTERY OF THE TRINITY
GAZETTEER P.140 · SITE NO.18

ST. SERGIUS MONASTERY
In the five years following Sergius' canonization in 1422, a white marble cathedral was erected over his tomb. The great princes of Moscow had their sons baptized there; they included Ivan the Terrible (in 1530) and his two sons.

ST. SERGIUS (1319–92) is the patron saint of Russia, and the Monastery of the Trinity dedicated to him is one of Russia's most famous religious buildings. Born a nobleman, Sergius, also called Sergiev, retired into the forest of Radonezh with his brother to live a life of prayer and contemplation. In 1340, they built a wooden church, and the site acquired such a reputation for holiness that pilgrims flocked there; other pious and holy men built their cells around the church.

But St. Sergius' fame was political as much as religious. At that time, Russia had for more than a century been devastated by the Mongols (Tartars). The Monastery of the Trinity became the symbol of religious renewal and national identity. Sergius urged the feuding princes to stop quarreling and combine against the Tartars. In 1380, he achieved success with the great Dmitri (of the Don), who defeated the Tartars at the Battle of Kulikovo. It was the beginning of the end of Tartar power and the beginning of a unified Christian Russia.

ICON OF CHRIST
The art of icon painting in Russia reached its peak in the 15th century, and the Trinity Monastery made a major contribution. Two monks from the monastery, Daniel Chorny and Andrei Rublev, were its greatest masters.

IPATEVSKY MONASTERY
ROYAL MONASTERY OF RUSSIA'S "GOLDEN RING"
GAZETTEER P.140 · SITE NO.16

THE GODUNOV FAMILY, whose most famous family member is Boris Godunov (Ivan the Terrible's successor as czar) were originally Tartars and therefore Muslims. The legend of the monastery tells how, in 1330,

IPATEVSKY MONASTERY
The St. Ipaty or Ipatevsky Monastery at Kostroma lies across the river from the main part of the city. The fire that burned the original monastery also destroyed much of the city of Kostroma.

Boris' ancestor Chet fell ill at Kostroma on his return from Moscow. St. Ipaty appeared with another saint and promised that the Muslim would recover if he became a Christian. Chet converted and his recovery followed. In thanks, Chet built the monastery to St. Ipaty on the banks of the Kostroma River. In the mid-17th century, its cathedral was blown up when careless monks went searching the powder magazine with candles. The monastery enjoyed the patronage of the Godunov family, whose family vault lies under the church, and later that of the Romanovs. In 1600, Boris Godunov exiled Fyodor Romanov to the monastery and Fyodor's son Michael happened to be there when he was elected czar. Michael transformed the drab building where he was crowned into the impressive Romanov Chamber, and all the Romanovs who succeeded him – down to the last one, Nicholas II – made it their duty to visit it.

KOSTROMA
Kostroma is the most northerly town of Russia's "golden ring," a circle of historic towns to the northeast of Moscow, many of which contain important religious buildings.

SOLOVYETSKY

MONASTERY-FORTRESS OF THE WHITE SEA

GAZETTEER P.140 · SITE NO.7

SITUATED ON THE WHITE SEA in northern Russia, the Solovyetsky Islands are bleak and rocky – a suitable site for a monastery whose dwellers wished to mortify the flesh. The Solovyetsky Monastery, on Solovets Island, is one of the largest in Russia. The austere group of buildings served as an important border post and a fortress in the Middle Ages, which explains why some of its architecture is distinctly military, with high windows like embrasures. It was founded in 1429 by St. Zosima (German) and St. Sabaty (Savvaty); a 16th-century icon of them stands beside the monastery building. The monastery has two 16th-century cathedrals, once linked by secret underground passages, and vaults for the storage of food and water in case of siege. It ceased to be a fortress in 1814, although it was attacked by the British during the Crimean War. In spite of its grim reputation as a prison for Stalin's political opponents, Solovyetsky Monastery is undoubtedly one of the most beautiful religious buildings in Russia.

USPENSKAYA CHURCH
This 16th-century church is part of the monastery compound. The people of the area, whose numbers approach 2,000, have only one place of worship – the Church over the Gate.

THE WHITE CHURCHES

"On the White Sea, where the nights are white for half a year at a time, Bolshoi Solovyetsky (Great Solovyetsky) Island lifts its white churches from the sea. . . Half a thousand years ago, the monks Savvaty and German crossed the mother-of-pearl sea in a tiny boat and came to regard this island that had no beasts of prey as sacred." So writes Solzhenitsyn in the *Gulag Archipelago*. The monks joined its lakes with canals and brought water to the monastery in wooden pipes. Inlets dammed off from the sea became the "Metropolitan's [Bishop's] Fishponds." In effect, the monastery turned into a small town, with its own trades – pottery, leatherwork, and carpentry. Vulnerable to attack from abroad, the many monasteries that had sprung up were turned into forts. The walls of the Solovyetsky Monastery were strengthened until they were 24 ft (7 m) thick; eight towers were raised on them. The bell tower of the monastery was manned as a lookout. In due course, the monastery also became a prison for heretics and political exiles, and the monks soon had the task of being jailers. It was only in 1903 that the monastery ceased to be a czarist prison, though it returned to that role under Stalin.

TRANSFIGURATION CATHEDRAL
The domes of the cathedral are seen on the left in the image. It is contemporary with St. Basil's Cathedral in Moscow (see pp.48-49) and, like St. Basil's, was built by Ivan the Terrible.

THE REMOTE PRISON

The Solovyetsky Islands were called "the Gulag Archipelago" by Alexander Solzhenitsyn, after the islands' history as a prison camp. The monastery-fortress of Solovyetsky has often played an important part in Russian history. The priest Sylvester, who had become a powerful influence on the teenage Ivan the Terrible after the Great Fire of Moscow in 1547, was exiled there when he fell from favor after the czarina's death in 1560. He was treated as a holy man, spending his remaining days there.

In later centuries, the remote position of the islands and its austere religious buildings made it an ideal prison or retreat for the enemies of the czar and Stalin.

THE SOLOVYETSKY ISLANDS
The Solovyetsky Islands lie in the White Sea in northern Russia. Despite the islands' northerly position, the White Sea is sheltered and the climate is far from harsh so that the monks of Solovyetsky Monastery were not only able to raise vegetables, but also roses.

ST. BASIL'S
IVAN THE TERRIBLE'S GREAT CATHEDRAL
GAZETTEER P.140 · SITE NO.22

IN THE CENTER OF RED SQUARE – so called before the Russian Revolution – stands the bizarre St. Basil's Cathedral, composed of 11 religious buildings combined into one incredible whole. Looking like something out of a fairy tale, it is a strange montage of domes, cupolas, arches, towers, and spires. Known properly as the Cathedral of the Virgin of the Intercession, it was built by Ivan the Terrible, and commemorates the capture of the Tartar city of Kazan on the Volga on 1 October 1552, the feast day of the Intercession. The popular name comes from a holy fool buried inside the church, a ragged prophet reputed to have foretold the Great Fire of Moscow in 1547. Legend states that when the cathedral was completed, Ivan had the architect blinded so that he could not create anything of comparable splendor. One traveler wrote: "There is no building in the world that compares with St. Basil's in its whimsical variety of shapes."

IVAN THE TERRIBLE
Ivan the Terrible only acquired his soubriquet in the latter half of his life after the death of his beloved wife. He seems to have developed into a sadist and tales of his cruelty are appalling – as in the notorious destruction of Novgorod in 1570, when he spent five weeks directing an orgy of murder and cruelty.

THE SIEGE OF KAZAN

Few admiring tourists are aware that the brightly colored domes of St. Basil's represent eight turbaned Muslim chieftains who were beheaded after Ivan the Terrible had conquered the middle Volga and forced its Muslim population to become Christian.

Although his title was Ivan (John) IV, Ivan the Terrible was the first to proclaim himself Russian czar – the title comes from the word Caesar. His predecessors had been called the grand dukes of Moscow. These grand dukes were the vassals of the Tartars, a Muslim people of Central Asia.

Moscow began in 1147 as a fortress on a hill overlooking the Moskva River, in the midst of forested plains. A small settlement of wooden huts soon grew around it, but was burned to the ground by Genghis Khan in 1237. The city that rose from the ashes became a Mongol protectorate. The first Ivan, Prince of Vladimir, built the Cathedral of the Assumption, the Uspensky Subor, and built a wooden wall around Moscow Hill – which in Mongol was called the "kreml." It enclosed two cathedrals, two churches, and the home of Ivan I, and was called the Kremlin.

THE DOMES OF ST. BASIL'S
St. Basil's embodied a new concept in architecture. Earlier Russian churches had been Byzantine in design, but wooden churches in northern Russia had brightly painted onion domes. St. Basil's is an amalgam of the two styles, but surpasses both in its sheer colorfulness and the scope of its imagination.

It was the fourth Ivan, "the Terrible", who decided to end the Tartar dominance once and for all by taking Kazan – a town that often called on the help of Tartars or Turks to help in its fight against Moscow. The siege began on 20 August 1552. The walls of Kazan were undermined by explosives and, on 1 October, the Russians poured through a tremendous breach. The news of the fall of Kazan brought rejoicing throughout Russia, and Ivan returned to Moscow and ordered the construction of St. Basil's.

ST. BASIL'S CATHEDRAL
The profusion of colored domes cover nine main chapels. The northeastern chapel covers the grave of St. Vasily the Blessed – the eponymous St. Basil. Although the church was built from 1555 to 1561, its array of onion domes were not painted until the 1670s.

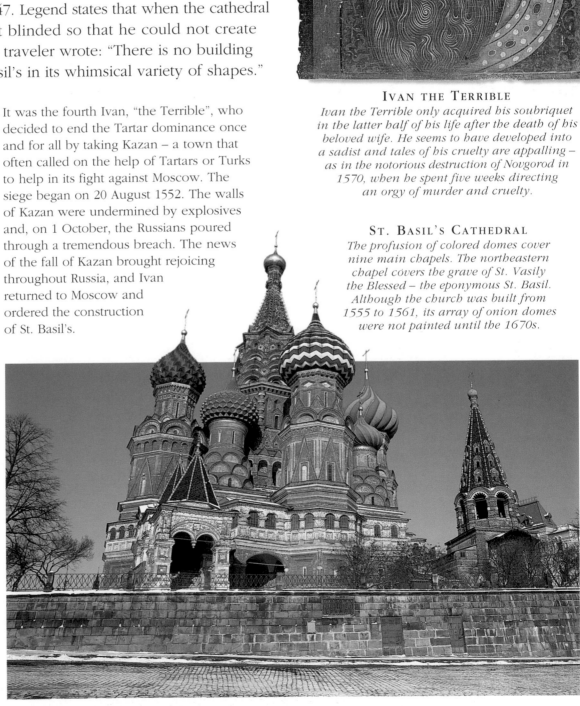

RILA MONASTERY
SACRED CENTER OF ST. JOHN OF RILSKI

GAZETTEER P.139 - SITE NO.49

AT THE AGE of 20, fed up with the life at court, Ivan Rilski (later St. John of Rilski) moved into a cave in a remote part of Bulgaria to do penance. His reputation for sanctity attracted many disciples, who built a hermitage a short distance southeast of the present monastery. Here, the saint's tomb can still be seen, together with his cell and a chapel dedicated to St. Luke.

In 1334–35, a ruler named Dragovol Hreljo rebuilt Rila after it had been destroyed by fire and avalanche, adding a great courtyard and a five-story tower – the only part of the original monastery that now remains. During this period, the monastery reached its greatest splendor. Hreljo was allegedly killed by jealous lords, and an inscription from his widow still survives. The monastery was granted a charter and more land in 1378, but it was attacked by Ottomans in the mid-15th century. The present version was built between 1816 and 1846, earlier versions having been destroyed by fire, avalanche, and invasions.

RIDGE-TOP MONASTERY
Surrounded by mountains covered with beech and pines, Rila stands on its mountain ridge like a fortress (left). In its heyday during the 14th and 15th centuries, it was a great religious and cultural center. Its walls were covered with scenes from clerical and secular life, and master craftsmen decorated its inner courtyard (right). The teachings of the monks served as a beacon to the surrounding area.

STONE FOREST
MYSTERIOUS PILLARS OF LAKE VARNA

GAZETTEER P.139 - SITE NO.46

THE UNIQUE AREA known as the Stone Forest lies in the region of the city of Varna on the coast of the Black Sea in Bulgaria. Here stand hundreds of limestone columns like a petrified forest, up to 16 ft (5 m) high and 10 ft (3 m) in diameter. They are, in fact, a kind of stalagmite. Fifty million years ago in the Eocene era, these columns were created by a shallow sea that covered the area (known as Dikilitash). It consisted of a bedrock of sandstone covered with two strata of chalk. Millions of years of sea currents deposited these strange shapes that resemble the sandstone columns in Arizona.

The fact that the pillars are almost all of equal height led early archaeologists to assume that they were looking at the remains of an ancient ruined temple. Local legend relates stories of dancing sinners who were turned to stone where they stood. The high number of snakes in the area may have contributed to the formation of this sinister legend.

BULGARIA'S PETRIFIED FOREST
The limestone columns of Dikilitash cover a space of 25 acres (10 hectares) and are divided into seven groups. They stand in an area of parched sand inhabited by snakes and lizards. The largest group is known as the "central bush."

SUCEVITA MONASTERY
ROMANIA'S SISTINE CHAPEL
GAZETTEER P.139 - SITE NO.38

SUCEVITA MONASTERY, one of the most magnificent religious buildings in Romania, is a monument to two 16th-century local chiefs and the murderess Elizaveta, who poisoned her husband so that her sons could inherit the throne. All of these figures are featured in splendid frescoes that adorn the walls of the complex. The monastery church was built in 1584, the outer walls a little later.

There is a certain savage splendor about the famous frescoes in the monastery: the well-preserved Ladder of Virtue has sinners falling through the rungs into the arms of grinning demons. The Last Judgment in the porch has angels smiting the heathen with swords, while Jews and Turks lament and the Devil gloats. Appropriately, tradition declares that the fresco was left unfinished because the artist fell off the scaffold and broke his neck. The murderous Elizaveta and her children can be seen on one of the walls to the right of the nave. The imagery of the monastery is a vibrant mixture of the religious and the secular.

THE FRESCOES OF SUCEVITA
The dazzling colored frescoes inside the church and on its exterior walls were painted by two brothers in 1596. The frescoes achieve a three-dimensional effect by laying brilliant reds and blues over an undercoat of green.

THE GREAT WALLS
The walls of this vast monastery are indicative of their protective function. The area was subject to raids from the Ottomans, and the monastery complex would also have served as a defensive compound for the people of the surrounding area.

ZBORNA GOMILA
BOSNIA'S STECCI STONES
GAZETTEER P.139 - SITE NO.56

IN THE 14TH CENTURY, the Vlachs of Herzegovina inherited an archaic cult of the dead, and delighted in placing ever-larger *stecci* or "tombstones" in traditional sacred places. The impressive Meeting Mound at Avtovac, Zborna Gomila, with its magnificent "portrait tombstones," was once a meeting place of congresses and parliaments that became a center for important burials. The coffer-shaped tombstone (below) has an inscription to the 14th-century Bosnian Prince Vukosav Pliscic.

The Vlach tombstones often have portraits of the deceased, while mourners are portrayed as dancers. Puzzled by these incongruously joyous scenes, Austrian historians decided that these were the tombs of a heretical sect called the Bogomils, who believed that this world was created by the Devil, and that therefore death is a joyful release. Unfortunately, this appealing theory has since been disproved – the dancers, in fact, express the simple joy of those who have reached heaven.

VLACH TOMBSTONE
We still do not understand the enigmatic scenes and figures that are depicted on Vlach tombstones and coffins in this area – dancers, magical symbols, and female genitalia are among the images.

THE BIHOVO CROSS
The famous Bihovo Cross, in the Trebinje region of Herzegovina, is a representation of a bearded elder carrying a staff – presumably a prince buried on his own land. It carries a shield of 15th-century design, and is placed in a position overlooking a valley, possibly the lands of his family.

TOMB OF POPE URBAN VIII
The Church of St. Peter contains the tombs of many Catholic popes. In 1629, Gian Lorenzo Bernini was appointed architect of St. Peter's and created the tomb of his friend Pope Urban VIII.

ST. PETER'S

"THE GREATEST CHURCH IN CHRISTENDOM"

GAZETTEER P.139 · SITE NO.72

ALTHOUGH THE CENTER of one of the world's greatest empires and the site of numerous temples and shrines, the city of Rome was more an administrative center than a religious one. It was not until the arrival of Christianity that Rome became one of the world's great centers of faith. Jesus' disciple Peter came to Rome to head the church there, and was persecuted with many other early Christians, being crucified upside down during the reign of Nero in A.D. 67. St. Peter's Church housed his tomb. Roman Catholic tradition claims St. Peter as the first of the popes. With the conversion of Constantine in A.D. 313, two and a half centuries of persecution ended and Christianity became the official religion of the Roman Empire. With the establishment of the papacy, St. Peter's became the religious center of the Catholic world, a status it retains to this day.

THE CHURCH OF ST PETER'S

Originally built to house the saint's tomb, the first Church of St. Peter was constructed by the emperor Constantine in the fourth century A.D. It suffered so many fires that in 1506 Pope Julius II asked the great architect Bramante to draw up plans for a new basilica. The dome was designed by Michelangelo who also painted the ceiling and end wall of the Sistine Chapel in the adjacent papal buildings, The paintings are considered one of the masterpieces of world art. The religious complex is part of the Vatican, a separate state within the city of Rome.

ST. PETER'S SQUARE

The immense ellipse of St. Peter's Square was designed by Bernini, a dominant figure of baroque art. In the center stands an obelisk brought from Alexandria in 37 B.C. and erected at the present site in 1586. At the papal palace, the Pope's window is the only one lit after dark.

THE ETERNAL CITY

It seems both a coincidence and a strange irony that Rome should have become the center of Christendom. Rome was tolerant of many other religions, and many gods from the East (for example, Isis and Serapis from Egypt) were worshipped. The Christians were

THE BALDACCHINO

The canopy over the altar is one of Bernini's most splendid works – as a piece of bronze casting it is extraordinary. In fact, there was insufficient bronze, and the Pope gave orders to strip some from the ceiling of the portico of the Pantheon, the temple of earlier Roman gods rebuilt by Hadrian.

persecuted because they refused to worship the Roman state gods (a perfunctory exercise) and they actively proselytized. The Jews did not recognize Roman gods, but they kept to themselves, did not seek recruits, and thus were not considered to be a menace to the Roman state. As Imperial Rome declined, the Christian Church was on hand to continue the history of Roman power and splendor. Later, the rebuilding of Rome during the 16th century and the inspiration of the Counter-Reformation gave new life to a city that echoed the Rome of the Caesars. Its spiritual and symbolic center was St. Peter's Church, planned as the "greatest church in Christendom."

CERVETERI

ANCIENT ETRUSCAN CITY OF CHAISRE

GAZETTEER P.139 · SITE NO.71

IN THE DAYS WHEN ROME was just a small group of villages scattered over the seven hills, a wealthy and powerful people called the Etruscans were the dominant civilization on the Italian peninsula. Some time after 750 B.C., Rome was ruled by Etruscan kings – the tombs below the Roman Forum date from this period. Yet within a few centuries, the Etruscans had vanished from history, eclipsed and conquered by Rome. For almost 2,000 years they were forgotten. However, in 1827 colored murals were discovered in Etruscan tombs at Corneto in Tuscany. More excavations soon followed – at Chiusi, Veii, Cerveteri, and Orvieto. As marvelous artistic treasures were unearthed, it became clear that the Etruscans had been as remarkable a people as the Greeks and Romans. Unfortunately, their language has still not been deciphered, so that even now they remain a mystery.

LEOPARD'S TOMB

In this tomb near Rome, at Tarquinia (called Tarxuna by the Etruscans), the fine murals illustrate the Etruscans' developed artistic skill. Dating from the fifth century B.C., after the last Etruscan tyrant had been expelled from Rome, they show feasts, dancing, and music being played.

ETRUSCAN BELIEFS

The Etruscans were a deeply religious people, and it was their common religion that held the 12 main cities together. An annual meeting took place at the Temple of Voltumna near Volsinii, whose chief business was the election of a new high priest. The "haruspices" – oracles or prophets – were as influential to the Etruscans as the Delphic oracle was to the Greeks. Lightning and the flight of birds were just two of the many natural "signs" that the Etruscans interpreted as messages of the gods.

According to Etruscan belief, the sky was a great dome, separated into 16 compartments, different parts of the heavens that were ruled by different types of gods. The Etruscan pantheon, with its numerous deities, included some Greek gods. The chief deity was Tinia, a figure equivalent to the Greek Zeus. There was also a mother goddess, Uni, equivalent to the Greek Hera. The Etruscans believed in an afterlife and a region populated by demons. They worshiped household gods who, like their later Roman equivalents, seem to have played an important part in domestic ritual.

WHO WERE THE ETRUSCANS?

Cerveteri, home of some of Etruria's most magnificent tombs, was once known as Chaisre, and was one of the great maritime centers of the Etruscans. Its wealth came from minerals, and by 650 B.C. it was one of the richest towns in Italy. There was an influx of exotic imports, such as Egyptian faience, Corinthian vases, Assyrian goldwork, and Phoenician silver. The art of the Etruscans shows us that they were a pleasure-loving people.

The Etruscans contributed to the civilization of Rome, creating the walls of the Capitoline Hill and the Cloaca Maxima, and brought many technological and cultural innovations. We do not know where the Etruscans came from; the Greek historian Herodotus (c. 485–425 B.C.) thought they were from Lydia in Asia Minor. Scholars now believe that they were an indigenous people.

GOLD ETRUSCAN BURIAL GOODS

ETRUSCAN NECROPOLIS

The Etruscans believed in a life after death similar to life in this world. The soft volcanic tufa around Cerveteri is honeycombed with chamber tombs surmounted by tumuli – the most remarkable, the Tomba dei Rilievi is decorated with lively wall paintings of everyday domestic life.

ALMENDRAS
ANCIENT IBERIAN STONES

GAZETTEER P.138 · SITE NO.154

LIKE NORTHERN FRANCE and the United Kingdom, Portugal and southern Spain have many ancient megalithic sites. Almendras is the largest and one of the most impressive stone circles in Portugal. Such circles are known in Portugal as cromlechs (although in northern Europe, the term refers to a flat, tablelike stone resting on two others). At Almendras, there are 95 stones, an unusually large number for a megalithic circle. These are arranged in a double oval, with "lobes" at either end – the eastern lobes being larger than the western. Excavations and the clearing away of vegetation have revealed fallen stones, some previously unknown. Many stones are decorated with "cup marks," small hollows in the stone, also found on megaliths from Scotland to Malta. No one knows the precise significance of the hollows, or of the stones' double-ringed circles.

ANTA GRANDE, ZAMBUJEIRO

This huge mound is one of the finest passage graves in Portugal. Since a large part of the mound has been removed, the enormous chamber, almost 20 ft (6 m) in height, has been exposed. A long stone slab near the mound has typical cup marks – it has been suggested that such marks may be intended to receive blood in some ritual sacrifice. Most passage graves are little more than 5 ft (1.5 m) high, so this is a splendid exception. Portugal contains some of the oldest *ante* (chamber tombs) outside Brittany – goods found in one of them have been dated to around 4150 B.C.

PRECISION CALENDAR

The Almendras circle could date to any time from 3500 to 1500 B.C. We cannot be certain about the precise function of the stones. It is now generally accepted that the purpose of most megalithic circles is astronomical: that is, the stones measured the movements of the stars and were used to establish a calendar. Many circles have 19 stones, corresponding to the moon's 19-year cyclic movement along the horizon. More than 90 stones, as at Almendras, is unusual. Alexander Thom, an acknowledged expert on megalithic circles, has pointed out that the clearer skies in the Mediterranean make stars far easier to view than in the north. More precise calculations – using a greater number of stones – could create a more accurate calendar than one based on simply the sun and the moon.

STANDING STONES

Like many groups of standing stones, the original function of the megaliths at Almendras was later forgotten, and they became a center for other rites, successively embroidered by local legend. Thus the site became a sacred center long after its inception.

SANTIAGO DE COMPOSTELA
"THE FIELD OF STARS"

GAZETTEER P.138 · SITE NO.145

SANTIAGO DE COMPOSTELA
The whole of Santiago de Compostela, except the tomb of the saint, was destroyed in 997 by the Moors. In 1078, the Romanesque cathedral began to be rebuilt over St. James' tomb.

STATUE OF ST. JAMES
St. James acquired an unsaintly reputation as a slayer of Moors after King Ramiro claimed that the saint had fought beside him at the Battle of Clavajo (A.D. 844) and killed 60,000 of them.

AROUND THE BEGINNING of the ninth century, a hermit saw a vision of stars on a hillside in Spain, and the place became known as Compostela – "the field of stars." Soon after, a buried altar containing human bones was found at the site where, according to an old legend, the corpse of Jesus's disciple St. James (Santiago in Spanish) had been brought from Egypt after his martyrdom by Herod. Spain was then almost entirely under the dominion of the Arabs, and Compostela became a place of political, as well as religious, importance. St. James was adopted as the champion of Christian Spain against the Muslims. King Alfonso II came to pay his respects and built a chapel. Alfonso III replaced it with a stone one. The town that grew up around the site became one of the major pilgrimage centers after Rome and Jerusalem. The legend soon included Charlemagne, who was supposed to have dreamt of St. James and learned the location of his tomb in Galicia. The route from France to Santiago was linked with pilgrims' hostels.

MONTSERRAT
MONASTERY OF THE BLACK MADONNA

GAZETTEER P.138 · SITE NO.138

SITE OF PILGRIMAGE
The monastery is visited by around 60,000 pilgrims a year who come to see Our Lady of Monserrat, the image around which the complex was built. It has been a site of pilgrimage for centuries. The present basilica was begun in 1560, and the monastery in 1755.

VIEW OF THE MOUNTAIN
The mountain itself was known to the Catalan people of the area as a sacred mountain before its Christian buildings were built. Remains at the site suggest it was inhabited in Prehistoric times.

PERCHED ON A TERRACE over 2,953 ft (900 m) above sea level and perched on a terrace among the fantastic saw-edges of the Montserrat mountains stands the magnificent monastery of Montserrat. The Romans called the location *mons serratus,* "saw-toothed mountain." It was later famous for a holy image of the Virgin, said to have been carved by St. Luke and brought to nearby Barcelona by St. Peter in A.D. 30. When the Moors invaded in 717, the image was hidden in a cave near Montserrat. The legend states that in 880, Gondemar, Bishop of Vich, drawn to the cave because of sweet sounds and flowery scents, rediscovered the image. He set out for Manresa with it, but at a certain point, the image refused to go any further, and a chapel was constructed to house it. A Benedictine convent was built around the chapel in 967. Positioned on one of the main routes to Compostela, the monastery became one of Europe's major pilgrimage centers. It is estimated that during the Middle Ages 50,000 pilgrims a year came there. It was

granted independence as an abbey by Antipope Benedict XIII in 1410. Later, the abbey went through many trials. It was despoiled during the Napoleonic Wars (1808–14), and in 1835, as a result of the Carlist insurrection, was deprived of its estates and revenues. The number of monks was reduced to 20. In 1874, it was made subject to the Bishop of Barcelona.

CARNAC

STONES OF MAGICAL POWER

GAZETTEER P.138 · SITE NO.133

THE GREATEST CONCENTRATION of upright stones (menhirs) in Europe – 3,000 of them in all – stands just to the north of Carnac, a small coastal town in Brittany. Unlike Stonehenge (see pp.68-69), all but 70 of the stones at Carnac are arranged in parallel rows. At Kermario, there are ten rows, each with 1,120 stones. The only Carnac mound to be dated so far is St. Michel, and the tests there placed its origin at about 5000 B.C. – at least 2,000 years older than was expected. Inevitably the area is full of legends – about how the stones were erected by spirits or giants, even how a former pope had changed his heathen pursuers to stones. Carnac was a religious center for the Romans, and later Christians carved crosses into the stones' surfaces. Yet folk memory holds clues to the pagan background of the site. On Midsummer Eve, bonfires are lit at the entrance to sunken roads, after which cattle and sheep are driven among the stones – ancient memories of festivals enacted to bring the protection of fertility gods.

FERTILITY STONES

Although we are still uncertain as to the actual use of the stones, it may be that the ancient religion with which they were associated worshipped an earth or moon goddess. The purpose of its ceremonies may have been to ensure fertility and to protect the crops from disasters that were probably attributed to hostile spirits. Even today, the stones are still associated with fertility: barren couples are advised to dance naked among the stones, and young married women to sit on them.

THE ENERGY OF THE STONES

All good dowsers will verify that the stones of Carnac are charged with some magnetic force. Native peoples in America and Australia believe that certain rocks have healing powers, and that the sick can touch them to use their power. The stones of Carnac may have been used for similar purposes.

THEORIES ON THE STONES

The purpose of these massive, parallel rows of stones has baffled antiquarians. In his book *Collection of Antiquities* (1761–67), the Count de Caylus speculated that Carnac was the monument of an unknown race of seafarers. He relates how they drove the Celts into the interior, and how they later went to Britain, where they built Stonehenge. Another writer declared that the seafarers were Egyptians, and the stones a temple in the form of a serpent. He pointed out that Carnac sounds like Karnak (see p.17), and when he found a statue of Isis in the grounds of a nearby castle, he was convinced of his theory. The scholar Jacques de Cambry stated that Carnac was a druid temple and had astronomical significance. This sounds like an inspired guess, though it was based on the dubious notion that the 11 rows of stones at Menec represented the signs of the zodiac. We now know that there was, in fact, a twelfth row. The Chevalier de Freminville, the creator of some fine drawings of Carnac, denounced it as romantic nonsense, declaring that the stones were obviously the graves of warriors.

At the turn of the century, a scholar named Zacharie Le Rouzie created confusion by marking and reerecting fallen stones; he often misplaced stones, and much of his work was unhelpful. Fortunately for later archaeologists, an earlier survey showed the original positions and his mistakes were corrected.

LINES OF ETERNAL RITUAL
Its original use may be a mystery, but Carnac has been used in rituals by subsequent cultures. The Romans carved deities on some of the stones, while Christians later added crosses to the site. Bretons held the stones in awe until recent times.

In 1970, the scientific methods of Alexander Thom, an expert on stone circles, revealed that Cambry had been right after all. Carnac had been set up by ancient astronomer-priests to observe the sun and moon. According to Thom, the Grand Menhir Brisé at nearby Locmariaquer was of central importance; once 68 ft (21 m) high, it may have been used as a marker for the rising and setting of the moon.

THE MYSTERY OF CARNAC

What the priests of this ancient religion did at Carnac remains a mystery. Thom has argued that the alignments were used as "stone graph paper" to calculate the position of the moon from observations over the Grand Menhir Brisé, with astronomer-priests noting the position of the moon behind the great megalith. Thom talks of two kinds of "megalithic lunar observatories": those at which the observer looked from the inside outward, like the ring at Stonehenge, and those which the observer looked from the outside inward, like Carnac.

Yet there can be little doubt that Thom had missed something. The people who built Carnac were obsessed by the moon because it affected them, as it affects tides and "lunatics" during a full moon. Experiments today prove that the area in which the stones of Carnac stand has a magnetic or electrical force that may have produced a similarly disturbing effect. Standing stones are often associated with legends of dancers; in fact, a festival is still held here during the midsummer solstice. What is clear is that the stones also had a ritual significance. Their role as a place of ritual may have resulted from their position at the center of a rich source of earth energy.

GAVRINIS PASSAGE GRAVE

The Chevalier de Freminville's belief that the stones of Carnac are graves of warriors is not as foolish as it sounds, for there are many tumuli in the area. The long tumulus at Gavrinis (above) to the east of Carnac is aligned to the midsummer solstice. One of the most beautiful passage graves in the world, the site includes slabs carved with spirals, axes, and other markings. The spirals represent the journey of the soul, moving from death to rebirth. The image on the right shows a representation of a goddess of the dead carved on another grave, farther up the Brittany coast at Barnenez. The builders of these mounds probably predate the makers of the stone rows.

GODDESS OF THE DEAD

LASCAUX

SANCTUARY OF ANCIENT HUMANS

GAZETTEER P.138 - SITE NO.123

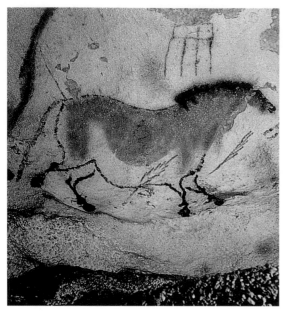

"CHINESE HORSES"

The three little horses on the ceiling of the Axial Gallery (the passage at the center of the main image, right) have been called "Chinese Horses" because they resemble horses found in Chinese paintings. One controversial interpretation of the "grid" in the top right of the image above is that of a tribal badge or a "magical" flight of arrows.

THE DISCOVERY

On September 12, 1940, four French teenagers decided to explore a hole left by an uprooted tree, near the little town of Montignac, in the Vézère Valley. An old woman had told them that a tunnel led from there to the château of Lascaux. Eighteen-year-old Marcel Ravidat widened it with a spade, then saw a narrower shaft at the bottom. He climbed in, dropping on soft earth, and lit his lamp. The light revealed a tunnel, leading into a grotto with paintings and engravings of animals on the walls. Five days later, Abbé Henri Breuil, a celebrated authority on cave art, came to inspect it, and realized at once that this was one of the greatest discoveries of cave art so far. Two tunnels lead off the "main hall" – with 65 tableaux of bulls, horses, reindeer, birds, even a man killed by a bison, and a multitude of mysterious signs. The paintings were in a better state of preservation and their colors (oddly enough, still damp), brighter than any discovered so far. These remarkable rock pictures – a "prehistoric Louvre" – date to about 15,000 B.C.

HIDDEN TREASURES

The caves are now closed to the public because of earlier damage caused by the presence of tourists. However, an exact replica, Lascaux II, is nearby. The continuous tapestry of paintings, crowded with hundreds of animals, brings an uncanny sense of the presence of the ancient artists.

WHILE IT IS PERHAPS the most famous of the caves decorated with paintings by early humans, Lascaux is also one of the most recently discovered – it was found in 1940. The discovery of cave art was one of the great archaeological watersheds of the late 19th century. Until then, early students of prehistory had concentrated on humans' physical evolution – assuming that modern humans were worlds away from their "primitive" forebears. These paintings revealed Stone Age humans who were, in their way, as sophisticated as any modern artist. The story began in 1878 when a Spanish nobleman, Don Marcelino de Sautuola, accidentally discovered the paintings in underground caves at Altamira in northern Spain. In 1895, similar discoveries made in French caves in the Vézère Valley confirmed the authenticity of Don Marcelino's find. These early discoveries pointed to the religious nature of many cave paintings. At first, it was assumed that other rock paintings had been worn away, while these had survived because of their sheltered location. But some scholars came to believe that the sites themselves may have been significant sanctuaries where rituals were performed.

LATE ICE AGE ARTISTS

Similarities in the art of different settlements of the late Magdalenian period – about 15,000 B.C. – have suggested the possibility that the artists were itinerant, making a living by their talents. Art may have lost its ritual significance, and carvings like this stylized mammoth, made from an animal's shoulder blade, may have been intended simply as talismans or good luck charms. Such art shows how ancient people progressed from a simple existence to abstract thought, expression, and a memory for myth.

NEOLITHIC MAMMOTH
BONE CARVING

Carved mammoth bones may have been used in ritual

THE FUNCTION OF THE CAVES

"Here is something other than a proof of a marvelous artistic disposition; there are unknown motives and aims at work." Thus spoke the prehistorian Emile Carthailac on seeing the engravings in the Laugerie Basse cave at Les Eyzies in the early 1890s. He had divined correctly that this was not merely a proof that Ice Age humans had an artistic disposition, but that the cave paintings had other uses. It was the Aborigines of Australia and the Native Americans who finally provided the clue, for their drawings serve magical and religious purposes. A drawing of a bison was intended to provide the magical link between the hunter and his prey. In the Three Brothers Cave (Trois Frères) in Ariege, in front of a picture of two bison coupling, footprints of dancers were found. There was also the famous painting of the "magician," a man wearing a bison skin. This suggested that before the hunters went out seeking their prey, the shaman led an elaborate ritual to ensure their success. But the pictures of mating bison – and even of men and women locked in an embrace – suggest that these magical rituals also concern reproduction. The caves were not the home of Ice Age humans, but a ritual site.

"MAN KILLED BY BISON"

This image of a prostrate – presumably dead – man, a disemboweled bison, and a bird on a kind of stick, is one of the most mysterious at Lascaux. It has been suggested that the bird represents the dead man's soul leaving his body.

BELIEFS OF ANCIENT PEOPLE

More than 100,000 years ago, *Homo sapiens* split into two distinct groups. *Homo sapiens sapiens* (modern humans) coexisted with *Homo sapiens neanderthalensis* (Neanderthals) in the Near East until the latter's extinction about 35,000 years ago. It is thought that hunter-gatherers were expert astronomers, since the passage of the seasons was important to them. Neanderthals seem to have been religious, burying their dead in graves. The first known burials are those found in the Middle East. *Homo sapiens sapiens* are thought perhaps to have had a decided advantage over their rivals in their more developed language skills. These skills played an important part in their survival and the emergence of abstract expression in the form of engravings on animal bones and early rock art. The earliest rock art has been discovered in the form of petroglyphs in northern Australia, and dates to possibly 45,000 years ago. Caves clearly attracted early people because they provided protection from the elements, but also developed a function as a sanctuary, where ancient knowledge and mythologies were recorded and rediscovered.

BLACK VIRGIN
The cult of the Black Virgin suddenly expanded in the 12th century, perhaps because crusaders brought black statues of the Virgin back from the Holy Land. Various sources suggest that the Black Virgin was originally a pagan goddess.

CHARTRES
THE BIBLE IN STONE

GAZETTEER P.138 - SITE NO.110

PERHAPS THE GREATEST of the French Gothic cathedrals, Chartres is among the masterpieces of world architecture. It was one of the results of a tremendous outpouring of religious energy that occurred around 1100. In effect, the building of the cathedral was a gigantic act of penitence, and those who contributed could feel assured of the forgiveness of their sins. If a man carried any bitterness in his heart, or if he refused to forgive his enemies, he was deprived of the right to help with the cathedral. For this work was not merely the building of a stone church; it was the building of a cathedral of the spirit, in which human beings were transformed. As an act of devotion to the Virgin Mary, to whom Chartres was dedicated, thousands of peasants from the area dragged the stones in carts so that they could be carved into the thousands of figures that adorn the building.

THE MASTER BUILDERS

Chartres poses many riddles. It carries the stamp of genius, yet we know nothing of those individuals who built it and carved its extraordinary sculptures. These include friezes of scenes from the Bible – like the Last Supper – grotesques of demons, and portraits of saints. Together with the beautiful stained glass windows, they make the cathedral a compendium of medieval theological imagery.

Yet not all of the imagery is explicitly religious. With the tremendous surge in cathedral building that began around 1100, the demands for architects, craftsmen, and masons suddenly became urgent. Bands of masons formed themselves into guilds and moved about Europe, taking work wherever it could be found. At a time when serfs were tied to the land they farmed, the masons became known as freemasons. Many abstract concepts were embodied in the cathedrals – ideas from alchemy and tones in music to theological and philosophical notions of harmony.

The art critic Kenneth Clark has argued that the faces carved at Chartres show a new stage in the ascent of Western culture – that their spirituality is "something entirely new in art."

THE CATHEDRAL SPIRES
The writer Paul Devereux has pointed out how the different heights of the two spires may illustrate an older symbolism. He claims that the dimensions of the taller tower relate to the solar calendar, while those of the shorter tower relate to the lunar cycle. The sun-moon, masculine-feminine symbolism carries echoes of older pagan traditions and suggests the cathedral may stand on a former pagan site.

THE LABYRINTH
The labyrinth in the church floor is 42 ft (13 m) across. Many churches have labryinths dating from this period. At the center is a rose where there was once a brass plate with figures of Theseus, the Minotaur, and Ariadne (see pp.36-37).

THE SACRED HILL

The cathedral's historian, Suchet, relates how there was once a sacred forest on the hilltop where Chartres now stands. Centuries earlier, it was known as Carnute, where – according to Julius Caesar – druids held their ceremonies. In the fourth century, a Christian church stood on the site. An old well behind the cathedral is believed to have been used by druids for purposes of divination. Druids studied the bubbling of water when it had been vigorously stirred by an oak rod. So it seems that Chartres, like so many of the world's sacred sites, is built on a place that had been regarded as sacred for centuries, perhaps for millennia.

AACHEN

CHARLEMAGNE'S HOLY CHAPEL

GAZETTEER P.139 · SITE NO.96

IT WAS THE HOT sulfur springs at Aachen that attracted its greatest patron, Charlemagne (A.D. 742–814) and convinced him to make it his second city. Aachen had previously been sacred to both Celts and Romans. It subsequently became one of the great centers of early European learning and culture. Charlemagne's father Pepin had laid the foundation of the immense wealth and power of the Catholic Church by conquering several Lombard towns in Italy and making a gift of them to the Pope. The son of Pepin – crowned in A.D. 768 – was just as good a friend to the papacy, and Pope Leo III rewarded him unexpectedly by crowning him as he knelt in prayer in St. Peter's on Christmas Day in A.D. 800. Aachen became one of the centers of the Holy Roman Empire. Its beautiful Palatine Chapel with its elegant proportions now forms the center of Aachen Cathedral.

AACHEN CATHEDRAL
Charlemagne admired the Roman palace at Trier, 100 mi (161 km) away, and used the design for his palace at Aachen. But the French name for Aachen, Aix-la-Chapelle, suggests the importance of Charlemagne's chapel.

DEVELOPMENT OF AACHEN

The chapel of Charlemagne's palace – the Palatine Chapel – is now the core of Aachen Cathedral. The chapel was based on the Byzantine church of San Vitale in Ravenna, Italy. Together with Rome, Ravenna had been one of the historical capitals of the Roman Empire, an importance that Charlemagne coveted for Aachen. The architect of the chapel, Odo of Metz, did not quite master the subtlety of the Italian church, and his chapel is massive and sturdy rather than light and airy. A ninth-century chronicler, Notke the Stammerer, records that skilled workmen were brought from all over the empire, so that the chapel should surpass any previously erected.

The symmetry, height, and grandeur of the chapel are overwhelming: the eight-sided dome is surrounded by a 16-sided walkway, above this is a two-tiered gallery, which is supported by eight columns.

After Charlemagne was canonized in 1165, so many pilgrims streamed into Aachen that the chapel had to be expanded. The Gothic choir was added between 1355 and 1414, modeled on St. Chapelle in Paris. A series of two-story chapels built encircling the octagon were also added, the finest being the Hungarian chapel of 1367. The dome was placed last. The rest of Charlemagne's palace has disappeared, and the Aachen *rathaus* (town hall) stands on the site of its banqueting hall. Its façade is lined with 50 statues of Holy Roman Emperors, 31 of them crowned in Aachen. From the tenth to the 17th century most of the German kings were also crowned here.

With all this Roman splendor, it is not surprising that Charlemagne was idealized more than any ruler since Alexander the Great. But his empire did not survive him, for it was too vast for any successors to hold together. And even at the time of his death, invaders called the Vikings were menacing northern Europe.

CHARLEMAGNE'S THRONE
The throne stood in the gallery of the chapel, looking west. On Midsummer Day, sunlight entering the east window would illuminate the head of the emperor.

COIN OF CHARLEMAGNE

INTERIOR OF THE CHAPEL
The contemporary biographer of Charlemagne, Einhard, describes the emperor's interests in astronomy. The writer Paul Devereux has made the startling suggestion that the ground plan of the chapel at Aachen has the same proportions as the inner horseshoe of trilithons at Stonehenge and shares similar astronomical alignments.

EXTERNSTEINE
SACRED ROCKS OF TEUTONIC MYTH

GAZETTEER P.139 - SITE NO.98

THE BIZARRELY TWISTED limestone rocks called the Externsteine have the look of forms from some strange fairy tale. This range of hills, set in the Teutoburger Wald, near Detmold in West Saxony has always been a center for heroic myths and Teutonic legend. It is also linked with many of the stories of the Scandinavian Eddas – Norse legends – and became associated with Aryan myth during the Nazi period. In ancient times this was a place of pagan worship, and later of Christian pilgrimage. Until the eighth century, this beautiful forest setting was the home of an Irmensul ("giant column," the German Tree of Life). The tree represents the entire world, its roots reaching down into the underworld and its branches stretching up toward the sky. It was cut down by the Frankish king Charlemagne (A.D. 742–814) as the first step toward Christianizing the site.

THE DEPOSITION OF CHRIST
This relief showing Christ being lifted from the cross was carved in the 12th century on the largest of the rocks, and the "stool" on which Nicodemus is standing is actually the pagan Irmensul tree bent at a right angle – presumably drooping in defeat before Christianity.

THE HISTORY OF THE ROCKS

In A.D. 9, the Teutoburger Wald was the site of a rousing defeat of the Roman troops by a local hero, Arminius. Understandably, he became a great German hero, and, in A.D. 185, a gigantic statue of him made of beaten copper was raised near the spot where the battle took place. After Charlemagne had Christianized the site, a replica of the holy places of Jerusalem was constructed at the Externsteine for the benefit of pilgrims, with remarkable bas-reliefs and chapels. For many years, monks and hermits lived in the caves. The Externsteine fell into disuse until the 1920s, when they became the center of a new cult. Inspired by the revival of romantic German nationalism, a vigorous German youth movement was spawned with a devotion to the countryside. Wilhelm Teudt, an evangelical parson, added his own gloss to this nationalism, declaring that the rock containing the chapel was a pagan solar observatory, and that "astronomical lines" linked numerous sacred sites throughout the Teutoburger Wald and northern Germany. His ideas inspired the Nazis, particularly Heinrich Himmler.

THE ANCIENT ROCK-HEWN CHAPEL
To the right of the bas-relief (above) is the rock-cut chapel, consecrated in 1115. In 1823, von Bennigsen noticed that from a niche in the chapel wall, a round window opposite would frame the moon in its northernmost position, as well as the sun at the summer solstice. From this, he deduced that the chapel had been used by ancient pagan priests as an "observatory." Wilhelm Teudt embraced this insight and enthusiastically extended it.

Originally a site of pagan worship, the rocks later became a place of Christian pilgrimage

This walkway leads to the rock-cut chapel inset at the bottom of the picture

THE SHAPES OF MYTH
The beautiful and bizarre shapes of the Externsteine, which once provided shelter for nomadic deerhunters, have always given rise to tales of magic and heroism. For Wilhelm Teudt, they were the home of the Stone Age Aryan civilization he so admired. He believed Aryans were great innovators, whose discoveries had influenced all of mankind.

THINGVELLIR
THE WORLD'S FIRST PARLIAMENT
GAZETTEER P.138 · SITE NO.1

EVERYMAN GORGE

Thingvellir, 30 mi (48 km) from Reykjavík, remained the site of the Icelandic parliament until 1798, when an earthquake took place, and the annual assembly moved from Everyman Gorge to the capital, Reykjavík. In 1944, the proclamation of the Republic of Iceland was read at Thingvellir.

ICELAND'S GREAT meeting place and site of religious celebration was established in A.D. 930, when its people still worshipped the Norse gods. At that time, Iceland had been settled for less than a century. When Ingolfur Arnason, a chieftain from west Norway, reached Iceland in 874, the only inhabitants were a few Irish hermits. He established himself at what is now the capital, Reykjavík. Other Norwegian and Irish settlers soon joined him. They lived by fishing and sheep farming. It was from here that the Vikings went on to discover North America.

In 930, the Icelanders decided they needed a parliament, and selected a 3 mi (5 km) long ravine in a field of volcanic lava on the northern shore of a lake. This became Thingvellir, their meeting place, and the site of *Althing*, the world's first parliament. The parliament was held there for 15 days following the summer solstice, presided over by the *godar*, religious leaders. The gorge was named Everyman Gorge, because everyone in the country could fit into it at the same time.

In A.D. 1000, it was at Thingvellir that the peaceful decision was made that Iceland should become Christian. In subsequent years, on this high plain surrounded by cliffs formed from lava, legal disputes were settled, bards read their epics, and religious rites took place.

LAKE THINGVALLAVATN

Althing, or parliament, took place on the northern shore of Lake Thingvallavatn. The lake, is 9 mi (14 km) long and up to 6 mi (10 km) wide, the largest in Iceland.

GOTLAND
THE NORSE SHIP OF NIGHT
GAZETTEER P.139 · SITE NO.13

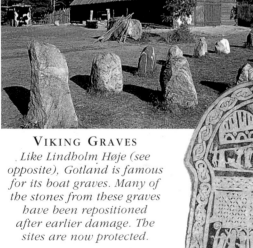

VIKING GRAVES

Like Lindholm Høje (see opposite), Gotland is famous for its boat graves. Many of the stones from these graves have been repositioned after earlier damage. The sites are now protected.

PICTURE STONE

This stone (right) is from Ardre in Gotland. At the top of the stone, Sleipnir, Odin's eight-legged horse, is seen carrying the god across the sky. The stone dates from the Viking era (A.D. 900–1050).

GOTLAND IS THE largest island in the Baltic Sea, and in the 12th century it was one of the greatest trading centers in Europe and a member of the Hanseatic League. The second-century historian Jordanes declared that the island was called Gotland because it was the home of the Goths, the barbarians who swept ruthlessly over Europe and contributed to the downfall of the Roman Empire.

Gotland was the center of an ancient Norse faith associated with a cult of the dead. At Klinthelm on the north coast of the island, there is an outline of a ship in stones – a ship intended to carry the souls of the dead to the underworld. It dates from around 1500 B.C., and is one of 350 boat burials on the island.

Local legend states that the island was once controlled by evil spirits, who made it sink during the day and reappear at night. Tjelvar, the first man to set foot on the island, broke the spell with a ritual involving fire, probably lighting up the island by night and driving away the evil spirits. The legend is certainly based on elements of Bronze Age sun worship, in which a wagon symbolized the sun's journey across the sky during the day, and a ship its journey through the underworld at night. The island itself was the ship of night, symbolizing the soul's journey to the land of the dead.

Even the famous stone maze at Trojeborg (near Visby, the capital of Gotland) is associated with the cult of the dead. Like the labyrinths depicted on megalithic tombs, it represents a path of the dead to the underworld. Since most stone mazes are close to the sea, it is probable that sailors used to enter them before a voyage, in a symbolic descent to the land of the dead, to propitiate its gods and prevent them from claiming the lives of sailors at sea.

LINDHOLM HØJE
NECROPOLIS OF BOAT GRAVES
GAZETTEER P.139 - SITE NO.20

ON A HILL OVERLOOKING the fjord near Ålborg in northern Denmark lies a great ancient necropolis. Although the 700 graves cover a period of more than four centuries, most of them are Viking and – like those of Gotland – 200 are shaped like boats.

Lindholm was clearly a major settlement from before A.D. 600 – as is implied by such a large graveyard. Many buildings have been found in an adjacent settlement, including long houses with convex sides and four straight shed buildings placed around a central yard. At the beginning of the 11th century, Lindholm was struck by a tremendous sandstorm that buried everything. It was abandoned and not rediscovered until the 20th century.

Around A.D. 800, at the time that the Vikings launched their devastating raids, Norway, Sweden, and Denmark were not separate countries with different languages; all were part of a greater Scandinavia where all the people spoke Old Norse and, with local variations, worshipped the same gods. It is believed the

Vikings embarked on their career of piracy because there was insufficient farmland to support the expanding population. Soon, no coastal area in Europe was safe from their raids. Terror was used as a deliberate weapon – for example, the sacrifice called the "blood eagle" involved opening the breast and spreading the lungs of the living victim like eagle wings.

The Norsemen often buried their dead on a headland within sight of the sea or a fjord. The Anglo-Saxon epic *Beowulf* describes what the Viking burials must have been like: warriors riding around the grave, dirges recited, and the heroic deeds of the dead man proclaimed. The boat-shaped graves, which mostly align north to south, represented the vessels that would carry the souls of the dead to Valhalla, the resting place of heroes.

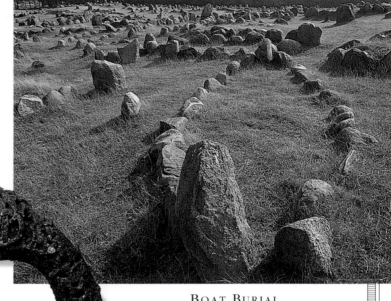

BOAT BURIAL
The necropolis includes hundreds of graves. Many contained burned burial objects – glass jewelry, swords, and animal bones.

BAROQUE HEAD
The purpose of this Viking animal head from a burial mound at Oseberg in Norway is unknown. It may have been used in religious processions.

THE NORTHERN LIGHTS
THE MAGICAL AURORA BOREALIS
GAZETTEER P.139 - SITE NO.4

IT WAS INEVITABLE that the spectacular light show called the aurora borealis should have been regarded by the ancient peoples of Scandinavia as a direct manifestation of their gods. In the latitudes farther south, where it is a less familiar sight, it was seen as a portent of coming calamities, particularly when it appeared red.

The northern (and southern) lights are caused by the glow of gases high in the earth's atmosphere. When atoms of hydrogen, oxygen, and nitrogen are struck by high-speed electrons from the sun, they glow like the gas in a neon sign. The solar "bullets" follow a curving path, due to the earth's lines of magnetic force. This produces beautiful auroral patterns, such as

LIGHT EFFECTS OF THE AURORA
The aurora rises to about ten degrees above the horizon, and turns brown or violet. A broad arch, first white, then yellow, encircles the dark segment. Rays emanate from it, and columns of flame appear to rise from the smoky arch, all flickering continuously in a sea of fire.

"curtains," "rays," and "crowns." Since the earth's magnetism is strongest over the poles, this is where the auroras can be seen most clearly.

The aurora is due to magnetic disturbance, registered by swings in a compass needle, i.e., to "telluric" magnetism (the magnetism of the earth). Experiments have shown that birds navigate by means of the earth's magnetism, and lose their way in the disturbances known as magnetic vortices. Similar experiments with human beings have shown a high sensitivity to magnetic fields, and that the ability to "dowse" is due to this sensitivity. For dowsers, sacred sites (like Stonehenge) reveal a vortex of "earth force." And since tribal shamans are chosen, among other things, for their sensitivity to this force, it can be seen why primitive people should see a connection between the sacred and magnetic disturbances.

The northern lights are, of course, not associated with one place, and can be seen in places as far apart as Scandinavia and Canada.

UNITED KINGDOM & IRELAND

THE UNITED KINGDOM AND IRELAND once stood on the dim outer limits of the known world, and were probably the place that about 300 B.C. the Greek explorer Pytheas called "Ultima Thule" – he referred to a great temple that may have been Stonehenge. Today when visiting Newgrange or Iona, it is still possible to capture some of the tradition of myth and mystery. Bronze Age paganism and Celtic beliefs seems to blend gently into early Christianity. Legends relate how King Arthur's magician Merlin brought the megaliths of Stonehenge from Ireland, while the historic site of Glastonbury was linked to the childhood of Christ and the Holy Grail. The county of Cornwall in southwest England still has many holy wells, believed to possess healing powers. Fragments of cloth are tied to branches around the well, the theory being that as they rot away, so the illness disappears. Throughout the Dark Ages, learning was kept alive in the Christian monasteries like Kells in County Meath, Ireland, where the Book of Kells was created in the seventh century. It is here that the modern British and Irish religious and cultural traditions began.

① IONA
St. Columba, an Irish monk, brought Christianity to Scotland via this remote and beautiful island.

NORTHERN IRELAND

DONEGAL BAY

LOUGH NEAGH

② NEWGRANGE
This great mound-barrow tomb is one of the most impressive prehistoric monuments in Europe.

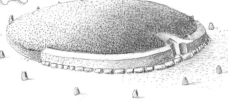

REPUBLIC OF IRELAND

ATLANTIC OCEAN

LOOP HEAD

③ THE HILL OF TARA
South of Newgrange, Tara is the most legendary of all sites in Celtic mythology. The seat of the high kings of Ireland, it has as many myths attached to it as King Arthur's Camelot.

BANTRY BAY

CELTIC SEA

GRAVE GOODS
This superbly crafted and astonishingly delicate boat was part of a hoard of golden objects found in Broighter, County Londonderry. It is made of solid gold and dates to the first century A.D. It may have been buried with the body of a chieftain in order to carry his soul safely to the underworld.

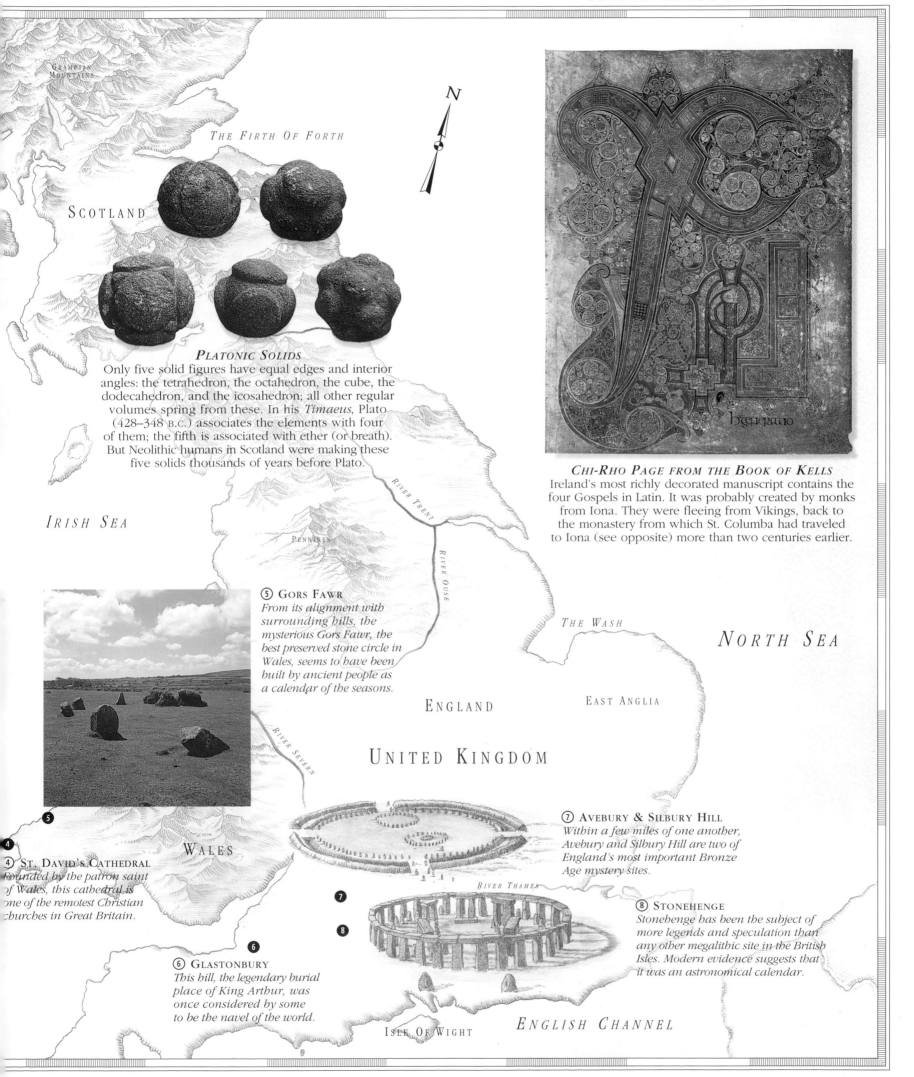

THE FIRTH OF FORTH

SCOTLAND

PLATONIC SOLIDS
Only five solid figures have equal edges and interior angles: the tetrahedron, the octahedron, the cube, the dodecahedron, and the icosahedron; all other regular volumes spring from these. In his *Timaeus*, Plato (428–348 B.C.) associates the elements with four of them; the fifth is associated with ether (or breath). But Neolithic humans in Scotland were making these five solids thousands of years before Plato.

IRISH SEA

RIVER TRENT

PENNINES

RIVER OUSE

CHI-RHO PAGE FROM THE BOOK OF KELLS
Ireland's most richly decorated manuscript contains the four Gospels in Latin. It was probably created by monks from Iona. They were fleeing from Vikings, back to the monastery from which St. Columba had traveled to Iona (see opposite) more than two centuries earlier.

⑤ **GORS FAWR**
From its alignment with surrounding hills, the mysterious Gors Fawr, the best preserved stone circle in Wales, seems to have been built by ancient people as a calendar of the seasons.

THE WASH

NORTH SEA

ENGLAND

EAST ANGLIA

RIVER SEVERN

UNITED KINGDOM

⑤

④

④ **ST. DAVID'S CATHEDRAL**
Founded by the patron saint of Wales, this cathedral is one of the remotest Christian churches in Great Britain.

WALES

⑦ **AVEBURY & SILBURY HILL**
Within a few miles of one another, Avebury and Silbury Hill are two of England's most important Bronze Age mystery sites.

RIVER THAMES

⑦

⑧ **STONEHENGE**
Stonehenge has been the subject of more legends and speculation than any other megalithic site in the British Isles. Modern evidence suggests that it was an astronomical calendar.

⑧

⑥

⑥ **GLASTONBURY**
This hill, the legendary burial place of King Arthur, was once considered by some to be the navel of the world.

ISLE OF WIGHT

ENGLISH CHANNEL

STONEHENGE

GLASTONBURY, AVEBURY & SILBURY

——— GAZETTEER P.143 · SITES NOS.61, 69 & 59 ———

ANCIENT STONE CIRCLES AND MEGALITHS (literally "large stones") are found all over the world. Yet despite this, little is known about them. For example, we know roughly who built the ancient British sites of Stonehenge, Avebury, and Silbury Hill and when, but not why. Some people have imagined the stones freeing concentrations of energy within the earth, much as acupuncture needles do in the body. Others suggest a possible connection to fertility rites and a religion of the Earth Mother – there are even suggestions of human sacrifice. The only thing that seems sure is that there was some connection to the seasons.

SACRED LINES
Ley lines link Silbury and Avebury (above, Silbury Hill is seen in the distance). Writer Paul Devereux suggests that ancient shamans used dream states to establish contact with a "paradise consciousness" where strange landscapes are seen, and that our Neolithic ancestors aligned major sites to create a symbolic landscape of sacred land art.

AVEBURY & SILBURY HILL

The great megalithic complex at the village of Avebury in Wiltshire was once even more impressive than Stonehenge, and its earliest part, "the Sanctuary," dates to about the same time (3000 B.C.). Inside the huge chalk ridge there once stood the largest stone circle known anywhere. It consisted of a main ring of 90 stone blocks, each weighing about five tons, and two smaller circles of 30 stones each. An avenue of upright stones once joined Avebury to a nearby temple on Overton Hill. During the Middle Ages, many of the stones were dragged away for building, or buried to discourage pagan rituals. This destruction continued into the 19th century. If the damage were restored, Avebury would be one of the most impressive temples in the world.

To the south of Avebury is Silbury Hill. Built around 2500 B.C., Britain's largest man-made mound is 600 ft (183 m) around the base and 180 ft (55 m) high. Traditionally it was the burial place of a king called Sil; local legend declared that inside was a golden treasure and a golden horse. When excavated in the 1990s, no treasure was found at the site.

The enduring masonry of Stonehenge is explained by the lintel stones on top of the sarsens being attached with mortise-and-tenon joints

Originally, 30 huge sarsen stones with lintels formed a ring around the five trilithons; they were brought to the site in about 2000 B.C.

Some of the original blue stones remain in position. This stone was hauled from the Preseli Mountains in southwest Wales

Lintel on outer ring of sarsen stones

GLASTONBURY TOR

According to legend, the town of Glastonbury was founded by Joseph of Arimathea (the man who helped bury Christ), although the tor was probably already a citadel for Celtic groups and a center for earlier mystery rites. Joseph is said to have brought the Holy Grail here and founded the world's first Christian church. In 1190, excavations in the abbey grounds uncovered a leaden cross with the words: "Here lies buried the renowned King Arthur." In a huge grave below, the monks are said to have uncovered the remains of King Arthur and his queen.

STONEHENGE

The building of Stonehenge, the most famous of ancient British stone monuments, must have been an arduous task. An extraordinary feat of engineering, it would have taken 1,500 men two months to drag each of the upright sarsen stones 24 mi (39 km) across the Marlborough Downs. Stonehenge is aligned with Old Sarum, Salisbury Cathedral, and Clearbury Ring. It is bound to the north by an even older cursus (a long earth avenue linking long hills). Early writers believed it was a temple where druids – Celtic nature priests – conducted human sacrifices. Not until the 20th century did the astronomer Sir Norman Lockyer suggest what is now believed to be the true nature of the site: a kind of calendar that enabled ancient priests to calculate the positions of the sun, the moon, and the planets at various times of the year. Gaps between the trilithons give accurate views of the solar and lunar rises, while the "Aubrey Holes" – a row of 56 filled pits – served as a sophisticated lunar eclipse calculator. The dual nature of Stonehenge as ceremonial site and astrological calendar illustrates how knowledge of the seasons and time itself was intimately linked to ancient religious and ceremonial practice.

SUMMER SOLSTICE
Lockyer discovered that the midsummer sun rises along the main avenue of Stonehenge. This is why it has been a traditional site for midsummer celebrations. The northeast axis, aligned with the sunrise at the summer solstice, is a line that links Stonehenge to Silbury Hill. At the winter solstice, the sun sets in the opposite direction.

A trilithon was a construction consisting of two upright stones and a horizontal lintel

Within the sarsen circle, five trilithons form a horseshoe shape

THE THREE VERSIONS OF THE HENGE
Around 3300 B.C. a wooden construction was built at Stonehenge. The first stone henge, comprising a circular ditch, 320 ft (98 m) across and enclosing the 56 "Aubrey Holes," was built in about 2200 B.C. Stonehenge II, two horseshoes of blue stone pillars, was built about 2000 B.C. Many of the blue stones were removed for Stonehenge III, the great circle of 30 megaliths with lintels and a horseshoe of five trilithons, built around 1900 B.C.

IONA

HOLY ISLAND OF ST COLUMBA

GAZETTEER P.142 · SITE NO.22

THIS TINY AND REMOTE ISLAND, 3½ mi (6 km) long by 1½ mi (2.5 km) wide, has an atmosphere of magic. It is associated with one man, the Irish saint Columba, who brought Christianity to Scotland and its pagan kings. In fact, its Gaelic name, Innis-nam Druidbneach, means "island of the druids," and it was sacred to these Celtic priests long before St. Columba appeared in A.D. 563 to Christianize it. There is also evidence of Roman occupation on the island. Unfortunately, its exposed and defenseless position off the west coast of Scotland later brought it to the attention of Viking raiders, who first sacked it in A.D. 794, and then massacred all of its monks in A.D. 986. Columba's conversion of the island did, however, have long-term consequences. As the Norsemen converted to Christianity, Iona's status as a holy place was assured, and the site became the burial place of Scottish, Irish, and Norwegian kings.

ST. COLUMBA

Born in A.D. 521, St. Columba was descended from one of the high kings of Ireland. By the age of 25 he had already founded the monastery of Derry in what is now Northern Ireland.

ST. COLUMBA'S JOURNEY

The reasons for St. Columba's departure from Ireland for Iona remain obscure. One story claims the saint had provoked a battle between two tribes of his kinsmen, which resulted in his banishment by the church; other sources claim he was looking for a new land to convert. Columba allegedly chose Iona because it was out of sight of his beloved Ireland. He set sail with 12 companions in a modest boat called a coracle and landed on the southern part of the island. On the nearby hill of Cnoc-an t-Sidhein, the saint is said to have had mystical experiences and visions of angels.

THE CROSS OF ST. MARTIN

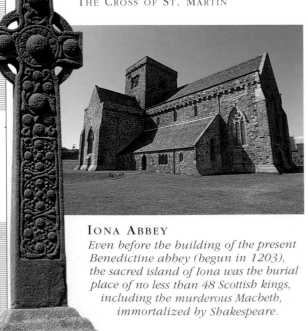

IONA ABBEY

Even before the building of the present Benedictine abbey (begun in 1203), the sacred island of Iona was the burial place of no less than 48 Scottish kings, including the murderous Macbeth, immortalized by Shakespeare.

COBHAN CUILTEACH HUT-CIRCLE

This hut-circle is associated with the place where St. Columba withdrew for prayer. It may be prehistoric and was probably used as a hermitage or monastic cell. Cairns built at different sites around the island have similar forms.

CONVERSION OF THE SCOTS

St. Columba had spent 17 years as a successful preacher in Ireland when he decided to try to convert the Scots. The monks established a life on the island by fishing, eating seal meat, and growing crops; their church was built of wood, and they lived in wooden huts. Nothing of this original settlement remains, but the present medieval abbey was built over the site.

At this time, Scotland was split between several different peoples: the Picts, the Celtic Britons, the Angles, and the Irish Celts. Columba travelled northeast along the Great Glen by Loch Ness, and there converted Brude, the king of the northern Picts. An impressive period of conversions followed, which led to the building of Scotland's earliest churches.

Columba's saintly reputation caused the community to flourish. When he died at the age of 76, his body was buried in a spot now covered by a shrine at the door of the abbey.

GORS FAWR
MOORLAND STONE CIRCLE
—— GAZETTEER P.143 - SITE NO.37 ——

LIKE ALL MEGALITHIC CIRCLES, Gors Fawr – the best preserved stone circle in Wales – is something of a mystery. "Fawr" means great, and "Gors" seems to be related to the Welsh word for throne. It is situated in the Preseli Mountains in Dyfed, the origin of the blue stones found at Stonehenge (see pp.68-69). The circle has 16 stones about 7 ft (2 m) apart. Like so many megalithic sites, the "circle" is not perfectly circular but is slightly pulled out of shape. To the northeast of the circle, two "entrance stones" stand apart from the main circle.

These two outliers, silhouetted against the gap in the hills beyond, make it clear that the purpose of the site was astronomical – to enable Stone Age or Bronze Age humans to mark the exact position of the sun and moon on the horizon, and to establish when the seasons began for the planting of crops. But there can be no doubt that the circle served some other function, perhaps of a religious or ceremonial nature, that has now been totally forgotten.

GORS FAWR STONE CIRCLE
The word "gors" with its suggestion of "gorsedd" – a meeting of bards – implies that the circle was used at some point as a druidic center, although many such circles are undoubtedly thousands of years older than the druids.

STONE DANCERS
One of the most frequent suggestions about stone circles is that they were the scene of dances, the outlying stones often being described as fiddlers or pipers. These rites were supposed to cause an interaction of energy between stones and dancers.

ST. DAVID'S
WALES' GREAT SITE OF PILGRIMAGE
—— GAZETTEER P.143 - SITE NO.35 ——

ST. DAVID'S CATHEDRAL lies at the extreme western point of southern Wales, 1 mi (1.5 km) from the sea. The area is so bleak and desolate that the visitor may be inclined to wonder why it was chosen as the site of a cathedral. The monastery was founded by St. David, and the site was chosen for its seclusion. Officially a city (because it is the seat of a bishop), St. David's is in fact a village with just three streets.

Most of what is known of St. David's (Welsh, *Dewi*) life is legendary. He was associated with King Arthur – usually as his uncle. Among the so-called "prophecies of Merlin," one stated that St. David would found a see (the diocese of a bishop) in Wales. Another legend tells how St. Gildas (born about A.D. 500) foretold David's birth when a pregnant woman came into the church as he was preaching. He was struck dumb, and on regaining his power of speech, predicted that she would give birth to a son "with a greater proportion of the divine spirit than has ever fallen to the share of a preacher."

The historical fact is that St. David was almost certainly the son of a local prince in Ceredigion. He grew up near Aberaeron, further north on the Welsh coast, and became a priest at the small monastery of Ty Gwyn. After a great deal of travel and preaching, he built the monastery at the site of the present cathedral. Intensely ascetic, he was known as Dewi Ddyfrwr, David the Water Drinker; he was a vegetarian, and refused to employ oxen to plow the ground, instead yoking his fellow monks to the plow. His followers had to observe a vow of silence, and were allowed no personal property. He traveled to Jerusalem and to Rome – where he was made a bishop. In about 588, he died at an old age.

The cathedral was burned down by the Danes in 1087 and rebuilt from 1175 onward, when it became an important pilgrimage site. The bones of St. David, which were hidden behind the altar during the time of the Reformation when the church was badly damaged, were found again in 1886.

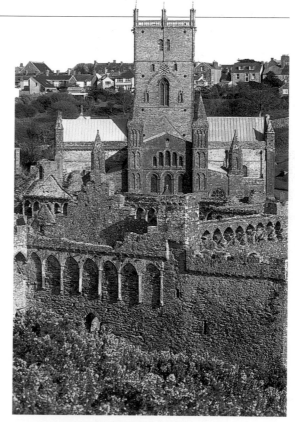

ST. DAVID'S CATHEDRAL
Although the exterior looks bleak and uncompromising, the interior compensates with its richly medieval atmosphere. For a long time the cathedral was a site of pilgrimage, two trips were regarded as the equal of one to Rome.

NEWGRANGE
& THE HILL OF TARA
GAZETTEER P.142 · SITES NOS. 8 & 9

THE GREAT BURIAL MOUND of Newgrange is one of the most impressive prehistoric monuments in Europe, ranking alongside Stonehenge (see pp.68-69) and the Ggantija Temple (see p.38). Although traditionally regarded as the burial place of the kings of Tara, it was built long before their time, in about 3200 B.C. In one sense it is a typical passage grave: a long tunnel under the mound leads to a high-domed burial chamber that has three recesses leading off it arranged like clover leaves. What distinguishes it from the hundreds of other passage graves is its immense size and the massive construction of the corbeled burial chamber. Modern archaeologists have suggested it may have been used as a solar observatory; if so, it would be the oldest of its kind in the world.

THE CORBELED CHAMBER
The heart of Newgrange is its "corbeled vault." The slabs of the vault are placed horizontally and overlap until the vault narrows to a single stone. The bones found here lead most archaeologists to assume this was a burial chamber; others claim that the absence of funerary objects suggests that Newgrange was a sun temple.

THE HISTORY OF NEWGRANGE

In 1699, a local landowner, Charles Campbell, ordered his men to remove stones from a giant circular mound on his land for roadbuilding. They soon discovered the entrance to a dark passage 60 ft (18 m) long with walls made of orthostats – huge, upright stones. It led to a burial chamber, whose corbeled roof soared upward like a chimney. The Welsh antiquarian Edward Lhwyd investigated the burial chamber soon afterward. It seemed to him that it was a "cave," and he noted the wealth of carvings – particularly the spirals, recurrent earth symbols in grave art – and three recesses containing "basins," or stone baths. The huge boulders had been placed with amazing precision; how this was done still remains a mystery.

Lhwyd concluded that it was "some place of sacrifice or burial for the ancient Irish." Others also speculated as to its use; in 1725, Thomas Molyneux declared that it had been built by Danish invaders in the Middle Ages. Later antiquarians even speculated that it could have been built by Egyptians or Indians.

A careful restoration by Michael O'Kelly in 1962 revealed clear astronomical alignments. At dawn on the day of the winter solstice, a pencil of light enters the roof box and the whole chamber is dramatically illuminated. The same alignment is found in two other nearby mounds, Knowth and Dowth. Local tradition refers to Newgrange as Bru na Boinne – the Mansion of the Boyne; some say it is the temple of the sun god Dagda.

SIDE AND AERIAL VIEWS OF NEWGRANGE
The wall around the front of Newgrange has been rebuilt using white quartz stones found on the site during excavations. At the base of this wall lie 97 stones laid end to end. Around the tumulus stand 12 stones; these are all that is left from an original circle of 35. They may have been associated with earlier structures on the site.

NEWGRANGE FOLKLORE

Three Irish sagas center around Newgrange. The first tells of Dagda, sun god and king of Ireland, and his love for Boand (Boyne). But Boand was married to Elomar, who lived in the palace at Newgrange. Dagda sent Elomar on an errand, using his magic to make it last nine months. Boand bore Dagda a child, Aengus, who was fostered out to a man named Midir. When Aengus grew up he was sent to woo the beautiful Princess Etain. In return for his daughter's hand, her father demanded the clearing of plains and opening of rivers, which Aengus did with the help of Dagda's magic.

In the second saga, Etain is reincarnated as the wife of King Eochaid of Tara. In the third saga, Midir steals Etain back, but will return her to Eochaid if he can pick her out from 50 lookalikes. He chooses Etain's daughter, who bears his child. The child is left out to die, but is found and raised by a cowherd and becomes the great Irish hero Conaire. One Irish scholar has identified Aengus with Apollo and Etain with a sun goddess. These myths, with their themes of incest, magic, and reincarnation, predate both Irish Christianity and the heroic Celtic legends, and offer us a glimpse of the primeval beliefs of the builders of Newgrange.

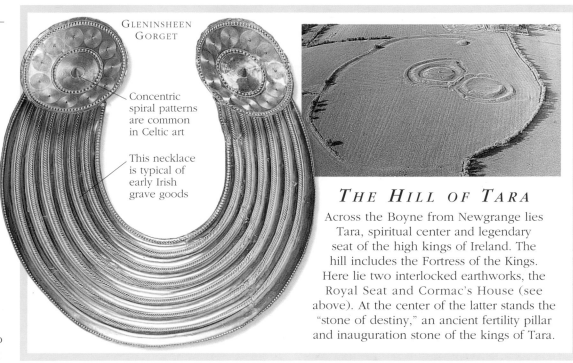

GLENINSHEEN GORGET

Concentric spiral patterns are common in Celtic art

This necklace is typical of early Irish grave goods

THE HILL OF TARA

Across the Boyne from Newgrange lies Tara, spiritual center and legendary seat of the high kings of Ireland. The hill includes the Fortress of the Kings. Here lie two interlocked earthworks, the Royal Seat and Cormac's House (see above). At the center of the latter stands the "stone of destiny," an ancient fertility pillar and inauguration stone of the kings of Tara.

SKILL OF THE ANCIENT IRISH

Like Stonehenge and the Egyptian pyramids, Newgrange used the labor of an immense, skilled workforce. Pollen from the tomb tells us that the area was once covered by a forest, cleared away to make room for Newgrange.

The tomb and passageway would have been built first with huge stone slabs, then covered with a cairn of huge boulders. Next, 35 upright megaliths were placed around the cairn in a large circle (this may have existed long before the tomb). Large slabs placed inside created an inner oval. The great earth mound, similar to those of North America, reached a height of 40 ft (12 m) above the whole structure. A facade of granite boulders was added; then the whole mound was covered with gleaming white quartz. It must have been an amazing sight, visible for some distance.

Martin Brennan argues that Newgrange was far too elaborate for a tomb and that it was a type of solar temple-observatory. It has many carvings of circles with rays suggesting the sun, and Dagda was proved to be the sun god, yet human bones found in the floor make it clear that Newgrange was indeed used as a tomb.

ENTRANCE TO NEWGRANGE

This huge curbstone originally covered the tomb entrance. It is elaborately carved with spirals, lozenges, and concentric arcs chipped into the stone with flint tools; the patterns are repeated on the walls of other tombs in the Boyne Valley. The stone, 10 ft (3 m) by 4 ft (1 m), is a wonderfully conceived work of art.

MYSTERIOUS BASINS

The purpose of the stone basins in the wings of the corbeled chamber remains a mystery. When Edward Lhwyd investigated, the basin in the right-hand wing stood in another wing, out of its original position. It has been suggested that they were for washing bodies, holding funerary offerings, or priestly ritual – we simply cannot tell.

NORTH AMERICA

TRACES OF EARLY humans in California have been dated as early as 43,000 B.C. but more commonly to 27,000 B.C. It is generally assumed, although by no means proven, that humans entered America from the far north across the Bering Strait. This would suggest that it happened before the last glaciation in Canada, around 40,000 B.C. Some authorities have linked Americans with the Ainu, the original inhabitants of Japan. If these early humans were related to the ancient peoples of Asia, then we may assume that their religion was shamanistic, based on worship of spirits and that the creator of the world was a Great Spirit, while their priests acted as contacts with the spirit world, entering a trance to establish contact. The sacred sites of North America, from the earth artwork called Serpent Mound to the Canadian petroglyphs of Peterborough and Sproat Lake, are often an integral part of the landscape. Other physical features of the land, such as the craters in Arizona and Hawaii, have even been interpreted as abodes of the gods.

N

PACIFIC OCEAN

② **GITANMAKS VILLAGE**
Many of Canada's indigenous peoples held potlatches – the giving of lavish gifts as a form of intertribal exchange.

① **SPROAT LAKE PETROGLYPHS**
These petroglyphs were created by the Nootka people. The Nootka believe their prey gives itself willingly and they thank it for allowing itself to be eaten.

③ **CHACO CANYON**
Home to the Anasazi people, who practiced rituals in circular kivas – ceremonial underground rooms.

④ **WUPATKI**

③

⑤ **SUNSET CR**

⑥

KILAUEA, HAWAII
Kilauea, the world's largest active volcano, is the home of the goddess Pele, and her devotees still leave her offerings of hibiscus flowers and tropical fruit. They believe that she lives inside the caldera, which is about 500 ft (150 m) deep.

PACIFIC OCEAN

NIIHAU
KAUAI

OAHU

MOLOKAI

MAUI

HAWAII
KILAUEA ⑪

N

200 KILOMETERS
0
200 MILES

⑥ **METEOR CRATER**
According to the Navajo, this immense crater was made by a serpent god who hurled a thunderbolt onto the land.

SASKATCHEWAN

ROCKY MOUNTAINS

BLUE MOUNTAINS

OREGON

UTAH

NEVADA

CALIFORNIA

ARIZONA

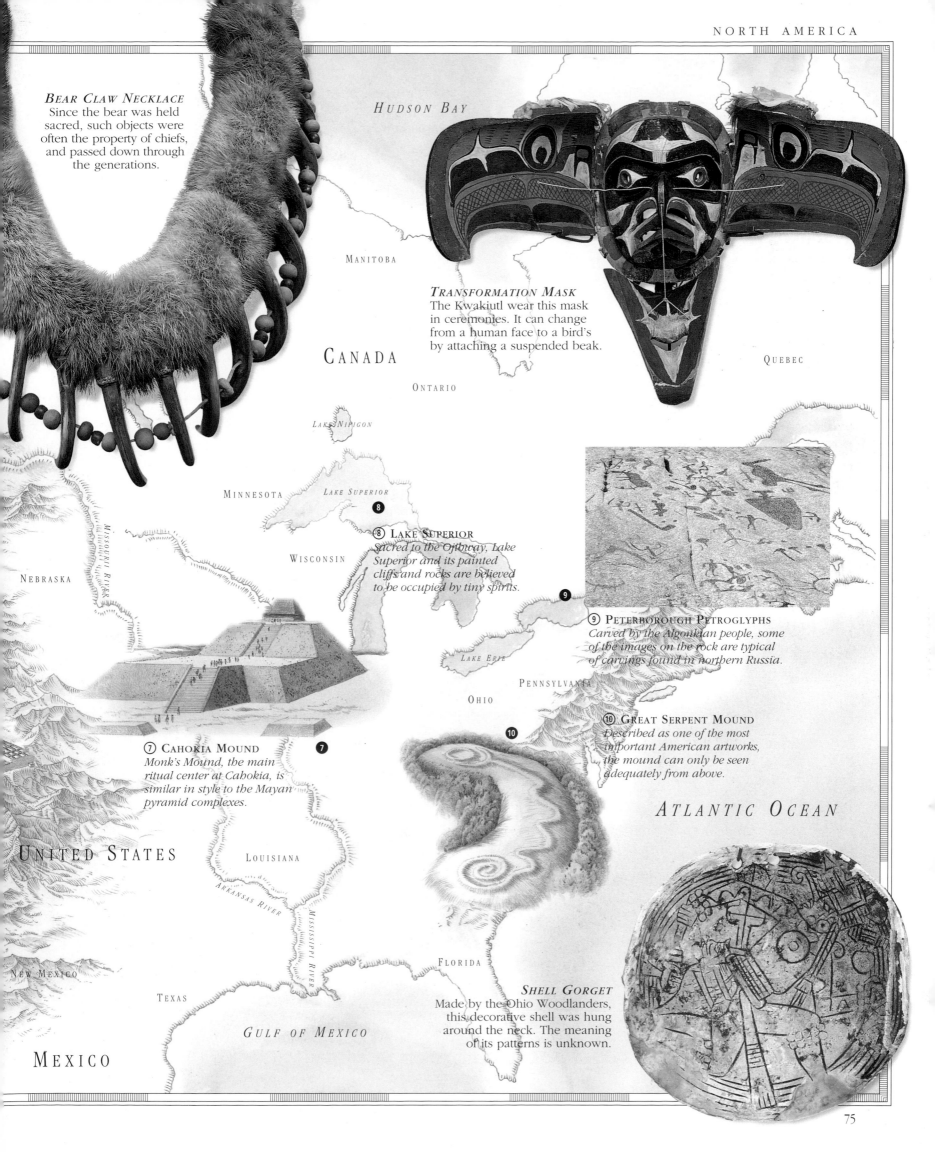

BEAR CLAW NECKLACE
Since the bear was held sacred, such objects were often the property of chiefs, and passed down through the generations.

HUDSON BAY

MANITOBA

TRANSFORMATION MASK
The Kwakiutl wear this mask in ceremonies. It can change from a human face to a bird's by attaching a suspended beak.

CANADA

ONTARIO

QUEBEC

LAKE NIPIGON

MINNESOTA

LAKE SUPERIOR

(8)

⑧ **LAKE SUPERIOR**
Sacred to the Ojibway, Lake Superior and its painted cliffs and rocks are believed to be occupied by tiny spirits.

WISCONSIN

(9)

⑨ **PETERBOROUGH PETROGLYPHS**
Carved by the Algonkian people, some of the images on the rock are typical of carvings found in northern Russia.

NEBRASKA

MISSOURI RIVER

LAKE ERIE

PENNSYLVANIA

OHIO

⑩ **GREAT SERPENT MOUND**
Described as one of the most important American artworks, the mound can only be seen adequately from above.

(7)

⑦ **CAHOKIA MOUND**
Monk's Mound, the main ritual center at Cahokia, is similar in style to the Mayan pyramid complexes.

(10)

UNITED STATES

LOUISIANA

ARKANSAS RIVER

MISSISSIPPI RIVER

ATLANTIC OCEAN

FLORIDA

SHELL GORGET
Made by the Ohio Woodlanders, this decorative shell was hung around the neck. The meaning of its patterns is unknown.

NEW MEXICO

TEXAS

GULF OF MEXICO

MEXICO

75

VIEWING THE SNAKE

As can be seen from the image above, the serpent is not visible from ground level. Visitors can now climb a tower to see its true shape. We can only speculate as to the inspiration for this giant earthwork effigy. Such imagery was prevalent among many of the Eastern Woodland peoples.

SERPENT MOUND
SACRED EFFIGY OF THE ANCIENT AMERICANS

GAZETTEER P.145- SITE NO.77

DURING THE 19TH CENTURY, Americans were mystified by the immense number of man-made mounds scattered from the Southeast to the Midwest of the United States. It was suggested that they had once been inhabited by a foreign race that had possibly arrived from Mexico, Scandinavia, or even Atlantis. Few people were willing to accept that these mysterious mounds may actually have been built by the Native American peoples. It was not until 1894 that Cyrus Thomas finally put the myths and speculations to rest by establishing their indigenous origins. Serpent Mound – called "one of the most important of American artworks" – and the thousands of other remains prove the complexity of the religions and funerary practices of early Native American societies.

PRESERVATION OF THE MOUND

The Serpent Mound of Ohio is now probably the most famous of the mounds. But when F. W. Putnam of the Peabody Museum visited it in 1886, he found it half destroyed by amateur excavators looking for treasure, and badly eroded by rain. The farmer who owned the mound was about to sell the land for growing corn, a fate that had already befallen hundreds of other mounds. Bostonians raised the money to buy the land and, in 1900, the mound was turned into a state park. Other sites in the area have led archaeologists to believe that most of the Ohio mounds were used as some form of sacred enclosure, or as ceremonial platforms rather than for burials.

THE HOPEWELLS

The early Adena culture almost certainly developed into the Hopewell people, merchants who traveled from the Great Lakes to the Mississippi and were also sophisticated artists and craftsmen. The extent of their trade is believed to have been linked to a need for luxury burial goods; they interred their dead with elaborate ornaments, jewelry, pottery, and clay figurines, like the one shown here. The topknot is distinctly Hopewell.

MOUND BUILDERS

Who built Serpent Mound? No one is quite certain, but the likeliest possibility is that the builders were the Adena people who existed from about the sixth century B.C. until around the beginning of the first century B.C.

The Adena were hunters and foragers and their remains have been found in the area. The tail of the serpent is coiled in the shape familiar all over the world as the symbol of the sacred forces of the earth, which may suggest that they also worshipped the earth as a divine mother. Although no Adenan artifacts have been found in the mound itself, to definitely

EFFIGY FOR THE GODS?

The mound is 1,200 ft (366 m) long and about 5 ft (1.5 m) high and is in the form of a snake with an egg-shaped form or frog in its mouth. Many have speculated that this vast earthwork was intended as an offering to the gods.

determine the site's origin, Adenan stone axes and a copper sheet have been unearthed in a nearby burial mound. From information garnered at other Adenan burial mounds in the surrounding area, it seems the Adenans buried their dead in large log tombs or clay-lined basins. The more important individuals were often painted in red ocher and accompanied by the most elaborate burial goods.

CAHOKIA MOUND
CEREMONIAL CITY OF THE MISSISSIPPIANS
GAZETTEER P.145 - SITE NO.61

CAHOKIA MOUND STATE PARK covers the area of the largest pre-Columbian community in North America. Built by the Middle Mississippi people, it contained over a hundred pyramid and burial mounds and was a ceremonial center for over 50 communities. Cahokia reached its peak between A.D. 1050 and 1250, but had declined well before the arrival of the Europeans. Monk's Mound was its center; as long as four city blocks and more than 108 ft (33 m) high, it covers 16 acres (6.5 hectares) and contains 22 million cu ft (623,000 cu m) of earth. The sacred mound was the temple of a ruling priest, who lived in a wooden structure on its peak. The remains of a circle of wooden poles and the alignment of the mounds suggest that Cahokians made calendrical observations.

THE SPLENDOR OF CAHOKIA
This aerial view of Monk's Mound shows the vast amount of labor involved in creating the structure. The Cahokians might have declined because of the resulting overexploitation of natural resources, as well as agricultural degradation and overpopulation.

MONK'S MOUND

Monk's Mound was so called after a group of French Trappist Monks who moved there in 1809. They left in 1813 apparently without experiencing any curiosity about the mound, on whose terraces they grew their vegetables. Carbon dating reveals that the mound was built between A.D. 900 and 1250 by the Middle Mississippians. Less sophisticated than earlier Native American cultures, the Mississippians had a social structure almost as rigid as that of the Maya or the ancient Egyptians. Their king was known as the "Great Sun," who ruled a graded aristocracy and a proletariat of slaves and commoners, known as "Stinkers."

MOUND OF THE RULER-PRIEST
It is likely that the ruler of Cahokia, the "Great Sun," lived on top of Monk's Mound. He was said to represent the sun on earth and was revered by the local peoples. Only the ruler and his priests were allowed to enter the temple on the summit.

STONE PIPE

This stone pipe is typical of artifacts from eastern North America. Pipes were often carved in the shape of animals or birds; this one is a raven. It belongs to a type called "platform pipes," which had a flat base on which the carved figures rested; the tobacco was pushed into a "chimney" on top, and the smoke drawn through a hole bored in the base.

CITY OF THE SUN

The Mississippian culture dates from the ninth century A.D., and is characterized by its flat-topped mounds, some of which served as temples and places of burial. When Cahokia was at its peak, it covered an area of 6 sq mi (15 sq km), and probably had a population of 20,000. The sacred fire that was kept burning atop Monk's Mound could be seen by the Mississippians from afar. It was a burial site for its ruler-priests and there is also evidence of human sacrifice.

In Mound 72, to the south of Monk's Mound and astronomically aligned with it, lay the skeleton of a person who was probably of high rank, resting on a bed of 20,000 shell beads, surrounded by grave goods including mica sheets and arrowheads, and accompanied by six sacrificial bodies. There were also the bones of 53 young women and four men in other pits; their heads and hands had been cut off. These ritual acts clearly show the importance of burial rituals to the Cahokians.

CHACO CANYON
HOME OF THE "ANCIENT ONES"

GAZETTEER P.145 - SITE NO.42

CHACO CANYON in New Mexico was the home of an indigenous people called the Anasazi – "Ancient Ones" – who inhabited the area from a few centuries B.C. until the 12th century A.D. The Great Houses of the canyon, which resemble modern apartment blocks, were built between A.D. 900 and 1115. Until A.D. 1884, when the first remains were discovered under the overhang of Mancos Canyon, Colorado, no one had heard of the Anasazi people, or suspected their existence. Abundant pottery and baskets woven so tightly that they would hold water, suggested that the Anasazi were highly advanced – although stone axes revealed they were a Stone Age culture. The remains of Pueblo Bonito in Chaco Canyon, a settlement covering over 3 acres (1.5 hectares)

confirmed that these people, ancestors of the Hopi and the Zuni, had occupied the area for over a thousand years.

One of the most puzzling features of the Chaco area are the "roads" – or what looks like a network of roads, 30 ft (9 m) wide, extending for several hundred miles around the canyon. Many of these can now only be seen from the air. They run in straight lines, then suddenly change direction. These might have been trade routes used by the inhabitants of Chaco Canyon, but the carefully engineered network needs further explanation. Moreover, at the edge of the canyon they often turn into flights of steep steps, too steep for everyday use. Legend claims that they were "tunnels" for the "Ancient Ones." It is possible that they served some ceremonial or religious purpose.

The sophistication of Chaco society when the Anasazi flourished suggests that Chaco Canyon may have been somewhat greener than it is today. The mystery of this ancient people, and why they vanished, has yet to be explained.

KIVAS
Kivas are circular underground chambers where male members of the Anasazi people performed their sacred rituals. The stones of the kivas often have a high level of radioactivity – especially for the granite of which they are made – and some writers have speculated that Anasazi shamans were sensitive to such forms of energy.

ANASAZI CARVING

METEOR CRATER
SIGN OF THE FLAMING SERPENT GOD

GAZETTEER P.145 - SITE NO.38

ABOUT 40,000 YEARS AGO, an immense meteorite slammed into the earth near present-day Flagstaff, Arizona, blasting out four million tons of earth and forming a crater 4,000 ft (1,220 m) wide and 600 ft (183 m) deep

– deep enough to hold a 50-story building. The crater is surrounded by a ridge of uplifted sediment – a kind of wall – rising up to 200 ft (61 m). The footpath down to the bottom is almost 3 mi (5 km) long. No meteorite iron has been found below the bottom of the pit, and for many years scientists suspected that the whole crater might have been formed by an immense explosion of volcanic steam. Yet the fact that the plain surrounding the crater was covered with chunks of iron, with a center of bright steel, should have convinced them otherwise. On impact with the earth the meteor had obviously exploded like a vast bomb.

The Navajo people regarded Meteor Crater as a sacred site, for according to their legend, the crater was made by a flaming serpent god who passed overhead and hurled a thunderbolt into the earth as a sign that he had been there.

SACRED CRATER
The local Navajo collected chunks of meteoric iron from around the crater and used it in local graves and at Sun Temple in Mesa Verde, 200 mi (322 km) away, a clear link between a people's sacred site and the burial of their dead.

SUNSET CRATER

This site in northern Arizona, an extinct volcano in the San Francisco range, is regarded by the Hopi people as a sacred mountain. A Hopi legend tells of how, in the remote past, the people became so degenerate that the gods were prepared to destroy them by fire. The only volcano in the region that has erupted recently enough to fit the legend is Sunset Crater. Strangely though, the eruption made the land more fertile, for the coating of ash trapped the water in the soil.

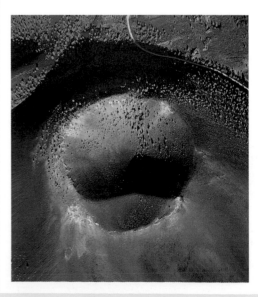

WUPATKI
THE TALL HOUSE OF THE HOPI
GAZETTEER P.145 · SITE NO.36

THE HOPI PEOPLE of Arizona are of local origin. Their migration eventually brought them to the San Francisco Peaks, north of Flagstaff, Arizona, in an area where the Anasazi people (see p.78) had once lived. Within sight

WUKOKI RUINS
The Wupatki National Monument is a collection of over 800 pueblos. The name of the ruin known as the Wukoki translates as the "Big House." In addition there is a center known as the Citadel, which remains unexcavated.

of the mountains at Wupatki, the Hopi built the "Tall House," now a ruin.

According to legend, when the Hopi first moved into the area, strange beings often wandered around the village. A warrior carrying prayer sticks went to investigate the top of the mountain, where he heard a voice calling him from a *kiva* – an underground ritual chamber. There he found a manlike being, who introduced himself as a spirit. Thus the Hopi established contact with the spirits of the mountains, the *kachinas*, represented as grotesque figures with large noses. These spirits answered the prayers of the Hopi, and brought rain and fertility to the region. Even today, the Hopi live close to the earth, and remain connected to their traditions.

THE WUPATKI "TALL HOUSE"
In Hopi, the word Wupatki means "Tall House." The original settlers may have come to the site after the eruption of the Sunset Crater in about the 11th century. The site seems to have been inhabited until the 13th century.

KILAUEA
SITE OF PELE'S SACRED LAKE
GAZETTEER P.151 · SITE NO.84

KILAUEA IN HAWAII is the world's largest active volcano. Although it erupts frequently, the result is usually simply a slowly advancing and nonthreatening sea of lava. However, as recently as 1790, the volcano exploded violently, killing with hot steam a Hawaiian army marching near the caldera.

Kilauea is the site of Halema'uma'u, a cooled lake of lava said to be the home of Pele, the goddess who is credited with creating Hawaii. Although the Hawaiian religion collapsed at the beginning of the 19th century, devotees of Pele still leave her offerings of hibiscus flowers and tropical fruit. Many Hawaiians claim her as an ancestor. During the 19th century, Kilauea's crater went through many cycles of overflow and collapse. It reached its present depth in 1919. Devotees of the goddess believe that she lives inside the caldera, a space 3 mi (5 km) long and over 2 mi (3 km) wide. Worshippers include followers of other religions, such as Christianity, who still maintain the ancient rites of the local tradition.

Pele is a kind of Hawaiian version of Venus, generous and highly sexed; her lover is the trickster demigod Maui (also an island), full of vitality and good humor, whose sexual potency is equal to the demands of his passionate mistress. Temples have traditionally been built along the lava flows and near the site of the lake itself. These flows have been interpreted as the goddess forming new lands and destroying her enemies with fire.

The ancient religion of Hawaii, the religion of the Huna, has been described in a number of fascinating books by Max Freedom Long, who speaks of the ability of the *kahunas* – Huna magicians – to kill their enemies with the "death prayer."

The Hawaiian Islands are a new land – little more than a million years old, and their physical features are still forming and changing. Even now, an underwater mountain called Loihi is forming, and will become an active volcano in a few thousand years – by which time the Kilauea volcano will be cold and silent.

LAVA FLOW
In 1955, an eruption and earthquakes caused lava to pour from fissures for 88 days, and destroyed a village and 6 sq mi (16 sq km) of fertile farmland. Four years later, it created a 400-ft- (122-m-) deep lake of molten lava.

PETERBOROUGH
ANCIENT PETROGLYPHS
GAZETTEER P.145 · SITE NO.14

A SLAB OF crystalline limestone, 180 ft (55 m) long and 100 ft (30 m) wide, near Peterborough in Ontario, contains over 900 images carved into what has been described as "white marble." They are believed to have been carved by the Algonkian people between A.D. 900 and 1400. Forgotten for centuries, the sacred stone was found again in 1924 by historian Charles Kingam. Boat figures among the petroglyphs do not resemble the traditional craft of Native Americans, but one solar boat – a stylized shaman vessel with a long mast surmounted by a sun – is typical of petroglyphs found in northern Russia and Scandinavia. There are similar figures of shamans (seen in the center of the image, left). Professor Barry Fell of Harvard, who studied the petroglyphs in his retirement, became convinced that these were inscriptions by a Norse king named Woden-lithi (Servant of Odin), who was said to have sailed from Norway and up the St. Lawrence River in about 1700 B.C.

SYMBOLIC WOMB
According to Romas and Joan Vastokas, the chief authorities on Peterborough, a fissure in the rock was interpreted as the entrance to the underworld or the symbolic womb of the Earth Mother.

LAKE SUPERIOR
SPIRIT HOME OF THE OJIBWAY
GAZETTEER P.145 · SITE NO.12

AROUND LAKE SUPERIOR, many rocks display fine examples of the rock art of the Canadian Native Americans. The Ojibway people believe that these rocks are inhabited by tiny spirits called *maymaygwayshiwuk*, who live in cracks in the cliffs and emerge to play tricks on humans. (Similarly, the Aborigines of northern Australia believe that a race of supernatural tricksters called the *mimi* live in the cracks of the Arnhemland escarpment.) Ancestors of the Ojibway are believed to be the painters of the red ocher figures on the rock. One cave in the region has been painted with figures of humans and animals that seem to be the expression of a dream or vision. Some Native Americans leave offerings of tobacco to propitiate the spirits, or pass by at a distance.

In studying the landscape art of the native peoples of the American and African continents, it is important to bear in mind that all share a shamanistic religion that accepts the reality of the spirit world, in which the shaman is able to travel to the world of the dead and bring

back messages. This is directly related to the cave art of early peoples in which there is a direct and close relation between nature, human beings, and the world of the spirits. Through religious ritual, human beings can learn to control natural forces and influence the results of a hunt.

The painting of rock constitutes a magical ritual, the power of the rock and the painter somehow combining together to create a great spiritual energy. This notion that certain rocks, or areas of rock, are sacred is worldwide. Two French priests of the late 17th century observed a human-shaped rock near Lake Erie that had been painted with red ocher to resemble a human being. Native Americans about to set out on the waters of the lake left offerings in front of it to ensure a safe passage. But in locations as diverse as Europe, Australia, and Africa, a "magical" attitude to natural formations exists, connected with a sense of the spiritual and healing forces of rocks and the earth.

LAKE SUPERIOR
The environs of Lake Superior are the home of the Ojibway people, who believe that the rocks of the lake house spirits. Their rich oral tradition, which tells of supernatural beings, is passed from generation to generation through the tribal elders.

SPROAT LAKE
PETROGLYPHS OF THE NOOTKA

GAZETTEER P.145 - SITE NO.3

THE PETROGLYPHS of Sproat Lake are one example of the numerous rock carvings that lie along the Pacific coast of North America. They were almost certainly carved by ancestors of the Nootka people who live in what is now British Columbia. The Nootka were named by Captain Cook in 1778 – Nootka seems to have been his attempt to pronounce their name Nuu-chah-nulth (meaning "all along the mountains"). As with most Native Americans of the coastal regions, fish play a vital part in their economy. When the first salmon of the year is caught, it is welcomed with an address of thanks, and the entrails thrown into the river, so they can return to the salmon's home and tell how well it was treated. Like some other Northwest peoples, the Nootka ventured out to sea in pursuit of whales, particularly the California gray and the humpback. The hunters had to row silently up to the whale, then the leader thrust in his harpoon, and the rowers paddled backward to escape the thrashing of its tail. The whaler prepared for his task with

a long period of fasting and sexual abstinence, and while he was on the hunt his wife had to remain totally still in bed to make the whale docile. The most important Nootka ceremony was the shaman's dance, representing the kidnapping of an ancestor by spirits, who bestowed shamanistic gifts before releasing him. It seems clear that the hunters (and fishermen) prepared themselves in much the same way as the Stone Age hunters, who painted the walls of Lascaux and Les Eyzies (see pp.58-59): with shamanistic ritual to ensure the success of the hunt. One function of the fish petroglyphs may have been magical – similar to that served by Stone Age paintings of bison and deer – suggesting that this site may have been a center for shamanistic ritual.

PETROGLYPHS OF SPROAT LAKE
The whale shaman of the Nootka people performed elaborate ceremonies that would propitiate the spirits of their ancestors, who had power over whales, and would cause them to make dead whales drift ashore near their village.

GITANMAKS VILLAGE
SITE OF THE POTLATCH CEREMONY

GAZETTEER P.145 - SITE NO.1

LIKE MANY OTHER North American peoples, the whole notion of status and rank among the Giksan people of northern British Columbia was bound up in the custom of *potlatch* (a Chinook word meaning gift). This ceremony involved the giving of lavish presents. While riches gained respect, giving them away gained even more. Great chiefs strove to outdo their rivals in distributing *potlatch*, "to make my name good." Not only did the *potlatch* bring the benefits of trade and exchange of each side's surplus, but it prevented tensions between different peoples. The sites of *potlatch* were often marked by totem poles and became centers for ritual. Although it was banned by the government in the last century, *potlatch* has subsequently been revived.

CHIEF GIT-DUM-KULDOAH
The totem pole of Chief Git-Dum-Kuldoah stood outside the potlatch *house in Gitanmaks Village, at Hazelton, British Columbia. Totem poles were erected as memorials, and the raising of the poles was accompanied by the* potlatch *ceremony.*

POTLATCH DISH

Art of the North American peoples often depicts animals from myths, or "crest animals," animals displaying a family crest, which was a jealously guarded family prerogative. This Tlingit feast dish in the shape of a canoe has stylized bears at either end, and a crest in the center. Such dishes were important symbols of rank and wealth, and, due to the excesses of the potlatch, could actually be as large as a small canoe. They would be placed in front of guest chiefs, together with decorated spoons of mountain-goat horn or wood.

CENTRAL & SOUTH AMERICA

THE ANCIENT NATIVE RELIGIONS of Central and South America – including those of the Aztecs, Maya, and Inca – may be symbolized by the ritual knife to the right. Captives were sacrificed, sometimes by the thousands, to propitiate the gods and avert some great universal catastrophe. The Aztecs, for example, believed that the world was in the final stage of the "fifth sun," the end of which would herald the end of the world. It has been suggested in some quarters that the similarities between these fatalistic beliefs may be linked to fragments of a comet that struck the earth 12,000 years ago. Many of the remaining South American native cultures, such as the Arawak, Carib, and Tupi peoples of Amazonia, have shamanistic religions that involve healing, divination, and rainmaking. But even these forest dwellers have legends of destruction, sometimes by fire, sometimes by water. Cave paintings at Monte Allegre on the Amazon, dated to 10,000 B.C., show a bright object falling from the sky. Oddly enough, the myths of South America reveal close similarities not only to those of North America, but also to the Melanesians. It is unlikely that we can solve the tantalizing puzzle of these shared beliefs. With the Spanish and Portuguese conquest of the Americas, the only clues we can gather are from the excavations of the extensive remains in Mesoamerica and Peru, which have left a wealth of information, and from the peoples of the Amazon who remain mostly untouched by post-Columbian America.

MEXICO

GULF O HONDUR

① TEOTIHUACAN
The Pyramids of the Sun and Moon were both topped by temple platforms, where the priests carried out ritual sacrifices.

CEREMONIAL KNIFE
On the handle of this ritual knife from Peru is the image of either a sun or a moon god.

MAYA CODEX TRO-CORTESIANUS
Codices contained information about divination and rituals for Mayan priests. This codex was made from bark paper covered in gesso.

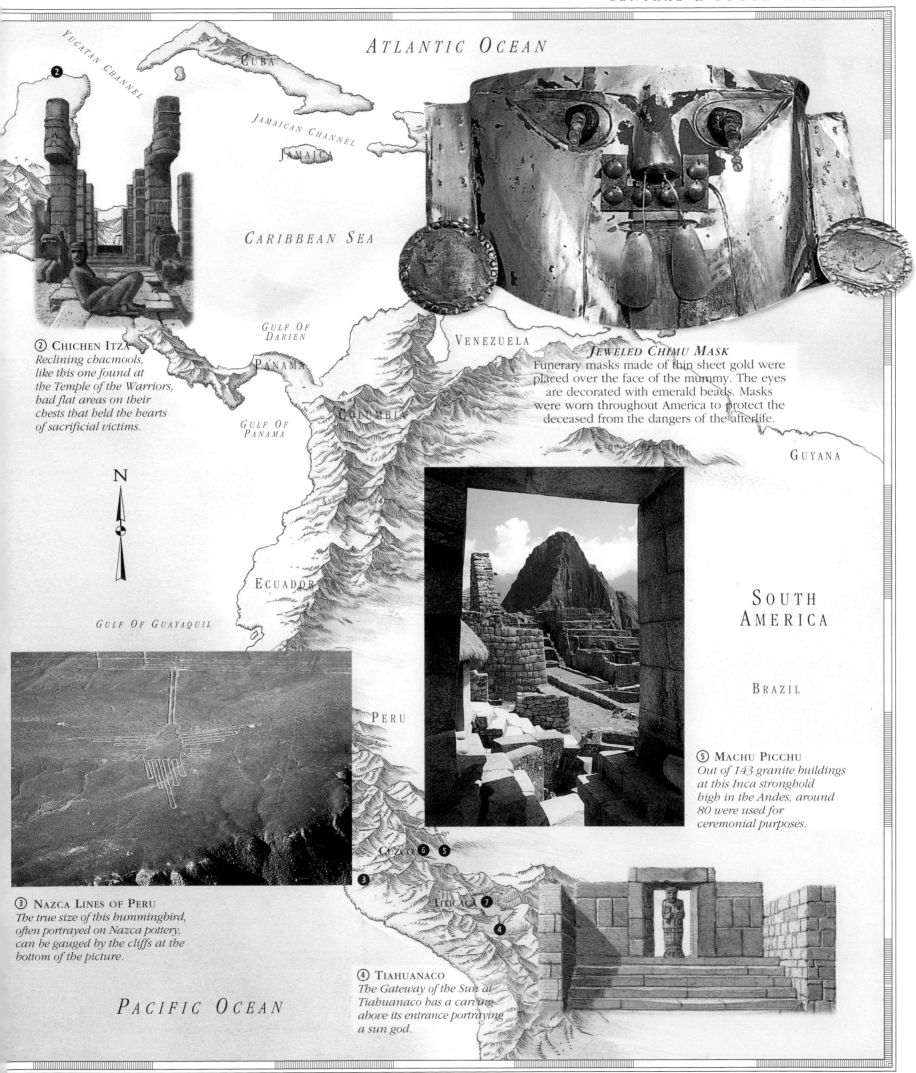

ATLANTIC OCEAN

YUCATAN CHANNEL

CUBA

JAMAICAN CHANNEL

JAMAICA

CARIBBEAN SEA

GULF OF DARIEN

VENEZUELA

PANAMA

COLOMBIA

GULF OF PANAMA

GUYANA

② **CHICHEN ITZA**
Reclining chacmools, like this one found at the Temple of the Warriors, had flat areas on their chests that held the hearts of sacrificial victims.

JEWELED CHIMU MASK
Funerary masks made of thin sheet gold were placed over the face of the mummy. The eyes are decorated with emerald beads. Masks were worn throughout America to protect the deceased from the dangers of the afterlife.

N

ECUADOR

SOUTH AMERICA

GULF OF GUAYAQUIL

BRAZIL

PERU

⑤ **MACHU PICCHU**
Out of 143 granite buildings at this Inca stronghold high in the Andes, around 80 were used for ceremonial purposes.

③ **NAZCA LINES OF PERU**
The true size of this hummingbird, often portrayed on Nazca pottery, can be gauged by the cliffs at the bottom of the picture.

CUZCO ⑥ ⑤

③

TITICACA ⑦

④

④ **TIAHUANACO**
The Gateway of the Sun at Tiahuanaco has a carving above its entrance portraying a sun god.

PACIFIC OCEAN

TEOTIHUACAN
CITY OF GODS

GAZETTEER P.147 · SITE NO.11

QUETZALCOATL, THE PLUMED SERPENT
Quetzalcoatl was perhaps the most revered of the Mesoamerican gods. According to legend, he was a tall, bearded white man who had once landed from the Atlantic, bringing civilization and peace to Mexico. Driven out by his enemies, he had promised to return. When the Spanish arrived, the Aztecs mistook them for the white gods they were awaiting. An earth and water deity, the god was also called the "Father of the Toltecs."

WHEN FERNANDO CORTÉS LANDED IN MEXICO with only 508 soldiers in 1519, the Aztecs, under their king Montezuma, had tens of thousands of warriors, yet by 1521 the Spaniards had destroyed his empire. Cortés entered the capital city of the Aztecs, Tenochtitlán (now Mexico City), and found it as sophisticated as Madrid or Venice. He seized Montezuma, who would die – wounded by his own followers – in Spanish hands. Driven north out of Tenochtitlán, the Spaniards came across the ruins of a great city – Teotihuacán, an ancient religious capital of the Teotihuacános and a pilgrimage site for the Aztecs, dating back to 200 B.C. It was dominated by two huge step pyramids – the Pyramids of the Sun and the Moon. The former was similar in size to the Great Pyramid at Giza. The Citadel, a vast precinct of temples and palaces that was the administrative and ritual center of Teotihuacán, stood around the Avenue of the Dead. The impressive Pyramid of Quetzalcoatl also lay within the Citadel. Cortés had stumbled across what was once the most important ceremonial center in the whole of Mesoamerica.

PYRAMID OF THE MOON
The Pyramid of the Moon stands at the end of the Avenue of the Dead in the shadow of the Cerro Gordo. Shorter than the Pyramid of the Sun, it stands on higher ground, so that the two structures are roughly level.

THE TEOTIHUACANOS

We do not know the original name of the city that was once the greatest religious center in Central America, covering an area larger than ancient Rome. It was the Aztecs arriving here in about A.D. 1320 who called it Teotihuacán, or City of Gods, and who made it a pilgrimage center. They believed the gods had gathered here to create the sun and the moon after the last great catastrophe that destroyed the world.

About 200 B.C., the fertile valley was first occupied by villages, their total population no more than about 7,000. Five hundred years later the city had become a great pilgrimage site, dominated by the Pyramid of the Sun, below which lay a holy cave, shaped like a four-leaved clover. The pyramid built over the cave suggests a deep religious significance – probably it was regarded as the place where the gods created the world.

The city peaked around A.D. 500, but its end is a mystery. The decline began in the seventh century A.D. Around 750 the city was destroyed by fire, and some of its greatest monuments were buried under millions of tons of earth. This suggests invaders who regarded the religion of Teotihuacán as a false one – the Toltecs have been suggested as the culprits.

THE AVENUE OF THE DEAD
This street was named by local people in the belief that the mounds were tombs. The street points at the setting of the Pleiades, and there is little doubt that the whole city is aligned astronomically. An alignment to the dog star Sirius, sacred to the ancient Egyptians, has caused some to suggest a link between the pyramids of Egypt and Mexico.

HUMAN SACRIFICE

Evidence from their murals suggests that the Teotihuacános were formidable warriors. Their aim was not the conquest of territory, but the capture of prisoners who were sacrificed to avert the end of the world. According to the mythology shared by most ancient peoples of Central America, there had been four great cycles (or suns) since the beginning of the world, lasting a total of 17,000 years; we are now in the age of the fifth sun. The first sun was destroyed by flood, the second by hurricanes, the third by fire, the fourth by a rain of fire and blood that led to starvation. The fifth sun will perish from earthquakes. Because they believed that the fifth sun was already old (symbolized by a wrinkle-faced sun with its tongue sticking out to taste human blood), they expected the end of the world at any moment.

Captives were sacrificed by the thousands. In the corner of each step of the Pyramid of the Sun, skeletons of children had been built into the fabric. Excavations below the Temple of Quetzalcoatl revealed three burial pits full of skeletons. Some time later, archaeologists found burials including 20 sacrifical victims, presumably intended as servants for deceased nobleman in the afterlife.

PRIEST'S SACRIFICIAL MASK

MASKS OF RITUAL
At its peak, in about 500 B.C., Teotihuacán was the largest city in the Americas. As in ancient Egypt, the priests were its most powerful caste. This mask, with eyes made of shell and pyrite and with sacrificial knives in the mouth and nose cavity, was almost certainly worn by the priest during ritual sacrifice.

WHO WERE THE OLMECS?

The Olmecs were the inhabitants of the coastal lowlands of eastern Mexico. Theirs is the earliest of the important Mesoamerican cultures. What we now know of them is mainly due to giant stone heads that they left behind. Carbon found in a layer with one of these heads has been dated to 1200 B.C., but the head could be far older. Many are taller than a human and weigh up to 20 tons. The city of La Venta, in Tabasco province, was an Olmec center, one of many, and there a great artificial mound was raised. That at San Lorenzo is more than 100 ft (30 m) high and 4,000 ft (1,220 m) long. Other sculptures found at La Venta include a group of figurines buried in a ritual formation; they are made of granite, serpentine, and jade.

CHICHEN ITZA

SACRED CITY OF THE MAYA & THE TOLTECS

TEMPLE OF KUKULCAN

Kukulcan is the Toltec name for Quetzalcoatl, the plumed serpent god. An hour before sunset at the two equinoxes, a shadow resembling a giant undulating serpent is thrown across the steps.

CHICHÉN ITZÁ was one of the greatest ruined cities in Central America. After being abandoned by the Maya in A.D. 900, it was rebuilt by the Toltecs almost a century later. A sacred road leads from the Temple of Quetzalcoatl (or Kukulcan, the plumed serpent) a sinister-looking sacred well used for human sacrifice which gives the site its name. (Chichén means "mouth of the well.") The remains of a road link this spot to another well. To the west of the temple lies the largest known ballcourt in Central America. To the east of the Temple was one of the most splendid monuments of the Toltec civilization: the Temple of the Warriors, a low pyramid flanked by columns depicting warrriors, and the location of the chacmool, an impressive sculpture where priests opened the chests of sacrificial victims and offered up their still-beating hearts to the gods.

THE MAYAN CITIES

No one knows why the Old Mayan Empire, which began around A.D. 300, came to an end, or why cities in its heartland (like Copán, Tikal, and Palenque) were abandoned around A.D. 900. All we know is that some time after A.D. 600 the Maya began to build new cities – like Chichén Itzá in the Yucatán peninsula. The city was built in the Late Mayan period, the "New Empire," when the Mayan civilization was nearing its end. In fact, three Chichéns had stood on the site, the earliest in A.D. 432.

Many theories have been proposed to explain the great abandonment of Mayan cities. At first, it was believed they were driven out by enemies, until it became clear that they had none – they were supreme within their vast realm. Earthquake and flood were also ruled out, since there were no signs of destruction; so had pestilence, since there were no mass graveyards. Most likely, combinations of these factors varied from place to place.

The Toltecs, warlike people who settled the city almost a hundred years after the Maya had left, originated from Tula. Reliefs carved into the walls of buildings at Chichén Itzá show scenes of warfare that typify the period.

TEMPLE OF THE WARRIORS

The reclining figure at the summit of the temple (right) was christened a chacmool by August Le Plongeon, the explorer who first discovered one at Chichén Itzá in 1875. Chacmools are now recognized as ritual figures, probably representing fallen warriors who act as messengers to the gods. The dish on the stomach is intended for the heart of a sacrificial victim.

THE BALL GAME

The Mesoamericans were obsessed by the ball game – not merely as a sport, but as a profound religious ritual. An unknown number of men played on either side in a court shaped like a capital letter I – at Chichén Itzá it had sloping walls – and when it was played as a religous ritual, the losing team was often sacrificed. The ball was originally made of stone, later of latex. It was thrown through circular discs – like that on the far right – attached to the sides of the ball court. The players had to strike the ball with the thigh or upper arm – or possibly with a kind of U-shaped stone yoke, worn around the waist. The tablet on the right shows the decapitated player-hero Hunahpu with blood gushing from his neck in the form of "seven serpents."

RELIEF OF HUNAHPU

BALLCOURT RING

MAYAN STAR WARS

Perhaps the most important building in Chichén Itzá was the Caracol, or observatory, with its domed top (the name means snail). The Maya attached enormous importance to astronomy – as most ancient peoples did – for it controlled their agriculture and thus their food supply. Their calendar was actually more exact than the European calendar of the time. Central to Mayan astronomy was the planet Venus, which in Mayan mythology was male and represented war. Venus' fortunes are described in the Mayan epic the *Popul Vuh*. The story relates how the hero Hun Hunahpu, who is identified with Venus, is decapitated. His severed head then spits at a goddess, impregnating her, and she gives birth to Venus once again. The legend explained the disappearance of Venus when it passed behind or in front of the sun.

At Chichén Itzá, the Maya arranged battles (literally star wars) to coincide with the appearance of Venus. The purpose of these staged fights was to bring about the rebirth of the planet – sometimes the battles were stylized and ritualistic, but often they were the real thing involving actual bloodshed. Experts on Mexican mythology, Mary Miller and Karl Taube speculate that these frequent star wars increased in the eighth century A.D. and contributed to the downfall of the Maya.

THE WELL OF SACRIFICE

In a book written in 1566, the Spanish bishop Diego de Landa described the "sacrificial well" at Chichén Itzá, where victims were hurled to appease the gods during plague or pestilence. In the 1860s, a young American, Edward Thompson, rediscovered the sacred well. But were the stories of sacrifices true? He decided to dredge the well using a contraption with metal jaws. At first, it came up full of mud, leaf mold, and dead branches. After many days he retrieved a ball of resinous incense. After that came pottery, sacred vessels, arrowheads, and idols. Finally, when it was clear the dredge had reached the bottom of the well, Thompson went down in a diving suit. Aided by two other divers he found hundreds of ritual objects – and dozens of skeletons and skulls. Some were of cripples and hunchbacks whom the Maya often sacrificed in their rituals. There were also the skeletons of young girls. Landa had mentioned that girls were thrown into the well at dawn as messengers to the gods, and pulled out – if they were still alive – at midday. Thompson also discovered the secret of the water's morbid appearance – every so often it was supposed to turn scarlet – a particular type of algae with red seeds turned the water the color of blood.

SACRED CENOTE
The Maya regarded wells as sacred to the rain god Chac. There are two in Chichén Itzá, although only one was used for sacrifice, the second being used for the water supply. A cenote is a natural well formed from the collapse of subterranean limestone caverns.

TIAHUANACO
& LAKE TITICACA
GAZETTEER P.149 · SITE NOS. 22 & 21

THE RUINED SITE of Tiahuanaco in the Bolivian Andes was built around A.D. 300 and was abandoned around A.D. 1000. It is 13 mi (21 km) from Lake Titicaca, which was once at sea level. The geological uplift that created the Andes 40 to 60 million years ago also altered the level of the lake. The presence of structures that may have been used for religious ceremonies and the area's relatively low soil fertility suggests that Tiahuanaco might have been unable to support a large population, and the site was probably a pilgrimage center rather than a city. It has been the subject of many theories over the years, but was most probably part of a culture related to the Mesoamerican peoples.

THE KALASASAYA COMPOUND
The Kalasasaya is a great courtyard that was designed as a kind of observatory. It contains two massive statues of the principal deity of Tiahuanaco. One of these has been positioned at the top of the megalithic stairway (see below and in the background of the image above).

THE TEMPLE

The sunken inner courtyard of the Kalasasaya compound (left) has been reconstructed to resemble its original layout. It looks like a large swimming pool; in the center are three pillars of red rock, one large and two smaller. The large pillar is actually a statue. It may represent an early version of the Incan sun deity Viracocha, who shares many qualities with Quetzalcoatl, the chief god of ancient Central America. The great courtyard was designed as a kind of astronomical observatory: two points in the Kalasasaya mark the summer and winter solstices. As with all early agricultural peoples, knowledge of the seasons was crucial for the planting of crops and thus survival of the group.

THE GREAT IDOL
OF TIAHUANACO

THE GATEWAY
AT KALASASAYA

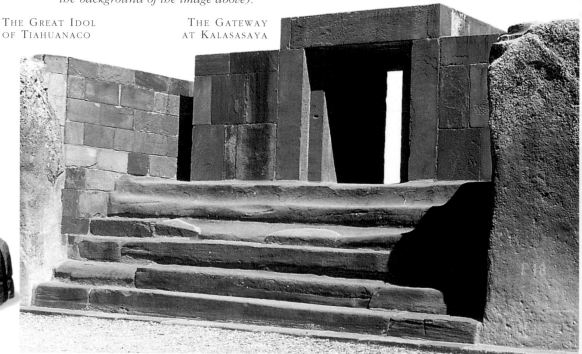

GATEWAY TO THE SUN
This gateway, 10 ft (3 m) high, carved from a single block, was probably the entrance to a sanctuary. It stands in a corner of the Kalasasaya. The figure on the side holds two staves and may represent the precursor of Viracocha.

THE LAKE

Lake Titicaca is the largest freshwater lake in South America and the world's highest large lake. This vast stretch of water, some 700 ft (213 m) deep, covers 3,200 sq mi (8,288 sq km). The Inca people, whose culture flourished after A.D. 1400, believed the lake to be the home of the god Viracocha. One myth says that he carved statues from nearby caves and brought them to life. These people populated the town of Cuzco, and were ruled over by the god's son, the Inca (Inca is a title meaning "king"). The god provided him with a wife so beautiful that he decided never to return to Cuzco; he went back to the sky, sending a man to rule in his place.

The lake is itself a mystery. An ancient "strand line" at 12,000 ft (3,658 m), with algae and calcareous deposits, reveals that it was once at sea level. In the 20th century, German engineer Hans Hoerbiger convinced thousands of people that the earth originally had many moons and that they came closer to the earth before crashing into it. According to Hoerbiger, the last of these moons, circling close to earth, caused a perpetual tide several miles high.

LAKE TITICACA
An island in the center of Lake Titicaca is called by the indigenous people the Island of the Sun. They declare that the sun god sent his son and daughter to this island with the mission of civilizing human beings, who lived like animals. They are said to have taught men the skills of agriculture and women how to weave clothes.

THEORIES ABOUT THE SITE

Who built Tiahuanaco and when? The Kalasasaya was clearly a ritual area (its name means Place of the Standing Stones, after the daggerlike stones that form its stockade). So was the Akapana Pyramid, a huge mound south of the Kalasasaya originally covered with steps made of andesite blocks. The name Akapana means "the place where men perish," so it may have been a site of human sacrifice.

In the early 20th century before the advent of archaeological training and sophisticated dating techniques, some people speculated that Tiahuanaco had been a great city peopled by refugees from the Old World or from Plato's mythical land of Atlantis.

Others drew conclusions based on what may have been coincidence. For example, in 1922 Arthur Posnansky dated the site of Tiahuanaco to 15,000 B.C. He argued that when the observation points on the Kalasasaya were made, the tropics of Cancer and Capricorn must have been positioned where they would have been in 15,000 B.C. Modern dating techniques suggest that humans did not live in the New World until long after that and that the Kalasasaya at Tiahuanaco is much later.

VIRACOCHA
Many of the statues and artifacts of Tiahuanaco seem to represent a principal deity. This may have been a representation of an early ancestor of the 15th-century Inca god, the mysterious "savior" and civilizer Viracocha. In Inca myth, the god is said to have risen from Lake Titicaca to create the sun, the moon, and the stars. He is sometimes portrayed with fish scales, a reference to his watery origins. The most famous representation of Viracocha is the "great idol of Tiahuanaco" (opposite) excavated in 1932. The idol was found in the underground temple that stands in front of the inner court of the Kalasasaya Temple.

THE INCAN GOLDSMITHS

It was the beauty and value of objects such as this that lured the greedy conquistadores to the Americas. The Inca, like other Mesoamerican cultures, used gold objects for ritual purposes.

MACHU PICCHU

THE LOST CITY OF THE INCA

GAZETTEER P.148 - SITE NO.1

THE FORTRESS OF MACHU PICCHU, high in the Peruvian Andes, is one of the most spectacular sites in the world. The city is enclosed on three sides by a steep gorge, half a mile (1 kilometre) deep, in which the Urabamba, a tributary of the Amazon, boils and surges; a mountain ridge acts as guardian on the fourth side. Discovered in 1911, this city once held several thousand people and contained towers, monuments, and religious shrines and temples. Hailed by some as the legendary Vilcabamba, last stronghold of the Inca, and as Tampa Tocco, the original Incan ancestral home (both since discovered elsewhere), it is unlikely that it was ever more than an important royal retreat. Yet its well-preserved ruins and sacred sites offer us a glimpse into the cultural and religious life of the Inca.

EARLY DISCOVERIES

In 1911, Hiram Bingham, a professor at Yale University, set out in search of the fabled Vilcabamba, the last refuge of the Inca. The Spaniards had captured Cuzco in 1532, murdering the Incan emperor Atahualpa. His brother Manco Capac withdrew to Vilcabamba, where he remained undiscovered by the Spanish. A local led Bingham to Machu Picchu, which was overgrown with forest. Once it was cleared, he found rows of agricultural terraces and many fine examples of Incan architecture. Further work in 1912 led to the discovery of the Temple of the Three Windows; a similar three-windowed cave, Tampu Tocco, was talked of by the Inca as the place of their origin. Other *huacas* (sacred places) like the Torreon and the Intihuatana, were found, and it became clear that natural boulders and caves were also worshipped.

But another discovery suggested to Bingham that Machu Picchu had been home to the Chosen Women – Mamacunas, dedicated to the worship of the sun god, the servant of Viracocha, the main Incan diety. Natural caves in slopes below the city were found containing burials of 173 skeletons, of which 150 were women. On a rock high above the city, they found the elaborate grave of a middle-aged woman, buried with ritual objects including a concave bronze mirror, a knife with a bird-shaped handle, and painted ceramics.

We now know that Machu Picchu was a royal estate built by the first Incan emperor Pachacuti, but the number of features at Machu Picchu that align with celestial formations indicates its importance as a religious center.

HITCHING POST OF THE SUN

The Intihuatana – the Hitching Post of the Sun – is an odd chunk of granite with geometrical carvings, surmounted by a vertical prong. It was possibly a form of astronomical marker used in important festivals. It has also been suggested that it was some form of sun dial used in a form of sun worship.

CUZCO
THE "NAVEL" OF THE INCAN WORLD
GAZETTEER P.148 - SITE NO.2

CAPITAL AND RELIGIOUS center of the Incan empire, Cuzco's name in Quechua (the Incan language) means navel. The Milky Way was a vital part of Incan cosmology. In Cuzco it arcs through the zenith of the sky overhead, and the Inca imagined Cuzco at the navel of the earth, corresponding to this zenith. A system of lines radiated from Cuzco, they were known as *ceques* and aligned *huacas,* and were the center of a religious system that integrated earthly features, social life, and the wider cosmos. At the center of Cuzco were the Huacapata and Cusipata precincts, where great religious festivals were presided over by the ruling Inca from his *usnu* (ritual throne).

Cuzco, the Inca declared, was founded by Manco Capac, but was also seen as the capital of Viracocha, "the Foam of the Sea" (and rain god). His marble statue once stood in the center of the Coricancha – the Temple of the Sun, the most sacred of Incan places; only a fragment now remains, surmounted by a later cathedral. One of the myths surrounding Virachoca is that he was a white-bearded god who appeared around the time of a great flood that destroyed the world, after which he created the sun, moon, and stars. He disappeared into the sea, but promised to return.

THE SACRED VALLEY
As its name suggests, the valley surrounding Cuzco was littered with areas considered sacred to the Inca. Thousands of huacas *could be found in its hills, mountains, rocks, and streams.*

SACSAHUAMAN
The sacred city of Cuzco was laid out to resemble the form of a puma. The fortress of Sacsahuaman lies north of the city and represented the head. It is an example of the Inca's fine stonemasonry.

NAZCA LINES
MYSTERY OF THE ANDES
GAZETTEER P.148 - SITE NO.3

THESE STRANGE LINES in the Peruvian desert have been called the greatest mystery in the world. Only recently rediscovered, when viewed from the air, hundreds of huge drawings in the sand and straight lines that radiate to the horizon can be seen, covering 193 sq mi (500 sq km). The images were made by arranging small stones on the flat, rainless plain, and include giant birds, fishes, flowers, mammals, and insects. The Nazca plain is windy, but the stones absorb enough sunlight to cause rising air to protect them. The stones have been carbon-dated to A.D. 350, but could be even older.

Linked to the Nazca culture, the lines may have been sacred ritual pathways. Some lines converge on a center, where offerings may have been left. Yet why could the lines only be seen from the air? In 1586, Spaniard Luis de Monzon said they were built in honor of the saintly "Viracochas," followers of the god, who expected him to return like a great bird from the air.

NAZCAN POT

IMAGES OF THE STARS
Dr. Phyllis Pitluga has suggested that the giant spider was based on the constellation Orion, and that the lines around it were designed to track its stars. There is little doubt that the lines had a ritual function that may have been astronomical.

MYSTERIOUS CULTURE
Nazcans were skilled potters, and some of their pottery found by researcher Maria Reiche has been dated to the first century B.C. Many of the animals featured in the Nazca lines appear in the same style on this pottery.

THE PACIFIC & AUSTRALASIA

SOUTHERN INDONESIA and Australia were not occupied by human beings until about 20,000 years ago. This was because of a deep trough in the sea between Borneo and Celebes that was 30 mi (48 km) wide even in the last Ice Age. Australia's isolation during subsequent millennia leads many to believe that its indigenous people represent the world's oldest continuous culture and religion. There is a sense in which the Aborigine religion may be regarded as the earliest. It springs out of a close relationship with the earth, which it regards as a living being. All Aborigine groups accept the concept of the Dreamtime, a time of creation that runs parallel to the present, where the earth is peopled by giant humans and animals, who are identified with major landmarks. Physical reality existed before creation, but was formless; the spirits gave it form, and could be regarded as artists who shaped reality.

The native religions of Pacific regions, such as Micronesia and Polynesia reflect a more stratified society, with a divine aristocracy. One fundamental concept is that of *mana*, a powerful and dangerous vital force that can nevertheless be controlled by human beings. Cannibalism, once practiced in the Pacific, involves absorbing the *mana* of the enemy.

PHILIPPINES

CELEBES SEA

INDONESIA

NEW GUINEA

ARAFURA SEA

TIMOR SEA

WESTERN AUSTRALIA

AUSTRALIA

NEW SOUTH WALES

SOUTHERN OCEAN

N

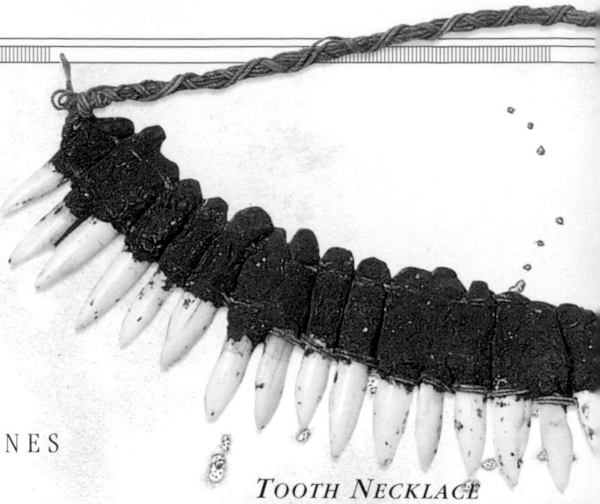

TOOTH NECKLACE
This Aboriginal tooth necklace, made of kangaroo teeth, comes from Queensland, in northeastern Australia. It is worn as a charm to ward off evil.

② *ULURU*
Uluru has been sacred to Aborigines from remote times. Many song lines and dreaming tracks come together here.

① *KATA TJUTA*
These mountains of "rounded minarets, giant cupolas, and monstrous domes" are believed to be the home of a giant male snake named Wanambi.

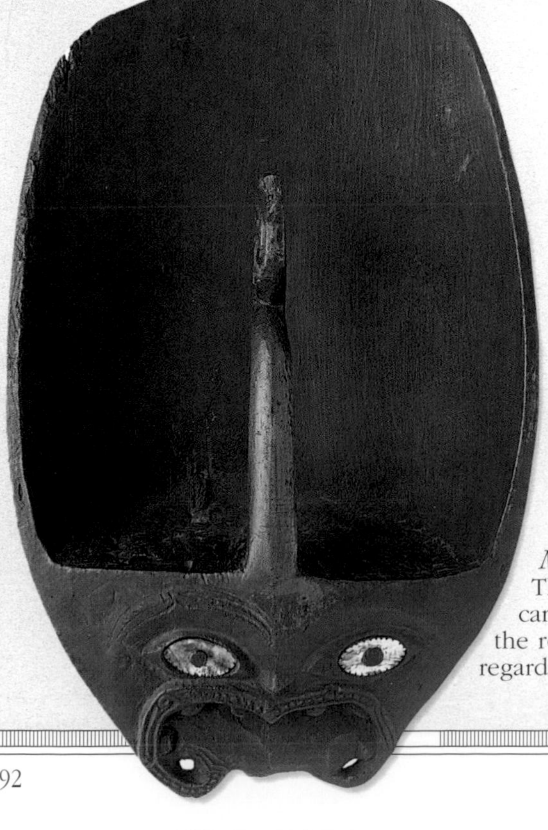

MAORI CANOE BAILER
The face carved on this wooden canoe bailer was intended to protect the rower from disaster. The Maoris regard carving as a semisacred task.

MICRONESIA

EASTER ISLAND

Until recently, Easter Island and its massive statues were one of the world's great mysteries. But modern scholars have begun to understand how and why the giant statues were erected, and how the islanders gradually destroyed their own environment through inter-tribal war and the prodigal use of their natural resources.

RANO AROI

RANO RARAKU

EASTER ISLAND

N

7 HANGA ROA

RANO KAU

PACIFIC OCEAN

2 MILES

0

3 KILOMETRES

③ NANDAUWAS
The vast artificial islets of coral on the island of Pohnpei and the mortuary compounds they support are among the world's great building achievements.

POLYNESIA

SAMOAN ISLANDS

SOCIETY ISLANDS

FIJI

TONGA

4

5

CORAL SEA

⑤ RAIATEA
This volcanic island is the legendary home of the god Oro. Worship of him includes human sacrifice and cannibalism.

④ TONGA
The huge trilithon of east Tongatapu is unique. It dates from about A.D. 1200 and is thought to have had some astronomical purpose.

PACIFIC OCEAN

CEREMONIAL AXE
The head of this Maori axe is made of nephrite, a similar mineral to jade, which is sacred to the Maoris.

6

TASMAN SEA

⑥ ONE TREE HILL
One Tree Hill is a Maori pa or fort on the slopes of an extinct volcano. It is found at modern Auckland on the North Island of New Zealand.

NEW ZEALAND

EASTER ISLAND

GUARDIAN STATUES & THE BIRDMAN CULT

GAZETTEER P.151 - SITE NO.98

STARING OUT ACROSS a remote island in the eastern Pacific, over 2,000 mi (3,219 km) from South America, stand 600 monolithic heads. Their origin remained a mystery for years. The islanders, who called their home *Te Pito o te Henua* ("Land's End"), claimed that the statues had walked there. Dutch explorers landed on the island on Easter Sunday in 1722; from their volcanic origins they speculated that the statues might have been dragged from local quarries on wooden sledges or rollers – yet the island had no trees. Not until the late 20th century did the mystery of the statues begin to unravel.

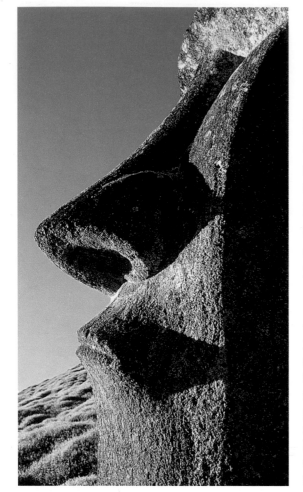

MOAI – SILENT STONE FIGURES

Built in honor of dead chiefs, not all the moai *held equal importance. Some tribes were more powerful and thus had more important leaders, who were honored as such. Statues in the south of the island have been found with stone topknots made from red volcanic rock that some believe are symbols of extra power.*

THE MYSTERIES SOLVED

In 1956, Norwegian explorer Thor Heyerdahl uncovered layers of charred wood on the island; it proved the existence of abundant forests and that the islanders had once practiced slash-and-burn farming. They had not sailed from the east as originally thought, but from the Polynesian Islands in the west around A.D. 450. It was not until about A.D. 1000 that they carved statues in honor of dead chiefs – seen as descendants of the gods – and it is believed they dragged them upright on sledges to their eventual resting places.

By 1500, their farming methods had leveled the island's forests, leading to widespread erosion and a shortage of the timber essential for building the canoes used for deep-sea fishing. As the inhabitants became prisoners on an island no longer able to support a large population, tribal warfare became the norm. It is believed many statues were torn down to destroy the *mana* (magic power) of rival tribes. The longing to escape the island led to the emergence of the birdman cult, expressing the wish to fly to freedom like the indigenous frigate bird. By the time the Dutch arrived in the 18th century, they found a divided culture, no longer in awe of its magnificent idols of stone.

PEDESTAL OF THE ANCESTOR GODS

Ahu Akivi, below, is one of the largest on the island. The ahu *– a temple platform – was used for the worship of the ancestors who protected the community. The number of ancestral idols often reflected the importance of the locality. Each community was linked by a common lineage.*

Though the eyes are now missing from these statues, the Easter Islanders originally placed white coral or red scoria rock in the eye sockets

There are 800 to 1,000 statues on the island. The average height is 13 ft (4 m). The largest is 65 ft (20 m) high

THE BIRDMAN CULT

As the construction of statues declined, so the birdman cult became increasingly important. Each year the tangata manu *festival took place at the ceremonial village of Orongo, where the bird petroglyphs were carved (see below). The island in the distance, Moto Nui, was where the sooty tern migrated to lay its eggs. The bird was believed to be an incarnation of Makemake, the island's principle deity, and its eggs were sacred. The chief of the first tribe to retrieve an egg from the island became the new birdman – effectively a man-god with much power over the island. Ceremonies took place in celebration with bird, or even human, sacrifices.*

RELIGIOUS HIERARCHY

The beliefs of the Easter Islanders differed significantly from the rest of Polynesia. Their main god, Makemake, was not found in the pantheon of any other island, even though he was believed to have evolved from the egg of Tangaroa, the most important Polynesian god.

According to legend, Hotu Matua was the first man to reach the island. The king, who lived in a sacred royal residence at Anakena, was always a member of the Honga clan, believed to be descendants of Hotu Matua, and inheritors of the divine power, the *mana*. The island was also divided into six districts called *mata*; Hotu Matua split the land between his six sons shortly before his death, and the power that each *mata* wielded varied accordingly. Each *mata* covered an area of coast, running back to the island's interior. Each district built its *ahu* near the shore so that the *moai*, which faced inland, could keep guard over the community. The *ahu* was also used as a

center of religious ritual and a place of burial for the most important members of the lineage. The number of *moai* on the *ahu* probably related to its importance; even in death the society was hierarchically divided. The houses of the priests and chiefs were nearest to the *ahu*, with the rest of the community housed further inland, according to their status.

Despite these social divisions, every islander was equally in awe of the gods. Every act was accompanied by a short prayer or ritual. Only in significant acts were the priests or kings called upon to use their *mana*.

RANO RARAKU QUARRY

Easter Island was created from the lava of the three volcanoes that form the corners of the island. The vast statues were cut from volcanic rock at the Rano Raraku quarry (below) and hauled to their respective ahu. *The effort required demonstrates the presence of considerable political power. Many, like those below, were never finished.*

Volcanic tuff was used as the material for most of the images

The classic *moai* was a distinctive male with an elongated head, thin lips, convex forehead, with the arms pressed tightly to the hips

The *ahu* is approached by a paved stone incline

The "tattooed" backs of the statues were often carved with reliefs

ULURU

SACRED SITE OF THE DREAMTIME

GAZETTEER P.150 · SITE NO.23

A GIANT MASS OF SANDSTONE, Uluru (Ayers Rock) is the world's most famous monolith. Covering an area 1¼ mi (2 km) wide and 2 mi (3 km) long, and rising 1,115 ft (340 m) above the desert plain, it has been sacred to Aborigines from time immemorial. Their legends describe how Uluru was created by two boys playing in the mud and rain during the Dreamtime, the Aboriginal time of creation that runs parallel to life. Dozens of dreaming tracks – the paths of their ancestors' journeys that connect sacred places – come together at Uluru in a unity of myth. A great battle fought here marks the end of the Dreamtime, when the Kuniya, the Carpet Snake people, were attacked by the Liru, venomous snake men. Rocks in the shape of a Kuniya woman's features, an attacking Liru man's wounded head, and the bodies of two other warriors are all found on the rock. To Aborigines, the Dreamtime is present in all aspects of Uluru.

AYERS ROCK
Known to Aborigines for thousands of years, Uluru was first seen by a European in 1872. It was named Ayers Rock after the premier of South Australia. In 1985, Uluru returned to its traditional Aboriginal owners, who leased it back to the government for 99 years.

KATA TJUTA

Also known as the Olgas, named after the Queen of Spain by Ernest Giles, Kata Tjuta can be found 31 mi (50 km) west of Uluru. Regarded as a female sacred place, from a distance it is said to resemble a giant female's body. Some of its domes are said to be food piles collected by the mice women, who are linked with fertility ceremonies. Mount Olga is home to the giant snake Wanambi, who lives in the waterhole on its peak during the wet season and in the gorge during the dry season; water channels are the hairs of his beard and the wind is his breath.

ABORIGINAL
SNAKE SPOON

THE DREAMTIME

The Dreamtime is the Aborigines' description of a time when the earth was created by spirit ancestors, who traveled across the landscape making its features and giving them names in song. These dreaming spirits are also responsible for the many different tribes, their customs, laws, and languages. The routes used are called dreaming tracks.

Aboriginal people commit to memory every detail of the dreaming tracks and, by repeating or singing the hundreds of different associated tales, can restate the philosophy of belonging to the land. There are thousands of such stories and songs in Australia, each clan having its own. Shamans called *karadjis* have access to the world of the dreaming spirits, so the stories can never be forgotten. Most Aboriginal men can lead the visitor across the landscape, pick out the features, and repeat the associated legends in song. Such routes are known as song lines and are associated with the idea of the spirits singing the world into existence – they are performing a religious ritual that brings forth the energy that renews the existence of the landscape.

One story associated with Uluru tells of a western people, the Windulka, growing angry with two peoples, the Kuniya and the Mala, who had failed to arrive for an important ritual. The Kuniya had camped on Uluru, where they had met some beautiful "lizard women." The Windulka made a dingo from the mud and sang evil into him; the dog then proceeded to kill the Mala. Later, the Liru people fought the Kuniya and killed their leader Ungata. As a consequence, the Kuniya sang themselves to death in an act of mass suicide. Certain boulders at Uluru are seen as Mala initiates lying asleep, others the dead bodies of Ungata and his mother Ingridi, while certain water stains are the blood of dying Liru warriors.

Another song line tells how two pigeons, a brother and a sister, wander along the Victoria River, passing through many different Aboriginal territories, changing each language accordingly. Such a song line is a common cultural inheritance of many Aboriginal peoples and serves to unite them.

The convergence of the song lines and dreaming tracks at these sites has been compared to wires of current being fed by a large node of power that gives life to the surrounding countryside. Uluru, the home of over 60 stories associated with the Dreamtime, is perhaps the most important of Aboriginal sacred places. The rock itself has a sunny side and a shady side, whose conflicts are resolved at the end of the Dreamtime.

CAVE PAINTING
Uluru is a living testament of Aboriginal ancestral history. The caves around the base of the rock have some of the finest examples of Aboriginal rock paintings, illustrating the borders and paths of the Dreamtime.

LAGARI, THE LAUGHING CAVE
Lagari, on the southern side of Uluru, is said to represent the open mouth of a Kuniya warrior. Inside rock paintings depict ingulbi, *native tobacco, which is mixed with* djunba *ash to make* karputa, *a chew to stave off thirst.*

RAIATEA
PLACE OF RITUAL SACRIFICE
—— GAZETTEER P.151 - SITE NO.97 ——

THE BIRTHPLACE of the Tahitian god of war and peace Oro, son of the creator Tangaroa, Raiatea in the Society Islands lies in a group of islands mostly dominated by volcanoes. In all the group, it is the island of greatest religious importance. The worship of Oro spread to most of the other islands, including Tahiti. The god was known as the killer of men, who delighted in human sacrifice. The religion that worshipped him included ritual cannibalism. The purpose of cannibalism is to allow the eater to absorb the attribute – strength, intelligence, etc. – of the eaten.

The islands were divided by a rigid caste structure, and intermarriage was forbidden. Tahitian chiefs were virtually high chiefs; they were carried around on their people's backs, and if they entered the house of a commoner, it was razed to the ground afterward, since the commoner was not worthy to live in a house honored by a chief. The chiefs were mummified after death.

A group known as the Arioi (founded by the priests of Oro) were also of considerable importance. These were young men and women who journeyed from village to village performing sacred plays and dances. They were fed and supported by the communities they visited, sometimes for years and had eight grades of initiation, suggesting a religious or magical group. Early reports speak of their greed, cruelty, and promiscuity. Children born as a result of the sexual activity were put to death, as were those born from the union of a chief and a commoner. Infanticide, however, was an accepted social practice.

RAIATEAN MARAE
The religion of Oro involved human sacrifice in a marae – sacred enclosure – performed to the beating of drums. Pigs were also sacrificed, and there was an ahu – a ceremonial platform – and a carved wooden board, representing the gods.

THE ISLAND OF RAIATEA
Although Tahiti was the most influential economically, Raiatea was the most sacred of the Society Islands. Its most powerful religion, the bloodthirsty cult of Oro, spread throughout the neighboring island groups.

TONGA
PREHISTORIC CORAL MOUNDS
—— GAZETTEER P.150 - SITE NO.63 ——

AS IN THE SOCIETY ISLANDS, in the Tongan Islands of the South Pacific, the chief was regarded virtually as a god. Commoners bent to touch the sole of his foot as he passed.

By A.D. 1200, the whole Tonga group was dominated by the Tonga Dynasty, which ruled from Tongatapu – where, in the district of Mu'a, the burial mounds of the kings can be seen. Many are concealed under huge steps of coral, and have burial chambers of coral slabs. Ha'amonga-a-Maui was also built around this time, said to have been constructed to symbolize the two sons of the ruling house of Tu'i Tonga. Even in prehistoric times, there existed a warlike aristocracy that developed a centralized government in the Tongan Islands, and a royal line continues in Tonga today.

HA'AMONGA-A-MAUI
This huge trilithon of eastern Tongatapu is made of massive blocks of coral. It dates from about A.D. 1200. The present king of Tonga has suggested that it has an astronomical purpose, recording the equinoxes against star positions.

NANDAUWAS
ROYAL TOMB OF NAN MADOL
GAZETTEER P.150 · SITE NO.55

THE SITE OF NANDAUWAS is one of the world's great religious buildings and certainly the greatest example of prehistoric architecture in Micronesia. It stands on the southeast coast of the island of Pohnpei. The island has been occupied for at least 2,000 years, but around A.D. 1300, a chief called the *saudeleur* (Lord of Delaur) made Nan Madol his capital, and began creating artificial sites on the coral that lay beneath the surface of the water. These islands covered areas equivalent to several football fields. Immense basalt walls were created as breakwaters, and the islets became the sites of temples, tombs, and other ritual sites. Several islets near the tomb compound probably served as priests' quarters. The site was abandoned some time after 1700.

THE GREAT MORTUARY TEMPLE
Walls up to 25 ft (8 m) high surround the royal tomb compound of Nandauwas. The central enclosure contains the island's largest crypt. Why the builders chose to create islands rather than building on land remains a mystery.

NEW ZEALAND
THE SACRED LAND
GAZETTEER P.150 · SITE NO.47

SINCE IT WAS ONE of the more remote parts of Polynesia, New Zealand was one of the last Pacific islands to be settled in about A.D. 800.

The indigenous Maori society had a priest caste, which included the tribal chiefs. The god they worshipped was called Io. He was invoked in birth, baptism, and marriage ceremonies for Maori of higher rank. The people also worshipped the nature gods, *tane-mahuta*, of forest, trees, birds, and Tangaroa, the Maori sea god. There were also dozens of minor nature spirits, *atua*, who might be malignant or otherwise. These nature spirits often sent omens, punished *tapu* (the Polynesian taboo – forbidden things), and were invoked in magic. (Maori magical ritual was extremely strict and precise; a mistake was serious and could even result in death.)

The Maori believe that man has several spirits; the *wairua* or soul, which vacates the body and wanders abroad in dreams, and the *mauri* and the *hau* – principles of vitality and intelligence that dissolve away at death. The

soul then passes to the Maori heaven, *Te Reinga*, a peaceful underworld beneath the sea, where life goes on as it did before.

Captain James Cook circumnavigated the two main islands in 1769–70, and the Europeans who poured in around the turn of the century were at first welcomed by the Maori. But the disease and the disintegration of social structures that accompanied them led the Maori to become increasingly hostile, and a series of wars – which the Maori lost – deprived them of much of their land, which they regarded as part of their sacred inheritance.

Like the Aborigines of Australia, the Maori consider the whole landscape sacred. The most distinctive historical Maori structures that remain are the *pa*, fortified villages, not unlike European hill-forts, frequently with terraces and ditches.

MAORI
AMULET

ONE TREE HILL
The slopes of extinct volcanoes were often chosen for the terraced type of pa, like this one found in Auckland on New Zealand's North Island.

THE FAR EAST

EARLY FAR EASTERN civilization was a creation of the Mongolian people. In China, the Shang Empire, dating from about 2500 to 1100 B.C., achieved considerable sophistication, with statues of jade and ivory, and a system of writing. Their preoccupation with the dead was as great as it was in ancient Egypt, and ancestor worship was a dominant form of religion. Oracle bones were the most important method of divination and shamans practiced rain-making. Both Hinduism and Buddhism reached China along the great trade routes, but it was the latter that made the greater impact, while the southeast Asian archipelago was powerfully influenced by both.

Because the Chinese were not seafarers, Japanese civilization remained isolated until the third century A.D., when influences from China infiltrated, probably via Korea. The introduction of rice and the growth of an agricultural economy led to the development of Shintoism, with its emphasis on the *kami* or spirits of natural locations. Shintoism later came to be associated with emperor worship, so that Japanese nationalism and religion remained closely associated. With the advent of Buddhism in the sixth century and in the Nara period that followed, Japanese life began to be slowly transformed, and a distinctive Japanese culture – and religion – began to emerge.

ASIA

IMPERIAL SEAL
This seal belonged to Qianlong, fourth emperor of the Manchu Dynasty, who ruled China as the Divine Emperor or Son of Heaven from 1736 to 1796.

RIVER GANGES

① **MINGUN PAGODA**
Built by an 18th-century tyrant, the Mingun Pagoda was intended to be the world's tallest religious building.

❶

BAY OF BENGAL

BURMA

INDIA

❷

② **SHWEDAGON**
Each year, devout pilgrims add to the gold of Burma's greatest religious shrine by covering it in gold leaf.

N

SRI LANKA

INDIAN OCEAN

THE HEART SUTRA
This scroll from the Horyuji Temple at Nara contains the Buddhist scripture known as the Heart Sutra. It shows the Buddha surrounded by bodhisattvas, with heavenly musicians, and a boat carrying devotees to heaven, all against a background of the temple complex.

MONGOLIA

⑩ **MOUNT FUJI**
This aerial view shows the volcano's crater; the temples and shrines at the bottom of it are sites of pilgrimage.

JAPAN

⑫ NIKKO

⑩

⑪ KAMAKURA

NARA ⑧

⑨

SOUTH KOREA

⑤ **TEMPLE OF HEAVEN**
Beijing's great temple was built for the personal worship of a Chinese emperor.

EAST CHINA SEA

YANGSTE RIVER

⑥ **EMEISHAN**
The most beautiful of China's sacred mountains, Emeishan is also the most arduous for pilgrims to climb.

⑦ **HENGSHAN**
On the steep cliffs of China's most northerly Taoist mountain sits the famous Hanging Monastery.

CHINA

⑨ **ISE**
Every 20 years for the last 14 centuries, Japan's most important Shinto shrine has been rebuilt.

TAIWAN

SOUTH CHINA SEA

PACIFIC OCEAN

HAINAN DAO

LUZON

MEKONG RIVER

VIETNAM

CAMBODIA

③

PHILIPPINES

③ **ANGKOR**
Hidden for centuries in the steamy jungles of Cambodia, this great temple city is sacred to the Hindu god Vishnu.

MINDANAO

LAYSIA

BORNEO

SULAWESI

INDONESIA

④ **BOROBUDUR**
Java's Temple of the Thousand Buddhas looks like a celestial city, with its profusion of bell-shaped domes and terraces.

INCENSE BURNER
Chinese Buddhists burn incense to household and ancestor gods, while the Japanese incorporate its use into Shinto ritual.

JAVA

④

NEW GUINEA

BOROBUDUR
IN THE FOOTSTEPS OF THE BUDDHA

GAZETTEER P.155 - SITE NO.47

HIDDEN STATUES
In all, there are 432 statues of the Buddha at Borobudur. Each of the bell-shaped miniature stupas (dagobas) at the summit also contains a statue, visible through the stone lattice.

THE PATH TO ENLIGHTENMENT

Borobudur was originally intended as a center of pilgrimage, a kind of Buddhist Mecca. The path to the summit of the temple was designed as a clockwise path of pilgrimage. Its main frieze, decorated with 1,400 stone carvings, is 3 mi (5 km) long, a narrative of the road to nirvana, with incidents from the lives of the Buddha and of other bodhisattvas. As the pilgrim ascends through the different layers of the temple, each completed level represents a progressively higher level of experience. Around the base of Borobudur, reliefs refer to the earthly realm or *kamadhatu*; carvings depict the actions of men, both good and bad, and their consequences. The four terraces that stand above this lower level represent the heavenly world or *ruphadhatu,* and the reliefs here display a concern with more spiritual matters, including passages from the life of the Buddha, from his birth to his first sermon. Levels two to four narrate the life story of the pilgrim Sudhana, whose journey toward enlightenment parallels that of the Buddha. The circular terraces at the apex of the temple represent the world of formlessness, or *aruphadatu,* a world beyond the heavens in which individual forms and identities dissolve.

THE TEMPLE OF BOROBUDUR
Borobudur is built in the form of a stupa – a structure created to house religious relics – itself derived from the shape of a burial mound. It may also be seen as a mandala (from the Sanskrit for circle), the circular figure symbolizing wholeness.

BOROBUDUR, IN THE CENTRAL highlands of Java, is the largest Buddhist shrine in the world. Its name means "Temple of the Countless Buddhas." Seen from above, it resembles some strange birthday cake. In its early days, painted white, it would have looked like a celestial city. The sheer profusion of bell-shaped domes, statues of Buddha, and other carvings make this stone pyramid striking to the eye. Built in the eighth to ninth century, it fell into neglect around the year 1000. It was rediscovered in 1815, and later rescued from the volcanic ash and vegetation that concealed it. Its base is not visible from the top, and vice versa. The temple was a symbol of the ascent through worldliness to the heights of enlightenment, in which the seeker would be unable to see – or even imagine – what existed at the end of the journey. Five terraces symbolize the levels that must be surmounted: worldly desire, malevolence, malicious joy, indolence, and doubt. When the seeker reached the top, earlier stages of nonperfection would no longer be visible.

TEMPLE RELIEFS
There are 3 mi (5 km) of wall carvings. Within each gallery, the outer wall contains two levels of reliefs, while the inner has one. Each gallery is invisible from the others, suggesting the separate layers of understanding.

HISTORY OF BOROBUDUR

Borobudur may originally have been built as a Hindu monument, its position on a hill an echo of the sacred Hindu mountain Mount Meru (see pp.106-107). Hindus regard the square as the perfect shape, the ultimate symbol of order, and claim that the circle is derived from it. Borobudur is built in square terraces leading to a circular summit – five large square terraces and three smaller circular ones, symbolizing the eightfold path. (A ninth "base terrace" was later built to stabilize it.) Borobudur has also been described as a mandala. In several religions, mandalas symbolize the harmony of the universe, usually in the form of a circle in a square.

The shape of Borobudur may also owe something to the line of volcanoes that lie to the north of the temple. The name of the ruling family who built it – Sailendra – means "Lords of the Mountains." Their wealth and power was legendary. Yet the temple was built – between A.D. 750 and 850 – at a time when Buddhism and Hinduism were in decline (both were eventually driven out by Islam).

When Borobudur was completed, it was only used for a few decades, and then abandoned. The reasons for this are not clear. One theory suggests that the rulers forced the peasants to work so hard on the temple that they preferred to flee to eastern Java, which became a trade center.

There is evidence that pilgrims from China continued to visit Borobudur long after it had ceased to be a great local religious center.

Then, for more than 800 years, the temple was forgotten. In the early 20th century, large-scale restoration began. But Java's heavy rainfall had taken its toll on the sacred hill, and it was obvious that, if left to itself, the temple would slide off it and collapse. In 1973, a $21-million restoration project was begun, and the temple was dismantled and reassembled. By the early 1990s, the plan was virtually completed.

BOROBUDUR AT DAWN
The site of Borobudur was obviously chosen because of its location amid mountains in a natural paradise. In the distance can be seen the volcano, whose eruption covered the site in volcanic ash, hiding it for many years.

LOROJANGGRANG

The remains of priests' quarters in the Lorojanggrang Complex at Borobudur suggests that it supported a large number of priests and, despite its unique structure, was used as a site of religious ceremony.

In fact, the site of Borobudur is a remarkably egalitarian example of temple architecture. While the structure of the temple at Borobudur suggests the hierarchy of religious thought, it is approached through the narrative of its many reliefs. The pyramid is experienced from the viewpoint of each individual pilgrim, and where he or she stands within its stepped framework. It therefore resists the hierarchy implicit in many religious ceremonies or rituals.

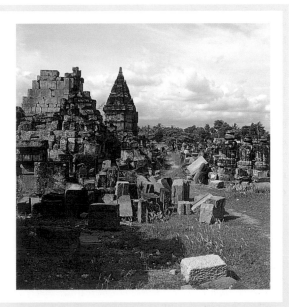

MINGUN

UNFINISHED PAGODA OF KING BODAWPAYA

GAZETTEER P.154 · SITE NO.1

HOME OF THE BUDDHA'S FOOTPRINT
Settawya Paya, seen above, is one building at Mingun that King Bodawpaya did finish. It was built in 1811 to house a footprint of the Buddha. In Theravada Buddhist countries like Burma, the feet represent the grounding of the transcendent. The worship of the stone footprint is a natural extension of animistic stone worship.

BURMA, NOW CALLED MYANMAR, is known as the land of the pagodas. These religious structures, often housing a relic of the Buddha, were regarded as places for worship, prayer, meditation, and spiritual refreshment. If it had been completed, the Mingun Pagoda, 7 mi (11 km) north of Mandalay, would have been the largest pagoda of all. Standing by the Irawaddy River, it was intended by its builder King Bodawpaya (died 1819) to be the greatest shrine in the world, and was to have reached a height of 500 ft (152 m), nearly 150 ft (46 m) taller than the Shwedagon Pagoda (see p.105). It fell short of achieving this feat, but nevertheless stands at 165 ft (50 m). However, its great iron bell, weighing 87 tons, now hung on iron beams in a building near the pagoda, is famous as the largest undamaged bell in the world.

REIGN OF TERROR

It seems appropriate that King Bodawpaya did not succeed in completing the huge pagoda, for posterity regards him as anything but a holy man. The sixth monarch of the Alaungpaya dynasty, he came to power in 1782 after murdering his grandnephew Maung Maung. He then embarked on a reign of terror, as he slaughtered his nearest rivals and burned the villages of any traitors. In 1784, he invaded Arakan, the maritime kingdom west of Lower Burma, taking 20,000 slaves, many of whom were called to work upon the Mingun Pagoda.

In spite of his cruelty, the king regarded himself as Arimittya, the reincarnated Buddha destined to conquer the world. He persecuted what he regarded as heretical sects and made capital crimes of drinking alcohol, smoking opium, and killing animals. The Mingun Pagoda, begun in 1795, was intended as the climax of his career as world savior. But he died in 1819, when only one third of the work had been carried out.

When the British eventually took over Rangoon in 1824, this gigantic religious monument was never completed as it had been intended, and instead was left to decay.

GUARDIANS OF MINGUN
Seen at the front of Settawya Paya are two griffin-like creatures called "chinthes" – a form of Burmese mythical animal. Two similar guardians, now in a ruined state, can be found in front of the unfinished pagoda.

HIDDEN TREASURES
Left in its unfinished state, it was not long before the pagoda was further damaged by an earthquake in 1838. The upper section of the building collapsed, but in doing so revealed a treasure vault that was filled with gold and silver images and precious stones.

The pagoda has been further damaged by trees growing in the cracks of the building

Each entrance led to a small shrine. Only the one facing the river is still used

The base of the temple covers 137 square metres (164 square yards)

SHWEDAGON
BURMA'S GOLDEN RELIGIOUS CENTER
GAZETTEER P.154 · SITE NO.9

THE GOLDEN PAGODA of Rangoon (now Yangon) is the world's tallest religious building at 386 ft (118 m). No one knows exactly when it was made, but it was repaired as early as 1362, and was built long before the city that grew up around it. The center of Burmese Buddhism, it possesses one of the holiest Buddhist relics – eight hairs of the Buddha's head. Shwedagon is literally covered with gold. In 1871, at a cost of several billion dollars in today's terms, King Mindon Min had the pagoda covered with gold. This is continually added to by pilgrims, who often save for years to afford a small packet of gold leaf to stick on its walls, or onto the dozens of pagodas and temples that now surround it. The spire is studded with precious stones, including diamonds, emeralds, and rubies, and the gold is renewed every generation by public conscription.

JOURNEY TO THE SHRINE
The Shwedagon Pagoda stands on a terraced artificial mound with four market streets that lead to the shrine; here pilgrims can buy offerings of lotus blooms, bowls of rice, and packets of gold leaf. The heart of the pagoda is a relic chamber containing eight hairs of the Buddha's head.

THE GOLDEN STUPA

The Shwedagon Pagoda stands on a hill that dominates the city of Rangoon, and it attracts pilgrims from all parts of the country. Like most of Burma's temples, it is built in the form of a stupa, a form which, according to the Burmese, was derived from a volcano called Mount Popa, also known as the Golden Mountain, or Mountain of Flowers. Before they became Buddhists, the Burmese worshipped nature spirits called *nats*. They were unwilling to totally abandon their older religion, and Shwedagon Pagoda has statues of *nats* in every corner and at every crossing, serving as protective spirits. Hundreds of temple bells on the terrace are struck to attract their attention and blessing.

Shwedagon Pagoda is made of bricks that are packed so tightly together that there is no room between them to insert a needle point. One king had his master builder executed when he discovered a pinhead-sized hole between the bricks. Tradition states that there is a relationship between the pagoda and the health of the person who builds on it (it has been rebuilt and raised higher many times),

so every defect causes an illness in the donor. Between the *nats* sit hundreds of alabaster and marble buddhas; seven of them were named after the seven then-known planets, and pilgrims lay offerings in front of the buddha under whose sign they were born. Shwedagon Pagoda is undoubtedly one of the most impressive religious centers in the world.

THE BELL OF SHWEDAGON
In a golden pagoda on the terrace (the main place of worship) hangs one of the largest bells in the world, weighing over 20 tons. At the top of the pagoda there are 100 gold and 1,400 silver bells. Echoing the bell motif, many other bell-shaped pagodas surround it. It is as if the whole site has been designed as a reminder of the bell that calls one to prayer and meditation. It seems appropriate that Yangon means "End of Strife."

SYMBOLIC ARCHITECTURE
The great achievement of the architects of Angkor Wat (left and above) was their ability to adapt a unique architectural setting to the sacred landscape of Hindu belief.

ANGKOR WAT
& ANGKOR THOM
GAZETTEER P.154 · SITE NO.31

FOR CENTURIES, the mighty religious center of Angkor lay hidden in the jungles of Cambodia. The temple complex called Angkor Thom covered an area 5 by 6½ mi (8 by 10.5 km); Angkor Wat, which is part of it, means "city temple." At Angkor, the Khmer rulers were worshipped and had their capital. The original city was centered on a mound or pyramid temple built to represent the sacred Hindu mountain of Mount Meru. The mountain symbolized the fertility of the soil on which the prosperity of the kingdom depended. Canals and reservoirs that served as irrigation for the capital also performed a symbolic function, representing the great ocean that surrounded the sacred mountain.

THE KHMER EMPIRE

For four centuries, from A.D. 800 to 1200, the Khmer Empire basked in a glory that recalls the French empire under Louis XIV. The great empire is pictured on the walls and in the galleries of the temple at Angkor as the center of a wealthy court, with armies on the march and with naval battles.

The Khmers were originally Hindus, and the great temple is dedicated to the god Vishnu. But the kings of Angkor, from the reign of Jayavarman II (A.D. 802–850) to Jayavarman VII (A.D. 1181–1218), may themselves have been regarded as gods. One modern writer speculates that the Khmer kings used their religious status to enslave the population of Cambodia, and that Angkor Wat was built by a vast army of slaves. The truth is simply that we do not know – we only know that Jayavarman VII, the king responsible for the structure that remains today, is represented as the Buddha (whom he adopted as his patron), and that following his death his kingdom was invaded by the Thais and was converted to Buddhism.

ANGKOR DISCOVERED
It was a French naturalist, Henri Mouhot, who penetrated to Angkor through the waterways and jungles in 1858. He realized that, for once, reality far outstripped myth – he declared that "it was grander than anything left to us by Greece or Rome." His diary, published after his death, caused a sensation and, by 1880, Angkor had become almost as famous as the pyramids of Giza.

ANGKOR THOM

Surrounded by the stone figures of its protector deities, Angkor Thom must have been one of the most beautiful temple complexes in the world. Its center was the Buddhist Bayon Temple (right), with four smiling faces sculpted on each of its towers, which faced the four cardinal points. These were the towers of its last great king, Jayavarman VII, and the whole population was required to parade in front of them every year.

CITY OF WATER
The Khmers relied on the flood waters of the Mekong River as the Egyptians did on the Nile. Without them, there would have been mass starvation during the six-month dry season. Angkor was a city of canals and reservoirs – two of which held well over 1,000 million gallons (4,550 million liters) each. The Khmers' genius for storing water may have caused their downfall: the Thais probably conquered Angkor by flooding it.

AERIAL VIEW
When the sacred chronicle Kojiki *was completed in A.D. 712, Ise had been a sacred place for centuries – the shrines are at least three centuries older. They are associated with the sun goddess.*

ISE

SHINTO, THE ANCIENT BELIEF of Japan, is a religion of nature worship; the objects of its veneration are the spirits – *kami* – of mountains, trees, rocks, springs, and other natural features. It follows that all the major Shinto shrines are found in surroundings of great natural beauty. The inner shrine at Ise, the most important Shinto site in Japan, is dedicated to the sun *kami* Amaterasu. Yet the simple, cabinlike shrines inside its wooden enclosure are not ancient; on the contrary, they are dismantled every 20 years – at enormous expense – and replaced with identical buildings on an adjacent plot. This has been happening for 14 centuries; it is a symbolic renewal, like the renewal of nature. Thus at Ise, it is not any single structure that is sacred, but the site itself.

THE SACRED MIRROR

Housed in the inner shrine at Ise, the sacred mirror has been part of the royal regalia of Japan for almost 2,000 years. The Shinto sacred book *Kojiki* tells how the sun *kami* Amaterasu was so disgusted by her brother Susanowo, the storm god – who damaged rice fields and defecated in her temples – that she retreated to a cave, plunging the world into darkness. To lure her out, the gods commissioned a smith to make a huge steel mirror. Then the goddess Ama no Uzume stood on a tub and began to perform an erotic dance. All the gods roared with laughter, and the sun goddess peeped out to see what was happening. Puzzled by the sight of herself in the mirror, she ventured out far enough for one of the gods to grab her and pull her out, restoring light to the universe.

The mirror was brought down to earth by the sun goddess's grandson Ninigi, who gave it to the emperor Sujin (first century A.D.). Since then it has been treasured by the royal family, who regarded Ise as their own special shrine. But in the Middle Ages, increasing poverty led the guardians of Ise to look for popular support. Little by little, it became a place of pilgrimage for the people, which it remains today.

TWIN ROCKS OF ISE

Before shrines and temples existed, natural objects were worshipped, like these "meota-iwa" (wedded rocks) in the sea near Ise. The rocks are believed to house the spirits of the two legendary progenitors of all things, the brother and sister Izanagi and Izanami, who gave birth to the islands of Japan and numerous gods. The last-born of their children was the god of fire, whose birth burned the goddess terribly, after which she died. The rocks are joined by a straw rope, which is renewed every year, while the larger of the two rocks is surmounted by a torii, a sacred gateway with two crossbeams.

INNER SHRINE
While the outer shrine is dedicated to the harvest goddess Toyuke, the inner shrine is dedicated to the sun goddess Amaterasu, and pilgrims are not permitted to pass beyond the torii. *The only individuals who can enter are Shinto priests and members of the Japanese royal household.*

NIKKO
SHRINE OF A SHOGUN WARRIOR
GAZETTEER P.153 · SITE NO.101

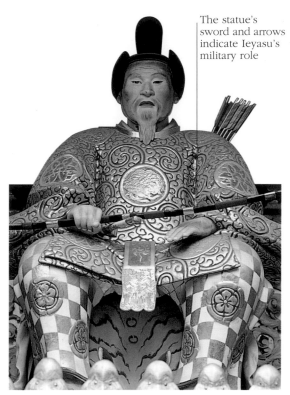

The statue's sword and arrows indicate Ieyasu's military role

THE NAME NIKKO means "sunlight." It is a fittingly beautiful name for one of Japan's greatest shrines. It is one of the most important pilgrimage centers in Japan, as well as one of the most beautiful. In the days when Tokyo was still a small town called Edo – albeit the capital of Japan – the great shogun or warlord Ieyasu decided that he wanted to be buried in Nikko. With the aid of his two great predecessors, Ieyasu had laid the foundations of a united Japan, while Nikko was, at that time, little more than a mountain village, about 60 mi (97 km) to the north of Tokyo. Ieyasu was buried there in 1617, and his famous tomb, the extraordinary Tosho-gu Shrine – built, according to one legend, by as many as 830,000 people in 15 months – became a center of pilgrimage. The third Tokugawa shogun, Iemitsu, was buried in the Daiyuin mausoleum in the year 1651. Gradually, other shrines, temples, and pagodas were constructed – most of these sites were originally Buddhist, although Nikko became predominantly Shinto in later centuries. Today, Nikko is one of Japan's major historical pilgrimage sites.

TOSHO-GU SHRINE
The colorful splendor of the Tosho-gu Shrine typifies the artistic magnificence that makes Nikko one of the great aesthetic experiences. Before the shrine there was an open court with a stage, on which a priestess performed religious dances.

LIFE OF A JAPANESE WARRIOR
It was remarked that the Japanese warrior caste "combined savage ferocity on the battlefield with an elegant and pleasing niceness in the home." Although Ieyasu spent most of his life on horseback, he was of a more contemplative disposition.

MOUNT FUJI
NATURE'S SLEEPING SOUL
GAZETTEER P.153 · SITE NO.98

THE LAKES OF FUJIYAMA
Mount Fuji is revered for its almost perfect symmetry. This quality is seen in the image above, where the mountain is reflected in the lake that lies before it. On the northern slopes of Mount Fuji are five other lakes (Fujigoko).

AT 12,388 FT (3,776 m) high, Mount Fuji (Fujiyama) is Japan's largest mountain; it is also the holiest. A dormant volcano that last erupted in 1707, it is revered above all other groups by Shintoists (see p.108), for whom Fuji is virtually the incarnation of the spirit of Nature. The Fujiko sect believe that the mountain is a sacred being with a soul. Holy to both Buddhists and Shintoists, the mountain has many temples and shrines – even at the bottom of its crater.

Buddhist tradition declares that Fuji rose out of the earth in 286 B.C. after an earthquake (which also left the hollow that became Lake Biwa, Japan's largest lake). In fact, geologists estimate that Fuji is at least 600,000 years old, formed during the Pleistocene era. It was originally the sacred mountain of the Ainu, the aboriginal inhabitants of Japan, who now live on the northern island of Hokkaido. Named after their fire goddess Fuchi, Buddhists believe that the mountain is the gateway to another world, while for Shintoists it is sacred to the goddess Sengen-Sama. Her nickname Konohana-Sakuahime means "causing the blossom to bloom brightly" – a reference to the cherry and plum blossoms that turn the five lakes on the mountain into a scene of dazzling beauty when they bloom against a background of snow. For most of the year, her shrine at the mountain top is covered with snow. In July and August, the snow clears and tens of thousands of pilgrims make the ascent to the summit, triggering fears that the number of pilgrims will cause environmental damage. Like the worshippers of many sacred mountains, these pilgrims are seeking the realm of the gods. There is a difference, however, for Fujiyama is not just the realm of the gods, but a god itself.

NARA

THE HORYUJI BUDDHIST TEMPLE

GAZETTEER P.153 - SITE NO.85

GOLDEN BUDDHA
Nara has many images of the Buddha. Pilgrims lay offerings in front of the statues, which are often made of gold or bronze. The images are particularly popular during Nara's many festivals, which occur throughout the year.

NARA'S BEAUTY LIES in its great Buddhist temples – some of the oldest in Japan. But it also gives its name to an important period in the history of Japan. Buddhism had come to Japan in the sixth century A.D., via China and Korea. In 645, the period described as the "era of the imitation of China" began and around 50 years later the court moved to Nara. The city became the imperial capital and a new culture began, absorbing many of the civilizing aspects of the great Chinese empire. During the brief Nara period (A.D. 710–784), culture flourished as never before. Nara blazed with the glory of its brilliantly painted roofs and outstanding temples. But it was the Buddhist teaching, and its yearning for spiritual enlightenment that epitomized the period, and this is characterized by the oldest wooden structure in the world, the Buddhist temple complex of Horyuji.

THE DAWNING OF BUDDHISM

Buddhism came to Japan in A.D. 552, when the Korean king of Paekche (Kudara) sent Buddhist scriptures to Kimmei-Tenno, 29th emperor of Japan, together with a bronze image of the Buddha. Fear that the new religion might offend the old *kami* (gods) of Japan seemed to be justified when a virulent plague broke out, and the emperor ordered the new Buddhist temple to be burned down. But over the next century, Buddhism slowly gained a foothold, so that during the Nara period Buddhism became Japan's dominant religion.

Thousands of Buddhist temples were built throughout Japan and there was little conflict with Shintoism – the indigenous religion of Japan. With its quest for spiritual enlightenment, Buddhism was more philosophically based than Shinto, but Buddhism's emphasis on the sacredness of all living things is similar to Shinto belief in the sanctity of nature. Shinto adopted the various buddhas as *kami,* and in many areas of Japanese religious life, the two systems blended. Though largely distinguished by the group of Buddhist temples and shrines built mostly in the eighth century, Nara still retains other Shinto shrines, such as the ancient Great Shrine of Kasuga.

GOJU NO TO
This five-story pagoda stands in the central compound of the eastern part of the Horyuji temple. The four sides of the main level of the pagoda are decorated with reliefs and terra-cotta sculptures depicting the life of the Buddha. During the last war, the pagoda was completely dismantled; it has since been reconstructed.

THE RISE AND FALL OF NARA

In A.D. 618, after many years of internal strife, China entered into a period of splendor and elegance, the T'ang period, which would last almost three centuries. The Chinese empire spread from the Yellow Sea to the shores of the Caspian. The whole of Asia admired its magnificence. At this time, Japan was regarded very much as the "little brother" of China, where local clans and feudal lords held as much influence as the imperial family. But the crown prince Shotoku (A.D. 573–621) had decided to change all that. He wanted to see the imperial family supreme, equal to the emperors of China and set about trying to turn Japan into a more centralized and efficient country.

Almost 90 years after Shotoku's death, Empress Gemmyo decided to emulate the Chinese by building herself a city modeled on the T'ang capital, Chang-an, built on a grid plan – like modern New York. Her own inherited "capital" Fujiwara, had also been constructed on the grid plan. In its brief history (649–710) this center had served three emperors, but it was too small for the new bureaucracy.

Until the move to Nara, the Japanese had known little of "capital cities." The capital was simply where the emperor's palace happened to be, and since most emperors built a new palace in a new spot, the capital moved regularly. But Heijo-kyo, to the west of the modern city of Nara, was consciously chosen as the site for a new beginning. A few decades after the Empress' decision, the population had

swollen to 200,000. A great flowering in the arts and religion took place. At the center of this revolution were the Buddhist monasteries and temples that disseminated learning and the Buddhist monks who formed part of the new bureaucracy. But Nara also sowed the seed of its own dissolution. To maintain such splendor – and the elaborate machinery of government that went with it – the people were heavily taxed. Japan had been a land of family clans who farmed their land jointly; the new government tried to create more organized farms, but farmers were destroyed by taxes. As they went bankrupt, their lands were taken by the aristocracy and the Buddhist monasteries. A Buddhist monk called Dokyo became chancellor and under his influence Buddhism spread through Japan. But his attempts to assume control of the court failed and his downfall followed. When the new emperor Kammu came to the throne he felt that the Buddhism of Nara had become too powerful, and that a new start was needed elsewhere. So he moved his capital to Nagaoka, then to Kyoto in 797. The oppressed Japanese peasants heaved a sigh of relief as the system of government became less rigid.

YUMEDONO, THE PAVILION OF DREAMS
This, the oldest octagonal religious building in Japan stands in the eastern part of the Horyuji Temple (to the left of the overview, below left). Here, Prince Shotoku meditated; apparitions aided his political and religious speculations.

BUDDHA OF KAMAKURA

This colossal representation of the Buddha, under the name of Amida, is considered the finest of its type in Japan. Cast of one-inch bronze plates in A.D. 1252, it is nearly 38 ft (11 m) in height, and weighs 450 tons. The eyes were of gold, the third eye of bossed silver. The Amida school preaches that man is powerless to save himself, and must rely on the compassion of the Buddha Amida – a view at variance with other forms of Japanese Buddhism.

The bronze plates are perfectly joined

The third eye signifies spiritual insight

AERIAL VIEW OF THE HORYUJI TEMPLE
This view of the temple complex's western quarter shows the oldest buildings: the middle cloisters, the kondo (main hall) at the side of the five-story pagoda, and the lecture hall in the background. Before it was burned down in 670, the temple was built in the style of Korean Buddhist structures, with the pagoda in front of the main hall.

LAMA TEMPLE
BEIJING'S TIBETAN TEMPLE
GAZETTEER P.153 - MAP REF.J4

IN THE NORTHEAST corner of the old Mongol city of Beijing lies the Buddhist Lama Temple, one of China's most famous religious buildings. Built in 1694, it originally served as the palace of the emperor Kangxi's son. But after he became the emperor Yongzheng, the building was converted into a temple, since an emperor's palace could not be used by his descendants. It has a remarkable Hall of Prayer, the Temple of the Great Buddha, and many gateways and staircases. The Great Buddha is 59 ft (18 m) high. The temple became a holy place for Tibetan lamas in 1744. Because of the explicit nature of many of the Tibetan statues, their genital regions are covered with silk scarves.

TIBETAN TEMPLE
The path to the temple used to be lined with the dwellings of lamas, and there is evidence of Tibetan influences throughout the temple. The decoration on the edge of the roof (see left above) shows the emperor followed by mythical beasts.

TEMPLE OF HEAVEN
THE UNION OF EARTH & SKY
GAZETTEER P.153 - SITE NO.44

The temple is painted blue to represent the color of heaven

THE TEMPLE OF HEAVEN, one of the most famous Chinese shrines, was built in Beijing in 1420 by the emperor Yunglo, third and most powerful emperor of the Ming Dynasty. The building was created to be the emperor's personal Confucian temple (where he was the sole worshipper), and it was completed in the same year as the imperial palace. The following year, Peking was declared the national capital.

The emperor, who was himself a kind of god, would come here to pray for good harvests and to atone for the sins of his people. Emperor Yunglo died in 1424 at the age of 64, returning from an expedition against the Mongols.

The temple is set in a park where the Son of Heaven would perform sacred ceremonies. Any hitch during these rituals was seen as a terrible omen for the coming year. In the building itself, everything is circular, in the image of heaven. The ground levels that surround the temple are square, representing the earth. Thus, the whole structure may be said to represent the union of heaven and earth.

SYMBOLIC ARCHITECTURE
The park of Tiantan (the Temple of Heaven) includes the Temple of the Earth and the Hall for Good Harvests. The large park has four gates that face the four cardinal points. The terraces of white marble (see left) represent, from bottom to top, humankind, earth, and finally heaven.

HENGSHAN

HOLY TAOIST MOUNTAIN

GAZETTEER P.153 - SITE NO.33

THE CHINESE REGARD mountains as living organisms; the earliest Chinese dictionary, the *Shuowen*, written about A.D. 100, defines *shan* (mountain) as *xuan* (the diffuser) because it diffuses vital breath, "dispersing and engendering the myriad things." For Taoists especially, mountains are a medium through which people communicate with immortals and the primeval powers of the earth. Where Confucianism lays emphasis on moral duties, social conduct, and government responsibility, Taoism stresses individual freedom, self-transformation, and mystical experience. The *tao* ("way") of humanity and nature is the path of balance – to live in accordance with the *tao* is to live in instinctive harmony with the universe. This cannot be expressed in words, only experienced – hence the importance of nature and mountains, whose divine summits reach to the clouds.

SACRED MOUNTAINS
The five holy Taoist mountains are Taishan (east), Hengshan (south), Huashan (west, above), Hengshan (north), and Songshan (south). The pronunciation of the northern and southern mountains is different in Chinese.

TEMPLES OF THE MOUNTAIN

Hengshan, the "Northern Guardian," was named by the Ming emperors in the 14th century A.D., after they overthrew the Mongol rulers of China and regained this lost territory. One of China's nine sacred mountains (five of which are Taoist, four Buddhist), Hengshan is about 44 mi (71 km) southeast of Datong, in the Hunyan District. It is approached through a limestone gorge known as the Magnet.

At the end of the gorge is Hengshan's most famous site, the Hanging Monastery, sometimes referred to as the Flying Temple – a monastery literally clinging to the face of the cliff. It was built by Taoist monks during the Toba-Wei Dynasty in the sixth century A.D. Its builders were known as *Yu Shih* ("the feathered scholars"), since their freedom led their contemporaries to compare them to birds – in fact, they are often depicted on early bronze mirrors as men with wings. From the monastery there is a long stone staircase – the "Pilgrim's Way" – that winds up to the twin summits of Hengshan, over 6,500 ft (1,980 m) high. En route it is possible to break the journey at the

shrine of Lu Tung-pin, one of the eight Taoist immortals. At the top of the steps of the northern peak is a bronze urn for incense and a temple with a red façade. The huge tablet over the entrance has a calligraphy inscription by the Emperor Kuang-hsü (1875–1907) rendering thanks to the god of agriculture. Tablets by earlier emperors are found in two pavilions on an upper ledge. On a clear day, from the summit (Heng-ting), one can see the Buddhist sanctuary of Wutaishan, 50 mi (80 km) to the south.

HANGING MONASTERY
With its roof tiles of turquoise blue and long rows of bright red, lacquered columns, the Flying Temple has a fairy-tale beauty. The visible part of the monastery consists of 40 wooden buildings. The cliff face behind them has been hollowed out to form monks' cells. Although the mountains were originally Taoist, all five now have Buddhist shrines as well. Hengshan (right) is the northernmost of the Taoist mountains.

EMEISHAN
SACRED BUDDHIST MOUNTAIN

GAZETTEER P.152 - SITE NO.22

GOLDEN PEAK (JINDING) TEMPLE
The name of the temple refers to its bronze-coated roof. Jinding means Gold Roof as well as Golden Peak. The main image (below) shows the view out across the mountain from the roof of the temple.

BUDDHISM WAS A latecomer to China; it did not arrive until the first century A.D. But with it came the idea of organized retreats in remote areas, where Buddhist monks spent their days in meditation. Emeishan (Lofty Eyebrow Mountain) is one of the four sacred Buddhist mountains – Wutaishan (north), Putuoshan (east), Jihuashan (south), and Emeishan (west) – that represent the four quarters of the universe. Each is associated with one of the great bodhisattvas. Emeishan is associated with Puxian, the god of universal kindness, who rides a white elephant.

THE SACRED PATHS

Those who visit China's sacred mountains should remember that for the Chinese, they are full of "telluric power," a sacred force inherent in the earth itself. The sacred force, known as the dragon current, permeates the landscape, and is studied by practitioners of *feng shui*, the science of "wind and water," who are basically geomancers. This notion is not confined to China; closely related ideas can be found among Australian Aborigines and among British "ley hunters." In China, the dragon current is of two kinds, yin and yang – female and male – and mountains are regarded as embodying the yang force.

THE WESTERN MOUNTAIN

There are nine sacred mountains in China, four are Buddhist and five Taoist. All are sites of pilgrimage. The highest of the four Buddhist sacred mountains, Emeishan is 10,164 ft (3,098 m) high, while the southern trail to the top is 40 mi (64 km). It is also one of the most beautiful – although one Ming poet once described it as "a hundred miles of mist." The mountain is on the southwest side of the Sichuan basin, and is thickly wooded with cool bamboo thickets full of butterflies and fast-flowing streams, two of which meet at the Pavilion of the Clear Singing Waters. Pandas live on the western slopes, although they are seldom seen. Of the many temples on the mountain the lowest is the Bauguosi, whose name means "protect the nation"; it was built in the Ming period (15th century). The Xianfeng (Fairy Summit or Magic Peak) Temple has many monkeys, whose rush for scraps has been known to hurl pilgrims off the cliffs. The oldest of the mountain's monasteries, the Wanniansi Monastery, was rebuilt in the ninth century. It is dedicated to the bodhisattva Puxian and contains a bronze and copper statue of him seated on a white elephant.

INTERIOR OF THE GOLDEN PEAK TEMPLE
The first Temple of the Golden Peak was built during the Eastern Han Period (A.D. 25–220). By the sixth century, the mountain had more than 100 temples, of which this was the most important.

THE LOFTY EYEBROW
Emeishan is usually covered with clouds. Locals describe it as "beautiful as the moth's wing, long and fine," perhaps referring to the eyebrowlike outline of the summit that is sometimes visible.

THE EAST

THERE IS AN IMMENSE GAP between the perception of both Hinduism and its sister religion Buddhism and that of the other world religions of Judaism, Christianity, and Islam. Hinduism, as epitomized in the Upanishads and the Bhagavad Gita (Song of God) is essentially a religion of asceticism, which teaches that the soul is of the same nature as God, and human misery arises from our failure to understand our own divine nature.

While neither Hinduism nor Buddhism spread to the west, Buddhism found ready acceptance in the east. In India, both Buddhist and Hindu arts flourished, especially during the Gupta Dynasty (fourth to sixth century A.D.), when many temples and monasteries were built, until Hinduism finally became the dominant religion. From the seventh century the influence of Islam spread across Asia from the Middle East to northern India, having particular influence during the medieval period. Islam is now the dominant religion in the populous states of Pakistan and Bangladesh and a major force in Indian religious life, although Hinduism remains dominant.

Many Hindu holy places are found near rivers or mountains – Varanasi, where the Ganges and the Yamuna meet, is especially sacred. Most Buddhist sites in India are still revered, though it is in its neighboring countries, like Tibet, that Buddhism still flourishes as it has not done in India for nearly 1,500 years.

TURKMENISTAN

UZBEKISTAN

RIVER AMUDAR'YA

① SAMARKAND
This Muslim center, crossroads of the east and west, contains the tomb of the bloodthirsty Timur.

AFGHANISTAN

PAKISTAN

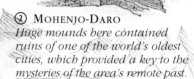

② MOHENJO-DARO
Huge mounds here contained ruins of one of the world's oldest cities, which provided a key to the mysteries of the area's remote past.

IRAN

RIVER INDUS

N

ARABIAN SEA

SCENES FROM THE RAMAYANA
This painting is a scene from the epic Hindu poem, the *Ramayana*. It shows Rama – an incarnation of the god Vishnu – being attacked. The *Ramayana* tells the story of Rama's attempts to win back his wife Sita, abducted by the demon Ravana.

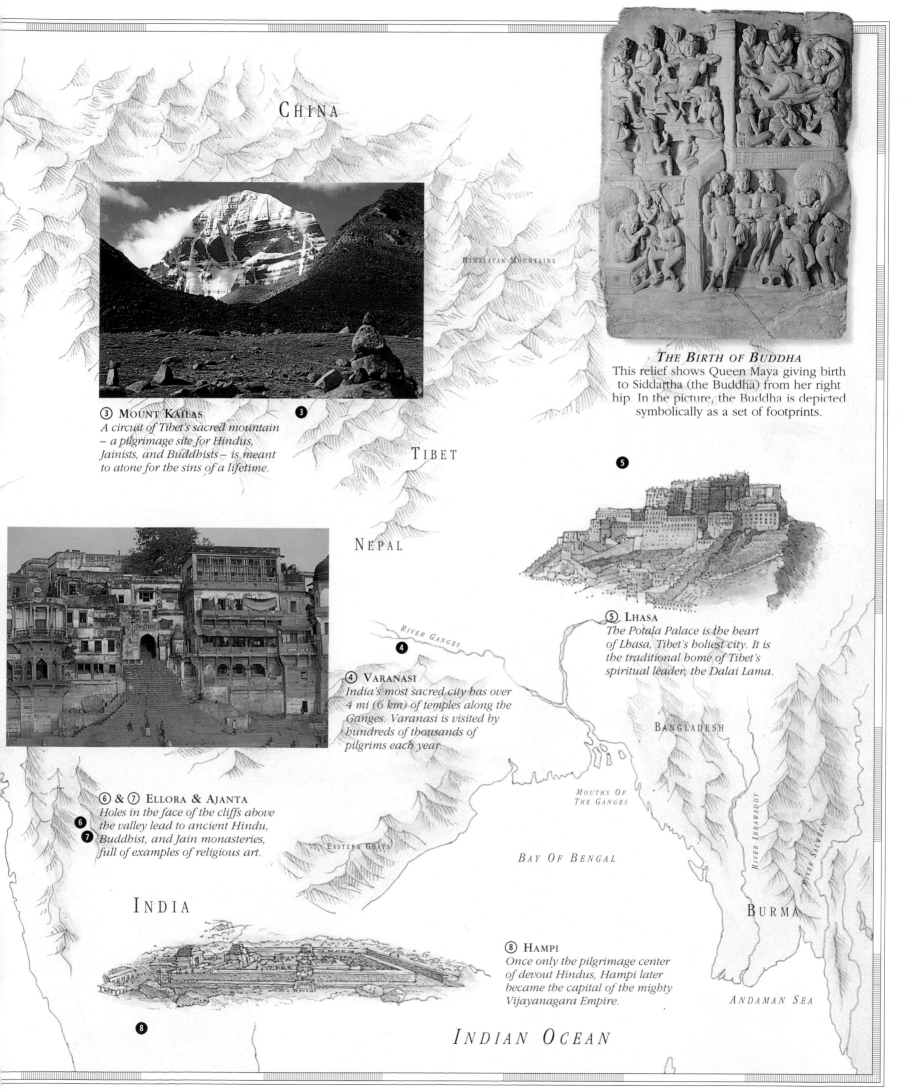

CHINA

③ MOUNT KAILAS
A circuit of Tibet's sacred mountain – a pilgrimage site for Hindus, Jainists, and Buddhists – is meant to atone for the sins of a lifetime.

HIMALAYAN MOUNTAINS

TIBET

NEPAL

THE BIRTH OF BUDDHA
This relief shows Queen Maya giving birth to Siddartha (the Buddha) from her right hip. In the picture, the Buddha is depicted symbolically as a set of footprints.

⑤ LHASA
The Potala Palace is the heart of Lhasa, Tibet's holiest city. It is the traditional home of Tibet's spiritual leader, the Dalai Lama.

RIVER GANGES

④ VARANASI
India's most sacred city has over 4 mi (6 km) of temples along the Ganges. Varanasi is visited by hundreds of thousands of pilgrims each year.

BANGLADESH

⑥ & ⑦ ELLORA & AJANTA
Holes in the face of the cliffs above the valley lead to ancient Hindu, Buddhist, and Jain monasteries, full of examples of religious art.

MOUTHS OF THE GANGES

EASTERN GHATS

RIVER IRRAWADDY

RIVER SALWEEN

BAY OF BENGAL

INDIA

BURMA

⑧ HAMPI
Once only the pilgrimage center of devout Hindus, Hampi later became the capital of the mighty Vijayanagara Empire.

ANDAMAN SEA

INDIAN OCEAN

VAJRAPANI

Vajrapani is one of the Dhyani bodhisattvas, a faithful companion of the Buddha. He represents power and is the scourge of the impious. In the main temple of the Potala Palace, he stands to the right of the central image of Avalokiteshvara.

LHASA
THE PURE LAND OF AVALOKITESHVARA
GAZETTEER P.152 - SITE NO.9

"THE ROOF OF THE WORLD," Tibet has always remained aloof from the rest of Asia. It lies on a high plateau 12,000–15,000 ft (3,660–4,750 m) high, surrounded by mountains that include Mount Everest. In early centuries, Tibet was a warlike country. In 763, the capital of China was captured by the Tibetan king Khri-srong. In the same year, he brought Buddhist teachers from India and China, and Tibet became a Buddhist stronghold, with Buddhism as the national ideology. At almost 12,000 ft (3,658 m), Lhasa is considered low-lying for Tibet. Until 1950, when Tibet was annexed by the Chinese, Lhasa was the political and religious center of the country and seat of its revered spiritual leader, the Dalai Lama. Tibetan Buddhists believe the Dalai Lama is a living god, the reincarnation of the bodhisattva Avalokiteshvara, the bodhisattva of compassion. The bodhisattvas are buddhas who postpone their own attainment of nirvana to further the spiritual path of ordinary humans. The Potala Palace, the traditional residence of the Dalai Lama, is literally the "Pure Land of Avalokiteshvara," a place roughly equivalent to the Western idea of paradise.

THE POTALA PALACE

The great golden-roofed Potala Palace, residence of the Dalai Lamas, built on the Marpori (Red Mountain), is one of the greatest palaces in the world. The present structure dates from the end of the 17th century. But as early as the seventh century, before Buddhism came to Tibet, King Srong-tsan-gampo built a small meditation pavilion on the site, and then a palace; this was burned down shortly after his death by Chinese invaders.

In 1642, the fifth Dalai Lama, Lobsang Gyatso, was enthroned by the Mongol conqueror Gu-shri, and the two set out to unify Tibet. Lhasa became its political, as well as religious, capital. The Dalai Lama began building the Potala Palace. The word Potala is derived from the Sanskrit *Potalaka*, meaning the abode of Bodhisattva Avalokiteshvara, who embodies the essence of enlightenment.

Lobsang Gyatso died in 1682. Anxious that work on the palace would be abandoned, his regent kept his death a secret, and a monk who resembled the Dalai Lama was found. The monk impersonated him for the ten years it took to complete the palace.

HOME OF THE DALAI LAMAS
The office of Dalai Lama is not hereditary. Tibetan Buddhists believe that the spirit of their leader moves into the body of a newborn child. This child – born soon after the death of the Dalai Lama – has to be found for succession to continue.

As the center of the Tibetan Buddhist faith, Lhasa is a place of constant pilgrimage. In their circuit of Lhasa's temples, some devotees choose the strenuous method of prostrating themselves flat, standing up at the point reached by their hands, and then prostrating themselves again.

THE JOKHANG TEMPLE

The Jokhang Temple, the most sacred temple in Lhasa, does not lie in the Potala Palace, but in the area called the Barkhor. Tibetan people still show their reverence for the site by their continuous circumambulations, called *Korwa*, all the while reciting prayers and mantras. King Srong-tsan-gampo, who built this temple in the seventh century, was regarded as the emanation of Avalokiteshvara and his Nepalese and Chinese wives the emanations of his companions, the female bodhisattvas Bhrkuti and Tara. Buddhist temples in Tibet were constructed at geomantically important points. In this way, they would literally pin down the earth energies of the female demon believed to lie prostrate beneath the surface of Tibet.

The female demon may represent the indigenous beliefs of Tibet demonized by Buddhism. At his death, the king and his wives were believed to have been absorbed into the statue of Avalokiteshvara in the Jokhang Temple ("The House of the Lord"). The statue was part of the dowry of the king's Nepalese wife and is the most revered image in Tibet. The temple stands on an east-west orientation and was allegedly built on the site of Lake Wothang, which was filled in at the queen's request.

THE TEMPLES OF THE PALACE

When the Chinese began to bomb Lhasa in 1959, the Dalai Lama fled his country and took up residence in India. Despite this, his residence remains a site of pilgrimage for many Tibetan Buddhists. Its importance is increased by the fact that it houses the spectacular tombs of the earlier Dalai Lamas. Perhaps most splendid among these is the tomb of the 13th Dalai Lama: its golden stupa is so high that it towers up into another floor and on the altar a beautiful mandala is encrusted with over 20,000 pearls.

Only two rooms of King Srong-tsan-gampo's original palace are said to remain. The first is the King's Meditation Cave, which includes images of the king and his two wives, who are both regarded as bodhisattvas. The other room to have survived the seventh-century construction – the most sacred in the palace – is a small chapel dedicated to Avalokiteshvara. Here, there stands an image of the bodhisattva said to date from the time of the original building. Pilgrims entering this temple prostrate themselves on the floor and touch the objects embedded there. This practice is believed to bestow blessings and good fortune upon them.

MOUNT KAILAS

With its four façades facing north, east, south, and west, Mount Kailas looks like an enormous diamond. Seventy-five percent as high as Mount Everest, the mountain is one of the tallest peaks in the Himalayas. Nearby is the source of the Indus, Sutlej, and Bramaputra Rivers. The source of the Ganges is not far away. On its southern face, a vertical gash crosses horizontal layers, creating the image of a swastika. The word comes from *svastika*, Sanskrit for well-being and good fortune. Buddhists regard the mountain as a mandala – the sacred circle from which the sacred rivers flow like the spokes of an eternal wheel.

PRAYER STONES
Inscribed with the words of the pilgrims, prayer stones are a common sight along the pilgrimage routes of Tibet. Pilgrims also write their worries or misfortunes on prayer flags (see pp.10-11). The wind then blows these troubles away.

SHIVA, CREATOR AND DESTROYER
*Shiva is the most revered Hindu deity at Varanasi.
Many temples and shrines there are dedicated to
him. He appears in a variety of incarnations.
Above, he is portrayed as the cosmic dancer of
creation within a circle of fire that represents
the destruction and re-creation of the world.*

VARANASI
CITY OF THE HOLY GANGES
GAZETTEER P.157 - SITE NO.51

THE GANGES IS INDIA'S most sacred river, and Varanasi, with its
4 mi (6 km) of riverside temples and palaces, is its most sacred city.
Hindus believe that to die there is to go straight to heaven. The area is
also important to Buddhists: Sarnath, where Buddha preached his first
sermon, is only 6 mi (10 km) away. The name Varanasi comes from the
names of the Varana and Asi Rivers, tributaries of the Ganges that lie to the
north and south of the city, respectively. Varanasi is dedicated to the god Shiva,
believed to have lived here in one of his human incarnations. Many of India's
730 million Hindus will make the pilgrimage here at least once in their lifetime.
Here, they drink the waters of the Ganges and bathe from the numerous *ghats*
(stone steps). A pilgrimage route called the Panchakosi encircles the city.

THE HOLY GANGES

One of the world's greatest rivers, the Ganges –
or Ganga – flows for over 1,600 mi (2,575 km),
from its source in the Himalayas, until it drains
through its many estuaries into the Bay of
Bengal. It supports 300 million people – more
than any other river in the world. There are
hundreds of pilgrimage sites dotted along the
holy river's journey to the sea.

Hindus regard the Ganges as the goddess
of purification Ganga, whose waters flow
through the locks of Shiva's hair, and have the
power to cleanse sin. Many temples along the
river are dedicated to Shiva, one of the most is
important situated at Hardwar. To bathe in the
Ganges sacred waters is to cleanse oneself of
sin, though pilgrims never bathe naked. A class
of brahmins, the Gangaputra, supervise the
bathing fairs held in honor of Ganga's birthday
in the spring, and the great festival held every
12 years when Jupiter enters Aquarius.

THE RIVER FRONT
*The stone steps, ghats, are always crowded with
pilgrims. It is considered a privilege to die at
Varanasi, gaining freedom from samsara – the
Hindu cycle of death and rebirth. Manikarnika
is the most sacred ghat; bodies are cremated here
and their ashes scattered in the holy river.*

HOLY CITY OF PILGRIMAGE

Varanasi is one of India's oldest cities and the most sacred, its history going back over 3,000 years. It has remained a place of pilgrimage throughout several sackings by Muslims from the 12th century A.D. on. But not until the 19th century did it fully reassert itself as a national religious center, and the city is littered with shrines and temples. It has been a center of Hindu learning since before the sixth century.

At Varanasi, the goddess Ganga (the Ganges) is known as Annapurna, goddess of food. Each spring, it is traditional to create clay images of Annapurna and give food to Shiva. In the autumn, devotees fill Shiva's most important shrine with rice, then give the sanctified food to the needy. Religious festivals are held throughout the year. There are many pilgrimage circuits, one involves praying at 108 shrines and lasts for five days.

THE VISHWANATH
Dedicated to Shiva, this temple was rebuilt in 1776 after the original had been destroyed by the Moghul emperor Aurengzeb. Pandit Malaviya, who built the new temple, wished to see Hinduism purged of its caste system – the result being that all castes are admitted to the temple.

THE FIRST SERMON
Siddartha Gautama (c. 563–483 B.C.) was the son of a local ruler. He came across an old man, a sick man, a dead man, and a holy man, and decided that life was a cheat. At the age of 29, he renounced the world. After his enlightenment at Bodh Gaya, Buddha, or "the enlightened one" (right), came to Sarnath, near Varanasi, where he preached his first sermon on abstention and correct living as the route to nirvana. A stupa was built here in the third century B.C.

THE HINDU PANTHEON

The Hindu pantheon can be very difficult to grasp, since its many gods have evolved and changed over thousands of years. Its roots lie in the Aryan tradition embodied in the Vedic hymns, which may date back as far as 7000 B.C. – the earliest texts of Hinduism. The pantheon gained importance between the sixth and 11th centuries A.D., when the Purana – myths and legends about the eternal trinity of Brahma, Shiva, and Vishnu – helped the spread of Hinduism. Each god incorporates many lesser cult figures and heroes from these myths. This expansion led to the personal worship of each god, and a spate of temple building during the Middle Ages, as Hinduism gradually replaced Buddhism in India.

Brahma, Shiva, and Vishnu are the most widely worshipped of the gods. Brahma is the creator god, whose four arms represent the four quarters of the universe. Vishnu can be found in ten incarnations – called avatars – the most important being Krishna, associated with altruistic love. Shiva, the Lord of Time, is creator and destroyer of all things. The female counterparts of these gods – Saraswati, Lakshmi, and Parvati, respectively – all play important parts in Hindu worship.

HAMPI
& THE GREAT CITY OF VIJAYANAGAR
GAZETTEER P.157 · SITES NOS.83 & 84

THE REMAINS OF VIJAYANAGAR, a stupendous ruined city set in a strange and beautiful landscape, was once the center of a Hindu empire and one of the greatest cities in southern India. It also includes Hampi, site of one of India's great temple complexes. The area itself was associated with stories from the Hindu epic the *Ramayana*. Shiva is alleged to have done penance on the nearby Hemakuta Hill before he married Parvati. Here, Shiva is also believed to have burned the god of lust. The sacred hill stands to the east of the Virupaksha Temple. When the Muslims began their conquest of India from the north in A.D. 1000, Vijayanagar – "City of Victory" – defied further Muslim expansion, becoming the embodiment of Hindu culture and resistance. In 1565, the city finally fell to a Muslim federation and was sacked, and this great cultural and religious center was abandoned.

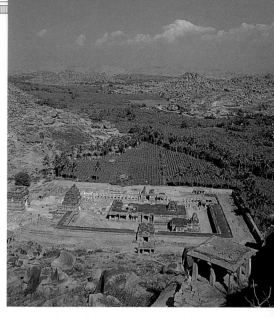

THE ACHYUTARAYA TEMPLE
At the center of the Hampi ruins stands the Achyutaraya Temple, seen here from the nearby Matanga Hill. This temple – like so many others in the sacred center – is dedicated to Vishnu.

VITTHALA TEMPLE
One of the most remarkable ruins at Hampi is the Vitthala Temple (above). The god Vishnu was allegedly so embarrassed by its ostentation that he refused to live there. Its construction was halted by the fall of Vijayanagar, so it was never consecrated. The outer pillars are known as "musical pillars" because they reverberate when tapped. The stone chariot (left) houses an image of Garuda, Vishnu's bird vehicle. The wheels of the chariot, now fixed, originally turned.

THE HISTORY OF VIJAYANAGAR

Hampi is the "sacred village" that lies at the center of Vijayanagar, once the most powerful city in southern India. Its ruins are still magnificent, with its long colonnaded street that serves as a bazaar, leading to entrance gateways capped with pyramidical towers called *gopuras*. The Virupaksha temple is perhaps its most spectacular monument, with a 171-ft- (52-m-) high *gopura*, and dates back to the "great period" of Vijayanagar.

This period started in the 1330s. Two brothers called Harihara and Bukka, had been captured by forces of the great Muslim ruler of Delhi, and forcibly converted to Islam. Sent back to the Deccan Plateau as governors, the brothers reconverted to Hinduism, and Harihara proclaimed himself king; he then established the city as his capital. Conquest expanded Vijayanagar, and for two centuries it became a showcase of magnificence and conspicuous consumption – particularly during the annual Mahanavami Festival, with thousands of troops, elephants, and horses. Its women, with their jewels and rich garments, were as much a part of the festival as the male nobles.

The great period is evident in the Royal Enclosure, a separate, later part of the ruins, with its many temples, the Enclosure includes Underground Temple and the Queen's Bath. The Elephant Stables, with 11 domed rooms for housing the royal elephants, also give some idea of the former magnificence of Vijayanagar. In 1565, Vijayanagar was finally defeated by an alliance of Muslim sultans at the battle of Talikota, and the city was sacked.

AJANTA

THE SACRED BUDDHIST CAVES

GAZETTEER P.157 · SITE NO.70

THE TRAVELER who leaves the village of Fardapur in central India soon finds himself in a magnificent wooded ravine, where the river Waghore descends over a series of waterfalls. Above the woods, in the almost vertical cliffs, a series of columns are visible, actually entrances to a series of monasteries and temples, hewn from the granite between 200 B.C. and the fifth century A.D. There are five *caityas* (Buddhist temples) and no less than 24 monasteries or *viharas* (dwelling places). The columns of the temples contain some remarkable carvings, but the most impressive features of the Ajanta Caves is the frescoes that cover almost all the walls. Those near the shrines depict Buddha, while the more worldly images in the main halls relate *jataka* (popular tales) of his previous lives. Rediscovered by Europeans in 1824, the buildings were completely overgrown and full of bats and snakes. The temples proved to be an amazing artistic discovery; incredibly, their frescoes were in a good state of preservation. Unfortunately they were allowed to deteriorate for many years before their value was fully recognized. Those that remain are now carefully preserved.

THE ROCK TEMPLES
Of the 29 caves at Ajanta, five contain temples. The oldest was first discovered in 1824 by European explorers. Number nine with its two Buddhas flanking the entrance, is also very old.

The posture of the bodhisattva is that of the enlightened

BODHISATTVA
Bodhisattvas are individuals who postpone their achievement of enlightenment in order to aid the spiritual path of ordinary humans.

ELLORA

THE ANCIENT CAVES OF SHIVA

GAZETTEER P.157 · SITE NO.69

CONSTRUCTED BETWEEN A.D. 600 and 1000, the Ellora Caves, like those at Ajanta, are also cut into a hillside in a horseshoe-shape curve, penetrating deep into the rock-face. Unlike the Ajanta Caves – also in Maharashtra state – which were hewn out of a vertical cliff, the 34 caves at Ellora are carved out of a sloping hill of tufa rock. They extend along the hillside for 1 mi (1.5 km), and include Buddhist, Hindu, and Jain temples. By the time the cave temples were constructed, Buddhism was in decline in India and the later caves are Hindu and Jain. The dominant figure is the Hindu god Shiva, to whom the largest temple, the Kailasanatha, is dedicated. The Russian philosopher Ouspensky describes Ellora: "Here are long corridors, narrow passages, inner courtyards; unexpected balconies and galleries with a view of the plains below; slippery staircases polished by bare feet thousands of years ago; dark wells beyond which one can sense hidden caves; twilight, silence undisturbed by a single sound."

THE CONSTRUCTION OF THE CAVES
The Ellora Caves are as famous for their sculptures as Ajanta is for its frescoes. It is believed that Ellora was constructed by the builders of the Ajanta Caves when they moved from the previous site.

LORD SHIVA
Shiva is the male generative force in the Hindu religion. He is represented by a silver-colored or white man, sometimes with five heads, each of which has a third eye in the forehead.

MOHENJO-DARO
THE HILL OF THE DEAD

GAZETTEER P.157 - SITE NO.21

IN 1922, ALONG THE VALLEY of the River Indus on the "hill of the dead," excavators uncovered the ruins of a Buddhist stupa, probably built in the third century B.C. But later excavations beneath the central mound revealed even more ancient remains, those of a rich Bronze Age civilization that no one had suspected. Details emerged of a site as sophisticated as a later Greek or Roman city. It was built on mud-brick platforms to protect it from floods with a grid pattern reminiscent of New York. The size of the city indicated that it held about 40,000 people. Mohenjo-Daro and Harappa had been twin cities of an ancient civilization unknown to history. Most interesting, however, were the characteristics of the site prevalent in later Hindu art and ritual. They suggested that excavators might have found the most ancient known forms of India's rich religious tradition.

PRIEST-KING
This rare bust made of steatite (soapstone) is one of the few surviving pieces of Indus Valley sculpture. It was found in a small house in the lower city. The main picture (below) shows the citadel of Mohenjo-Daro, with its central mound that was later used as a Buddhist stupa.

THE LOST RIVER

To the east of the Indus lies a vast, arid, and salt-encrusted landscape, the Thar Desert. When remains of towns were found in this area, there was puzzlement as to how they had survived such conditions. Satellite photographs revealed that the desert had once been a fertile plain, traversed by a great river. Scholars concluded that the river which has now vanished was the Sarasvati, mentioned in the Vedic hymns. In the heyday of Mohenjo-Daro and Harappa, this plain was one of the richest areas in the world. It seems that some great catastrophe destroyed this civilization some time after 1900 B.C. Evidence shows that the earth buckled, due to the pressure of the tectonic plate that raised the Himalayas. A series of earthquakes and volcanic eruptions resulted that caused the river to literally sink into the ground.

BUDDHA TEACHING

This relief from the upper levels at Mohenjo-Daro belongs to the Gandhara period of Buddhist art. Buddhism came to this region in the third century B.C. in the reign of the great emperor Ashoka. The Gandhara style flourished in north-west Pakistan and eastern Afghanistan from the first century B.C. to the seventh century A.D. Figures and clothing in the relief betray contact with Roman styles of representation.

THE INDUS CIVILIZATION

After the discovery of Mohenjo-Daro in 1922, further excavations along the 1,800 mi (2,900 km) of the Indus River Valley revealed more than 150 sites, half a dozen of them cities. The whole area, from the Arabian Sea to the foothills of the Himalayas, was once the home of a great civilization that rivals those of Egypt or Greece in importance. This lost civilization has been called the Indus Valley culture. These discoveries threw doubt on the accepted view of Indian history.

Earlier versions of ancient Indian religion had mentioned the Dravidians, a primitive, phallus-worshipping people. The large number of female statuettes found suggest that an earlier female deity – probably a moon goddess – was worshipped here. Seals found at the site portray a seated yogi surrounded by animals in a representation reminiscent of the Hindu god Shiva. Others depicting sacred bulls recall the Vedic god Rudra who is referred to as a bull. In later Hinduism, Shiva also rides a bull. The city itself was built on two mounds. The higher of these contained the Great Bath and a granary. The size of the baths suggest that they played a part in some religious ritual.

If so, this may have been a precursor of modern Hindu bathing rituals, such as the washing carried out before Hindus enter a temple. And the baths themselves may be an early form of the sacred pools found in many Indian villages. Evidence of the structures and artifacts found at Mohenjo-Daro and similarities between the early Indus religion and Hindu ritual suggest that the roots of Indian religion may go back much further than was originally thought.

AERIAL VIEW OF THE RUINS
This aerial view of the residential area clearly shows its grid pattern. The main streets were very broad, while the houses were separated by narrow lanes, often shaped like a dog's leg to prevent the wind howling through them. In 2500 B.C., the city would have been surrounded by vegetation, while the River Indus – now 2 mi (3 km) away – would have flowed close by.

SAMARKAND

ANCIENT CAPITAL OF TIMUR THE LAME

GAZETTEER P.141 - SITE NO.49

KNOWN AS MARAKANDA by the ancient Greeks, and as Afrasiyab for many centuries after, Samarkand is one of the oldest cities in the world. It has been in existence since the fourth millennium B.C.; its ancient ruins lie to the north of the present city. Like Palmyra in Syria, it owed its importance to its position on the Silk Road – the main trade route from the Middle East to China. Its central location made it inevitable that it should change hands again and again down the ages; it was conquered by the Greeks under Alexander the Great, by the Samanids of Persia, and by the Khwarazm-shahs, before being devastated by Genghis Khan in A.D. 1220. However, it was under the equally brutal reign of Timur (Tamberlaine) in the 14th century that it reached the height of its splendor. While Timur conducted his bloody campaigns abroad, under his tutelage Samarkand became the cultural center of Islam in central Asia. It was transformed into a city of Islamic schools, mausoleums, and mosques with brightly colored domes and minarets. This work was continued by his grandson Ulugh-beg in the 15th century. Despite its eventual decline, Samarkand retains much of its original splendor in its extraordinary religious architecture.

SYMBOL OF GOD'S SUPREMACY

Minarets are found on mosques throughout the world. The writing just below its top bears the name of God (Allah). In the Islamic world, minarets symbolize the oneness of God; to associate God with anything else is one of the greatest sins.

Representations of animals and humans are prohibited on Shiite Islamic buildings. These images of tigers are unusual

THE MAGICAL CITY

Samarkand has always been regarded as something of a magical place. When Alexander the Great first set his eyes upon the ancient walled city, he said, "Everything I have heard is true, except that it is more beautiful than I had ever imagined." Yet Alexander was never able to observe the later transformation of a ruined city that was started by Timur and continued by his descendants.

As well as the Registan madrasas and Timur's tomb, Samarkand is also home to the Bibi-Khanum Mosque, one of the world's largest mosques, named after Timur's Chinese wife. Nearby is the cemetery complex Shah-i Zinda ("the living prince"). Its innermost shrine is the home of Kutham ibn Abbas, the man said to have brought Islam to the surrounding area. Many other Islamic buildings were built by the Uzbeks, who took over the city in 1500. Later the city went into decline, and not until its restoration in the 19th century did Samarkand return to its former splendor.

THE MADRASAS OF REGISTAN

The first madrasa, or Muslim school, was set up by Ulugh-beg, Timur's grandson, in 1420. Under each dome is a lecture hall, while at the back is a large mosque. It was the construction of religious learning centers such as this that made the city the intellectual and religious capital of central Asia.

ISLAM IN CENTRAL ASIA

The Mongol people of central Asia had largely accepted Islam by the end of the 13th century, yet their nomadic roots and expansionist ethos brought a new age in the central Asian Islamic world. Timur (who was of Mongol descent) regarded himself as a devout and pious Muslim. On their excursions into other countries, from the Mediterranean to the subcontinent, Timur and his descendants gleaned a vast amount of cultural knowledge. Their disruptions of the balances of power led to the movement of craftsmen and architects, whose religious buildings at Samarkand became the model for religious architecture in central Asia.

ISLAMIC LEARNING

Arabic calligraphy is an important element in the teaching of Islam – Allah cannot be represented through iconography, only the written word. The sacred text of the Qur'an is often inscribed on the walls of mosques. Early Muslims were also interested in religious science, not least astronomy. Ulugh-Beg's ruined sextant for observing the stars is still preserved at Samarkand. The astrolabe, shown below, was used for orientation on land and sea.

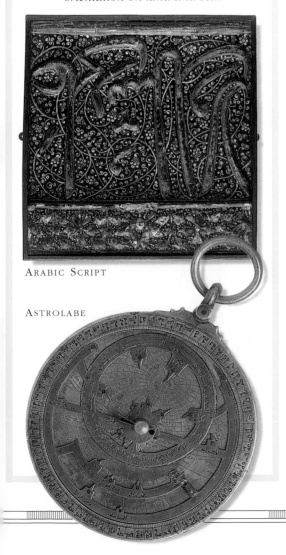

ARABIC SCRIPT

ASTROLABE

TIMUR THE LAME

Born in A.D. 1336, Timur Lenk (Timur the Lame) was a descendant of Genghis Khan, one of the most ruthless leaders in history. As a young man he took part in Chatagai Khan's (Genghis's son) campaign in Transoxiana (now roughly in Uzbekistan, in which Samarkand is found), and he soon took control of the area. He turned his attention to East Turkestan and spent seven years subduing it, and then joined the Mongol Khan of the Crimea, Tokhatmysh, against the Russians and Lithuanians.

Soon nothing could stop him: Persia, Iraq, Azerbaijan, Georgia, and Armenia all fell. Timur treated his defeated enemies with a particular cruelty and violence that suggest he was not entirely sane. One of his cruelest actions came in 1383 when he had 2,000 prisoners built into a living mound, then bricked in. In the same year, he had 5,000 captives beheaded and stacked into a huge pyramid. In 1386, he had all the inhabitants of a conquered town massacred; prisoners were hurled over a cliff. In Delhi, Timur is said to have massacred a hundred thousand prisoners. He had invaded India in 1398 on the excuse that the Muslim sultans of Delhi were showing too great a tolerance to their Hindu subjects. He marched into Delhi and reduced the city to rubble.

In 1399, his attention turned to the Mediterranean and the lands of the Sultan of Egypt. Aleppo and Damascus were sacked. In 1400 he took the Christian garrison of Sivas and its 4,000 defenders were buried alive. When he took Baghdad in 1401, 20,000 of its inhabitants were massacred and all its greatest monuments destroyed. He invaded Turkey, capturing Ankara and Smyrna, and received an offer of surrender from the Sultan of Egypt. The history of carnage only came to an end with the death of Timur in 1405; he was 68.

REGISTAN SQUARE
Samarkand's most impressive showpiece, the Registan square is surrounded by the three madrasas – the one built by Ulugh-beg is found on the left. One writer has described the city as having "almost an overload of mosaics and vast, perfectly proportioned spaces."

More than 500 years later, Timur's tomb was opened in 1941 by Russian archaeologists. They found his skeleton under a huge but broken slab of jade. There is a story to the effect that they also found an inscription declaring that whoever disturbed his bones would "be defeated by an enemy more formidable than I." The next day, Hitler invaded Russia. Whether there is truth in such a tale, there is no doubting the power which Timur wielded over the whole of central Asia and his influence on its culture.

THE MAUSOLEUM OF TIMUR
Timur left an impressive architectural legacy; his tomb, the Gur-i Amir, is small but exquisite. At first built for one of his nephews, Timur himself was placed in it after his death. Also buried here are three of his sons and his grandson Ulugh-beg.

PART TWO

THE GAZETTEER

WHEN I BEGAN RESEARCHING THIS book, I had no doubt that most of the world's greatest religious sites could be included between two covers – Jerusalem, Mecca, Rome, Mount Fuji, Varanasi, Teotihuacan, Mount Kailas... But as the list swelled to well over 1,000 sites, I began to realize that even with a large gazetteer section, it was going to be impossible to cover them all, and any selection must be partial and, to a certain extent, personal. I began to stumble across fresh sites in my casual reading, and realized that having included one site from a particular area, I had excluded others. Thus some sites must be seen as representative of a type. In spite of these misgivings, I think I can claim that what has been included is not only a fairly comprehensive introduction to the world's sacred geography, but also to its spiritual history.

SPIRITUAL CENTER
Many medieval maps showed Jerusalem as the center of the world – even those, like this German example from the 16th century, that postdated the discovery of America. This is clearly intended as a spiritual map rather than an accurate guide. The countries of the world fold out from the Holy City like the petals of a flower. The "New World" is shown in the bottom left-hand corner.

HOW TO USE THE

GAZETTEER

THE FOLLOWING PAGES (132-157) include the 16 gazetteer maps on which are plotted over 1,000 sacred sites. The map below shows how the globe is divided. On pages 158-185, gazetteer listings give details of each sacred site. Every site in the listings is given a number, which corresponds to a point on the relevant map. There is also a map reference, indicated by a letter and a number. In most cases, the listings give the first recording of the site – in some instances, this is simply the period in which the site is known to have been used. There follow general notes about the site's history and importance.

The maps and listings have been researched to cover all areas of the world. Special attention is paid to areas with concentrations of sacred centers that have a unique historical significance, such as Egypt. In other areas, such as Australia, the vast number of sacred sites and the sacred nature of the land have made it necessary to choose a representative sample. Emphasis has been given to historically important sites rather than modern religious places. For example, the map and listings for South America concentrate on Incan and Aztec sites, rather than the many Christian churches that exist in the area today.

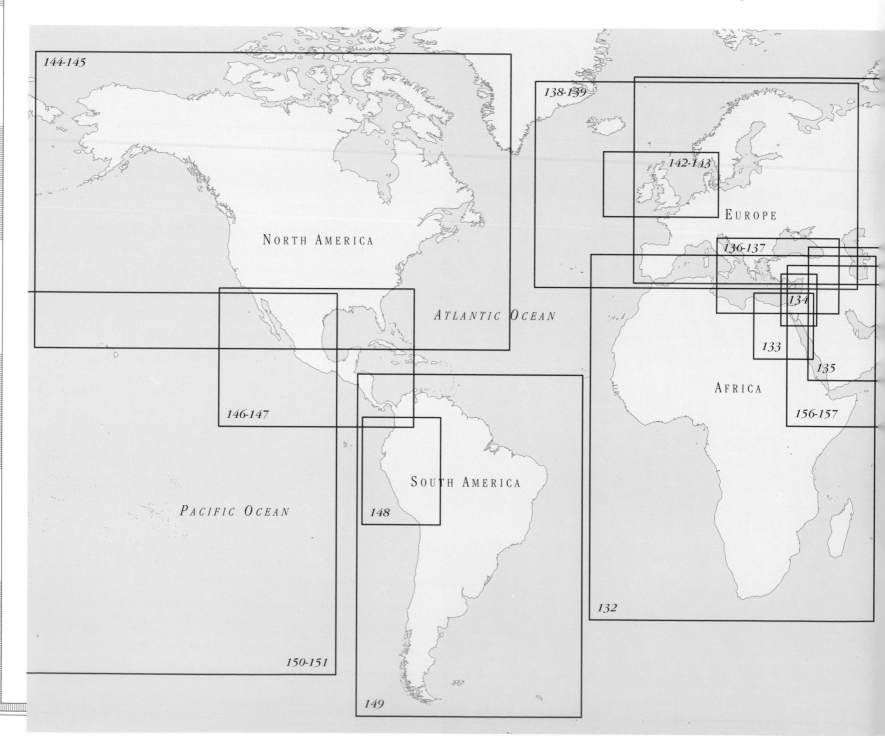

THE MAP SECTION

The world map below shows the area covered by each of the 16 maps in this section of the book. Each box refers to a map that is spread over one or two pages. The text box in the bottom right-hand corner of this page gives the title of every map, and the pages on which it can be found with the relevant listings. Each map carries the following information:

• The locations of up to 150 sacred sites.

• Whether the site is still in use. If it is, the site number appears in a circle; if not, the number appears in a square.

• The historical periods when sites were first used or built. These are indicated by the color of the square or circle. A key to the colors is given on each map.

• Arrows at the sides of the maps indicate the page numbers of adjacent geographical areas covered by other maps in the book.

• A short paragraph of text introduces the historical background of the religions in the area and the changes in its belief systems. Page numbers at the end of each paragraph refer to relevant listings pages.

• A globe at the side of each introductory paragraph indicates the area covered by the map in terms of the whole globe.

THE LISTING SECTION

For each map there is a corresponding list. This list provides information about any of the sites plotted on the maps. These listings start on page 158 and the text box below shows the pages on which particular listings can be found. Sites covered in detail in the front section of the book are only named in the listings section, although the reader will find that these sites are plotted on the gazetteer maps. The listings give the following information on the sites:

• The name of the site, its location, and the specific date for the site, if it is known.

• A grid reference to help locate the position of the site on the relevant map.

• Notes, including a brief description of the site and its importance as a sacred center.

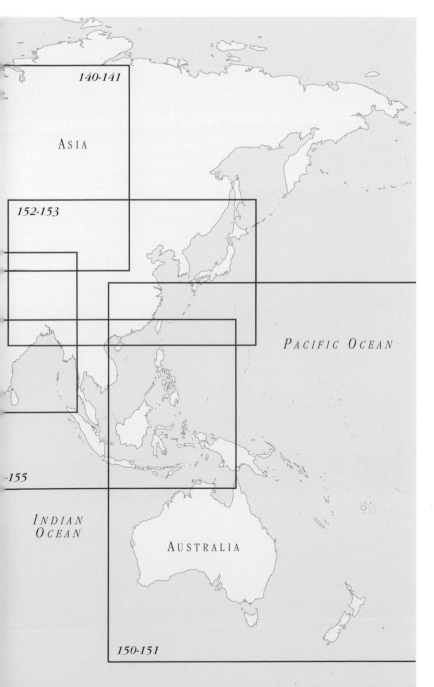

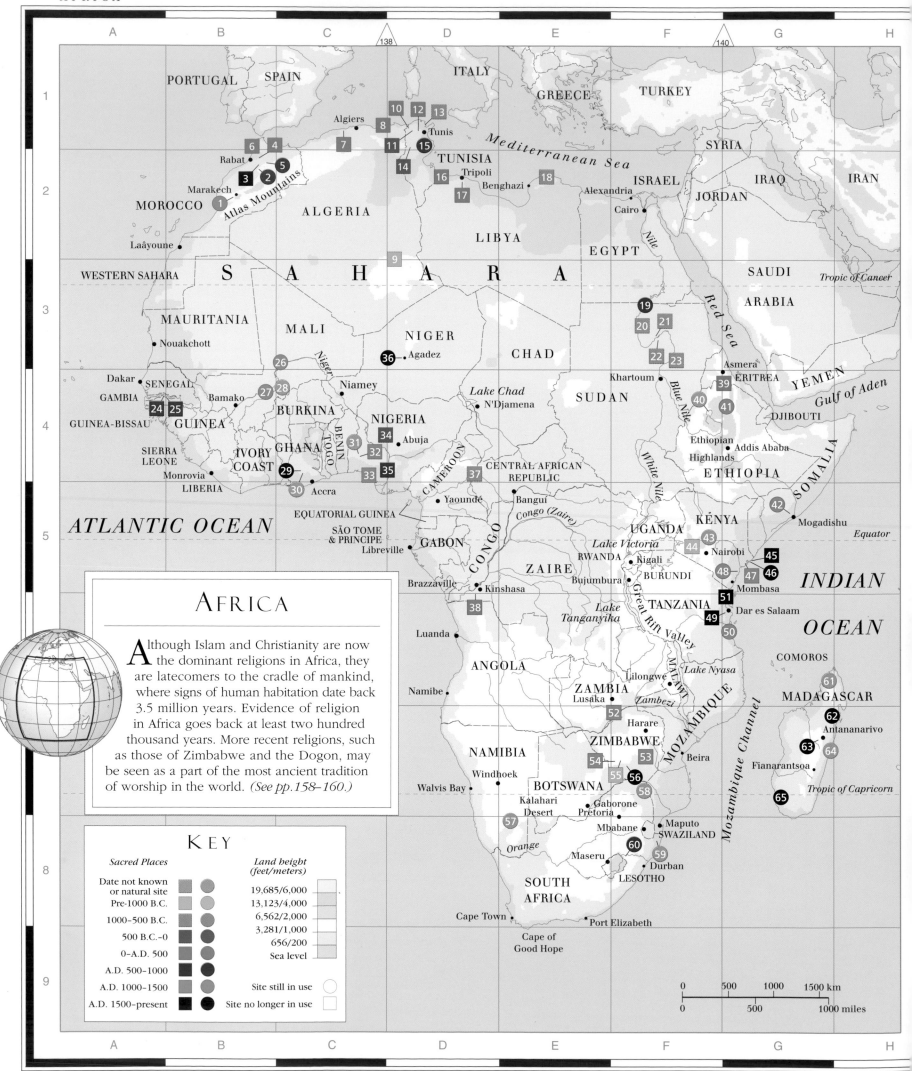

A B C D E F G H

1

PORTUGAL SPAIN ITALY GREECE TURKEY

Mediterranean Sea SYRIA

10 12 13
Algiers 8
6 4 7 11 Tunis IRAQ IRAN
Rabat 5 15 TUNISIA ISRAEL
3 2 14 Tripoli JORDAN
2 Marakech 16 17 Benghazi Alexandria
1 18 Cairo

MOROCCO ALGERIA LIBYA EGYPT

Laâyoune

2

WESTERN SAHARA S A H A R A SAUDI Tropic of Cancer

9 ARABIA

3

MAURITANIA 19 Red Sea
MALI 20 21
Nouakchott NIGER 22 23 Asmera
36 Agadez CHAD Khartoum 39 ERITREA
26 Niger Khartoum 40 YEMEN
Dakar SENEGAL Niamey Lake Chad SUDAN 41 Gulf of Aden
GAMBIA 27 28 N'Djamena DJIBOUTI
24 25 BURKINA NIGERIA 34 Ethiopian Addis Ababa
GUINEA-BISSAU GUINEA 31 Abuja CENTRAL AFRICAN Highlands ETHIOPIA
SIERRA IVORY GHANA 32 REPUBLIC SOMALIA
LEONE COAST 33 35 37 CAMEROON
Monrovia 29 Bangui 42
LIBERIA 30 Accra Yaoundé Congo (Zaire) KENYA Mogadishu
EQUATORIAL GUINEA UGANDA Equator

4

5

ATLANTIC OCEAN SÃO TOME GABON 44 43 Nairobi INDIAN
& PRINCIPE Libreville RWANDA Kigali 45
CONGO ZAIRE Bujumbura BURUNDI 48 47 46
Brazzaville Kinshasa 38 TANZANIA 51 Mombasa OCEAN
Lake Great Rift Valley 49 Dar es Salaam
Tanganyika 50

AFRICA

Although Islam and Christianity are now
the dominant religions in Africa, they
are latecomers to the cradle of mankind,
where signs of human habitation date back
3.5 million years. Evidence of religion
in Africa goes back at least two hundred
thousand years. More recent religions, such
as those of Zimbabwe and the Dogon, may
be seen as a part of the most ancient tradition
of worship in the world. (See pp.158–160.)

Luanda COMOROS 61
ANGOLA Lilongwe Lake Nyasa MADAGASCAR
Namibe ZAMBIA 62
Lusaka Zambezi 52 MALAWI Antananarivo
Harare 63 64
ZIMBABWE 53 MOZAMBIQUE Fianarantsoa
NAMIBIA 54 Beira Mozambique Channel 65
Windhoek 55 56 Tropic of Capricorn
Walvis Bay BOTSWANA 58
Kalahari Gaborone 57
Desert Pretoria Mbabane Maputo
Orange 60 SWAZILAND
Maseru 59 Durban
SOUTH LESOTHO

6

7

8

AFRICA

Cape Town Port Elizabeth
Cape of
Good Hope

9

KEY

Sacred Places

Date not known or natural site	▢	⬤
Pre-1000 B.C.	▢	⬤
1000–500 B.C.	▢	⬤
500 B.C.–0	▢	⬤
0–A.D. 500	▢	⬤
A.D. 500–1000	▢	⬤
A.D. 1000–1500	▢	⬤
A.D. 1500–present	▢	⬤

Land height (feet/meters)

19,685/6,000
13,123/4,000
6,562/2,000
3,281/1,000
656/200
Sea level

○ Site still in use
□ Site no longer in use

0 500 1000 1500 km
0 500 1000 miles

A B C D E F G H

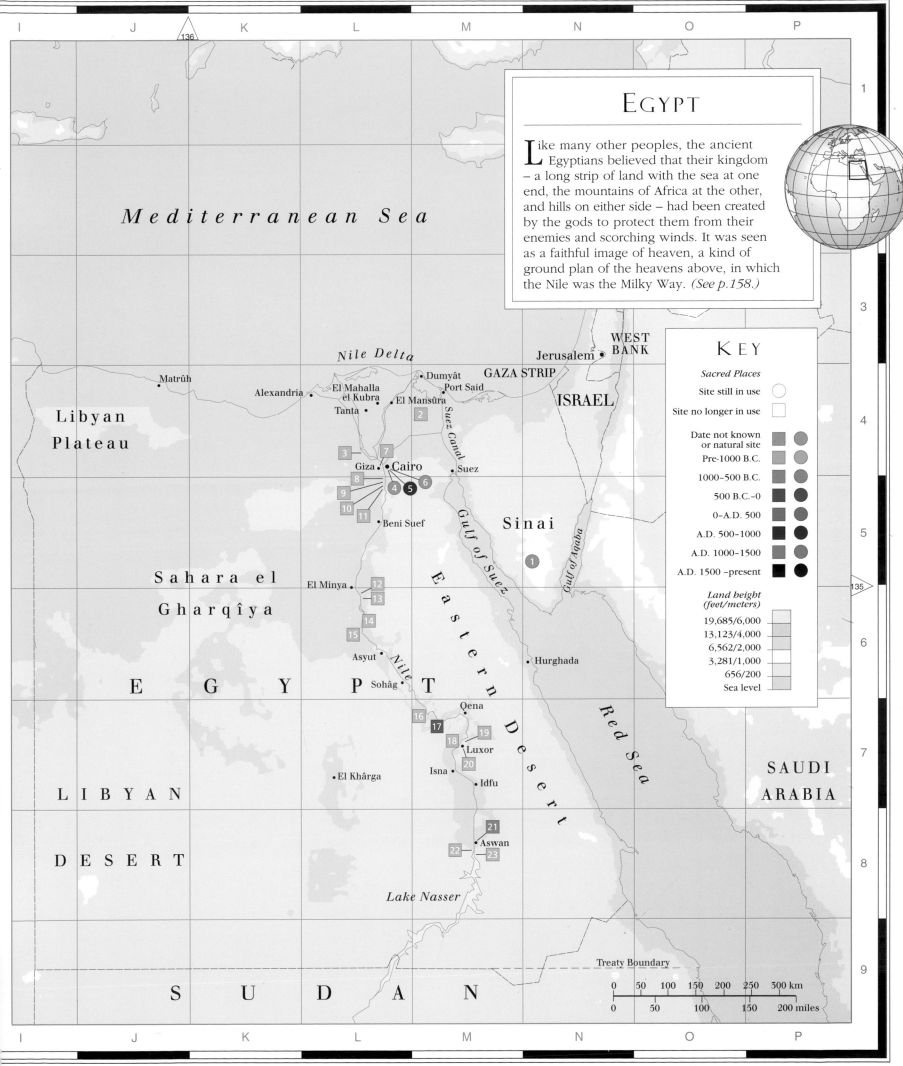

Mediterranean Sea

Nile Delta

Matrûh

Alexandria

El Mahalla el Kubra

Dumyât
Port Said

Tanta

El Mansûra

GAZA STRIP

Jerusalem

WEST BANK

ISRAEL

Libyan Plateau

Giza

Cairo

Suez

Beni Suef

Sinai

Gulf of Suez

Gulf of Aqaba

Sahara el Gharqîya

El Minya

Asyut

Sohâg

Hurghada

Red Sea

E   G   Y   P   T

El Khârga

Qena

Luxor

Isna

Idfu

SAUDI ARABIA

L I B Y A N

D E S E R T

Aswan

Lake Nasser

Eastern Desert

Nile

Treaty Boundary

S   U   D   A   N

EGYPT

Like many other peoples, the ancient Egyptians believed that their kingdom – a long strip of land with the sea at one end, the mountains of Africa at the other, and hills on either side – had been created by the gods to protect them from their enemies and scorching winds. It was seen as a faithful image of heaven, a kind of ground plan of the heavens above, in which the Nile was the Milky Way. *(See p.158.)*

KEY

Sacred Places

Site still in use

Site no longer in use

Date not known or natural site

Pre-1000 B.C.

1000–500 B.C.

500 B.C.–0

0–A.D. 500

A.D. 500–1000

A.D. 1000–1500

A.D. 1500 –present

Land height (feet/meters)

19,685/6,000

13,123/4,000

6,562/2,000

3,281/1,000

656/200

Sea level

0   50   100   150   200   250   300 km

0   50   100   150   200 miles

133

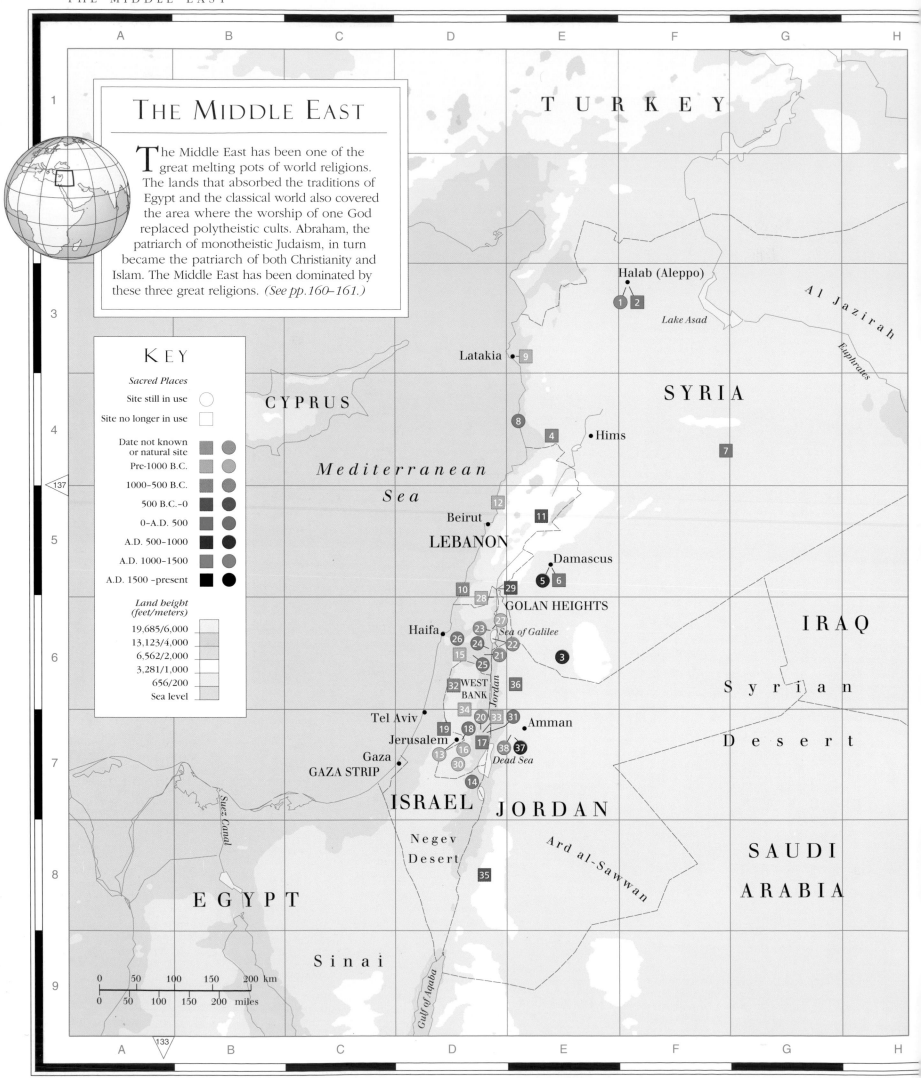

THE MIDDLE EAST

T he Middle East has been one of the
great melting pots of world religions.
The lands that absorbed the traditions of
Egypt and the classical world also covered
the area where the worship of one God
replaced polytheistic cults. Abraham, the
patriarch of monotheistic Judaism, in turn
became the patriarch of both Christianity and
Islam. The Middle East has been dominated by
these three great religions. *(See pp.160–161.)*

KEY

Sacred Places

Site still in use

Site no longer in use

Date not known
or natural site

Pre-1000 B.C.

1000–500 B.C.

500 B.C.–0

0–A.D. 500

A.D. 500–1000

A.D. 1000–1500

A.D. 1500 –present

*Land height
(feet/meters)*

19,685/6,000

13,123/4,000

6,562/2,000

3,281/1,000

656/200

Sea level

TURKEY

SYRIA

CYPRUS

Halab (Aleppo)

Lake Asad

Al Jazirah

Euphrates

Latakia

Mediterranean

Sea

Hims

IRAQ

Beirut

LEBANON

Damascus

GOLAN HEIGHTS

Haifa

Sea of Galilee

S y r i a n

Tel Aviv

WEST
BANK

Jordan

Amman

D e s e r t

Jerusalem

Gaza

GAZA STRIP

Dead Sea

ISRAEL

JORDAN

*Negev
Desert*

Ard al-Sawwan

SAUDI

ARABIA

EGYPT

S i n a i

Suez Canal

Gulf of Aqaba

0   50   100   150   200 km

0   50   100   150   200 miles

137

133

134

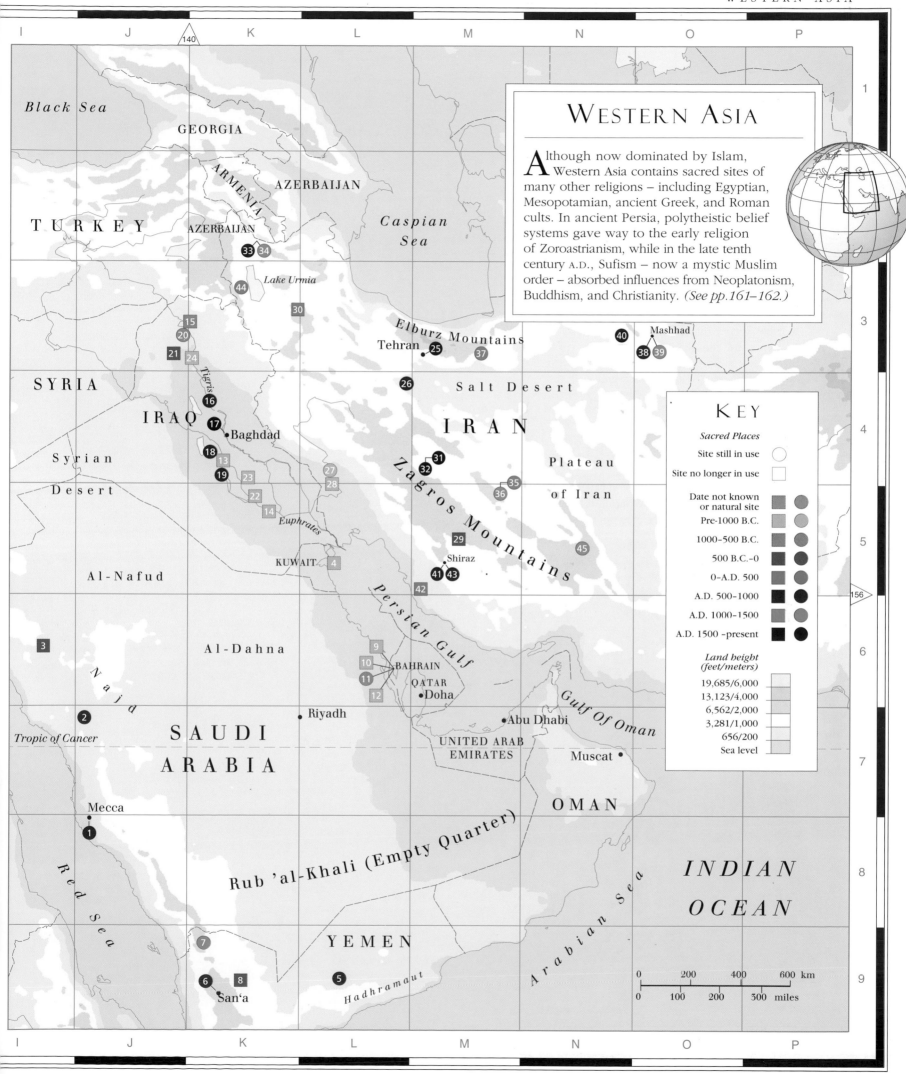

WESTERN ASIA

Although now dominated by Islam, Western Asia contains sacred sites of many other religions – including Egyptian, Mesopotamian, ancient Greek, and Roman cults. In ancient Persia, polytheistic belief systems gave way to the early religion of Zoroastrianism, while in the late tenth century A.D., Sufism – now a mystic Muslim order – absorbed influences from Neoplatonism, Buddhism, and Christianity. *(See pp.161–162.)*

KEY

Sacred Places

○ Site still in use

□ Site no longer in use

Date not known or natural site	
Pre-1000 B.C.	
1000–500 B.C.	
500 B.C.–0	
0–A.D. 500	
A.D. 500–1000	
A.D. 1000–1500	
A.D. 1500 –present	

Land height (feet/meters)

19,685/6,000
13,123/4,000
6,562/2,000
3,281/1,000
656/200
Sea level

Black Sea

GEORGIA

ARMENIA

AZERBAIJAN

TURKEY

AZERBAIJAN

Caspian Sea

Lake Urmia

Elburz Mountains

Mashhad

Tehran

SYRIA

Tigris

IRAQ

Baghdad

IRAN

Salt Desert

Plateau of Iran

Syrian Desert

Zagros Mountains

Al-Nafud

Euphrates

KUWAIT

Al-Dahna

Najd

BAHRAIN

Persian Gulf

QATAR
Doha

Gulf Of Oman

Riyadh

SAUDI ARABIA

Tropic of Cancer

Abu Dhabi

UNITED ARAB EMIRATES

Muscat

OMAN

Mecca

Red Sea

Rub 'al-Khali (Empty Quarter)

INDIAN OCEAN

Arabian Sea

YEMEN

San'a

Hadhramaut

0	200	400	600	km
0	100	200	300	miles

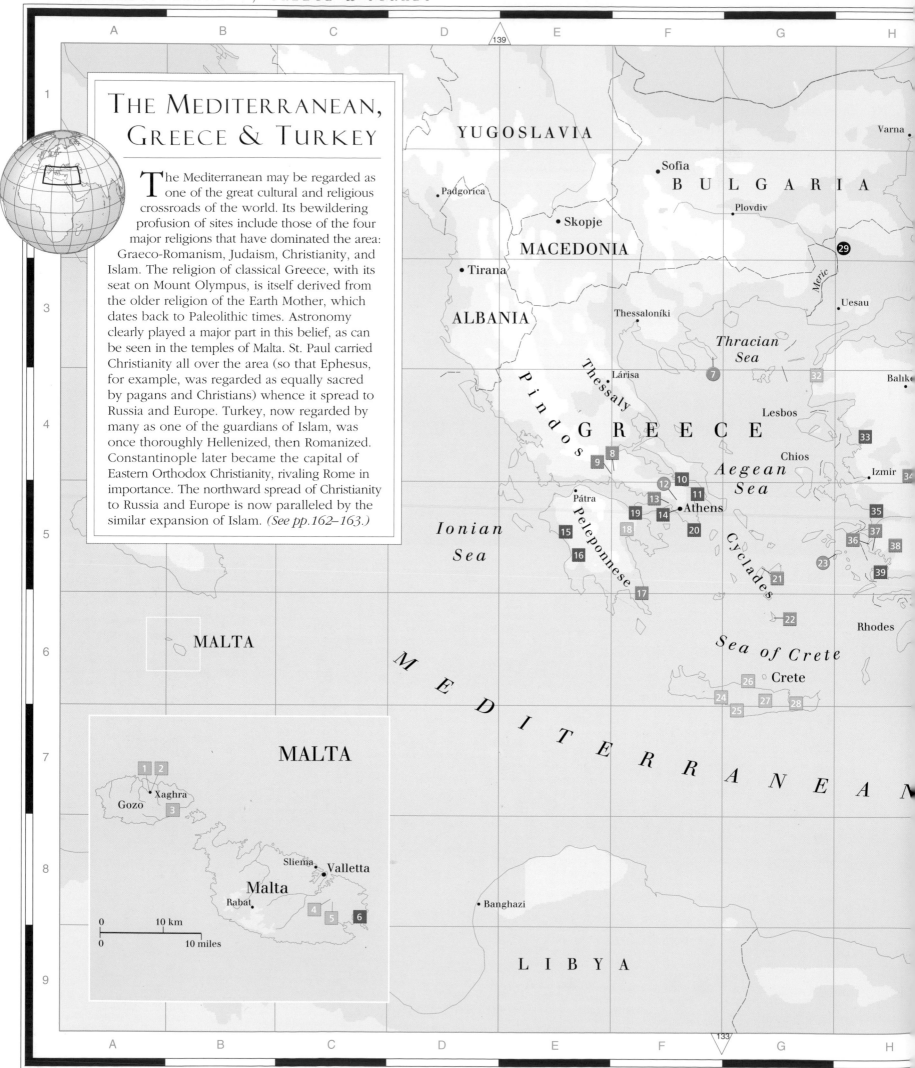

THE MEDITERRANEAN, GREECE & TURKEY

The Mediterranean may be regarded as one of the great cultural and religious crossroads of the world. Its bewildering profusion of sites include those of the four major religions that have dominated the area: Graeco-Romanism, Judaism, Christianity, and Islam. The religion of classical Greece, with its seat on Mount Olympus, is itself derived from the older religion of the Earth Mother, which dates back to Paleolithic times. Astronomy clearly played a major part in this belief, as can be seen in the temples of Malta. St. Paul carried Christianity all over the area (so that Ephesus, for example, was regarded as equally sacred by pagans and Christians) whence it spread to Russia and Europe. Turkey, now regarded by many as one of the guardians of Islam, was once thoroughly Hellenized, then Romanized. Constantinople later became the capital of Eastern Orthodox Christianity, rivaling Rome in importance. The northward spread of Christianity to Russia and Europe is now paralleled by the similar expansion of Islam. *(See pp.162–163.)*

YUGOSLAVIA

BULGARIA

Varna

Sofia

Padgorica

Plovdiv

Skopje

MACEDONIA

29

Tirana

Meric

Uesau

ALBANIA

Thessaloníki

Thracian Sea

Pindos

Thessaly

Lárisa

7

32

Balhk

Lesbos

GREECE

Aegean Sea

Chios

Izmir

34

8

9

12 10

11 Athens

33

Pátra

13

Peleponnese

19 14

35

18

20

37

36

38

15

Ionian Sea

16

Cyclades

23

21

39

17

22

Rhodes

Sea of Crete

MEDITERRANEAN

MALTA

Crete

26

24 27 28

25

MALTA

1 2

Xaghra

Gozo

3

Sliema Valletta

Malta

Rabat

4 5 6

Banghazi

0   10 km

0   10 miles

LIBYA

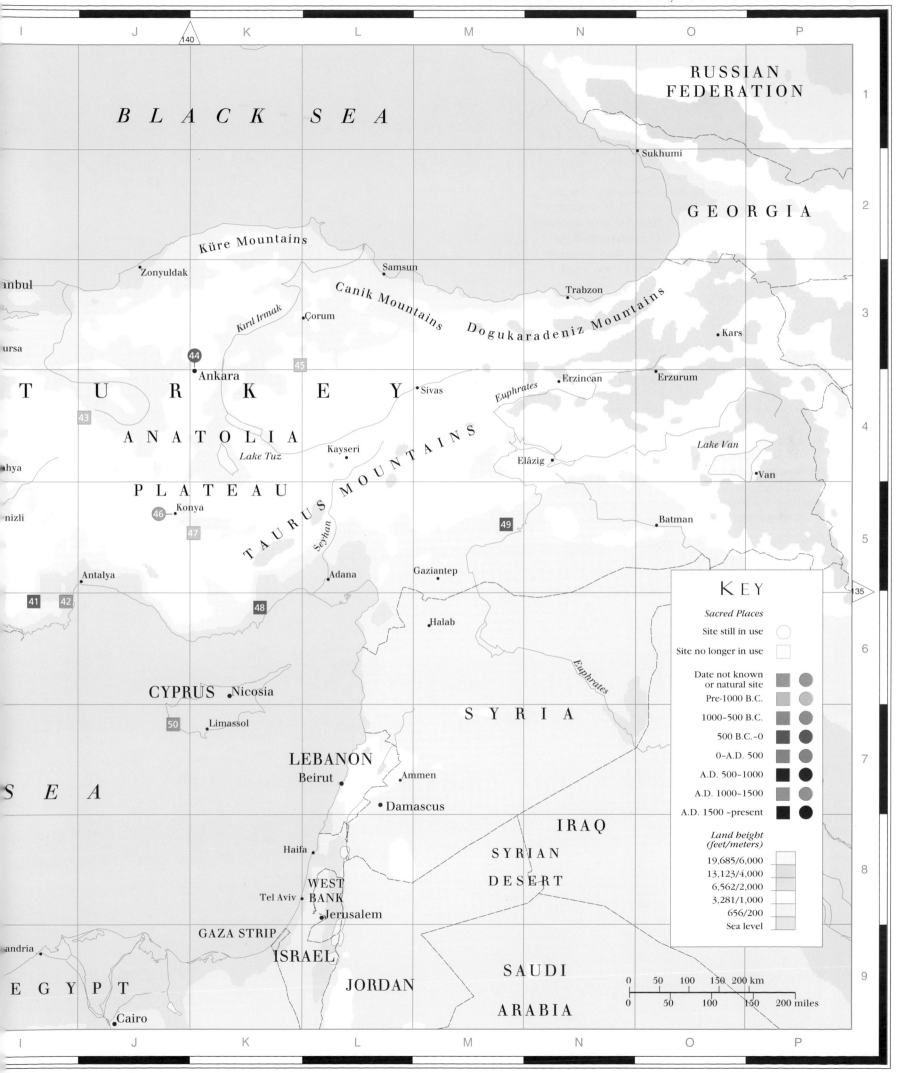

RUSSIAN
FEDERATION

BLACK SEA

• Sukhumi

GEORGIA

Küre Mountains

• Zonyuldak

• Samsun

• Trabzon

Canik Mountains

Dogukaradeniz Mountains

Kızıl Irmak

• Çorum

anbul

ursa

• Kars

44

45

• Erzincan

• Erzurum

TURKEY

• Ankara

• Sivas

Euphrates

43

ANATOLIA

Lake Van

Kayseri

TAURUS MOUNTAINS

• Elâzig

ahya

Lake Tuz

• Van

PLATEAU

46 • Konya

47

Seyhan

49

• Batman

nizli

• Antalya

• Adana

• Gaziantep

41

42

48

135

• Halab

KEY

CYPRUS • Nicosia

SYRIA

Euphrates

50 • Limassol

LEBANON

• Beirut

• Ammen

• Damascus

SEA

• Haifa

IRAQ

SYRIAN
DESERT

WEST
BANK

Tel Aviv •

• Jerusalem

GAZA STRIP

ISRAEL

andria

EGYPT

JORDAN

SAUDI

ARABIA

• Cairo

Sacred Places

Site still in use

Site no longer in use

Date not known
or natural site

Pre-1000 B.C.

1000–500 B.C.

500 B.C.–0

0–A.D. 500

A.D. 500–1000

A.D. 1000–1500

A.D. 1500 –present

Land height
(feet/meters)

19,685/6,000
13,123/4,000
6,562/2,000
3,281/1,000
656/200
Sea level

0   50   100   150 200 km

0   50   100   150   200 miles

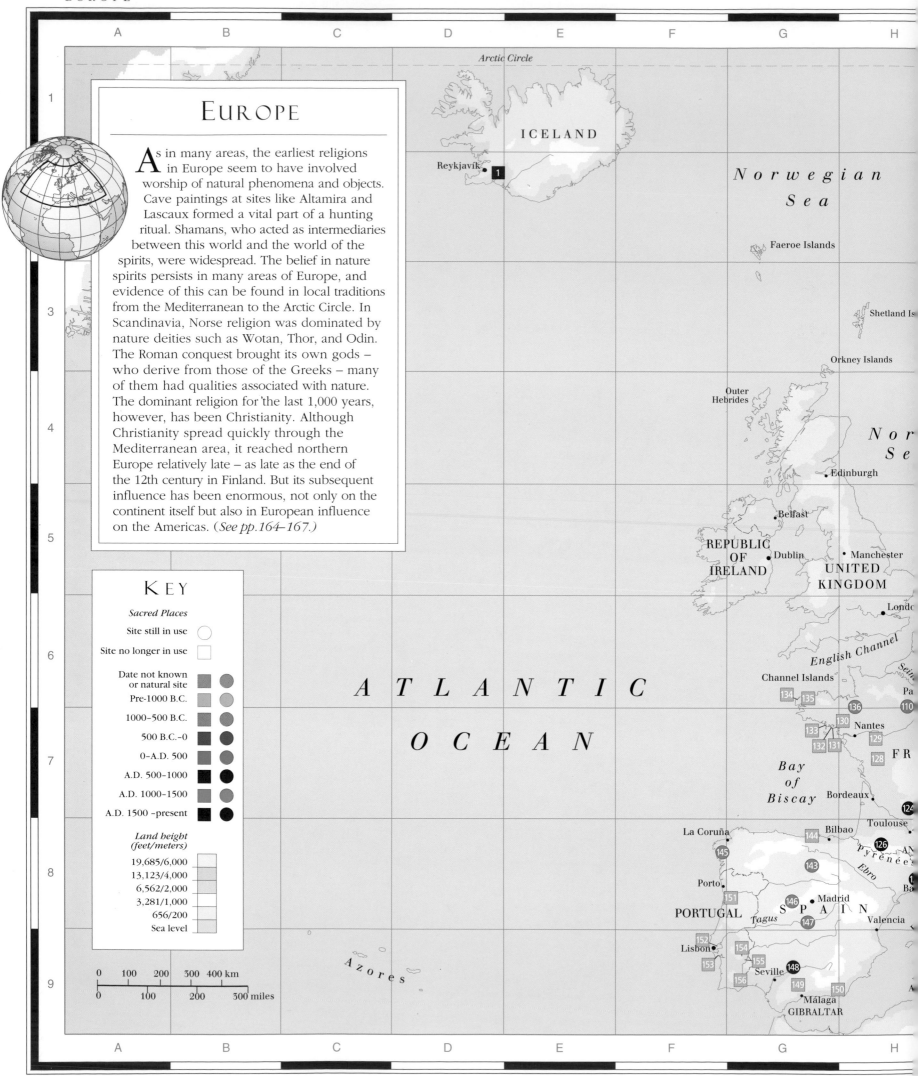

EUROPE

As in many areas, the earliest religions in Europe seem to have involved worship of natural phenomena and objects. Cave paintings at sites like Altamira and Lascaux formed a vital part of a hunting ritual. Shamans, who acted as intermediaries between this world and the world of the spirits, were widespread. The belief in nature spirits persists in many areas of Europe, and evidence of this can be found in local traditions from the Mediterranean to the Arctic Circle. In Scandinavia, Norse religion was dominated by nature deities such as Wotan, Thor, and Odin. The Roman conquest brought its own gods – who derive from those of the Greeks – many of them had qualities associated with nature. The dominant religion for the last 1,000 years, however, has been Christianity. Although Christianity spread quickly through the Mediterranean area, it reached northern Europe relatively late – as late as the end of the 12th century in Finland. But its subsequent influence has been enormous, not only on the continent itself but also in European influence on the Americas. (*See pp.164–167.*)

KEY

Sacred Places

Site still in use ◯

Site no longer in use ▢

Date not known or natural site		●
Pre-1000 B.C.		●
1000–500 B.C.		●
500 B.C.–0		●
0–A.D. 500		●
A.D. 500–1000		●
A.D. 1000–1500		●
A.D. 1500 –present		●

Land height (feet/meters)

19,685/6,000	
13,123/4,000	
6,562/2,000	
3,281/1,000	
656/200	
Sea level	

0 100 200 300 400 km

0 100 200 300 miles

Norwegian Sea

ICELAND

Reykjavík • ▢ 1

Faeroe Islands

Shetland Is

Orkney Islands

Outer Hebrides

Nor Se

• Edinburgh

• Belfast

REPUBLIC OF IRELAND

Dublin • • Manchester

• Londo

UNITED KINGDOM

English Channel

Channel Islands

Se

134 135 136 110

A T L A N T I C

O C E A N

133 130 Nantes •

132 131 129

128 FR

Bay of Biscay

Bordeaux •

124

Toulouse

La Coruña • • Bilbao

144 126 AN

Pyrénées

145 *Ebro*

143

B

Porto •

151 146 • Madrid

PORTUGAL S P A I N

Tagus 147 Valencia •

152 154

Lisbon •

153 155 148

156 Seville •

149 150

• Málaga

GIBRALTAR

Azores

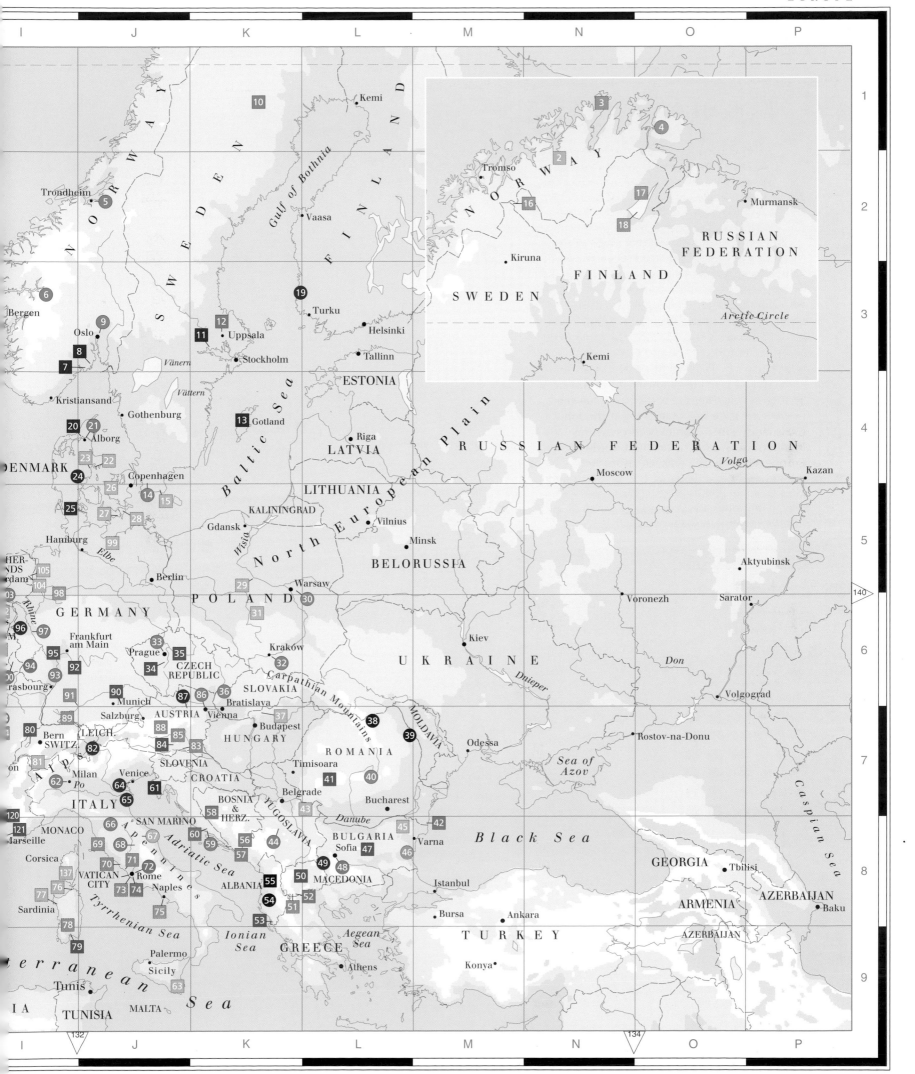

I J K L M N O P

1
2
3
4
5
6
7
8
9

140

Kemi

3

4

2

Tromso

16

17

18

Murmansk

RUSSIAN FEDERATION

Kiruna

FINLAND

SWEDEN

Arctic Circle

Kemi

10

Gulf of Bothnia

N O R W A Y

S W E D E N

F I N L A N D

Trondheim

5

6

Bergen

9

8

7

Oslo

Vaasa

19

Turku

Uppsala

11

12

Helsinki

Stockholm

Tallinn

Vänern

Vättern

Kristiansand

Gothenburg

20 21

Alborg

13 **Gotland**

ESTONIA

Riga

LATVIA

Moscow

Volga

Kazan

Baltic Sea

23 22

24

Copenhagen

14 15

DENMARK

26

25

27 28

LITHUANIA

KALININGRAD

Vilnius

Minsk

BELORUSSIA

RUSSIAN FEDERATION

Aktyubinsk

Hamburg

99

Elbe

Wisla

Gdansk

105

104

98

103

NETHER-LANDS
rdam

Berlin

29

Warsaw

30

Sarator

GERMANY

96 97

Frankfurt am Main

95

94

93

92

91

strasbourg

P O L A N D

North European Plain

31

Kiev

U K R A I N E

Voronezh

Don

Dnieper

33

Prague

35

34

CZECH REPUBLIC

Kraków

32

Carpathian Mountains

SLOVAKIA

Volgograd

90

Munich

87 86

36

Bratislava

Salzburg

89

AUSTRIA

Vienna

37

Budapest

38

MOLDAVIA

Odessa

Rostov-na-Donu

80

Bern

SWITZ.

LEICH.

88

85

82

84

83

HUNGARY

39

81

Milan

A l p s

62

Po

64

65

61

Venice

ITALY

SLOVENIA

CROATIA

ROMANIA

Timisoara

41

40

Sea of Azov

Caspian Sea

Belgrade

Bucharest

66

SAN MARINO

58

BOSNIA & HERZ.

43

Danube

42

120

121

MONACO

Apennines

Adriatic Sea

60

59

56

44

45

YUGOSLAVIA

BULGARIA

Sofia

47

Varna

Black Sea

GEORGIA

Tbilisi

Marseille

69

68

67

70

71

72

Corsica

137

VATICAN CITY

Rome

Naples

73 74

57

55

50

ALBANIA

49

48

MACEDONIA

46

Istanbul

ARMENIA

AZERBAIJAN

Baku

77

76

Sardinia

Tyrrhenian Sea

75

54

52

51

53

Bursa

Ankara

AZERBAIJAN

78

79

Palermo

Sicily

Ionian Sea

Aegean Sea

GREECE

T U R K E Y

Konya

Athens

Tunis

63

MALTA

terranean Sea

TUNISIA

132

I J K L M N O P

134

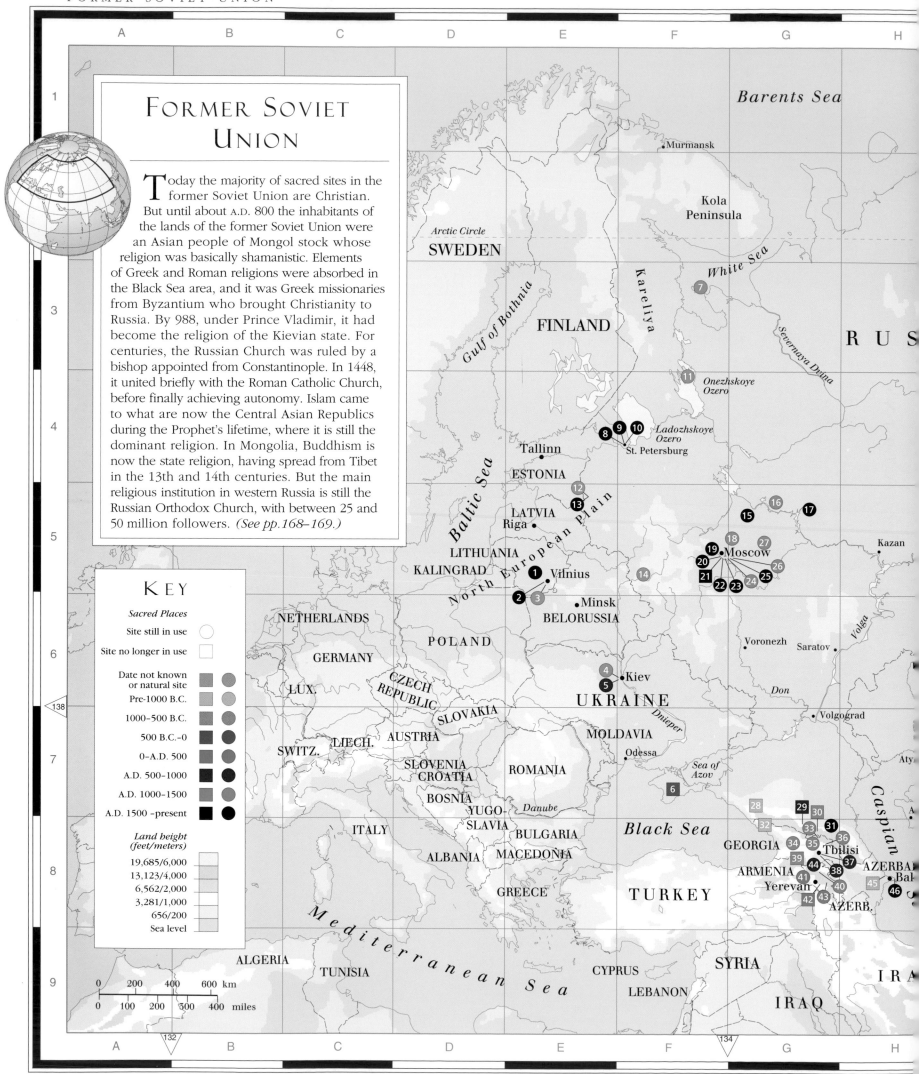

FORMER SOVIET UNION

Today the majority of sacred sites in the former Soviet Union are Christian. But until about A.D. 800 the inhabitants of the lands of the former Soviet Union were an Asian people of Mongol stock whose religion was basically shamanistic. Elements of Greek and Roman religions were absorbed in the Black Sea area, and it was Greek missionaries from Byzantium who brought Christianity to Russia. By 988, under Prince Vladimir, it had become the religion of the Kievian state. For centuries, the Russian Church was ruled by a bishop appointed from Constantinople. In 1448, it united briefly with the Roman Catholic Church, before finally achieving autonomy. Islam came to what are now the Central Asian Republics during the Prophet's lifetime, where it is still the dominant religion. In Mongolia, Buddhism is now the state religion, having spread from Tibet in the 13th and 14th centuries. But the main religious institution in western Russia is still the Russian Orthodox Church, with between 25 and 50 million followers. *(See pp.168–169.)*

KEY

Sacred Places

Site still in use ○

Site no longer in use ☐

Date not known or natural site

Pre-1000 B.C.

1000–500 B.C.

500 B.C.–0

0–A.D. 500

A.D. 500–1000

A.D. 1000–1500

A.D. 1500 –present

Land height (feet/meters)

19,685/6,000
13,123/4,000
6,562/2,000
3,281/1,000
656/200
Sea level

Barents Sea

Murmansk

Kola Peninsula

White Sea

Arctic Circle

SWEDEN

Kareliya

FINLAND

Severnaya Dvina

R U S

Gulf of Bothnia

Onezhskoye Ozero

11

7

Ladozhskoye Ozero

8 9 10

St. Petersburg

Tallinn

ESTONIA

12

16

17

13

15

LATVIA

North European Plain

Riga

18

27

LITHUANIA

19 Moscow

20

KALINGRAD

1 Vilnius

14

26

21

25

2 3

22 23 24

Minsk

BELORUSSIA

Kazan

NETHERLANDS

POLAND

Voronezh

Saratov

Volga

GERMANY

LUX.

CZECH REPUBLIC

4 Kiev

5

UKRAINE

Don

Dnieper

Volgograd

SLOVAKIA

SWITZ. LIECH.

AUSTRIA

SLOVENIA

CROATIA

MOLDAVIA

Odessa

Sea of Azov

Aty

ITALY

BOSNIA

YUGO-SLAVIA

Danube

ROMANIA

Black Sea

6

Caspian

BULGARIA

28

29

ALBANIA

MACEDONIA

32

30

GEORGIA

33 31

34 35

36

Tbilisi

GREECE

TURKEY

39

44 38

37

AZERB

Bal

ARMENIA

41 40

45

Yerevan

46

42 43

AZERB.

Mediterranean Sea

ALGERIA

TUNISIA

CYPRUS

SYRIA

IRA

LEBANON

IRAQ

0 200 400 600 km

0 100 200 300 400 miles

138

132

134

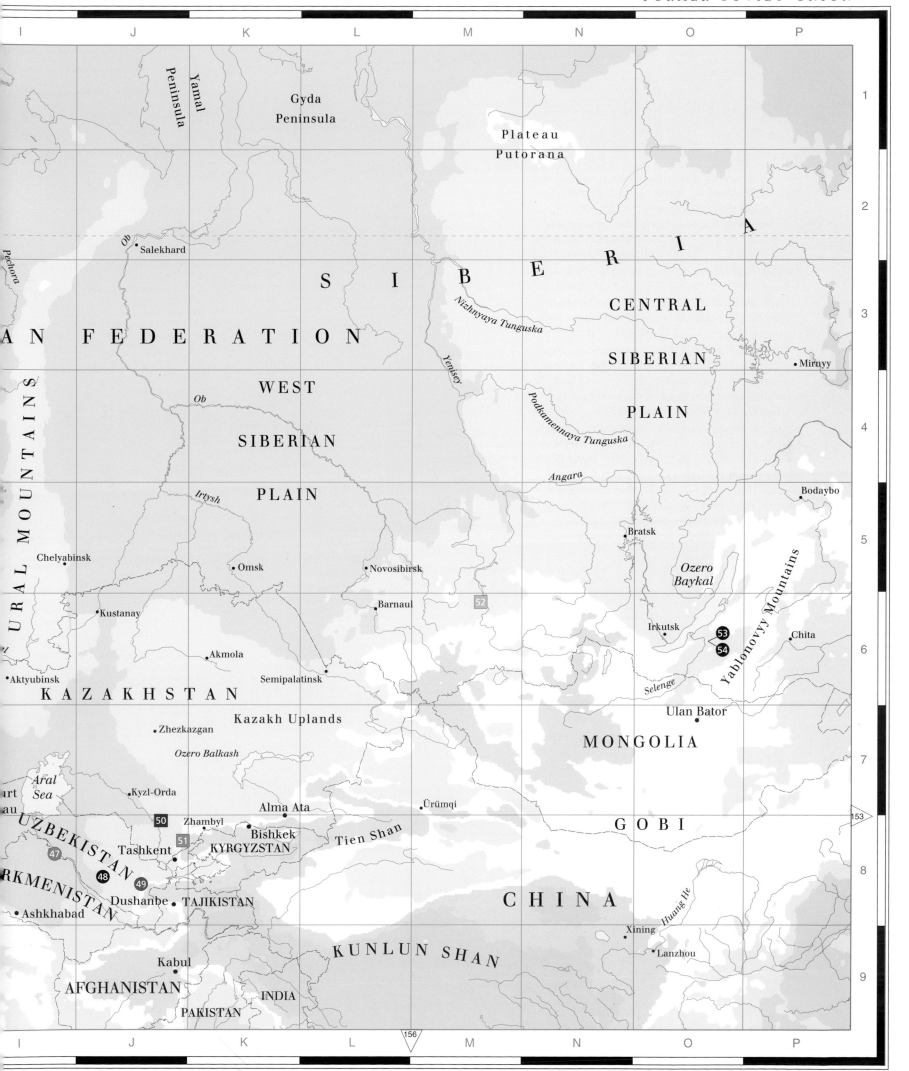

Yamal Peninsula

Gyda Peninsula

Plateau Putorana

S I B E R I A

CENTRAL

SIBERIAN

PLAIN

Pechora

Ob

• Salekhard

S I B E R I A

AN F E D E R A T I O N

Nizhnyaya Tunguska

Yenisey

• Mirnyy

WEST

Ob

SIBERIAN

Podkamennaya Tunguska

Irtysh

PLAIN

Angara

• Bodaybo

U R A L   M O U N T A I N S

• Chelyabinsk

• Omsk

• Novosibirsk

• Bratsk

Ozero
Baykal

• Barnaul

52

Yablonovyy Mountains

• Kustanay

Irkutsk

53
54

• Chita

• Akmola

K A Z A K H S T A N

• Aktyubinsk

Semipalatinsk

Selenge

Ulan Bator

• Zhezkazgan

Kazakh Uplands

M O N G O L I A

Ozero Balkash

Aral
Sea

• Kyzl-Orda

• Ürümqi

G O B I

153

art
au

50

Zhambyl

Alma Ata

Tien Shan

U Z B E K I S T A N

51

Bishkek

47

Tashkent

KYRGYZSTAN

C H I N A

RKMENISTAN

48

49

Huang He

• Ashkhabad

Dushanbe • TAJIKISTAN

• Xining

• Lanzhou

K U N L U N   S H A N

• Kabul

AFGHANISTAN

INDIA

PAKISTAN

156

UNITED KINGDOM & IRELAND

Ranging from ancient megaliths to some of the greatest Christian cathedrals, the British Isles have a broad variety of sacred places. The earliest religion was a form of nature worship; certain rocks and wells were believed to have healing and numinous qualities derived from the earth itself. Many of the megalithic circles of Britain and Ireland predate the Great Pyramid of Giza. These early temples were sacred centers where ceremonies took place at certain seasons to ensure the earth's fertility – seasons for which the stones themselves provide an astronomical calendar. Around 600 B.C., Celtic druids began to worship in sacred groves. Many Celtic sacred sites and those dedicated to earlier pagan gods became sites of Christian churches. Even today churches may have carvings of fertility gods and goddesses, while some altars have been found to contain what appear to be phallic stone objects. Many Christian sites of Britain and Ireland may thus be part of a more ancient tradition of religious custom. *(See pp.169–171.)*

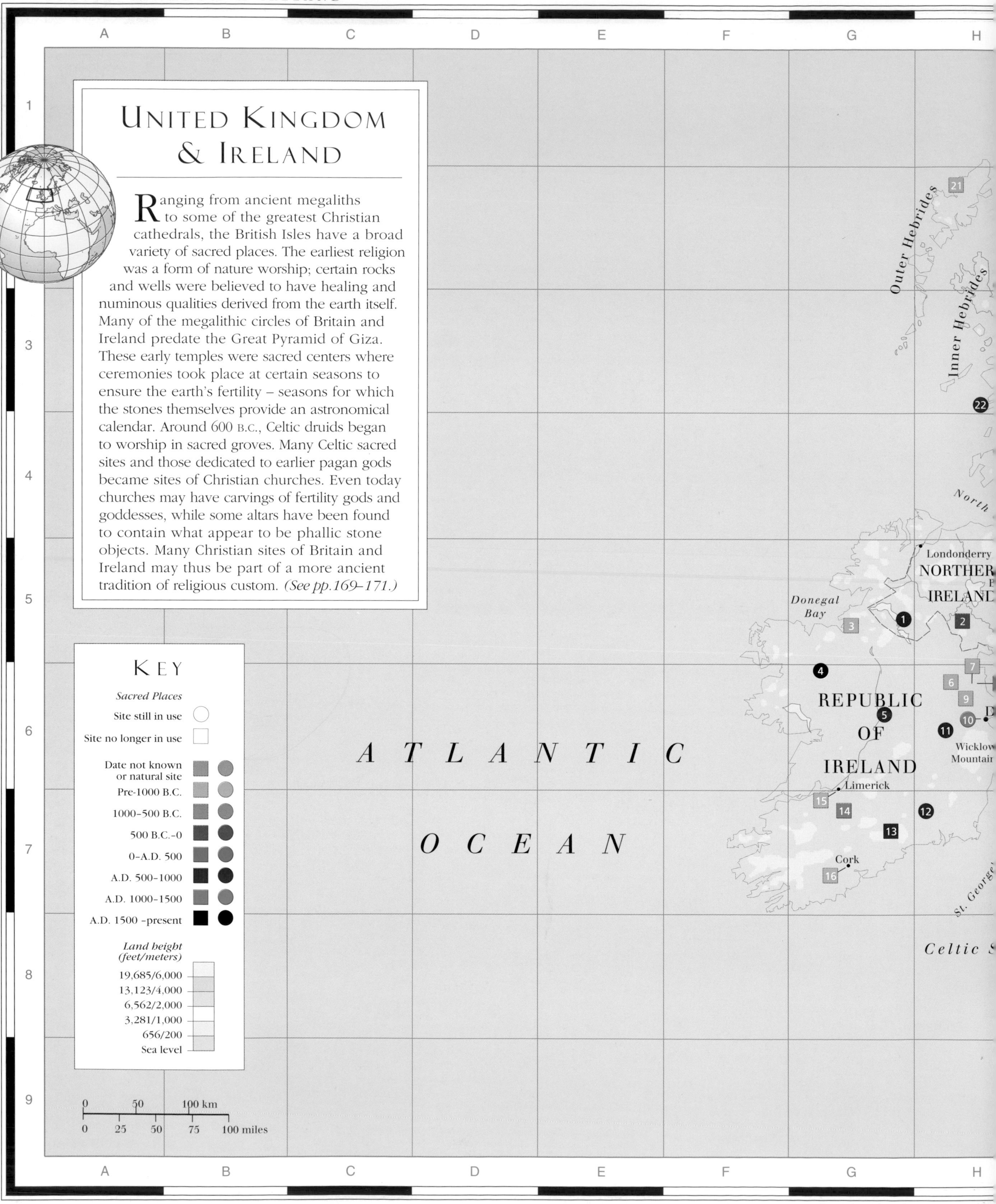

KEY

Sacred Places

Site still in use ⭕

Site no longer in use ⬜

Date not known or natural site	▨	⬤
Pre-1000 B.C.	▨	⬤
1000–500 B.C.	▨	⬤
500 B.C.–0	◼	⬤
0–A.D. 500	◼	⬤
A.D. 500–1000	◼	⬤
A.D. 1000–1500	▨	⬤
A.D. 1500 –present	◼	⬤

Land height (feet/meters)

19,685/6,000
13,123/4,000
6,562/2,000
3,281/1,000
656/200
Sea level

0   50   100 km
0   25   50   75   100 miles

ATLANTIC

OCEAN

Outer Hebrides

Inner Hebrides

North

Londonderry
NORTHER
IRELAND

Donegal Bay

REPUBLIC
OF
IRELAND

Limerick

Wicklow Mountain

Cork

St. George's

Celtic S

NORTH AMERICA

It was once believed that humans were relative latecomers to the American continent – no more than 2,000 years ago. We now know that it was populated much earlier, perhaps even before the end of the last Ice Age, about 12,000 years ago. Religions of the native North Americans, such as the Ojibway, Pueblo, and Navajo are based on a deep sense of people's dependence on the earth and the forces of nature. As in Australia, the majority of North America's sacred sites are earth sites and many are still venerated today, often independently of any organized belief system. In the area now covered by the United States, the predominant historic sacred sites fall into two main areas. The first group are the great mounds of the Hopewell and Adena cultures based on the land around the Ohio and Mississippi rivers. The other is the Pueblo culture in the south-west United States. In Canada, many of the oldest sites are petroglyphs or natural features of the landscape. Canada is also famous for its medicine wheels; many of these have astronomical alignments. *(See pp.171–173.)*

KEY

Sacred Places

Site still in use ○

Site no longer in use ☐

Date not known or natural site

Pre-1000 B.C.

1000–500 B.C.

500 B.C.–0

0–A.D. 500

A.D. 500–1000

A.D. 1000–1500

A.D. 1500 –present

Land height (feet/meters)

19,685/6,000
13,123/4,000
6,562/2,000
3,281/1,000
656/200
Sea level

0 100 200 300 400 km

0 100 200 300 miles

Beaufort Sea

• Atqasuk

Bering Strait

Brooks Range

• Inuv

ALASKA

• Dawson

Alaska Range

21

Mac

• Anchorage

Coast

Juneau

Alaska Peninsula

Kodiak Island

Gulf Of Alaska

Alexander Archipelago

Aleutian Islands

Queen Charlotte Island

Vanc Isl

PACIFIC OCEAN

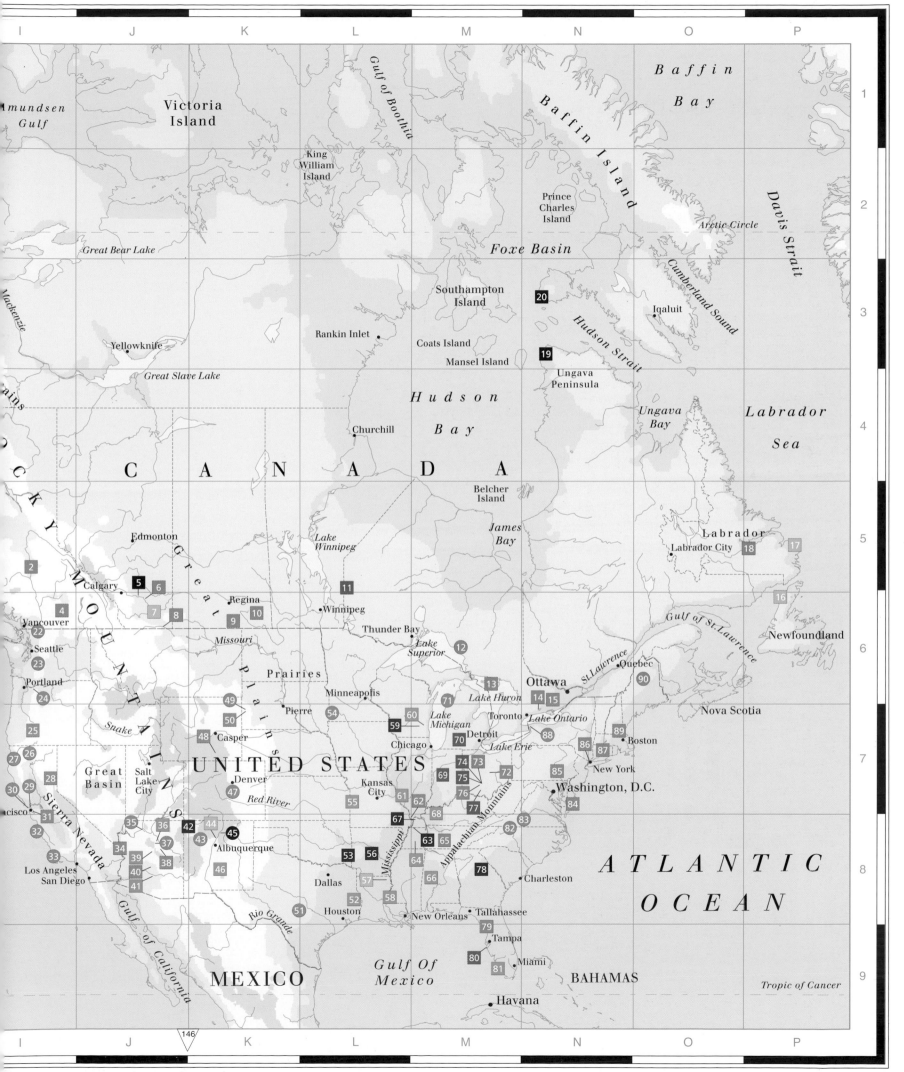

Amundsen Gulf

Victoria Island

Gulf of Boothia

King William Island

Baffin Island

Baffin Bay

Prince Charles Island

Davis Strait

Great Bear Lake

Foxe Basin

Arctic Circle

20

Yellowknife

Southampton Island

Iqaluit

Rankin Inlet

Cumberland Sound

Coats Island

19

Mansel Island

Hudson Strait

Great Slave Lake

Hudson

Ungava Peninsula

Ungava Bay

Labrador Sea

Bay

Churchill

C A N A D A

James Bay

Belcher Island

Labrador

Labrador City

18

17

Edmonton

Lake Winnipeg

2

5 **6**

Calgary

Great Plains

Regina

Gulf of St. Lawrence

4

7 **8**

11

16

9 **10**

Winnipeg

Newfoundland

Vancouver

22

Thunder Bay

Missouri

Lake Superior

12

Seattle

23

Prairies

13

Ottawa

St. Lawrence

Quebec

Portland

Minneapolis

71

Lake Huron

14 **15**

90

24

49

Pierre

54

60

Lake Michigan

Toronto

Lake Ontario

Nova Scotia

50

59

88

89

Snake

25

48

Casper

70

Detroit

Lake Erie

86

Boston

U N I T E D S T A T E S

69 **74** **73**

72

87

27 **26**

Great Basin

Salt Lake City

Denver

85

New York

28

75

30 **29**

47

Red River

61

76

Washington, D.C.

Sierra Nevada

31

55

Kansas City

62

77

84

cisco

32

35 **36** **42** **44**

67

68

83

34

37 **43** **45**

63 **65**

82

A T L A N T I C

33

39 **38**

Albuquerque

53 **56**

64

78

Los Angeles

40

46

Mississippi

66

Charleston

O C E A N

San Diego

41

Dallas

58

Tallahassee

Gulf of California

52

57

51

Houston

New Orleans

79

Tampa

Rio Grande

80

Miami

81

M E X I C O

Gulf Of Mexico

BAHAMAS

Tropic of Cancer

Havana

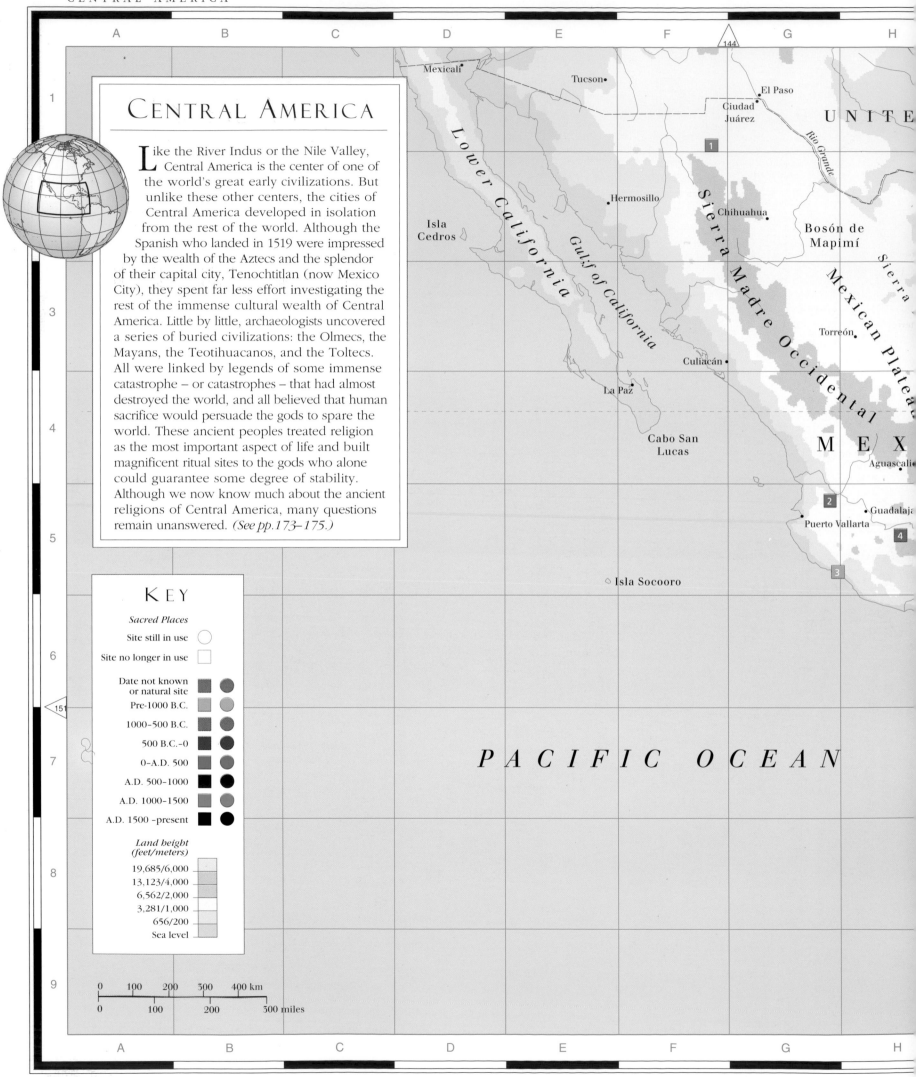

CENTRAL AMERICA

Like the River Indus or the Nile Valley, Central America is the center of one of the world's great early civilizations. But unlike these other centers, the cities of Central America developed in isolation from the rest of the world. Although the Spanish who landed in 1519 were impressed by the wealth of the Aztecs and the splendor of their capital city, Tenochtitlan (now Mexico City), they spent far less effort investigating the rest of the immense cultural wealth of Central America. Little by little, archaeologists uncovered a series of buried civilizations: the Olmecs, the Mayans, the Teotihuacanos, and the Toltecs. All were linked by legends of some immense catastrophe – or catastrophes – that had almost destroyed the world, and all believed that human sacrifice would persuade the gods to spare the world. These ancient peoples treated religion as the most important aspect of life and built magnificent ritual sites to the gods who alone could guarantee some degree of stability. Although we now know much about the ancient religions of Central America, many questions remain unanswered. *(See pp.173–175.)*

KEY

Sacred Places

Site still in use

Site no longer in use

Date not known or natural site

Pre-1000 B.C.

1000–500 B.C.

500 B.C.–0

0–A.D. 500

A.D. 500–1000

A.D. 1000–1500

A.D. 1500 –present

Land height (feet/meters)

19,685/6,000
13,123/4,000
6,562/2,000
3,281/1,000
656/200
Sea level

0   100   200   300   400 km

0   100   200   300 miles

Map labels:

Mexicali
Tucson
El Paso
Ciudad Juárez
UNITE
Río Grande
Lower California
Hermosillo
Chihuahua
Sierra Madre Occidental
Isla Cedros
Gulf of California
Bosón de Mapimí
Mexican Plateau
Sierra
Torreón
Culiacán
La Paz
Cabo San Lucas
M E X
Aguascali
Guadalaja
Puerto Vallarta
Isla Socooro
PACIFIC OCEAN

TATES OF AMERICA

Colorado

• Houston

New Orleans

Red River

Mississippi

Mississippi Fan

Jacksonville

• Tampa

Brownsville

terrey

Matamoros

Gulf of Mexico

Tropic of Cancer

• Miami

• Havana

C U B A

Tampico

Bay of

Campeche

Merida

Yucatan Channel

Yucatan
Peninsula

JAMAICA

Mexico City

Villahermosa

BELIZE

• Belmopan

Gulf of
Honduras

Bay Islands

C A R I B B E A N

Acapulco

Sierra Madre Del Sur

GUATEMALA

San Pedro Sula

HONDURAS
Tegucigalpa

S E A

Gulf of
Tehuantepec

Guatemala City

San
Salvador

**EL
SALVADOR**

NICARAGUA
Managua

• Bluefields

Lake Nicaragua

**COSTA
RICA**

San José

PANAMA

• Panama City

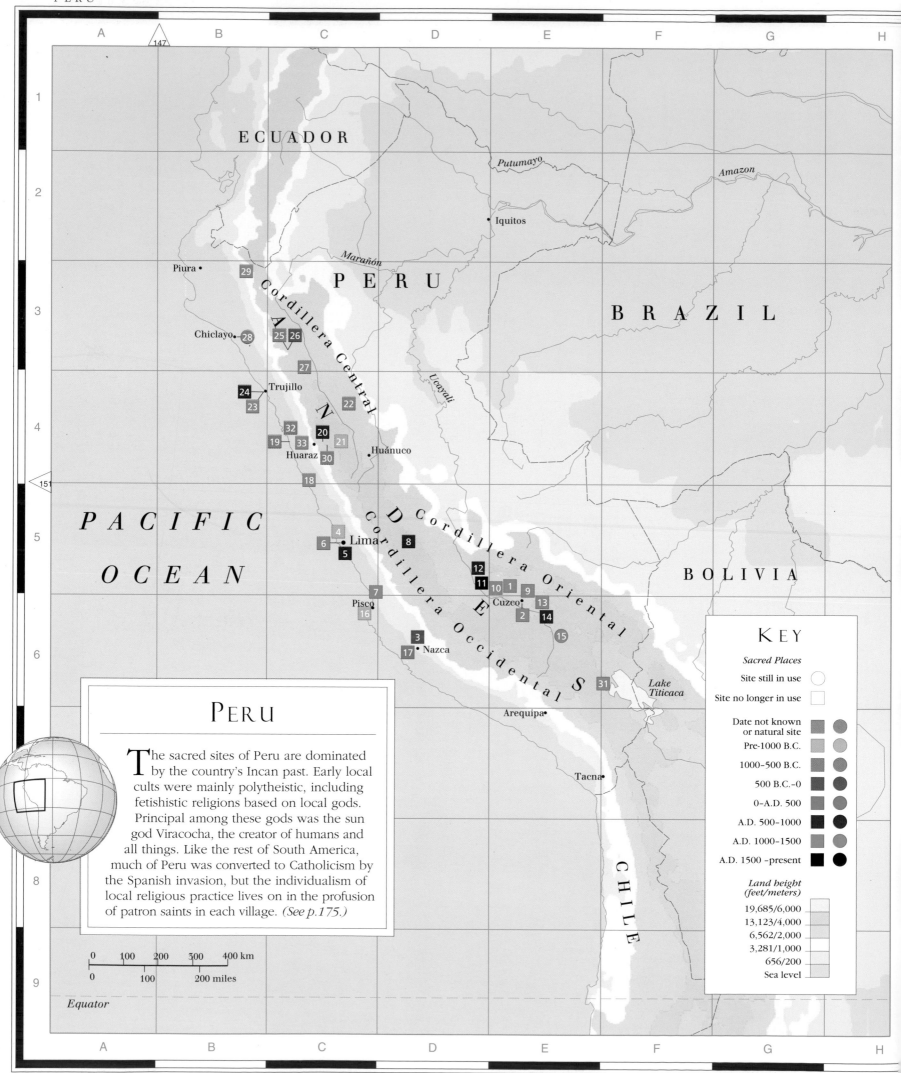

PERU

A B C D E F G H

1

ECUADOR

Putumayo

Amazon

2

• Iquitos

Marañón

Piura • 29

P E R U

B R A Z I L

3

Chiclayo • 28   25 26

Cordillera Central

27

24 Trujillo

23

Ucayali

22

32 20

19 33 21

Huaraz   30

• Huánuco

18

151

PACIFIC

OCEAN

4

6 Lima

5

8

Cordillera Oriental

BOLIVIA

Cordillera Occidental

12

11 10 1

9

Cuzco • 13

7

Pisco

16

2 14

15

Arequipa •

31

Lake Titicaca

3

17 • Nazca

PERU

T he sacred sites of Peru are dominated by the country's Incan past. Early local cults were mainly polytheistic, including fetishistic religions based on local gods. Principal among these gods was the sun god Viracocha, the creator of humans and all things. Like the rest of South America, much of Peru was converted to Catholicism by the Spanish invasion, but the individualism of local religious practice lives on in the profusion of patron saints in each village. *(See p.175.)*

Tacna •

C H I L E

| 0 | 100 | 200 | 300 | 400 km |
| 0 | | 100 | | 200 miles |

KEY

Sacred Places

Site still in use ○

Site no longer in use □

Date not known or natural site

Pre-1000 B.C.

1000–500 B.C.

500 B.C.–0

0–A.D. 500

A.D. 500–1000

A.D. 1000–1500

A.D. 1500 –present

Land height (feet/meters)

19,685/6,000

13,123/4,000

6,562/2,000

3,281/1,000

656/200

Sea level

Equator

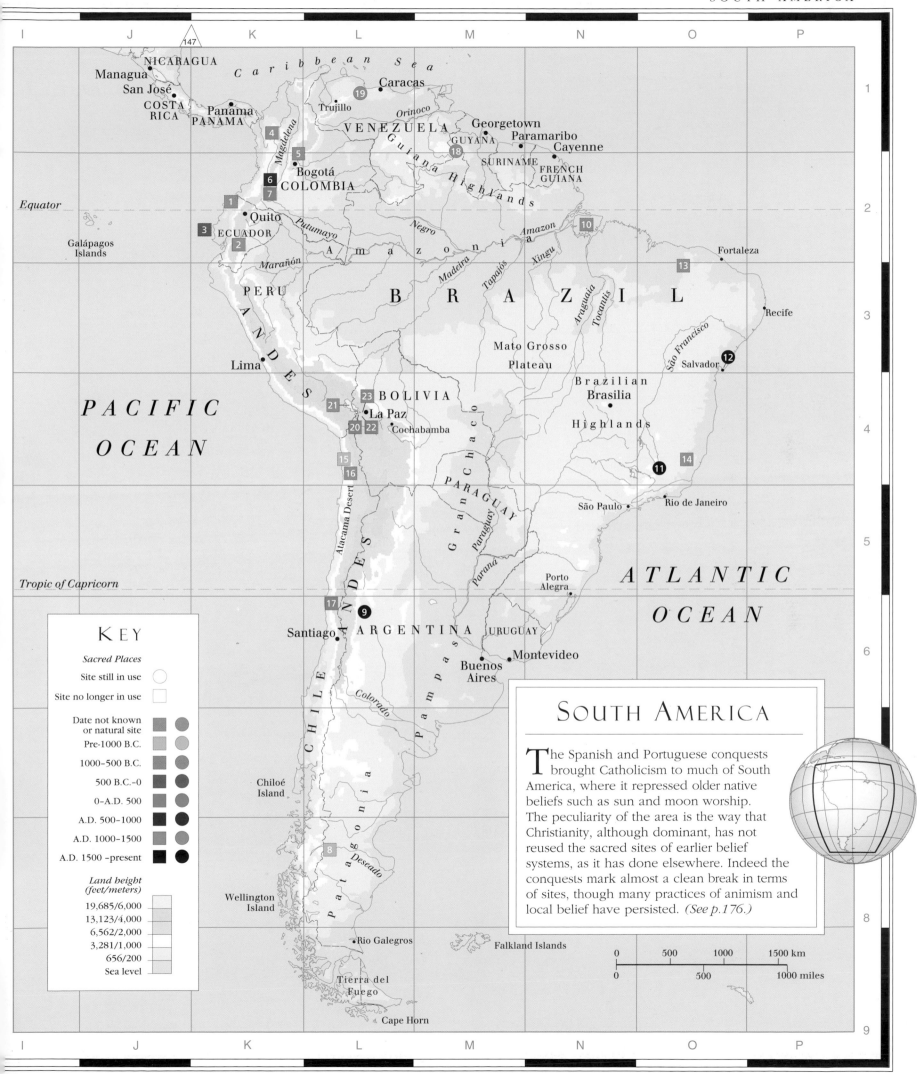

NICARAGUA
Managua
San José
COSTA
RICA
Panama
PANAMA

Caribbean Sea

Caracas
Trujillo
VENEZUELA
Georgetown
GUYANA
Paramaribo
Cayenne
SURINAME
FRENCH
GUIANA

Orinoco

Guiana Highlands

4
5
Bogotá
6
COLOMBIA
7
1
Magdalena

Equator

3 ECUADOR
2
Quito
Putumayo

Marañón

Negro
Amazon
10
Amazon
Fortaleza

13

Recife

PERU
Madeira
Tapajós
Xingu
Araguaia
Tocantins

B R A Z I L

Lima

Mato Grosso
Plateau

São Francisco
12 Salvador

PACIFIC

OCEAN

23 BOLIVIA
21
20 22 La Paz
Cochabamba

Brazilian
Brasilia
Highlands

15
16
Atacama Desert
A N D E S

Gran Chaco

PARAGUAY
Paraguay

11 14

São Paulo
Rio de Janeiro

Paraná

Porto
Alegra

ATLANTIC

OCEAN

17
9
Santiago
CHILE ARGENTINA URUGUAY
Montevideo

Pampas
Buenos
Aires

Colorado

Chiloé
Island

8
Deseado
Patagonia

Wellington
Island

Galápagos
Islands

Tropic of Capricorn

Rio Galegros
Falkland Islands

Tierra del
Fuego

Cape Horn

KEY

Sacred Places

○ Site still in use

□ Site no longer in use

Date not known
or natural site
Pre-1000 B.C.
1000–500 B.C.
500 B.C.–0
0–A.D. 500
A.D. 500–1000
A.D. 1000–1500
A.D. 1500 –present

*Land height
(feet/meters)*

19,685/6,000
13,123/4,000
6,562/2,000
3,281/1,000
656/200
Sea level

SOUTH AMERICA

The Spanish and Portuguese conquests brought Catholicism to much of South America, where it repressed older native beliefs such as sun and moon worship. The peculiarity of the area is the way that Christianity, although dominant, has not reused the sacred sites of earlier belief systems, as it has done elsewhere. Indeed the conquests mark almost a clean break in terms of sites, though many practices of animism and local belief have persisted. *(See p.176.)*

0   500   1000   1500 km
0   500   1000 miles

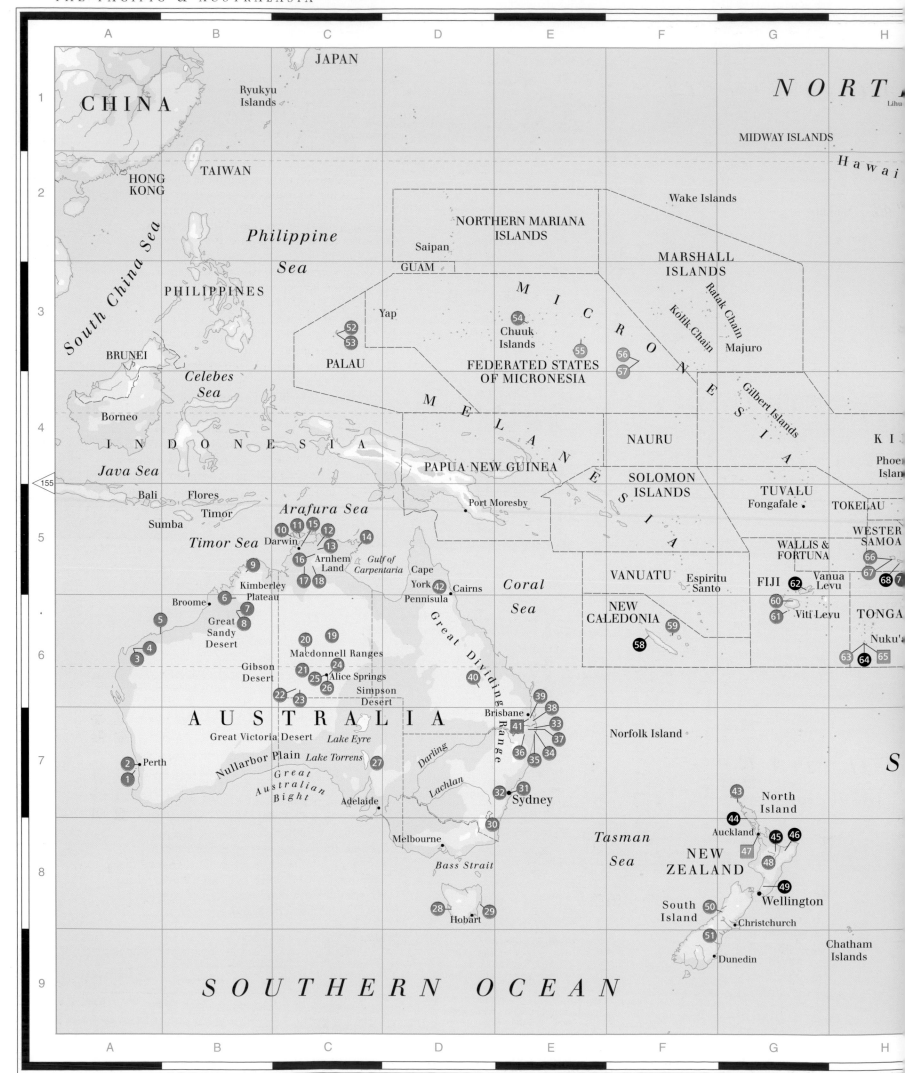

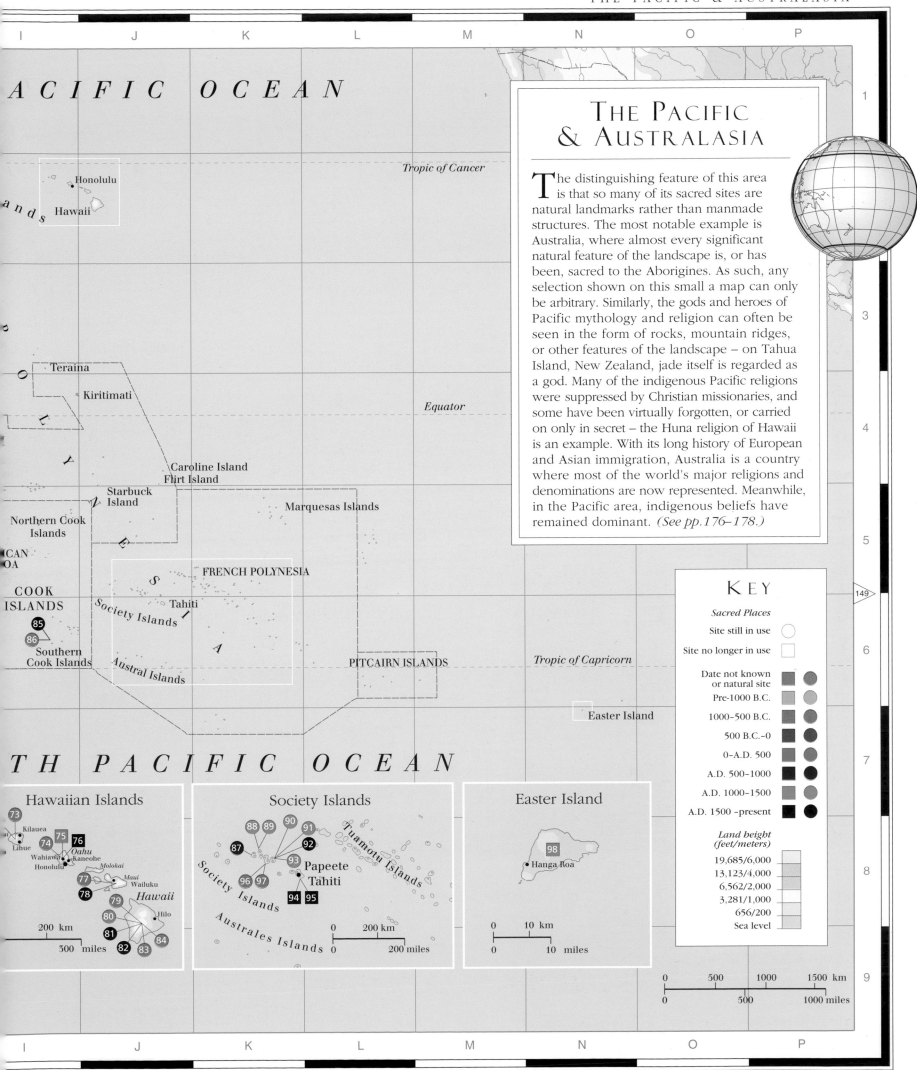

P A C I F I C   O C E A N

Tropic of Cancer

Honolulu

Hawaii

Teraina

Kiritimati

Equator

Caroline Island
Flirt Island

Starbuck
Island

Marquesas Islands

Northern Cook
Islands

CAN
OA

COOK
ISLANDS

FRENCH POLYNESIA

Society Islands

Tahiti

85

86

Southern
Cook Islands

Austral Islands

PITCAIRN ISLANDS

Tropic of Capricorn

Easter Island

TH   P A C I F I C   O C E A N

THE PACIFIC & AUSTRALASIA

The distinguishing feature of this area is that so many of its sacred sites are natural landmarks rather than manmade structures. The most notable example is Australia, where almost every significant natural feature of the landscape is, or has been, sacred to the Aborigines. As such, any selection shown on this small a map can only be arbitrary. Similarly, the gods and heroes of Pacific mythology and religion can often be seen in the form of rocks, mountain ridges, or other features of the landscape – on Tahua Island, New Zealand, jade itself is regarded as a god. Many of the indigenous Pacific religions were suppressed by Christian missionaries, and some have been virtually forgotten, or carried on only in secret – the Huna religion of Hawaii is an example. With its long history of European and Asian immigration, Australia is a country where most of the world's major religions and denominations are now represented. Meanwhile, in the Pacific area, indigenous beliefs have remained dominant. *(See pp.176–178.)*

149

KEY

Sacred Places

Site still in use ○

Site no longer in use □

Date not known
or natural site

Pre-1000 B.C.

1000–500 B.C.

500 B.C.–0

0–A.D. 500

A.D. 500–1000

A.D. 1000–1500

A.D. 1500 –present

*Land height
(feet/meters)*

19,685/6,000

13,123/4,000

6,562/2,000

3,281/1,000

656/200

Sea level

Hawaiian Islands

73

Kilauea

74 75 76

Lihue

Wahiawa *Oahu* Kaneohe

Honolulu Molokai

77 *Maui* Wailuku

78

79 *Hawaii*

80 Hilo

81

82 83 84

200 km

300 miles

Society Islands

88 89 90 91

92

87 *Tuamotu Islands*

93 Papeete
Tahiti

*Society
Islands* 96 97

94 95

Australes Islands

0   200 km

0   200 miles

Easter Island

98

Hanga Roa

0   10 km

0   10 miles

0   500   1000   1500 km

0   500   1000 miles

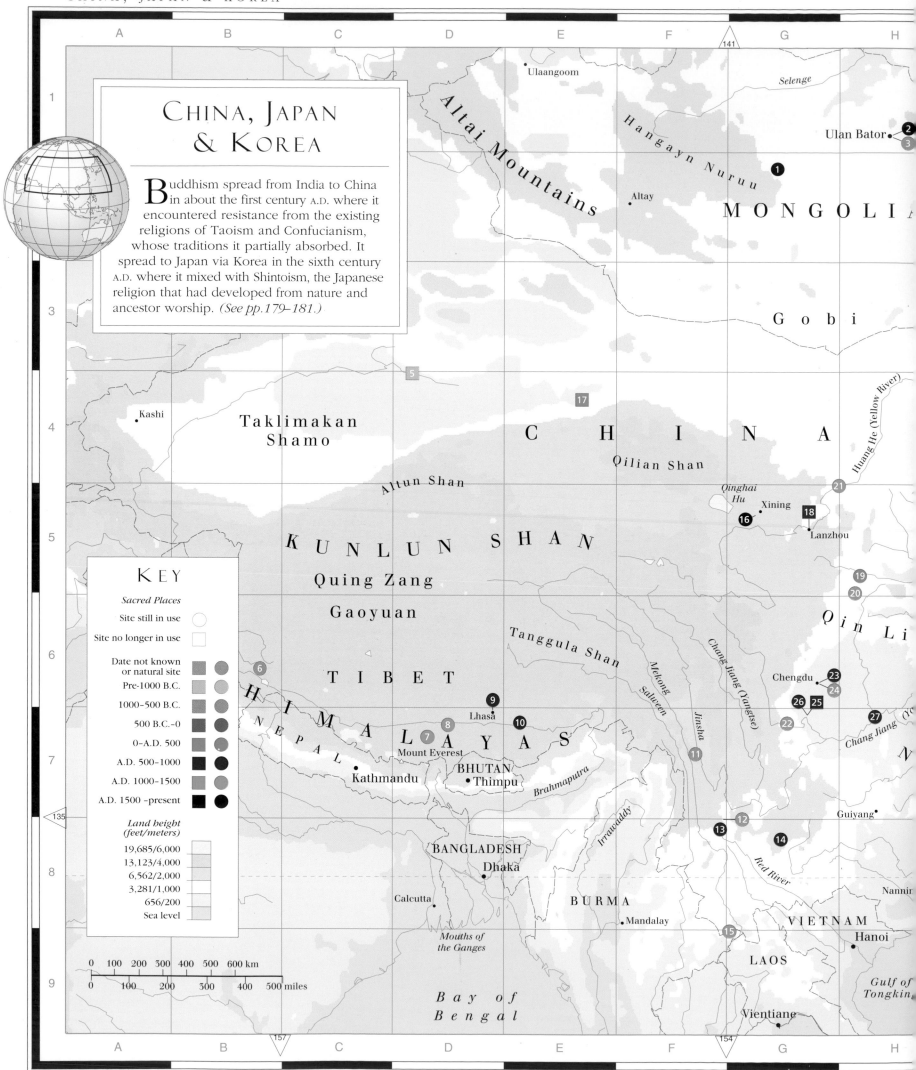

CHINA, JAPAN & KOREA

Buddhism spread from India to China in about the first century A.D. where it encountered resistance from the existing religions of Taoism and Confucianism, whose traditions it partially absorbed. It spread to Japan via Korea in the sixth century A.D. where it mixed with Shintoism, the Japanese religion that had developed from nature and ancestor worship. *(See pp.179–181.)*

KEY

Sacred Places

○ Site still in use

□ Site no longer in use

Date not known or natural site
Pre-1000 B.C.
1000–500 B.C.
500 B.C.–0
0–A.D. 500
A.D. 500–1000
A.D. 1000–1500
A.D. 1500 –present

Land height (feet/meters)
19,685/6,000
13,123/4,000
6,562/2,000
3,281/1,000
656/200
Sea level

0 100 200 300 400 500 600 km
0 100 200 300 400 500 miles

Altai Mountains

Ulaangoom

Selenge

Hangayn Nuruu

Ulan Bator ● ②
③

①

Altay

MONGOLIA

Gobi

⑤

⑰

Kashi

Taklimakan Shamo

CHINA

Qilian Shan

Altun Shan

Qinghai Hu

Xining ●

㉑

⑯ ⑱

Huang He (Yellow River)

Lanzhou

KUNLUN SHAN

⑲
⑳

Quing Zang

Qin Li

Gaoyuan

Tanggula Shan

Mekong

Salween

Chang Jiang (Yangtze)

Jinsha

Chengdu ● ㉓
㉔

TIBET

⑨

Lhasa

⑩

⑥

HIMALAYAS

⑧
⑦
Mount Everest

Kathmandu ●

NEPAL

BHUTAN
● Thimpu

Brahmaputra

⑪

㉖ ㉕

㉒

㉗

Chang Jiang (Ya

N

Guiyang ●

⑫

⑬

⑭

Irrawaddy

Red River

BANGLADESH
Dhaka ●

Calcutta ●

BURMA

Mandalay ●

VIETNAM

Hanoi ●

Nanni

⑮

Mouths of the Ganges

LAOS

Bay of Bengal

Vientiane ●

Gulf of Tongkin

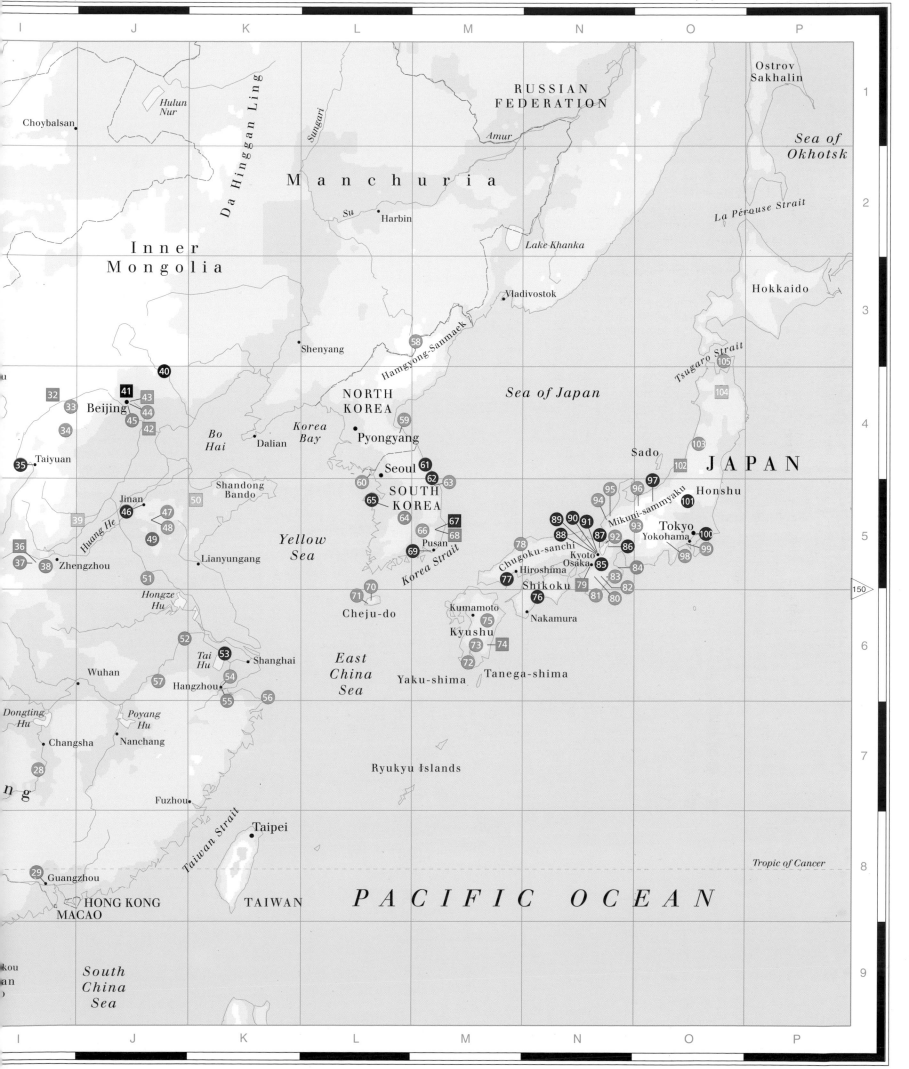

I J K L M N O P

Choybalsan

Hulun Nur

Da Hinggan Ling

RUSSIAN
FEDERATION

*Ostrov
Sakhalin*

*Sea of
Okhotsk*

M a n c h u r i a

Sungari

Amur

La Pérouse Strait

Su

Harbin

I n n e r
M o n g o l i a

Lake Khanka

Hokkaido

Vladivostok

Tsugaro Strait

Shenyang

Hamgyong-Sanmaek

105

40

NORTH
KOREA

Sea of Japan

104

32

41 **43**

Beijing

33 **44**

45 **42**

Pyongyang

59

*Korea
Bay*

Sado

103

102

JAPAN

34

35 Taiyuan

Dalian

*Bo
Hai*

Seoul **61**

62 **63**

60 SOUTH
KOREA

97

95 **96**

94 Honshu

93

Jinan

50

*Shandong
Bando*

65

89 **90** **91**

88

87 **92**

100

Tokyo
Yokohama

101

46

39

47
48

64

66 **67**

68

86

85

99

36

49

*Yellow
Sea*

78

Chugoku-sanchi

Kyoto
Osaka

84

98

37

38 Zhengzhou

69 Pusan

Korea Strait

77

Hiroshima

83

82

150

51

79

81 **80**

*Hongze
Hu*

71 **70**

Shikoku

76

Kumamoto

75

Nakamura

Cheju-do

52

*Tai
Hu*

53

Shanghai

Wuhan

57

Hangzhou

54

55 **56**

*East
China
Sea*

Kyushu

73 **74**

72

Yaku-shima

Tanega-shima

*Dongting
Hu*

*Poyang
Hu*

Changsha

Nanchang

Ryukyu Islands

n g

28

Fuzhou

Taipei

Taiwan Strait

Tropic of Cancer

29 Guangzhou

HONG KONG
MACAO

TAIWAN

P A C I F I C   O C E A N

*South
China
Sea*

I J K L M N O P

1 2 3 4 5 6 7 8 9

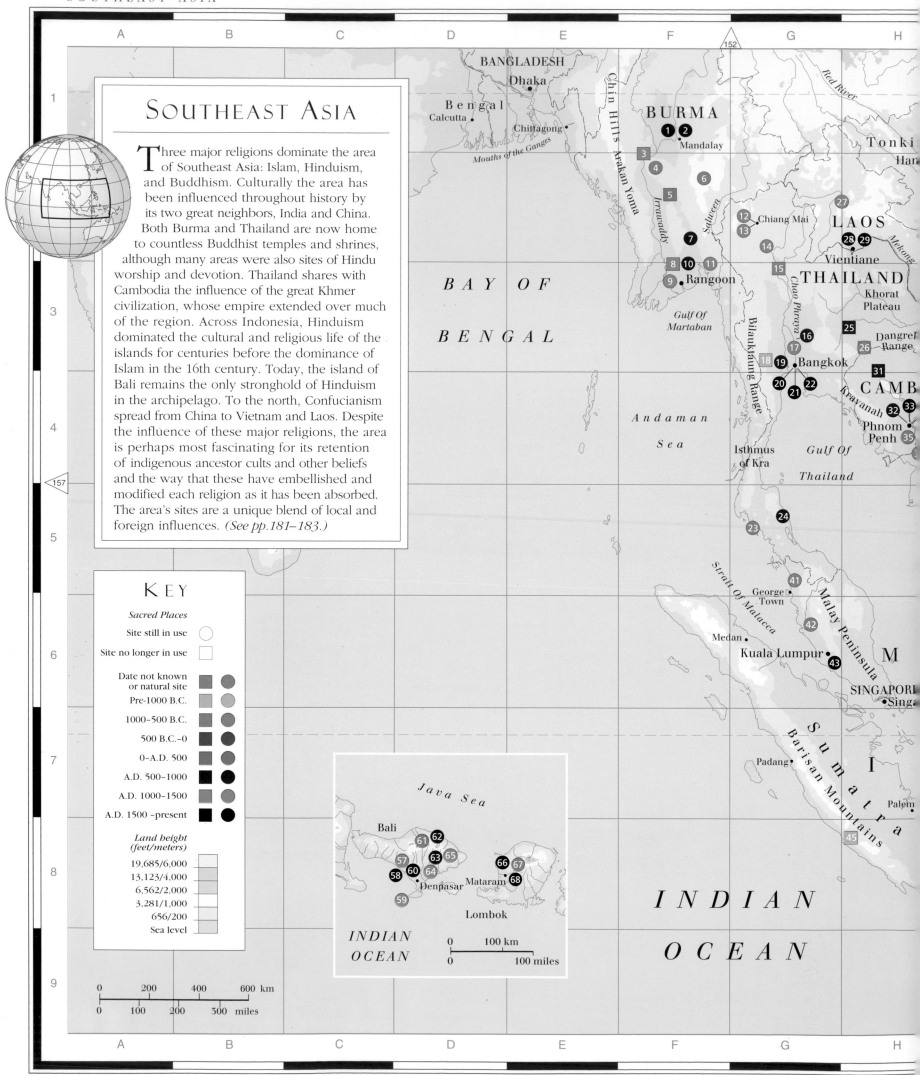

SOUTHEAST ASIA

Three major religions dominate the area of Southeast Asia: Islam, Hinduism, and Buddhism. Culturally the area has been influenced throughout history by its two great neighbors, India and China. Both Burma and Thailand are now home to countless Buddhist temples and shrines, although many areas were also sites of Hindu worship and devotion. Thailand shares with Cambodia the influence of the great Khmer civilization, whose empire extended over much of the region. Across Indonesia, Hinduism dominated the cultural and religious life of the islands for centuries before the dominance of Islam in the 16th century. Today, the island of Bali remains the only stronghold of Hinduism in the archipelago. To the north, Confucianism spread from China to Vietnam and Laos. Despite the influence of these major religions, the area is perhaps most fascinating for its retention of indigenous ancestor cults and other beliefs and the way that these have embellished and modified each religion as it has been absorbed. The area's sites are a unique blend of local and foreign influences. *(See pp.181–183.)*

KEY

Sacred Places

Site still in use ◯

Site no longer in use ☐

Date not known or natural site	◼ ⬤
Pre-1000 B.C.	◼ ⬤
1000–500 B.C.	◼ ⬤
500 B.C.–0	◼ ⬤
0–A.D. 500	◼ ⬤
A.D. 500–1000	◼ ⬤
A.D. 1000–1500	◼ ⬤
A.D. 1500 –present	◼ ⬤

Land height (feet/meters)

19,685/6,000	
13,123/4,000	
6,562/2,000	
3,281/1,000	
656/200	
Sea level	

BANGLADESH

Dhaka

B e n g a l

Calcutta

Chittagong

Mouths of the Ganges

Chin Hills

Arakan Yoma

BURMA

1 2

Mandalay

3

4

6

5

27

Irrawaddy

Salween

12 Chiang Mai

13

LAOS

28 29

Vientiane

14

7

15

THAILAND

Khorat
Plateau

8 10 11

9 Rangoon

Chao Phraya

16

25

Dangr
Range

26

17

Bilauktaung Range

18 19 Bangkok

31

CAMB

20

21 22

Kravanah

32 33

Phnom
Penh

35

Tonki

Red River

Han

Mekong

B A Y   O F

B E N G A L

*Gulf Of
Martaban*

A n d a m a n

S e a

Isthmus
of Kra

Gulf Of

Thailand

24

23

41

George
Town

42

Strait Of Malacca

Medan

Kuala Lumpur

43

Malay Peninsula

M

SINGAPORE

Sing

S u m a t r a

Barisan Mountains

Padang

Palem

45

I N D I A N

O C E A N

Java Sea

Bali

62

61

57

63 65

60

58 64

59

Denpasar

66 67

68

Mataram

Lombok

INDIAN
OCEAN

0   100 km

0   100 miles

I N D I A N

O C E A N

0   200   400   600 km

0   100   200   300 miles

I J K L M N O P

1

HINA

Nanning

Guangzhou

MACAO   HONG KONG

Taiwan Strait

TAIWAN

Tropic of Cancer

PACIFIC

2

r Of

Haikou

Hainan

kin

OCEAN

Da Nang

39 40

3

VIETNAM

Luzon

Manila

PHILIPPINE SEA

Minh City

38

4

PHILIPPINE
ISLANDS

SOUTH CHINA SEA

Palawan

5

Sulu Sea

Mindanao

Davao

PALAU

Sabah

Bandar Seri

BRUNEI   Begawan

Celebes

150

6

AYSIA

44

Sarawak   *Iran Mts*

Sea

Borneo

Schwaner Mts

D   O   N   **E**   **S**   **I**   **A**

Equator

7

Sulawesi

M o l u c c a s

Molucca
Sea

Seram Sea

Irian Jaya   *Maoke Mts*

70

New Guinea

8

Java Sea

arta

andung

49

48   52

51

47   50   53

Surabaya

55

56

54

Lesser Sunda Islands

Bali

Sumbawa

Flores

Arafura Sea

va

Lombok

9

Sumba

69

Timor

Timor Sea

I J K L M N O P

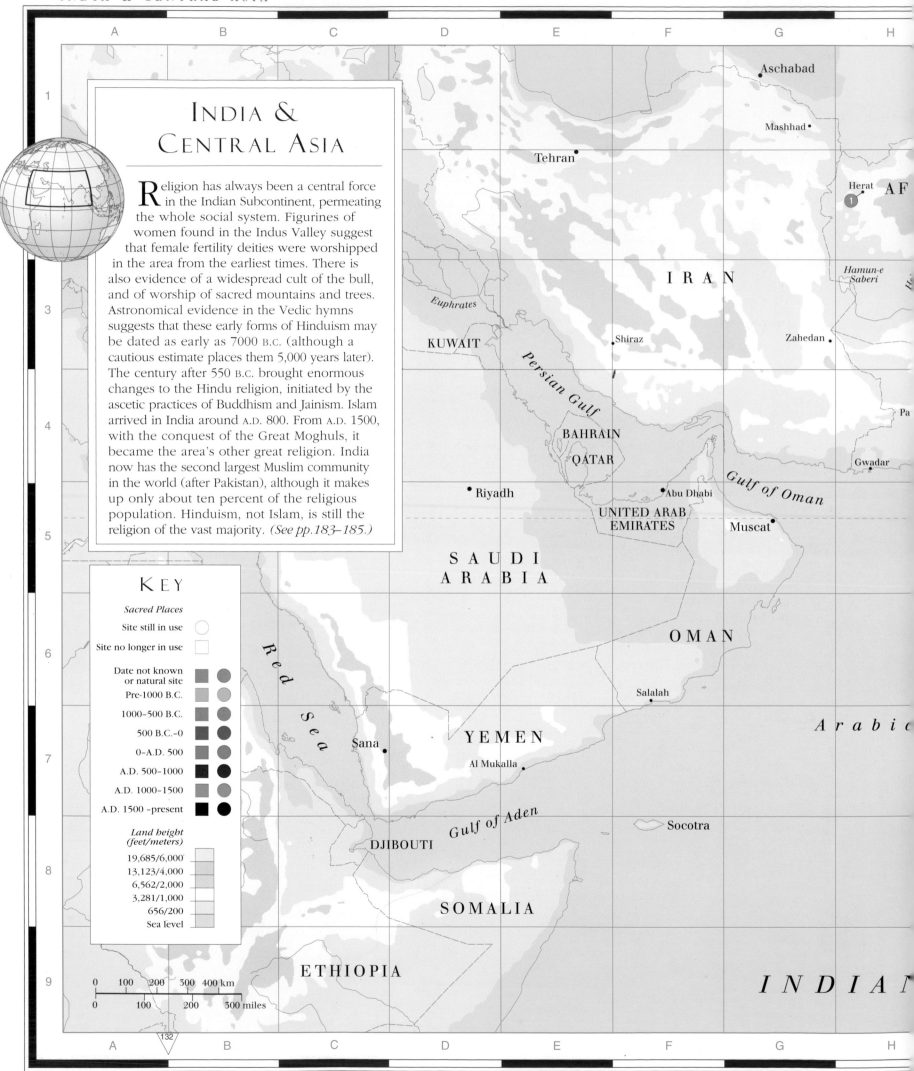

INDIA & CENTRAL ASIA

Religion has always been a central force in the Indian Subcontinent, permeating the whole social system. Figurines of women found in the Indus Valley suggest that female fertility deities were worshipped in the area from the earliest times. There is also evidence of a widespread cult of the bull, and of worship of sacred mountains and trees. Astronomical evidence in the Vedic hymns suggests that these early forms of Hinduism may be dated as early as 7000 B.C. (although a cautious estimate places them 5,000 years later). The century after 550 B.C. brought enormous changes to the Hindu religion, initiated by the ascetic practices of Buddhism and Jainism. Islam arrived in India around A.D. 800. From A.D. 1500, with the conquest of the Great Moghuls, it became the area's other great religion. India now has the second largest Muslim community in the world (after Pakistan), although it makes up only about ten percent of the religious population. Hinduism, not Islam, is still the religion of the vast majority. *(See pp.183–185.)*

KEY

Sacred Places

Site still in use ○

Site no longer in use ☐

Date not known or natural site	◼	●
Pre-1000 B.C.	◼	●
1000–500 B.C.	◼	●
500 B.C.–0	◼	●
0–A.D. 500	◼	●
A.D. 500–1000	◼	●
A.D. 1000–1500	◼	●
A.D. 1500 –present	◼	●

Land height (feet/meters)

19,685/6,000
13,123/4,000
6,562/2,000
3,281/1,000
656/200
Sea level

0   100   200   300   400 km

0   100   200   300 miles

Aschabad

Mashhad

Tehran

Herat

IRAN

Euphrates

Hamun-e
Saberi

KUWAIT

Shiraz

Zahedan

Persian Gulf

BAHRAIN

QATAR

Gwadar

Riyadh

Abu Dhabi

Gulf of Oman

UNITED ARAB
EMIRATES

Muscat

SAUDI
ARABIA

OMAN

Red Sea

Salalah

Arabi

Sana

YEMEN

Al Mukalla

Gulf of Aden

Socotra

DJIBOUTI

SOMALIA

ETHIOPIA

INDIAN

132

156

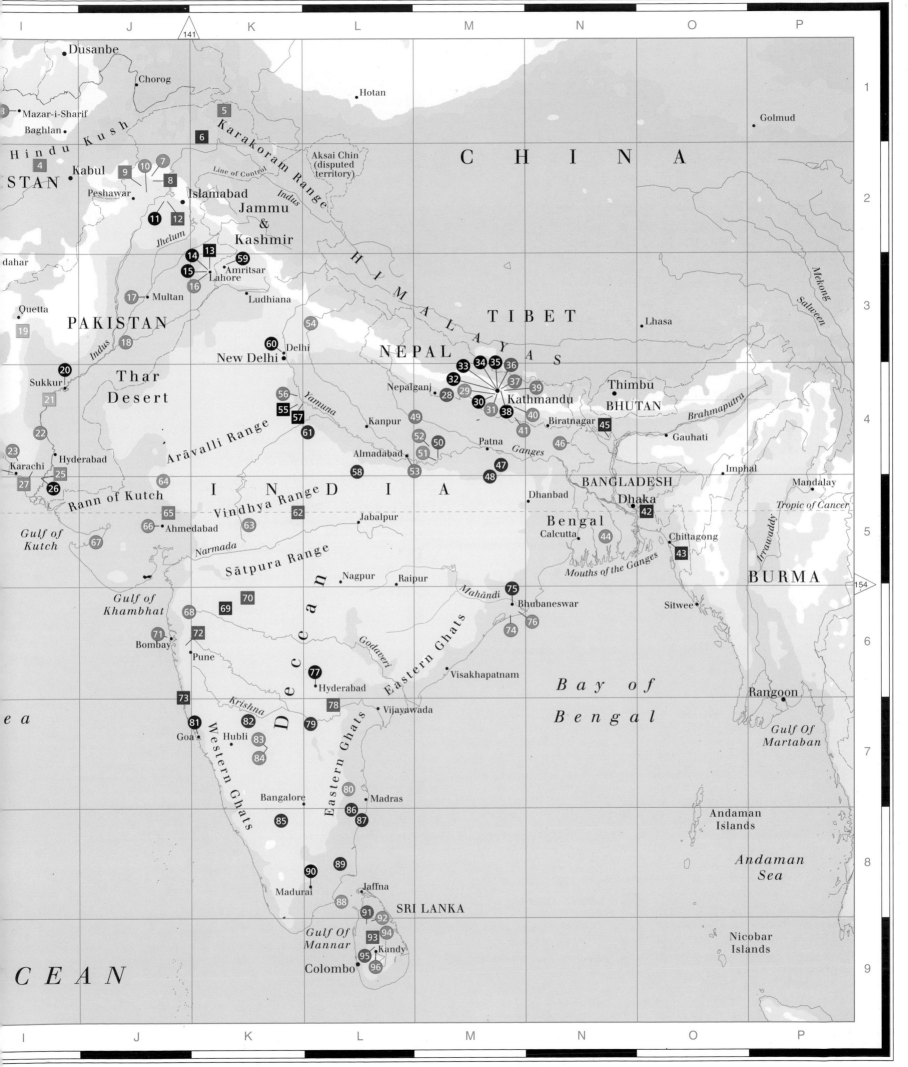

Dusanbe

Chorog

Hotan

C H I N A

Golmud

Mazar-i-Sharif
Baghlan

Karakoram Range

Aksai Chin
(disputed
territory)

5

6

Hindu Kush

Kabul

4

9 10 7
8

Peshawar

Islamabad

**Jammu
&
Kashmir**

Line of Control

Indus

11 12

Jhelum

14 13
15 59
16

Amritsar

Lahore

Ludhiana

17 Multan

Quetta

PAKISTAN

19

Indus

18

54

60 Delhi

New Delhi

H I M A L A Y A S

T I B E T

Lhasa

NEPAL

33 34 35 36
32 37
29 39
28 30 31 38 40
41

Nepalganj

Kathmandu

Thimbu

BHUTAN

Brahmaputra

45

Gauhati

Mekong

Salween

20

Sukkur

21

**Thar
Desert**

56
55 57
61

Yamuna

Arāvalli Range

Kanpur

49

52 50
51

Almadabad

53

58

Patna

46

Ganges

Biratnagar

Imphal

Mandalay

22

23

Karachi

Hyderabad

25
27 26

Rann of Kutch

64

65

66 Ahmedabad

I N D E **D I A** **A**

Vindhya Range

62

63

Jabalpur

Narmada

47

48

BANGLADESH

Dhaka

42

Dhanbad

Bengal

Calcutta

44

Chittagong

43

Mouths of the Ganges

BURMA

Tropic of Cancer

Irrawaddy

*Gulf of
Kutch*

67

Sātpura Range

Nagpur

Raipur

Mahāndi

75

Bhubaneswar

76

74

Sitwee

70

68 69

71

Bombay

72

Pune

Krishna

Godāveri

Eastern Ghats

77

Hyderabad

78

79

Vijayawada

Visakhapatnam

**B a y   o f

B e n g a l**

Rangoon

*Gulf Of
Martaban*

*Gulf of
Khambhat*

D e c c a n

73

81

Goa

82

Hubli

83

84

Western Ghats

Eastern Ghats

80

Bangalore

Madras

85

86
87

89

90

Madurai

88

Jaffna

91 92

93 94

95 96

Kandy

SRI LANKA

*Gulf Of
Mannar*

Colombo

**Andaman
Islands**

*Andaman
Sea*

**Nicobar
Islands**

C E A N

ea

a

1
2
3
4
5
6
7
8
9

141

154

THE LISTINGS

The listings in this section correspond to sites plotted on the maps of the preceding pages (132-157). After each number in the listings a map reference is given. The page number of the relevant map is given under the title of each section.

EGYPT

The map for these listings is on p.133.

● Site still in use

■ Site no longer in use

① N5 MOUNT SINAI (JEBEL MUSA)
NATURAL SITE
LOCATION: Egypt
NOTES: The Sinai Peninsula is the area in which Moses and the Israelites wandered for 40 years. Mount Sinai is the mountain on which Moses saw God in a burning bush, and received the Tablets of the Law containing the Ten Commandments. At the bottom of the mountain is the Greek Orthodox Monastery of St. Catherine, founded in the fourth century A.D. by Empress Helena, mother of Constantine.

② M4 TANIS
2300-0 B.C.
LOCATION: Egypt
NOTES: City where the ancient Israelites were persecuted by the pharaoh and from which they fled, led by Moses. Once one of the largest cities in the Delta area, excavations have revealed sacred lakes, the foundations of temples, and a royal necropolis.

③ L4 TEMPLE OF RA
C. 2400 B.C.
LOCATION: Abu Ghurab, Egypt
NOTES: Several of the pharaohs of the period built temples to the sun god Ra; this is the most famous.

④ L4 MAUSOLEUM OF QA'IT BEY
A.D. 1474
LOCATION: Cairo, Egypt
NOTES: Site of the Mausoleum of Qa'it Bey, the last sultan of the Mamluks, a warrior caste who were dominant from 1250 to the early 16th century.

⑤ L4 MOSQUE OF IBN TULUN FUSTAT
A.D. 879
LOCATION: Fustat, Egypt
NOTES: One of the largest mosques in the world. It once had a magnificent fountain in its inner courtyard for ablutions.

⑥ L4 SULTAN HASAN MOSQUE
A.D. 1546-63
LOCATION: Cairo, Egypt
NOTES: Originally a theological school, this mosque has four vaulted halls surrounding a central court. Construction of this large structure took many years

to complete, and specialists from every part of the Islamic world were enlisted to help in its construction.

⑦ L4 THE PYRAMIDS AND SPHINX
C. 2540-2470 B.C.
LOCATION: Giza, Egypt
NOTES: *See pp.14-15.*

⑧ L5 ABU SIR
2494-2345 B.C.
LOCATION: Egypt
NOTES: Site of a number of rich burials. Four royal pyramids were built here some time between 2565 and 2420 B.C.

⑨ L5 PYRAMIDS OF SAQQARA
C. 3000 B.C.
LOCATION: Saqqara, Egypt
NOTES: *See p.15.*

⑩ L5 BENT PYRAMID AND RED PYRAMID OF SNOFRU
2550 B.C.
LOCATION: Dahshur, Egypt
NOTES: Two pyramids attributed to Snofru, father of Khufu (Cheops). The angle of the Bent Pyramid may have been changed halfway up to avoid the same collapse that had happened to the pyramid at Meidum. This theory, though plausible, is not universally accepted.

⑪ L5 THE COLLAPSED PYRAMID
2600 B.C.
LOCATION: Meidum, Egypt
NOTES: Previously known as the Unfinished Pyramid, not until recently was it established why it remained unfinished – it had fallen down in the last stages of construction, probably with immense loss of life. The ancient Egyptians ascribed it to Snofru (or Snefru). More recent research suggests it was built by Huni, last of the Third-Dynasty Kings.

⑫ L6 ZAWYET EL-AMWAT
2500-2000 B.C.
LOCATION: Egypt
NOTES: Site on the Nile mainly noted for a step pyramid, possibly of the Third Dynasty, and a necropolis of rock-cut tombs from the end of the Old Kingdom, which belonged to ancient Hebenu.

⑬ L6 BENI HASAN TOMBS
C. 2000-1900 B.C.
LOCATION: Egypt
NOTES: A 200-mi (370-km) stretch containing the rock-cut tombs of Beni Hasan. There are 39 tombs. All have impressive wall paintings.

⑭ L6 TELL EL-AMARNA
1353-35 B.C.
LOCATION: Egypt
NOTES: Former religious capital of the rebel pharaoh Akhenaton, who ruled with his wife Queen Nefertiti. He abandoned the polytheistic religion of ancient Egypt and instituted a monotheistic worship of the sun god Aten (also known as Ra). He began building his capital on the east bank of the Nile in about 1370 B.C. – it lasted

only 15 years. After his death, the priests of Karnak regained their ascendancy and persuaded his son-in-law Tutankhamen to re-establish the old religion at Thebes.

⑮ L6 MEIR
2300-1873 B.C.
LOCATION: near el-Qusiya, Egypt
NOTES: Groups of tombs, the most important of which are the rock-cut tombs of the Sixth to 12th Dynasties.

⑯ M7 TEMPLE OF SETY I AND THE OSIREION
1291-79 B.C.
LOCATION: Abydos, Egypt
NOTES: *See p.17.*

⑰ M7 TEMPLE OF HATHOR
30 B.C.-A.D. 14
LOCATION: Dendera, Egypt
NOTES: *See p.17.*

⑱ M7 COLOSSI OF MEMNON
C. 1400 B.C.
LOCATION: Egypt
NOTES: Across the Nile from Thebes and Luxor, remains of temples stretch for over 5 mi (8 km). The area includes the Valley of the Kings. Two great statues known as the Colossi of Memnon – images of Amenhotep III – are all that remains of a great mortuary temple. The northern colossus was shattered in a great earthquake in A.D. 27.

⑲ M7 TEMPLE OF AMUN
2ND MILLENNIUM B.C.
LOCATION: Karnak, Egypt
NOTES: Temple complex, one of the most impressive in Egypt, built over a period of nearly 1,500 years, beginning in the reign of Sesostris I (c. 1980–1935 B.C.).

⑳ M7 LUXOR TEMPLE
1370-1250 B.C.
LOCATION: Egypt
NOTES: *See p.16.*

㉑ M8 ASWAN
C. 700 B.C.
LOCATION: Egypt
NOTES: Old Kingdom rock tombs are on the west bank of the Nile. The Temple of Isis at Philae was built at some point between 380 B.C. and the second century A.D. It is still one of the most perfect Egyptian temples. When the Temple of Isis was threatened by Lake Nasser, created by the Aswan Dam, an international consortium raised money to move it from its original island to the higher island of Algikia.

㉒ M8 TEMPLES OF EL-SEBU'A
2ND MILLENNIUM B.C.
LOCATION: Egypt
NOTES: On the west bank of the Nile, the great temple of Rameses II was moved to a new site farther to the west during the campaign to save the monuments of Nubia from being submerged by the waters of the Aswan Dam. The temple is dedicated to Amun.

㉓ M8 ABU SIMBEL
1290-1224 B.C.
LOCATION: Egypt
NOTES: In the Nubian desert stand the last and greatest of the New Kingdom temples, most of them built under the pharaoh Rameses II. The magnificent facade of the Abu Simbel Temple has four vast colossi cut into the cliff face. Each of them taller than the Colossi of Memnon at Thebes.

AFRICA

The map for these listings is on p.132.

● Site still in use

■ Site no longer in use

① B2 KUTIBAYAH MOSQUE
12TH CENTURY A.D.
LOCATION: Marrakesh, Morocco
NOTES: Mosque built by the Almohad Islamic dynasty. Its vast prayer hall has 17 naves.

② B2 MOULAY IDRISS
9TH CENTURY A.D.
LOCATION: near Meknes, Morocco
NOTES: Town named after the revered saint who brought Islam to the area. It has many shrines and mosques, including the mausoleum of Moulay Idriss himself. A major pilgrimage site.

③ B2 Q'UBBA OF SIDI BEN AISSA
AFTER 1500 A.D.
LOCATION: Meknes, Morocco
NOTES: Sanctuary where one of the most extreme cults in Moroccan history was situated. During one period, the followers would swallow glass and even snakes.

④ B2 VOLUBILIS
2ND-3RD CENTURY A.D.
LOCATION: near Meknes, Morocco
NOTES: Site of Roman ruins, once inhabited by the Carthaginians. Its mixture of peoples practiced Christianity until the advent of Islam.

⑤ B2 QARAWIYYIN MOSQUE
A.D. 859-862
LOCATION: Fez, Morocco
NOTES: The main mosque of the city, it is said to hold up to 20,000 people. The university is considered one of the best centers of religious teaching for Muslims.

⑥ B1 LIXUS
C. A.D. 0-500
LOCATION: near Larache, Morocco
NOTES: Important religious site settled by prehistoric sun worshippers (whose stone circle still exists), the Phoenicians, and the Romans. There are ruins of a Roman temple and sanctuaries.

⑦ C1 TIPASA
C. 2ND-4TH CENTURY A.D.
LOCATION: near Algiers, Algeria
NOTES: Early Christian site until a Vandal invasion; taken over by Muslims in the sixth century A.D. It has the ruins of two Roman temples, a Christian basilica, and a Christian chapel.

⑧ C1 DJEMILA
C. 3RD CENTURY A.D.
LOCATION: Algeria
NOTES: Roman site with several sacred areas. The Temple of Septimien is the largest religious building. A Christian basilica and baptistry were built later. In the center of the old forum is an altar with reliefs of sacrificial animals.

9 D2-3 TASSILI N'AJJER
C. 6000 B.C.
LOCATION: Sahara, Eastern Algeria
NOTES: Site of ritualistic cave paintings drawn by an ancient people of the lakes once found in the area. Over 15,000 examples of art including depictions of human figures with featureless heads.

10 D1 BULLA REGIA
A.D. 0-500
LOCATION: near Jendouba, Tunisia
NOTES: Site of temples to Apollo and Isis, the latter interestingly adapted by the Romans as they extended their pantheon.

11 D1 DOUGGA
C. 400-200 B.C.
LOCATION: Tunisia
NOTES: Roman Temple of Saturn built on the site of a previous pagan temple dedicated to the Carthaginian god Baal. The Temple of Minerva has a couple of megalithic monuments nearby.

12 D1 THUBURBO MAJUS
2ND-3RD CENTURY A.D.
LOCATION: near Tunis, Tunisia
NOTES: Site of a large Roman settlement with a number of temples. The Capitol Temple, the Temple of Mercury, and the sanctuaries of Baal and Caelestis served both Carthaginians and Romans.

13 D1 CARTHAGE
C. 814 B.C.
LOCATION: Tunisia
NOTES: Legendary city, later a decadent Roman site after its destruction in the second century B.C. Remains from many eras can be found here. There are many churches, such as the famous Karita Basilica and the Basilica of St. Cyprian.

14 D1 MAKTAR
2ND CENTURY B.C.
LOCATION: Tunisia
NOTES: Founded by a Numidian king and later Romanized, it once had a temple to the Carthaginian god Hathor Miskar. The fifth-century Basilica of Hildeguns was used for Byzantine burials, and there is also a Roman Temple of Bacchus.

15 D1 QAIROUAN MOSQUE
A.D. 836
LOCATION: Tunisia
NOTES: The foremost Muslim mosque in north Africa, it is also one of the oldest. Built after Muslims conquered the north African coast around the eighth century, it has been restored many times since, though its minaret belongs to the original building.

16 D2 SABRATHA
1ST-2ND CENTURY A.D.
LOCATION: Libya
NOTES: Sacred Roman site, including the Mausoleum of Bes, the South Forum Temple, the fifth-century Basilica of Apuleius, the Antonine Temple, the Temple of Liber Pater (Dionysus), the Temple of Serapis, based on a cult from Memphis in Egypt, and the Capitolium – the temple dedicated to Jupiter.

17 D2 LEPTIS MAGNA
2ND CENTURY A.D.
LOCATION: Libya
NOTES: Once one of the most important centers outside Rome. The Nymphaeum was used for the worship of nymphs, and the Temple of Magna Mater contains an old forum church. The Temples of Liber Pater, Rome, and Augustus, and Jupiter, Serapis, Isis are also found on the site.

18 E2 CYRENE
7TH CENTURY B.C.
LOCATION: Libya
NOTES: Greek site founded by Battus I, whose tomb is here with an altar for animal sacrifice. In the sanctuary of Apollo is a temple and a sacred fountain. Nearby are a necropolis and the Temple of the Three Generals.

19 F3 FARAS
C. 543 A.D.
LOCATION: Nubia, Sudan
NOTES: The original church was partly demolished and converted into a pagan palace. In A.D. 707, it became the foundation of a major cathedral.

20 F3 KERMA
C. 7TH CENTURY B.C.
LOCATION: Sudan
NOTES: Castle containing the royal cemeteries of the kings of Kush as well as elaborately constructed tumuli. There are traces of human sacrifices.

21 F3 TEMPLE OF JEBEL BARKAL
C. 750 B.C.
LOCATION: Sudan
NOTES: Temple sacred to the Meroitic Kingdom. Here, the worship of the sun god Amun was revived.

22 F3 ROYAL NUBIAN CEMETERY
700-300 B.C.
LOCATION: Nuri, Sudan
NOTES: Site with tombs of 19 kings and 53 queens. In the center stands the pyramid of King Taharqa, steeper than the classic Egyptian examples.

23 F3 PYRAMIDS OF MEROE
C. 500 B.C.
LOCATION: Meroë, Sudan
NOTES: Capital of the Nubian kingdom of Kush. After about 670 B.C., it was deeply influenced by Egyptian culture, and pyramids were built over the tombs for kings. They first appeared in Meroë several centuries after pyramid-building had ceased in ancient Egypt.

24 A4 WASSU STONE CIRCLE
C. 9TH CENTURY A.D.
LOCATION: Gambia
NOTES: A burial site that includes a dozen or so standing stones.

25 B4 SINE-SALOUM
C. 8TH CENTURY A.D.
LOCATION: Gambia
NOTES: An area around the River Gambia where over 4,000 megalithic tombs have been discovered filled with grave goods.

26 C3 TIMBUKTU
C. 12TH-16TH CENTURY A.D.
LOCATION: Mali
NOTES: Famed "city of gold" on the River Niger, and the trade, intellectual, and religious center of the Songhai Empire. In the 14th century, Mansa Musa fostered Muslim culture in the town. The Friday Mosque attracted teachers and students of law, logic, and rhetoric. After its capture by Morocco in the late 16th century, its importance faded.

27 B4 JENNE
14TH CENTURY A.D.
LOCATION: Mali
NOTES: *See p.23.*

28 C4 BANDIAGARA
NATURAL SITE
LOCATION: Mali
NOTES: *See p.22.*

29 C4 BREMEAN ROYAL MAUSOLEUM
17TH CENTURY A.D.
LOCATION: Kumasi, Ghana
NOTES: Burial place of the Ashanti kings. Legendary origin of the Ashanti people.

30 C4 LAKE BOSUMTWI
NATURAL SITE
LOCATION: Ghana
NOTES: Sacred to the Ashanti, who believe that their dead souls come here to bid farewell to the god Twi.

31 C4 OSHOGBO
NATURAL SITE
LOCATION: Nigeria
NOTES: Forest containing shrine complexes sacred to the Yoruba. Its main shrine is to the river goddess Oshuno. A sacred river runs through its center.

32 C4 IFE
C. A.D. 1000-1250
LOCATION: Nigeria
NOTES: The original state of Ife expanded into the Oyo empire. In Yoruba creation myth, the "god of the sky," Olokun, lowered the Yoruba founding ancestor, Oduduwa, down to earth at Ife.

33 C4 BENIN
12TH CENTURY A.D.
LOCATION: Nigeria
NOTES: After the foundation of Ife, one of the sacred ruling princes, Oranmiyan, left Ife and went to the neighboring Edo-speaking city state of Benin, thus making the state a sacred center.

34 C4 NOK
C. 4TH CENTURY B.C.
LOCATION: Taruga, Nigeria
NOTES: On the Jos Plateau, 150 beautifully constructed figurines of terracotta have been found. These ritual figurines are mainly seminaturalistic human heads, elephants, and other animals.

35 C4 IGBO UKWU
8TH-9TH CENTURY A.D.
LOCATION: Nigeria
NOTES: Rainforest village in southeast Nigeria where more than 40 ninth-century bronze ritual objects were discovered buried in an underground chamber.

36 D3 THE GREAT MOSQUE
A.D. 1515
LOCATION: Agadez, Niger
NOTES: Later rebuilt in the 19th century, this mosque includes an impressive 81-ft (27-m) high minaret.

37 D4 BOUAR
500 B.C.
LOCATION: Central African Republic
NOTES: A set of tall standing stones believed to indicate a tumulus burial.

38 D6 SANGA
4TH CENTURY A.D.
LOCATION: Lake Kisale, Zaire
NOTES: A necropolis here contained rich burials with heavy cruciform copper ingots, jewelry, and ceremonial items.

39 G4 AXUM
4TH CENTURY A.D.
LOCATION: Ethiopia
NOTES: *See p.19.*

40 F4 SOURCE OF THE BLUE NILE
NATURAL SITE
LOCATION: Ethiopia
NOTES: Considered a holy site by the Ethiopian Orthodox Church. From the source, the stream, then called the Abay, flows down to another sacred site, the Lake Tana.

41 G4 CHURCH OF ST. GEORGE
13TH CENTURY A.D.
LOCATION: Lalibela, Ethiopia
NOTES: *See pp.18-19.*

42 G5 FAKHR AL-DIN
A.D. 1269
LOCATION: Mogadishu, Somalia
NOTES: Mosque with domes constructed in coral concrete.

43 F5 MOUNT KENYA
NATURAL SITE
LOCATION: Kenya
NOTES: Masai, Kikuyu, Kimeru, and Kiembe legends claim that Ngai the one god, creator of all things, dwells on Kirinyaga, the highest point of Mount Kenya. It is believed by the Kiembe that humans were created at the summit of the mountain.

44 F5 HYRAX HILL
BEFORE 1000 B.C.
LOCATION: Rift Valley, Kenya
NOTES: An Iron Age settlement with a number of burial pits containing 19 skeletons, most of them decapitated.

45 G5 MANDA ISLAND
A.D. 1683
LOCATION: Kenya
NOTES: Ruins of a town in which all the houses and huts were aligned toward Mecca. Its mosque dates from 1683.

46 G5 LAMU
AFTER 1500 A.D.
LOCATION: Lamu Island, Kenya
NOTES: Stone-built town, the site of many mosques. A center for Islamic study.

47 G5 SHANGA RUINS
14TH-15TH CENTURY A.D.
LOCATION: north of Lamu Island, Kenya
NOTES: Ruins of a large town with a well-preserved mosque. There are palaces, mosques, and hundreds of tombs.

48 G5 GEDI
14TH CENTURY A.D.
LOCATION: Kenya
NOTES: Ruins of a prosperous Islamic Swahili trading town, probably founded in the 12th century. Many of the ruins remain intact, including a palace, six mosques, and three pillar tombs.

49 G6 KUNDUDHI RUINS
16TH CENTURY A.D.
LOCATION: Dar es Salaam, Tanzania
NOTES: Ruined 16th-century mosque and an 18th-century graveyard, unique for its graves marked with stone obelisks.

50 G6 DOMED MOSQUE OF KILWA
15TH CENTURY A.D.
LOCATION: Kilwa Island, Tanzania
NOTES: One of the most beautiful medieval Swahili mosques, built of coral rock.

51 G6 TONGONI RUINS
16TH CENTURY A.D.
LOCATION: Tanga, Tanzania
NOTES: Site of ruined mosque and large concentration of tombs.

52 F7 INGOMBE ILEDE
14TH CENTURY A.D.
LOCATION: Zambia
NOTES: Later Iron Age site with many graves richly furnished with jewelry, iron hoes, copper ingots, and ornaments.

53 ■ **F7 GREAT ZIMBABWE**
14TH–15TH CENTURY A.D.
LOCATION: Zimbabwe
NOTES: See pp.20–21.

54 ■ **F7 KHAMI RUINS**
15TH CENTURY A.D.
LOCATION: Zimbabwe
NOTES: Founded by migrants from Great
Zimbabwe, the remains of a sacred
king's house can also be found here.

55 ■ **F7 MATOPOS**
BEFORE 1000 B.C.
LOCATION: Bulawayo, Zimbabwe
NOTES: Rock paintings of figures whose
many symbolic shapes and patterns may
be emanations of energy or emotion.

56 ■ **F7 GULUBABWE CAVE**
17TH–19TH CENTURY A.D.
LOCATION: Zimbabwe
NOTES: Cave containing ritual paintings,
one of a multicolored snake with
humans and animals riding on its back.

57 ● **E8 MUKUROB (GOD'S FINGER)**
NATURAL SITE
LOCATION: near Asab, Namibia
NOTES: Strange pillar of rock resembling
a finger pointing to heaven.

58 ● **F7 LAKE FUNDUDZI**
NATURAL SITE
LOCATION: Venda, South Africa
NOTES: Sacred lake of the python god
who holds an important position in
the matriarchal culture of the area.

59 ● **F8 GHOST MOUNTAIN**
NATURAL SITE
LOCATION: Mkuze, South Africa
NOTES: Mountain used as a burial site,
believed to be spiritually powerful.
There is talk of mysterious lights.

60 ● **F8 DRAKENSBERG MOUNTAINS**
7TH CENTURY A.D.
LOCATION: Natal, South Africa
NOTES: Area with large concentration
of Bushman sacred art. Images represent
elements of San mythology, especially
their veneration of the eland antelope.

61 ● **G6 MONT PASSOT**
NATURAL SITE
LOCATION: Nosy-Bé, Madagascar
NOTES: Mountain, site of sacred volcanic
lakes. Also said to be home to the spirits
of Antakarana and Sakalava princes.

62 ■ **G7 IRAVOANDRIANA**
C. 1700 A.D.
LOCATION: Imerina, Madagascar
NOTES: Village with megaliths standing at
the cardinal points. Each house's position
was determined by an astronomer.

63 ■ **G7 ROVA (THE QUEEN'S PALACE)**
A.D. 1873
LOCATION: Antananarivo, Madagascar
NOTES: Palace of Queen Ravalona I, with
mausoleums and sacred houses covering
the tombs of queens and kings.

64 ● **G7 LAC ANIVORANO**
NATURAL SITE
LOCATION: Madagascar
NOTES: Sacred lake, believed to have
once been a semiarid desert until a
thirsty traveler, refused drink by the
locals, flooded the area in revenge.

65 ■ **G7 MAHAFALY TOMBS**
C. A.D. 1800
LOCATION: Betioky, Madagascar
NOTES: Site of painted ancestor tombs.

MIDDLE EAST

The map for these listings is on p.134.

● Site still in use
■ Site no longer in use

1 ■ **F3 JAMI'AT ZAKARIYYA**
A.D. 1090
LOCATION: Aleppo (modern Halab), Syria
NOTES: Great Mosque reputed to hold
the head of Zacharia, John the Baptist's
father, after whom the mosque is named.

2 ■ **F3 QAL'AT SAMAAN**
5TH CENTURY A.D.
LOCATION: Syria
NOTES: Early Christian martyr St. Simon
Stylites (St. Simeon) sat on top of a
pillar for 36 years, with an iron collar
around his neck to stop him from falling.
Fed by monks, he celebrated mass on
his pillar twice a week. He died in
A.D. 459. Four basilicas were built around
the pillar in the shape of a cross. It was
an early site of Christian pilgrimage.

3 ■ **E6 MOSQUE OF 'UMAR**
A.D. 720
LOCATION: Bosra, Syria
NOTES: Formerly a monastery, built in
the fourth century, where Muhammad
is said to have met the monk Buhayra.
One of the oldest mosques in the world.

4 ■ **E4 CRAC DES CHEVALIERS**
A.D. 1150–1250
LOCATION: Qal'at al-Hisn, Syria
NOTES: Castle of the Knights, a vast
crusader castle that served as a base,
for, among others, Richard Lion-Heart.
The religious part of the structure is the
small chapel, converted into a mosque
after the Muslim conquest of 1271.

5 ■ **E5 UMAYYAD MOSQUE**
8TH CENTURY B.C.
LOCATION: Damascus, Syria
NOTES: Temple built by the Aramaeans
to their god Hada. A temple to Jupiter
was built on the same site by the Romans
in the third century A.D. and a Christian
church dedicated to John the Baptist was
built in the fourth century. In 636, the
eastern part became a mosque. Another
mosque was built in 705, said to contain
the head of John the Baptist.

6 ■ **E5 KANISAT HANANYA**
1ST CENTURY A.D.
LOCATION: Syria
NOTES: Old cellar of the house of Ananias,
an early Christian disciple who restored
the sight of Saul of Tarsus (St. Paul).

7 ● **F4 PALMYRA**
2ND CENTURY A.D.
LOCATION: Syria
NOTES: See p.27.

8 ● **E4 TARTUS**
4TH CENTURY A.D.
LOCATION: Syria
NOTES: Twelfth-century cathedral built

on the site of a chapel devoted to
the Virgin Mary. The altar and icon
had been objects of pilgrimage for
the crusaders since the fourth century.

9 ■ **E3 RAS SHAMRA (UGARIT)**
16TH CENTURY B.C.
LOCATION: near Lattakia, Syria
NOTES: Once the most important city on
the Mediterranean coast; offerings were
sent from Egypt to the Temple of Baal,
storm god and chief god of Canaanites,
Phoenicians, and Aramaeans. Another
temple on the site was dedicated to
Dagon, father of Baal, associated with
fertility of crops. Destroyed by the
Philistines in the 12th century B.C.

10 ■ **D5 TELL AL-MA'SHUK (HILL OF THE BELOVED)**
9TH CENTURY B.C.
LOCATION: Tyre, Lebanon
NOTES: Phoenician temple dedicated to
Melqart (Bel-Shamin of the Starry Tunic
– the starry tunic was the sky). The
Greeks called Melqart Heracles and built
a temple to him on top of the earlier site.

11 ■ **E5 BAALBECK**
4TH CENTURY B.C.
LOCATION: Lebanon
NOTES: Reputedly founded by Cain after
Jehovah banished him. Astarte, El, and
Baal were worshipped here; there was
also an oracle. The Greeks called the
town Heliopolis, "city of the sun" (Baal
was the sun god) and changed the gods'
names to Zeus, Aphrodite, and Hermes.
The Romans in turn worshipped Jupiter,
Venus, and Mercury here, and it is the
three temples to these gods that survive;
that to Venus is the most complete
Roman temple remaining in the world.

12 ■ **D5 BYBLOS (JBAIL)**
2800 B.C.
LOCATION: Lebanon
NOTES: The Egyptians called it "God's
Country." The Phoenicians called it Jbail,
meaning "little mountain." The Greek
name Byblos means "paper" (it was a
major producer of papyrus). A partner
in the cedar trade with the Egyptians,
the chief goddess of the city, Baalat
(the Lady) was also worshipped in
Egypt. Her temple, built in 2800 B.C.,
was followed 100 years later by one to
Baal. There is a sacred pool to Astarte
and another temple to Reshef (Egyptian
name for the Amorite sun god Amurru)
consisting of stone obelisks, onee
containing bronze statuettes covered
in gold leaf.

13 ● **D7 JERUSALEM**
1800 B.C.
LOCATION: Israel
NOTES: See pp.24–25.

14 ■ **D7 MASADA**
1ST CENTURY A.D.
LOCATION: Israel
NOTES: See p.25.

15 ■ **D6 MEGIDDO**
4000 B.C.
LOCATION: Israel
NOTES: Site of the biblical Armageddon,
mentioned in the Book of Revelation
where the final battle between good
and evil will be fought. The word
Armageddon comes from the Hebrew
Har Megiddo (Mount of Megiddo).
Originally inhabited about 4000 B.C.,
Megiddo was captured by the Egyptians
and was also part of Solomon's kingdom.
It fell into disuse around 1200 B.C.

16 ● **D7 BETHLEHEM**
14TH CENTURY B.C.
LOCATION: West Bank
NOTES: Birthplace of Christ and King
David. Burial place of the matriarch
Rachel. Sacred to both Christians and
Jews, it is a major pilgrimage site. After
Christ's death, the town became a center
for paganism until the dedication of its
first Christian church in A.D. 339.

17 ■ **D7 QUMRA'N**
1ST CENTURY A.D.
LOCATION: West Bank
NOTES: Site where the first of the Dead
Sea Scrolls were discovered in 1947 by
a Bedouin shepherd. One of the most
important archaeological finds in history,
the 400 manuscripts contained almost
the entire Old Testament, various
psalms, other sectarian writings, and
legal documents. The caves were
inhabited by a Jewish sect, the Essenes,
who studied the scriptures and lived
apart from the Jewish establishment.
The Scrolls have been crucial in
establishing the history of Palestine
between the fourth century B.C. and
the first century A.D., and the relationship
of the Christian and Jewish traditions.

18 ● **D7 BETHANY**
1ST CENTURY A.D.
LOCATION: Israel
NOTES: Site of the Raising of Lazarus,
of the anointment of Christ with oil,
and of Christ's ascension.

19 ■ **D7 EMMAUS**
1ST CENTURY A.D.
LOCATION: Israel
NOTES: On the road between modern
Tel Aviv and Jerusalem, the site where
Christ appeared after his resurrection.

20 ● **D7 MOUNT OF TEMPTATION**
NATURAL SITE
LOCATION: West Bank
NOTES: Site of Christ's 40-day fast in
the desert and temptation by the Devil.
There is a stone here on which Christ
allegedly sat while he refused to turn
stones into bread, and a monastery built
around the cave, the site of his fast.

21 ● **D6 MOUNT TABOR**
NATURAL SITE
LOCATION: Israel
NOTES: Traditional site of Christ's
transfiguration, where he was seen with
the prophets Elijah and Moses. Its capture
by Muslims in 1187 led to the Third
Crusade. On the summit is a Franciscan
monastery, a Greek Orthodox church,
and remains of a Byzantine monastery.

22 ● **D6 SEA OF GALILEE**
NATURAL SITE
LOCATION: Israel
NOTES: Place where Christ is said to have
walked on water. Here, he taught from
Peter's boat and calmed the storm. His
disciples made a miraculous catch of fish.

23 ● **D6 TABGHA AND THE MOUNT OF THE BEATITUDES**
NATURAL SITE
LOCATION: Israel
NOTES: Site where Christ is alleged to
have fed 5,000 people with five loaves
and two fish, and where he later
conferred the leadership of the Christian
Church on St. Peter. Churches on the
site commemorate both events. The
Mount of the Beatitudes is the place
where Christ delivered his Sermon
on the Mount.

24 D6 CANA
1ST CENTURY A.D.
LOCATION: modern Kafer Kanna, Israel
NOTES: Site of Christ's first miracle, in which he turned water into wine.

25 D6 NAZARETH
1ST CENTURY A.D.
LOCATION: Israel
NOTES: Capital of Galilee during Herod's reign and home to Mary and Joseph before the birth of Jesus. The town remained Christian until the third century and became a pilgrimage site again in the sixth century.

26 D6 SEPPHORIS
1ST CENTURY A.D.
LOCATION: Tzipori, Israel
NOTES: The capital of Galilee in Herod's time was the traditional home of Joachim and Anna and birthplace of Mary.

27 D6 CAPERNAUM
13TH CENTURY B.C.
LOCATION: Israel
NOTES: Birthplace of St. Peter and the starting point of Christ's ministry. Also said to be the burial place of the Jewish prophet Nahum. Capernaum is a Greek rendering of the Hebrew *Kefar Nahum* (village of Nahum).

28 D5-6 DAN
1200 B.C.
LOCATION: Israel
NOTES: Ancient Leshem or Laish, cult center for the northern tribes of Israel. "From Dan to Beersheba" described the limits of the kingdom of Israel. Jeroboam set up a golden calf here.

29 E5 PANIAS
3RD–4TH CENTURY B.C.
LOCATION: Israel
NOTES: Named after Pan, a goat-footed Greek god, it was originally a Phoenician settlement. Renamed Caesarea Philippi by the Romans, it was here that Peter identified Christ as the Messiah and converted the first gentile to Christianity, a centurion called Cornelius.

30 D7 TOMB OF THE PATRIARCHS
2000 B.C.
LOCATION: Hebron, West Bank
NOTES: Site of David's capital before Jerusalem. At Hebron, God made his covenant with Abraham that he would be the father of the Chosen People. It is the burial place of Abraham, Isaac and his wife Rebecca, and Jacob and his wife Leah. The Cave of Machpelah and the Tomb of the Patriarchs are very important sites for Jews, Christians, and Muslims. According to tradition, God told Abraham that Adam and Eve had been buried here.

31 D7 BETH ARABAH
1ST CENTURY A.D.
LOCATION: River Jordan, West Bank/Jordan
NOTES: Frequently mentioned in both Old and New Testaments; the site of Christ's baptism by John the Baptist.

32 D6 SEBASTIYA
876 B.C.
LOCATION: Israel
NOTES: Burial place of the head of John the Baptist, it is also the former site of a ninth-century B.C. Israelite city. It passed through Assyrian, Persian, Greek, and Roman hands, falling to Herod in 30 B.C. Also believed to be the burial place of the Old Testament prophets Obadiah and Elisha.

33 D7 JERICHO
6000 B.C.
LOCATION: West Bank
NOTES: Considered both the oldest city on earth and the farthest below sea level. Traces of hunters at the site date to 9000 B.C. Around 6000 B.C., the skulls of ancestors were set into the walls of the city and venerated in a form of ancestor worship. In the Old Testament, it was the first town attacked by the Israelites after crossing the River Jordan. To storm the city, they blew their trumpets and the walls fell down.

34 D6-7 ALA-SAFAT
BEFORE 1000 B.C.
LOCATION: West Bank
NOTES: Neolithic cemetery that measures 2½ mi (4 km) by 1¼ mi (2 km). It includes over 200 burials, including 164 chamber tombs.

35 D8 PETRA
4TH CENTURY B.C.
LOCATION: Jordan
NOTES: *See p.26.*

36 E6 JERASH
2ND CENTURY A.D.
LOCATION: Jordan
NOTES: Site of the Temple of Zeus built by the Greeks; its lower level included a holy sacrificial altar. Jerash also contains the remains of the Temple of Artemis, patron goddess of the city. Its materials were used for 13 Christian churches built here in the sixth century.

37 E7 CHURCH OF ST. GEORGE
560 A.D.
LOCATION: Madaba, Jordan
NOTES: Greek Orthodox church containing mosaic map of Palestine and Lower Egypt, with a plan of Jerusalem showing the Church of the Holy Sepulchre.

38 E7 MOUNT NEBO
NATURAL SITE
LOCATION: Jordan
NOTES: One of the three peaks on Mount Nebo, Siyagha is supposedly the site of the tomb of Moses. The mountain includes the ruins of a fourth-century church and a later sixth-century Byzantine church and monastery.

WESTERN ASIA
The map for these listings is on p.135.

● Site still in use
■ Site no longer in use

1 J8 MECCA
7TH CENTURY A.D.
LOCATION: Saudi Arabia
NOTES: *See pp.28-29.*

2 J7 MEDINA
7TH CENTURY A.D.
LOCATION: Saudi Arabia
NOTES: Holy city (*madinat-al-nabi* means City of the Prophet) that formed the earliest base of the Muslim faith. A mosque is built on the site where Muhammad and his family were said to have settled. An important pilgrimage center, it is the second most sacred Muslim site after Mecca.

3 I6 MADAIN SALAH
1ST CENTURY B.C.–1ST CENTURY A.D.
LOCATION: Saudi Arabia
NOTES: Most important Nabataean city after Petra, the site of rock-cut tombs.

4 L5 TEL SA'AD
14TH CENTURY B.C.
LOCATION: Failaka Island, Kuwait
NOTES: Site with remains of a temple to Anzak, the main Dilmun god. The ancient Greeks built a temple to Artemis here.

5 L9 FRIDAY MOSQUE
A.D. 904
LOCATION: Shibam, Yemen
NOTES: Built by Caliph Harun ar-Rashid on the site of an earlier mosque.

6 K9 GREAT MOSQUE OF SAN'A
A.D. 630
LOCATION: San'a, Yemen
NOTES: Built during Muhammad's lifetime, two years after Islam arrived in Yemen.

7 K9 GREAT MOSQUE OF SA'DA
12TH CENTURY A.D.
LOCATION: Sa'da, Yemen
NOTES: Burial place of Imam Yahya, founder of Zaydism, a Shiite sect that followed the leadership of Zayd, one of Muhammad's direct descendants.

8 K9 TEMPLES OF SUN AND MOON
400 B.C.
LOCATION: Ma'rib, Yemen
NOTES: Both temples are named after a Saban queen.

9 L6 AD-DIRAZ TEMPLE
2ND MILLENNIUM B.C.
LOCATION: near Qal'at Al-Bahrain, Bahrain
NOTES: Dilmun temple with an altar; there is evidence of sacrifice here.

10 L6 BARABAR TEMPLES
3RD–2ND MILLENNIUM B.C.
LOCATION: near Qal'at Al-Bahrain, Bahrain
NOTES: Three megalithic temples, one dedicated to Dilmun god of wisdom Enki.

11 L6 TREE OF LIFE
NATURAL SITE
LOCATION: Bahrain
NOTES: Tree fed by an underground spring and the alleged site of the Garden of Eden. Its exact location is uncertain.

12 L6 A'ALI BURIAL MOUNDS
3RD MILLENNIUM B.C.
LOCATION: Bahrain
NOTES: Bahrain has 85,000 burial mounds dating from 2800 B.C. to the arrival of Islam in the seventh century A.D. This is the site of the royal tombs.

13 K4 BABYLON
EARLY 2ND MILLENNIUM B.C.
LOCATION: Iraq
NOTES: *See p.30.*

14 K5 UR
4TH MILLENNIUM B.C.
LOCATION: Iraq
NOTES: *See p.31.*

15 K3 NINEVEH
7TH CENTURY B.C.
LOCATION: Iraq
NOTES: *See p.30.*

16 K4 SAMARRA
A.D.836-83
LOCATION: Iraq
NOTES: This 'Abbasid capital is famous for its Great Mosque, the largest in Islam.

17 K4 KAZIMAYN MOSQUE
A.D. 1515
LOCATION: Baghdad, Iraq
NOTES: The third most important mosque in Iraq after Kerbela' and Najaf. Contains the shrines of the two imams, Musa al-Kazim and Muhammad al-Jawad.

18 K4 KERBELA'
7TH CENTURY A.D.
LOCATION: Iraq
NOTES: Site of battle in A.D. 680 in which Husayn, son of Muhammad's cousin and son-in-law 'Ali ibn Abi Talib, was killed. Shiite Muslims mourn his death here each year, re-enacting his assassination.

19 K4 NAJAF
A.D. 791
LOCATION: Iraq
NOTES: Mosque containing the tomb of 'Ali ibn Abi Talib, cousin and son-in-law of Muhammad and first Imam of Shiite Islam. It is an honor for a Muslim to be buried here. The town is full of shrines.

20 J3 MOSQUE OF NABI YUNUS
12TH CENTURY A.D.
LOCATION: Mosul, Iraq
NOTES: Supposed burial place of Jonah. The mosque housing the shrine is built over older – probably Assyrian – ruins.

21 J3 HATRA
250 B.C.–A.D. 250
LOCATION: Iraq
NOTES: Ancient Parthian city with a temple precinct, a religious center for nomadic Arab tribes. There were temples to a trinity of deities: father, mother, and son.

22 K5 URUK
5TH MILLENNIUM B.C.E
LOCATION: modern Tall al-Warka, Iraq
NOTES: Ancient Mesopotamian site. In myth, the walls were built by the hero Gilgamesh. The White Temple, which stood atop the ziggurat was dedicated to Anu, a sky god. The other ziggurat was dedicated to Inanna, goddess of love and war and Queen of the Sky.

23 K4 NIPPUR
5TH MILLENNIUM B.C.
LOCATION: modern Nuffar, Iraq
NOTES: According to Sumerian myth, earth and heaven were separated here during the creation. Enlil, leader of the gods, made a hole in the earth from which humankind sprang. The religious right to rule was bestowed on kings here.

24 K3 ASHUR
2500 B.C.
LOCATION: modern Qal'at Sharqat, Iraq
NOTES: Religious capital of the Assyrian Empire and site of 34 temples. Principal temples were to Enlil (also called Ashur) and Inanna (Ishtar). Enlil was later identified with the city's protection and its people's political ambitions.

25 M3 KELISA-YE HAZRAT-E SARKIS
A.D. 1964–70
LOCATION: Tehran, Iran
NOTES: Armenian cathedral and a place of pilgrimage; the most important non-Islamic religious building in Tehran.

26 L4 QUM
9TH CENTURY A.D.
LOCATION: Iran
NOTES: Holy city, center of Shiism. Burial place of Fatima, sister of Imam 'Ali Reza, and site of the Astana shrine complex built by Safavid sultans.

27 L4 SUSA
4TH MILLENNIUM B.C.
LOCATION: Iran
NOTES: Prehistoric settlement, later the Achaemenid capital captured by the Assyrians in the seventh century B.C. For centuries a place of Jewish learning. The tomb of the prophet Daniel is here.

28 L5 CHOGHA ZAMBIL
13TH CENTURY B.C.
LOCATION: Iran
NOTES: Ziggurat that functioned as a sacred mountain, surrounded by 11 temples dedicated to various deities. A medieval religious center, it is now chief pilgrimage site for the Elamites.

29 M5 PERSEPOLIS
5TH CENTURY B.C.
LOCATION: Takht-i Jamshid, Iran
NOTES: Great festival city built by Darius. The rock-face houses rock-cut tombs of Darius and other Achaemenid kings.

30 K3 FORTIFIED FIRE TEMPLE
3RD CENTURY A.D.
LOCATION: Takht-i Sulaiman, Iran
NOTES: Site of Atur Gushnap, sacred fire of the warriors, believed to be the birthplace of Zoroaster. An important religious complex stood here during the Sassanian period (A.D. 226–642).

31 M4 MASJID-I IMAN
A.D. 1638
LOCATION: Isfahan, Iran
NOTES: Remarkable mosque covered in pale blue tiles that took 26 years to build, based on the mosque at Mashhad.

32 M4 KELISA-YE HAZRAT-E LUGHA
20TH CENTURY A.D.
LOCATION: Isfahan, Iran
NOTES: Church of St. Luke, head of the Episcopal Church of Iran.

33 K2 KELISA-YE VANK
A.D. 1655–64
LOCATION: Jolfa, Iran
NOTES: Armenian Cathedral, precursor of the Armenian Church in Tehran.

34 K2 KELISA DARRE SHAM
14TH CENTURY A.D.
LOCATION: Jolfa, Iran
NOTES: Church of St. Stephanos, an Armenian monastery allegedly founded by St. Bartholemew in the first century.

35 M4 ATESHKADE
A.D. 470
LOCATION: Yazd, Iran
NOTES: Ancient fire temple, the flame has allegedly been kept burning since the fifth century. A major site of pilgrimage for the 12,000 Zoroastrians who live in the area.

36 M4 MAGHBARE-YE DAVAZDAH EMAM
11TH CENTURY A.D.
LOCATION: Yazd, Iran
NOTES: Site of the tomb of the 12th Imam.

37 M3 MASJID-I TANKHURE
A.D. 0–500
LOCATION: Semnan, Iran
NOTES: Pre-Islamic site with one of the oldest functioning mosques in Iran, restored in the 11th century.

38 O3 HARAM-E MOTAHHAR-E EMAM REZA
9TH CENTURY A.D.
LOCATION: Mashhad, Iran
NOTES: Shrine of Imam 'Ali Riza who died here in A.D. 817. Mashhad is the main Shiite pilgrimage center in Iran.

39 O3 MASJID-I AZIME GOHAR SHAD
EARLY 15TH CENTURY A.D.
LOCATION: Mashhad, Iran
NOTES: Built for Empress Gohar Shad, wife of Tamerlane's eldest son Shah Rokh and a unique patron of the arts.

40 N3 BOGH'E-YE KHAJE GHADAMGAH (PLACE OF THE FOOT)
17TH CENTURY A.D.
LOCATION: near Nishapur, Iran
NOTES: Named after a stone slab containing footprints of Imam Riza. A place of pilgrimage for Muslims.

41 M5 BOGH'E-YE SHAH-E CHERAGH
9TH CENTURY A.D.
LOCATION: Shiraz, Iran
NOTES: Site of a congregational mosque and the mausoleum of Sayyed Mir Ahmad, brother of Imam Riza. Shiraz is a major Shiite pilgrimage center.

42 M5 KUH-E KHAJE
5TH CENTURY A.D.
LOCATION: Iran
NOTES: Early Sassanian island complex with a palace and Zoroastrian fire temple.

43 M5 MASJID-I JAME-E ATIGH
9TH CENTURY A.D.
LOCATION: Shiraz, Iran
NOTES: Ancient mosque, the Khodakane or "House of God," was a repository for Qur'ans. Rebuilt in the 14th century.

44 K3 GHARA KELISA
1ST CENTURY A.D.
LOCATION: Orumiyé, Iran
NOTES: The Church of St. Thaddeus, a disciple of Christ; its name, the Black Church, refers to an earlier structure.

45 N5 MAHAN
15TH CENTURY A.D.
LOCATION: Iran
NOTES: Community formed by Sufi poet and mystic, Shah Ni'matullah Wali. His tomb is the hub of a religious complex.

THE MEDITERRANEAN, GREECE, & TURKEY

The map for these listings is on pp.136–137.

● Site still in use
■ Site no longer in use

1 B6 GGANTIJA TEMPLES
3500–2500 B.C.
LOCATION: Gozo, Malta
NOTES: See p.39.

2 B6 BROCHTORFF CIRCLE
C. 3000 B.C.
LOCATION: Gozo, Malta
NOTES: Neolithic rock-cut tomb complex, with twin chambers containing the crushed bones of 60 human burials. Underground caves were uncovered full of niches and caverns also filled with burials. In a central shrine was a cache of idols, including a stone pig's head with tusks, a carved human head on a pillar base, and a small bag of red ocher. Twin-seated obese goddesses carved into limestone and a large stone jar that once contained a liquid for burial rituals were placed on an altar. Burials were mainly of women and babies.

3 B6 MGARR
C. 2000 B.C.
LOCATION: Gozo, Malta
NOTES: Impressive megalithic monument, consisting of a temple tomb with a central passage, from which transepts with apsidal chambers open out. A Neolithic model of the temple was found at the site. Also a triangular stone, probably used as an anchor and dedicated to the mother goddess after a successful voyage or escape from shipwreck.

4 B6 HAL SAFLIENI
C. 2000 B.C.
LOCATION: near Valletta, Malta
NOTES: Part-temple, part-tomb cut into soft rock, remains of skulls and bones indicate that over 7,000 Neolithic people were buried. The site was dedicated to a cult of fertility and the dead. Small clay figurines have also been found.

5 B6 TARXIEN
C. 2000 B.C.
LOCATION: near Valletta, Malta
NOTES: Megalithic temples where excavations revealed a giant statue of a temple goddess wearing a pleated skirt, broken at the waist but originally about 10 ft (3 m) high. In the apse of one of the southern temples stood a large altar and a stone block decorated with running spirals. In front of this was a cupboard, where a sacrificial flint knife was found. On top of the block was a stone niche with a porthole slab, which may have contained a perishable image. A cremation cemetery existed here in about 1400 B.C.

6 B6 TAS SILG
6TH–2ND CENTURY B.C.
LOCATION: Valletta, Malta
NOTES: Inscriptions were found here to the Phoenician goddess Astarte and many plates inscribed to her and Carthaginian goddess Tanit. The sanctuary included a sacrificial area, where remains of offerings were found. However, in origin, Tas Silg is a prehistoric shrine linked to the Carthaginian phase of Malta's history. The site was later used in Roman and Byzantine times.

7 F3 MOUNT ATHOS
NATURAL SITE
LOCATION: Halkidikai Peninsula, Greece
NOTES: Holy mountain, site of various Byzantine monasteries. The first was founded in A.D. 961 by St. Athanasius.

8 F4 MOUNT PARNASSUS
NATURAL SITE
LOCATION: Greece
NOTES: Holy mountain once sacred to Apollo, Dionysus, and the Muses.

9 E4 DELPHI
6TH CENTURY B.C.
LOCATION: Greece
NOTES: See p.42.

10 F4 ERETRIA
400 B.C.
LOCATION: Euboea, Greece
NOTES: Major archaeological site, with the remains of a palace, a temple, and a theater with a subterranean passage. In the center of the town lie remains of the Temple of Dafniforos Apollo.

11 F5 RHAMNOUS
5TH CENTURY B.C.
LOCATION: Attica, Greece
NOTES: Ancient fortress-town to the north of Marathon, where the Greeks fought against overwhelming odds in 490 B.C., and wiped out 6,000 Persians. Among the ruins is the Doric Temple of Nemesis, the goddess of retribution and mother of Helen of Troy. Nearby are ruins of a smaller fifth-century temple dedicated to Themis, goddess of justice.

12 F5 DAPHNI MONASTERY
C. 11TH CENTURY A.D.
LOCATION: Attica, Greece
NOTES: One of the greatest monuments of Greece's Byzantine period built on the Sacred Way from Athens to Eleusis, and covering the site of a sanctuary to Apollo (daphne laurels were sacred). The Christos Pantocrator (Christ in Majesty) in the dome of the church is regarded as a masterpiece of Byzantine art.

13 F5 ELEUSIS
C. 10TH CENTURY B.C.
LOCATION: Athens, Greece
NOTES: One of the great ancient Greek mystery sites dedicated to the cult of Demeter, mother of Persephone. The ruins of the Sanctuary of Demeter, and the Sacred Way were once the site of one of the world's greatest mystery religions ("mystery" derived from the fact that its rituals were a secret, whose disclosure was punished by death). It flourished from 1000 B.C. to A.D. 400.

14 F5 THE ACROPOLIS
447–438 B.C.
LOCATION: Athens, Greece
NOTES: Once a town in itself, undoubtedly the most remarkable site in Greece. Its buildings were burned by the Persians in 480 B.C. Pericles recreated the

Acropolis as we know it. The Parthenon ("Parthenos" means virgin) was dedicated to Athena, goddess of war, the Erectheon to Erectheus, mythical king of Athens. The nearby Temple of Hephaestus, the blacksmith god (the Roman god Vulcan), is the best-preserved Doric temple in Greece, and was once surrounded by foundries and metal workshops.

15 E5 OLYMPIA
C. 5TH CENTURY B.C.
LOCATION: Greece
NOTES: See p.43.

16 E5 TEMPLE OF APOLLO
420 B.C.
LOCATION: Bassae, Arcadia, Greece
NOTES: Perhaps the most isolated temple in Greece. Designed by the architect of the Parthenon, it was dedicated to Apollo Epikiouros by the villagers of Phigalia in return for deliverance from pestilence.

17 F5 EPIDAURUS
C. 600 B.C.–C. 5TH CENTURY A.D.
LOCATION: Greece
NOTES: Temple-sanctuary dedicated to the god of medicine Asclepius. Those in need of healing came from all over the Mediterranean. A *kategogeion* (a two-story hostelry for sanctuary visitors) was built in the fourth century B.C. The priests urged the pilgrims to think positively, in accord with the Greek belief in the power of mind over body.

18 F5 MYCENAE
1500–1100 B.C.
LOCATION: Greece
NOTES: See pp.40–41.

19 F5 CORINTH
C. 5TH CENTURY B.C.
LOCATION: Greece
NOTES: Business center of ancient Greece. The most striking ruin here is the Temple of Apollo. But in the fortress Acrocorinth overlooking the city, the Temple of Aphrodite surmounts the higher of its two summits. St. Paul objected to its trade in temple prostitutes – male and female – but his preaching had little effect.

20 F5 TEMPLE OF POSEIDON
444 B.C.
LOCATION: Cape Sounion, Greece
NOTES: Built on a spur overlooking the sea. Byron referred to it as Sunium, and carved his name on one of the columns.

21 G5 PAROIKIA
NATURAL SITE
LOCATION: Paros, Greece
NOTES: Site of the spectacular Church of Ekatontapyliani (Our Lady of the Hundred Gates). The complex includes three churches. There are in fact only 99 doors or gates; a legend relates that when the hundredth gate is found, Constantinople will return to Greece.

22 G6 SANTORINI
NATURAL SITE
LOCATION: Greece
NOTES: Called Thera by the ancient Greeks, and Santorini since medieval times, the island received its first visitors in 3000 B.C. The Minoans arrived in 1800 B.C. Some scholars claim it was the site of Plato's Atlantis. A monastery sits atop the highest peak.

23 H5 MONASTERY OF ST. JOHN
1088 A.D.
LOCATION: Patmos, Greece
NOTES: St. John the Divine was banished to Patmos in A.D. 95 and is said to have written the Book of Revelation in a cave. The Monastery of St. John the Theologian was founded by an abbot called the Blessed Christodoulos, who was Turkish.

24 F6 ZEUS' CAVE
2ND MILLENNIUM B.C.
LOCATION: Mount Ida, Crete, Greece
NOTES: See p.37.

25 G7 PHAESTUS
2ND MILLENNIUM B.C.
LOCATION: Crete, Greece
NOTES: Minoan palace (c. 2000 B.C.), rebuilt in 1700 B.C. after an earthquake, and destroyed in 1400 B.C. by a volcanic eruption. The central court was probably an arena for the sacred bull sports, as at Knossos. Much later, a temple to the Greek goddess Rhea was built here.

26 G6 PALACE OF KNOSSOS
2ND MILLENNIUM B.C.
LOCATION: Crete, Greece
NOTES: See pp.36–37.

27 G6 ARKALOCHORI
C. 2000–1000 B.C.
LOCATION: near Knossos, Crete, Greece
NOTES: Cave sanctuary destroyed when an earthquake caused the roof to fall in. Offerings, including objects in bronze, silver, and gold, were then deposited in front of the entrance until the 11th century B.C.

28 G6 GOURNIA
C. 1650 B.C.
LOCATION: Crete, Greece
NOTES: Small Bronze Age town, site of a shrine sanctuary in which a terra-cotta altar was discovered almost intact, together with a snake goddess figurine, sacred symbols, offertory tables, and ritual vessels. The town was inhabited from 3000 B.C. and flourished during the Minoan period, but, like other Cretan settlements, was burned down.

29 H2 SELIMIYE MOSQUE
C. A.D. 1574
LOCATION: Edirne, Turkey
NOTES: Built by Sinan, architect of the Süleymaniye in Istanbul (see below), for the sultan Selim II. It stands on a small hill, once the site of a pagan shrine.

30 I3 SULEYMANIYE CAMII
A.D. 1550–57
LOCATION: Istanbul, Turkey
NOTES: Largest mosque in the Ottoman Empire and one of the largest mosques in the world. Built during the reign of Süleyman I the Magnificent, it was based on the Santa Sophia built 1,000 years earlier. It was a hospital, and included schools and a kitchen for the poor.

31 I3 SANTA SOPHIA
A.D. 537
LOCATION: Turkey
NOTES: See p.33.

32 G4 TROY
3000–300 B.C.
LOCATION: Turkey
NOTES: Legendary site of Homeric Greek myth, excavations have revealed an ancient city rebuilt several times. Its main temple in the Hellenistic period was dedicated to Athena.

33 H4 PERGAMON
4TH CENTURY B.C.–2ND CENTURY A.D.
LOCATION: Bergama, Turkey
NOTES: Capital of the dynasty established by the Attalids, a Greek family from the Hellenistic period, Pergamon was home to a library, temples, and altars. An altar to Zeus was built on the acropolis in the second century B.C. It also housed the famous Asclepion, an ancient medical center where Galen practiced. Patients awaiting a cure or diagnosis slept in a room dedicated to Telesphorus.

34 H4 SARDIS
7TH CENTURY B.C.–3RD CENTURY A.D.
LOCATION: Turkey
NOTES: Former capital of the Lydian king Croesus, later conquered by Alexander the Great. The Temple of Artemis, despite its size, was never completed. It was built beside an ancient altar, and the site as a whole is believed to have been sacred to a variety of religions and cults.

35 H5 EPHESUS
5TH CENTURY B.C.–5TH CENTURY A.D.
LOCATION: Turkey
NOTES: See p.32.

36 H5 MILETUS
7TH CENTURY B.C.–3RD CENTURY A.D.
LOCATION: Turkey
NOTES: Once an important city, colonized by Greeks. The ruins of a Hellenistic temple can be found here. The 14th-century Ilyas Bey Camil Mosque is situated to the south of the ruins.

37 H5 DIDYMA
8TH CENTURY B.C.–3RD CENTURY A.D.
LOCATION: Turkey
NOTES: Site of an unfinished Temple of Apollo and oracle rivaling the one at Delphi. It remained a pilgrimage center until the Byzantines quashed paganism.

38 H5 LABRANDA
7TH CENTURY B.C.
LOCATION: Turkey
NOTES: Site of a sanctuary and temple of the god Zeus Statius and an oracle. The First and Second Androns – religious game sites – are still here, as is a large tomb from the fourth century B.C.

39 H5 THE MAUSOLEUM
4TH CENTURY B.C.
LOCATION: Bodrum, Turkey
NOTES: The vast tomb of King Mausolus of Caria was one of the Seven Wonders of the Ancient World. Destroyed by an earthquake, little remains.

40 I5 APHRODISIAS
9TH CENTURY B.C.
LOCATION: Turkey
NOTES: Major center of the cult to Greek goddess of love Aphrodite. Her temple was built on a prehistoric mound of the Early Bronze Age (2800–2200 B.C.) and became a place of pilgrimage for over 1,000 years. It was transformed into a Christian church under Byzantine rule.

41 I6 PINARA
4TH CENTURY B.C.
LOCATION: Turkey
NOTES: Ancient city of Lycia and site of temples to Aphrodite and Athena, which include heart-shaped columns. The rock face behind the city is riddled with rock-cut tombs, some of which are decorated with reliefs.

42 I6 OLYMPOS
NATURAL SITE
LOCATION: Turkey
NOTES: Site of the Chimaera, a naturally occuring gas flame that springs from the earth just outside the city. It was named after the grandson of the earth goddess Gaia. In the second century B.C. it was a center for the worship of the Roman god Vulcan.

43 J4 YAZILIKAYA
13TH CENTURY B.C.
LOCATION: Turkey
NOTES: Ancient religious site with natural rock galleries; monumental gateways and temples were built in front of these. The larger of the temples contains bas-reliefs of numerous conehead deities marching in procession. This was the Hittites' most holy sanctuary. The Hittites had 1,000 deities, but less than 100 are represented here. The most important were the storm god Teshub and the sun goddess Hepatu.

44 K4 ANKARA
4TH CENTURY B.C.
LOCATION: Turkey
NOTES: The modern capital of Turkey is the center of the order of Bayramiye dervishes founded by the Muslim saint Haci Bayram Veli in the city around A.D. 1400. The saint's tomb was formerly a shrine to Cybele, to Men (a Phrygian phallic god), the emperor Augustus, and then a Byzantine church.

45 K3 HATTUSAS
14TH CENTURY B.C.
LOCATION: Turkey
NOTES: Former Hittite site of an immense temple complex of the storm god Buyuk Mabed, with ritual altars and elaborate water channeling and drainage systems.

46 J5 MEVLANA TURBESI
13TH CENTURY A.D.
LOCATION: Konya, Turkey
NOTES: One of the most sacred sites in the Muslim world, the tomb of mystic philosopher Jalaleddin Rumi (called Mevlana by his followers), leader of a dervish order. He is buried next to his son and surrounded by the tombs of his disciples. Their tombs are covered in great velvet shrouds. Mevlana and his son have great symbolic turbans on their tombs.

47 K5 CATAL HUYUK
7500 B.C.
LOCATION: Southern Anatolia, Turkey
NOTES: Site of the earliest known human community. Buildings identified as shrines were decorated with paintings of leopards, bulls' heads and horns, and female figures. Artifacts from the site include earth mother figures.

48 K6 OLBA
4TH CENTURY B.C.
LOCATION: Turkey
NOTES: Center of worship to Zeus Olbius this ancient Greek temple city was ruled by priest-kings. A site of pilgrimage and burial, the area is covered with tombs.

49 M5 NEMRUT DAGI
1ST CENTURY B.C.
LOCATION: Mount Nimrod, Turkey
NOTES: The mountain summit was formed when King Antiochus I Epiphanes cut two ledges in the rock and filled them with colossal statues of himself and the gods (who he believed were his relatives). He then ordered an artificial monument peak of crushed rock 164 ft (50 m) high to be piled between them.

50 J7 ROCK OF APHRODITE
NATURAL SITE
LOCATION: Cyprus
NOTES: See p.39.

EUROPE

The map for these listings is on pp.138-139.

● Site still in use

■ Site no longer in use

■1 D2 THINGVELLIR
A.D. 850-900
LOCATION: Iceland
NOTES: *See p.64.*

■2 (SEE BOX) ALTA
4200-500 B.C.
LOCATION: Finnmark, Norway
NOTES: Large numbers of rock engravings have been discovered here, accredited to the Saami culture, whose main religion was a type of shamanism. The shaman's burial was often accompanied by special ritual items.

●3 (SEE BOX) NORDKAPP
NATURAL SITE
LOCATION: Finnmark, Norway
NOTES: Northernmost point in Europe, once a Saami sacrificial site.

●4 (SEE BOX) NORTHERN LIGHTS
NATURAL SITE
LOCATION: Northern Hemisphere
NOTES: *See p.65.*

●5 J2 NIDAROS CATHEDRAL
A.D. 1075
LOCATION: Trondheim, Norway
NOTES: Scandinavia's largest medieval building, dedicated to King Olaf I, its founder. It soon became a burial place for royalty and gained importance as a pilgrimage center in the Middle Ages.

●6 I3 BORGUND STAVE
A.D. 1150-1200
LOCATION: Norway
NOTES: Famous stave church, built of timber; the oldest surviving church of its kind in Scandinavia.

■7 J3 OSEBERG
C. A.D. 850
LOCATION: near Oslo, Norway
NOTES: The famous Oseberg ship, now fully excavated, was removed from this burial mound. The burial boat was filled with grave goods, while the remains of two female bodies at the stern suggest that the burial was royal, perhaps for Queen Asa. The ship itself, unlike most, was not burned but buried whole and anchored, perhaps waiting for some future resurrection.

■8 J3 GOKSTAD
9TH CENTURY A.D.
LOCATION: Vestfold, Norway
NOTES: Viking tumulus including a royal burial ship. It is possible that the Viking King Olaf I was buried here.

●9 J3 GAMLE AKER KIRKE
A.D. 1100
LOCATION: Oslo, Norway
NOTES: Oldest stone church in the country.

■10 K1 GRATRASK
A.D. 1000-1300
LOCATION: Västerbotten, Sweden
NOTES: Ancient site of sacrifice for the Saami culture.

■11 K3 ANUNDSHOGEN
A.D. 600-700
LOCATION: Västerås, Sweden
NOTES: Megalithic remains of stone ships, including one of the largest found in Scandinavia. A runestone has also been found here. Like Gamla, it was evidently a place of pagan worship.

■12 K3 GAMLA
5TH CENTURY A.D.
LOCATION: Uppsala, Sweden
NOTES: Huge mound where early kings were buried. Later became a ceremonial center for the Vikings. Also a ritual site with nine sacrifices made every year to appease the gods.

■13 K4 GOTLAND
A.D. 900
LOCATION: Sweden
NOTES: *See p.64.*

●14 J4 LUND CATHEDRAL
A.D. 1145
LOCATION: Lund, Malmöhus, Sweden
NOTES: Considered Scandinavia's finest medieval building, it includes a mosaic of Christ and a 15th-century altar.

■15 J5 HAGESTAD
C. 2500 B.C.
LOCATION: Löderup, Scania, Sweden
NOTES: Carlshögen, the most famous of these burial monuments, was divided into nine chambers and contained the remains of up to 50 people. They are likely to have been separated according to social divisions.

●16 (SEE BOX) SAANA
NATURAL SITE
LOCATION: Finland
NOTES: Mountain that was once sacred to the Lapps.

●17 (SEE BOX) KALLIOPARTA
NATURAL SITE
LOCATION: Lake Inari, Finland
NOTES: One of a number of sacred islands on Lake Inari. It has a large cave where sacrifices were made for good luck in hunting and fishing and is seen as the residing place of Ukko, the ancient sky god, who restored fire to mankind after it was taken from the earth by an evil spirit. The god was depicted as an old man holding a hammer in the sacrificial pictures on the shaman's drums.

●18 (SEE BOX) UKKOSAARI ISLAND
NATURAL SITE
LOCATION: Inari, Finland
NOTES: Once a Lapp site of sacrifice; as its name suggests, it was probably sacred to the god Ukko.

●19 K3 VASARAINEN
A.D. 500-1000
LOCATION: Rauma, Finland
NOTES: Around 600 barrows exist nearby, but in this particular area there are five large stone tables on top of some cliffs, thought to have been used for ritual sacrifice. Local people still occasionally bring offerings to the stones.

■20 J4 LINDHOLM HØJE
C. A.D. 500-900
LOCATION: Jutland, Denmark
NOTES: *See p.65.*

●21 J4 BUDOLFI CATHEDRAL
11TH CENTURY A.D.
LOCATION: Ålborg, Jutland, Denmark
NOTES: Built on the site of an 11th-century church with tombs; a number of Celtic ritual objects have been found nearby.

■22 J4 MOLS GROUP
3500-1500 B.C.
LOCATION: Knebel, Denmark
NOTES: Large chamber likely to have been used for communal burial. A circle of 23 stones nearby surrounds an earth mound covering two chamber tombs.

■23 J4 TUSTRUP GROUP
3200 B.C.
LOCATION: Århus, Jutland, Denmark
NOTES: A number of megalithic remains are found here, including a burial chamber, a dolmen, a passage grave, and a horseshoe-shaped "temple" that may have been either a funerary structure or a sanctuary; it was certainly some form of cult building.

●24 I-J4 JELLING
A.D. 700-1000
LOCATION: Vejle, Denmark
NOTES: Site of the Viking royal capital with a number of burial mounds and runestones that are good examples of Nordic pagan culture. A tenth-century church here shows the influence of Christianity on the same people.

■25 I5 HEDEBY
C. A.D. 800
LOCATION: Denmark
NOTES: One of the largest Viking settlements, it contains a number of religious remains, including a pagan cemetery, boat burials, and runestones.

■26 J5 BILDSØ
3500-3000 B.C.
LOCATION: Zealand, Denmark
NOTES: A simple set of small chambers found in a long mound predating most megaliths in Scandinavia.

■27 J5 FREJLEV SKOV GROUP
C. 3000 B.C.
LOCATION: Nysted, Lolland, Denmark
NOTES: Burial site containing 13 dolmens, five passage graves, and a stone circle.

■28 J5 TRUNDHOLM
1800-1600 B.C.
LOCATION: Denmark
NOTES: Ritual site where a number of objects have been found, including a sun disc – it suggests that some form of sun worship was practiced here.

■29 K5 SARNOVO
C. 2000 B.C.
LOCATION: Wloclawek, Poland
NOTES: Nine huge mounds make up this necropolis; the remains of Neolithic dwellings have been found under two of them. Evidence suggests that these are the remnants of a culture that inhabited the area for over a millennium.

●30 K5 ST. ANNE'S CHURCH
A.D. 1454
LOCATION: Warsaw, Poland
NOTES: Beautiful church that was destroyed in 1656 and then rebuilt. Polish princes used to swear homage to their monarch here.

■31 K6 GAJ
2500 B.C.
LOCATION: Kolo District, Poland
NOTES: Kujavian megalithic tomb.

The remains of a large mortuary house, or perhaps a sanctuary, can be found at one end of the site.

●32 K6 CHURCH OF THE VIRGIN MARY
A.D. 1497
LOCATION: Kraków, Poland
NOTES: Famous for its stained-glass windows, the church was previously destroyed during the Tartar invasions. Its Chapel of Our Lady has a venerated image of the Black Madonna.

●33 J6 PRAGUE CATHEDRAL
C. A.D. 1350
LOCATION: Prague, Czech Republic
NOTES: Gothic cathedral, important in the 14th century, where Charles IV is buried with many of his Bohemian ancestors.

■34 J6 ZAVIST
C. 500-200 B.C.
LOCATION: Zbraslav, Czechoslovakia
NOTES: Large Celtic fortress area which contained a sacred sanctuary similar to those found in western Europe.

■35 J6 LIBENICE
3RD CENTURY B.C.
LOCATION: Kolín, Czech Republic
NOTES: Celtic sanctuary with an oblong enclosure, including a female burial site and a sacrificial area. The site was approached by a ramp. Remains of several animals, mostly bulls, have been found along with those of humans.

●36 K6 ST. EMERAN CATHEDRAL
11TH CENTURY A.D.
LOCATION: Nitra, Slovak Republic
NOTES: Complex of three churches; the oldest remaining is an 11th-century chapel. The first Christian church in the country was founded here in the ninth century.

■37 K7 BODROKERESZTUR
C. 3300 B.C.
LOCATION: East Hungary
NOTES: The remains of at least 50 humans have been discovered at this prehistoric cemetery.

●38 L7 SUCEVITA MONASTERY
16TH CENTURY A.D.
LOCATION: near Putna, Romania
NOTES: *See p.51.*

●39 L7 CHURCH OF THE THREE HIERARCHS
A.D. 1639
LOCATION: Iasi, Moldavia, Romania
NOTES: The exterior of the church is covered with intricate patterned stone. It holds the tombs of the two princes who founded modern Romania. A small building nearby is painted with a number of 17th-century frescoes.

●40 L7 THE BLACK CHURCH
A.D. 1384-1477
LOCATION: Brasov, Romania
NOTES: Possibly built by the father of Vlad, the basis for the character of Count Dracula. Its strange appearance was a result of a fire in 1689. It is still used by German Lutherans.

■41 L7 SARMIZEGETHUSA
100 B.C.-A.D. 106
LOCATION: Romania
NOTES: City of the Dacians found on the steep slopes of the Carpathian Mountains. Its sanctuaries were said to have housed sacred groves. Also here are two round structures, the larger being the Great

Round Cult Building, with two rings of pillars believed to have been built for calendrical purposes. The smaller shrine is likely to have had astronomical importance, with a smaller stone nearby that is said to represent the sun, and was probably used in sacrificial ritual.

42 M8 MANGALIA
4TH–6TH CENTURY A.D.
LOCATION: Romania
NOTES: While the fourth-century Roman necropolis has been destroyed, the ruins of a sixth-century Paleo-Christian basilica still remain.

43 L7 LEPENSKI VIR
5000–5000 B.C.
LOCATION: Serbia
NOTES: A farming and fishing community found on the banks of the River Danube that was the center for a form of ritual carving, examples of which were placed next to the hearths of local dwellings. Little is known about the religion here, but the figures are likely to have represented a local river deity.

44 K8 STUDENTICA MONASTERY
A.D. 1209
LOCATION: Serbia
NOTES: Oldest of the medieval Serbian monasteries, it houses the grave of its founder, King Stefan Nemanja.

45 L8 MADARA
2ND MILLENNIUM B.C.–14TH CENTURY A.D.
LOCATION: Bulgaria
NOTES: Debate has raged over who carved this mysterious bas-relief 330 ft (100 m) up a cliff face. Some believe it to have been carved in the eighth century, while others say that it is a nameless rider-god of the Thracians. Near the relief is a large cave that was filled with Thracian offerings, while the remains of a 14th-century monastery can also be found nearby. There is evidence of a settlement at the top of the cliff itself.

46 L8 STONE FOREST
NATURAL SITE
LOCATION: Varna region, Bulgaria
NOTES: See p.50.

47 L8 KAZANLUK
4TH CENTURY B.C.
LOCATION: Bulgaria
NOTES: Thracian tombs associated with the Great Goddess. It is covered by a beehive dome depicting a funerary feast and a chariot race.

48 L8 ROTUNDA OF ST. GEORGI
4TH CENTURY A.D.
LOCATION: Sofia, Bulgaria
NOTES: A rotunda (a building with a circular ground plan) was first built here by the Romans on the site of a previous pagan temple. It was converted into the Church of St. George in the 14th century.

49 L8 RILA MONASTERY
C. A.D. 950
LOCATION: Bulgaria
NOTES: See p.50.

50 K-L8 STOBI
1ST CENTURY B.C.–6TH CENTURY A.D.
LOCATION: Macedonia
NOTES: Important Roman site that declined in the sixth century. It has a series of church buildings, including a fourth-century basilica with a geometric design. A number of terra-cotta figures were found in its pagan cemetery.

51 K8 TREBENISTE
C. 7TH CENTURY B.C.
LOCATION: Macedonia
NOTES: Celtic burial site where a number of gilded funerary masks were found.

52 K8 HERACLEA NECROPOLIS
4TH CENTURY A.D.
LOCATION: Bitola, Macedonia
NOTES: Founded by Philip II, it includes a sculpture of the goddess Nemesis, as well as two early Christian basilicas.

53 K8 BUTRINT
4TH CENTURY B.C.
LOCATION: near Sarande, Albania
NOTES: Ruins of ancient city ruled by Greeks and then Romans before becoming a Byzantine ecclesiastical center. There is a sixth-century Paleo-Christian baptistry and a basilica.

54 K8 BERAT-ST. MARY BALCHERNA
16TH CENTURY A.D.
LOCATION: Albania
NOTES: The church contains 16th-century Byzantine frescoes by the painter Onufri. Also found in its grounds is the Church of St. Michael.

55 K8 KRUJE-DOLLMA TEKKE
18TH CENTURY A.D.
LOCATION: north of Tirana, Albania
NOTES: Bectashi Sufi shrine allegedly founded by a dervish who killed a dragon on the site. Focus of Muslim, Christian, and pagan beliefs.

56 K8 ZBORNA GOMILA
11TH–15TH CENTURY A.D.
LOCATION: near Stolac, Bosnia
NOTES: See p.51.

57 K8 MEDJUGORIE
11TH–15TH CENTURY A.D.
LOCATION: Bosnia
NOTES: Site of the Hill of Apparitions and the Hill of the Cross. The former is also seen as a sight of miracles, while the latter is a 46-ft (14-m) high cross.

58 K7 MITHRAIC TEMPLE
4TH CENTURY A.D.
LOCATION: Jajce, Bosnia
NOTES: Sacred site for the Bogomil sect of Christianity, paralleling the mystic elements of Orthodox Christianity, while distorting its values. The temple contains imagery with some elements that mocked Christ's crucifixion, others that showed the importance of victory and sacrifice.

59 K8 SPLIT CATHEDRAL
12TH CENTURY A.D.
LOCATION: Croatia
NOTES: The cathedral stands on the site of the mausoleum of Diocletian, a third-century Roman emperor whose bust is the only remaining relic.

60 K8 SATONA
4TH CENTURY A.D.
LOCATION: Split, Croatia
NOTES: Center of Christianity on the site of a Roman town that was sacked in the sixth century. Among the ruins are a necropolis for Christian martyrs and piles of sarcophagi situated around a fifth-century basilica.

61 J7 BASILICA OF EUPHRASIUS
6TH CENTURY A.D.
LOCATION: Porec, Croatia
NOTES: Byzantine structure with a well-preserved gold mosaic floor, dating from the fourth century. It has an earlier Christian basilica in its grounds.

62 I7 MILAN CATHEDRAL
A.D. 1390–1400
LOCATION: Milan, Italy
NOTES: An extremely impressive Gothic cathedral, whose façade was transformed in the 17th century when it was given a Renaissance uplift.

63 J9 CASTELLUCCIO
1800–1400 B.C.
LOCATION: Sicily, Italy
NOTES: Cemetery of several hundred rock-cut tombs that were constantly reused, each burial being accompanied by offerings, often of pottery or copper ornaments. Two of the tombs that are carved with reliefs have been compared to the tombs at Tarxien in Malta.

64 J7 ST. MARK'S CATHEDRAL
9TH CENTURY A.D.
LOCATION: Venice, Italy
NOTES: In the ninth century, Venetian merchants brought the remains of St. Mark the Evangelist from Alexandria, and a shrine was built to house them. The church that replaced it, begun in 1063, has become one of the most famous Italian religious sites, mixing Byzantine and Romanesque architecture with Middle Eastern influences.

65 J7 SAN VITALE
A.D. 547
LOCATION: Ravenna, Italy
NOTES: A modest building, but its spectacular mosaics make it perhaps the most famous Byzantine church outside Istanbul. During the first half of the fifth century, Ravenna itself became the western capital of the Roman Empire as the emperor fled the invading Goths. It thus became the effective center of the Christian Church in the West.

66 J8 FLORENCE CATHEDRAL
A.D. 1294
LOCATION: Florence, Italy
NOTES: The colored marble facade of this famous Gothic cathedral is proportioned geometrically. Its marvelous dome is the work of Filippo Brunelleschi (1377–1466).

67 J8 PIANELLI DI GENGA
2000–1000 B.C.
LOCATION: Gola del Sentino, Italy
NOTES: Bronze Age cemetery of several hundred burial cremations. The Grotta Frasassi remains a pilgrimage site and is large enough to contain a church.

68 J8 ASSISI
13TH CENTURY A.D.
LOCATION: Umbria, Italy
NOTES: Once the site of the Roman Temple of Minerva, it is more famous as the birthplace of St. Francis of Assisi, "the most saintly among saints." The 13th-century Basilica of St. Francis is here, as are a number of other churches. Still a place of Christian pilgrimage.

69 J8 POPULONIA
1000–100 B.C.
LOCATION: Italy
NOTES: Site of an Etruscan city that includes in its ruins rock-cut tombs and the neighboring San Cerbone urnfield cemetery. The graves were made in a flat-stone circular wall around a square chamber, with a tumulus above.

70 J8 TARQUINIA
10TH–4TH CENTURY B.C.
LOCATION: Italy
NOTES: See p.53.

71 J8 CERVETERI
9TH–4TH CENTURY B.C.
LOCATION: near Rome, Italy
NOTES: See p.53.

72 J8 ST. PETER'S
C. A.D. 349
LOCATION: Rome, Italy
NOTES: See p.52.

73 J8 VEII
10TH–4TH CENTURY B.C.
LOCATION: near Rome, Italy
NOTES: Site of the first Etruscan city. By a spectacular waterfall are the remains of the fifth-century B.C. Temple of Apollo, while one of its cemeteries contains the seventh-century Campana-painted tombs.

74 J8 THE CATACOMBS
2ND–5TH CENTURY A.D.
LOCATION: Rome, Italy
NOTES: Underground cemetery containing the bodies of several early popes. It is a maze of underground galleries with niches where bodies of saints and martyrs were sealed in. Large tomb chambers – loculi – housed generations of the same families. A number of paintings depict Lazarus rising from the dead and other biblical scenes. It was considered a place where the dead must expiate their sins, while their prayers would help the living.

75 J8 VESUVIUS
NATURAL SITE
LOCATION: near Naples, Italy
NOTES: The volcanic mountain that destroyed the city of Pompeii was also considered sacred before and after Roman occupation.

76 I8 LI LOLGHI
2000–1000 B.C.
LOCATION: Arzachena, Sardinia, Italy
NOTES: Largest of the "giant" graves – long megalithic chambers surrounded by large "Cyclopean" figures with long, curved wings.

77 I8 ANGHELU RUJU
2500–2000 B.C.
LOCATION: Sardinia, Italy
NOTES: Cemetery of rock-cut tombs known locally as the "fairies' houses." Mostly shaft tombs, the main chambers were often elaborately decorated, occasionally with carved reliefs. Attributed to the Ozieri culture, links have also been made with cultures from the south of France.

78 I8 BARUMINI
10TH–6TH CENTURY B.C.
LOCATION: Sardinia, Italy
NOTES: A nuraghi, a circular stone tower examples of which are found throughout Sardinia. This example contained a gigantic tomb, where the dead were interred in gallery graves. Also within the complex were a number of sacred wells.

79 I9 CAGLIARI
5TH CENTURY B.C.
LOCATION: Sardinia, Italy
NOTES: Phoenician site later occupied by the Romans. There is a necropolis, the tomb of Atilia Pomptilia, and the Cave of the Vipers, so called after the two snake carvings that adorn its entrance.

80 I7 LA TENE
5TH CENTURY B.C.–1ST CENTURY A.D.
LOCATION: Switzerland
NOTES: Site that gives its name to the Celtic La Tène culture, where evidence

of a ritual vehicle burial has been found. The remains of weapons have also been discovered in the burials.

81 I7 LE PETIT CHASSEUR

C. 4000 B.C.

LOCATION: Sion, Valais, Switzerland

NOTES: Cemetery whose cists were aligned with some standing stones; 12 megalithic coffers were built at a later date. Fine examples of megalithic art were also found here.

82 J7 CONVENT OF ST. JOHN

10TH CENTURY A.D.

LOCATION: Mustair, Switzerland

NOTES: Part of the St. John the Baptist Monastery, it is one of the oldest churches in the country.

83 J7 KLEINKLEIN

7TH CENTURY B.C.

LOCATION: Austria

NOTES: Celtic cemetery where a number of vessels have been found enscribed with scenes of ritual processions and mythical hunts. A human funerary mask was also found here.

84 J7 MAGDELENBURG

C. 500 B.C.

LOCATION: Black Forest, Germany

NOTES: Huge barrow over 330 ft (100 m) in diameter, consisting of a main chamber surrounded by a number of subsidiary chambers. The barrow also contained a funerary wagon.

85 J7 STRETTWEG

9TH–6TH CENTURY B.C.

LOCATION: Austria

NOTES: Celtic cremation site that contained a funerary wagon showing a Celtic goddess bearing a scent burner.

86 K7 ST. STEPHEN'S CATHEDRAL

A.D. 1304

LOCATION: Vienna, Austria

NOTES: Adapted from a Romanesque building, this is probably the most famous of the Gothic buildings in Austria.

87 J6 MELK

A.D. 935

LOCATION: Austria

NOTES: The largest abbey in Austria, it became Benedictine in 1089. The abbey was rebuilt in 1702. In the famous Nibelung legends, it is known by the name Medelike.

88 J7 HALLSTATT

10TH–5TH CENTURY B.C.

LOCATION: Austria

NOTES: Ancient burial grounds and salt mine that give their name to the period of Celtic Hallstatt culture. The site was later known as Heidenbirge – pagan mountain. Some of the earliest metalwork has been found among the burial goods.

89 I7 STOCKACH

C. 900 B.C.

LOCATION: Tübingen, Germany

NOTES: Tumulus site associated with the early Hallstatt cremations. Parts of a figure found here suggest that some form of ancestor worship may have been practiced.

90 J6 MANCHING

2ND CENTURY B.C.

LOCATION: Germany

NOTES: One of the largest Celtic centers in Germany, it contains a large rectangular Celtic shrine.

91 I6 HEUNEBERG

C. 6TH CENTURY B.C.

LOCATION: Germany

NOTES: Large prehistoric citadel that was surrounded by 11 tumuli.

92 I6 MUMLING-GRUMBACH

C. 500–0 B.C.

LOCATION: Odenwald, Germany

NOTES: Holy well from the Celto-Roman period with a stone relief showing three fertility goddesses.

93 I6 SPEYER CATHEDRAL

A.D. 1025

LOCATION: Speyer, Germany

NOTES: The largest cathedral in Germany. It has been a place of worship since pre-Roman times; a temple to the Celtic goddess Nantosvelta was built here. It is believed by some to be positioned on an alignment with holy blue stones, situated at the centers of some medieval towns.

94 I6 TRIER

1ST CENTURY A.D.

LOCATION: Germany

NOTES: Provincial Roman capital that flourished at the beginnning of the first millennium A.D. A fourth-century basilica, the Altbachtal religious complex with over 50 Celto-Roman shrines, and a first-century temple were built here. The Porta Nigra – a fortified town gateway – was later converted into a two-story church and an 11th-century cathedral.

95 I6 GOLORING

4TH CENTURY B.C.

LOCATION: near Mainz, Germany

NOTES: Religious cult center dating to the end of the Hallstatt period. There is a henge monument, 656 ft (200 m) in diameter, with a central terrace.

96 I6 AACHEN

A.D. 805

LOCATION: Germany

NOTES: See p.61.

97 I6 COLOGNE CATHEDRAL

A.D. 1248

LOCATION: Cologne, Germany

NOTES: Beautiful cathedral heavily influenced by French religious architecture. A five-aisled basilica, it stands on the site of a Romanesque church. The Chapel of the Holy Cross holds a crucifix from the earlier church.

98 I5 EXTERNSTEINE

NATURAL SITE

LOCATION: Germany

NOTES: See pp.62-63.

99 J5 EVERSTORFER FORST GROUP

C. 2200 B.C.

LOCATION: Mecklenberg, Germany

NOTES: Tomb complex containing ten burial chambers, three dolmens, one large burial chamber, and a stone circle.

100 I6 RINDSCHLEIDEN

12TH CENTURY A.D.

LOCATION: Luxembourg

NOTES: Church with 15th-century frescoes that also includes the holy well of St. Willibord, which remains a pilgrimage site to the present day.

101 I6 WERIS, EREZEE, AND OPPAGNE

4500-2500 B.C.

LOCATION: Marche-en-Famenne, Belgium

NOTES: Megalithic complex that is probably related to the Seine-Oise-Marne culture. The site consists of five standing stones, three tombs, and three horizontal stones.

102 I6 TOTERFOUT-HLAVE MIJL BARROWS

16TH–11TH CENTURY B.C.

LOCATION: Veldhoven, Netherlands

NOTES: Bronze Age barrow cemetery that once included mortuary houses, ritual burial pits, and temporary wooden circles. Linked to the Hilversum culture, an offshoot of English Wessex culture.

103 I5 UTRECHT CATHEDRAL

A.D. 1254

LOCATION: Utrecht, Netherlands

NOTES: One of the best examples of Gothic architecture in the country, much of its structure was influenced by the cathedral at Amiens in France.

104 I5 PAPELOZE KERK

3300-2800 B.C.

LOCATION: Sleen, Drenthe, Netherlands

NOTES: The name of the megalithic site means "priestless church". It also contains six huge capstones, one of them weighing 25 tons.

105 I5 SCHIMMERES

C. 4000-3500 B.C.

LOCATION: Emmen, Drenthe, Netherlands

NOTES: Two burial chambers in the shape of a huge longboat. Some standing stones can be found near the site.

106 H6 RIBEMONT-SUR-ANCRE

3RD CENTURY B.C.

LOCATION: Somme, France

NOTES: Large Celtic sanctuary where the bones of over 1,000 humans have been found, likely to have been sacrificed before being placed within an eerie cubic monument.

107 H6 AMIENS CATHEDRAL

A.D. 1220-1270

LOCATION: France

NOTES: At the time of its construction, it was the largest Gothic cathedral in France. It combines elements of Romanesque and Gothic designs.

108 H6 NOTRE DAME DE PARIS

A.D. 1163-1250

LOCATION: Paris, France

NOTES: Probably the most famous of the Gothic cathedrals. Built on the site of two basilicas, the foundation stone was laid by Pope Alexander III. Probably a previous pagan ceremonial site.

109 H6 GOURNAY-SUR-ARONDE

3RD CENTURY B.C.

LOCATION: Oise, France

NOTES: Belgic-type Celtic sanctuary with a wooden decorated temple in its middle. In its ritual pits bent swords have been found – believed to have been broken at the time of their owner's death. There are also a number of relics from sacrifices, some of which may have been human.

110 H6 CHARTRES

A.D. 1194-1260

LOCATION: France

NOTES: See p.60.

111 I7 VIX

C. 520-510 B.C.

LOCATION: Mont Laissois, France

NOTES: Hill-fort where a fascinating grave of a princess has been found. Along with the body itself, a golden diadem, jewelry, and parts of a funerary chariot were found. Many examples of Greek art were also found, mostly from the nearby Greek settlement at Marseille.

112 I7 VEZELAY CHURCH

A.D. 1100-1150

LOCATION: France

NOTES: A popular pilgrimage site in the Middle Ages, it is decorated with sculptures depicting biblical scenes; the most famous shows Christ as arbiter between the blessed and the damned.

113 I7 ABBAYE DE FONTENAY

A.D. 1118

LOCATION: Saône-et-Loire, France

NOTES: The oldest Cistercian abbey in Europe, founded by St. Bernard. Cistercian monks renounced the world and espoused poverty.

114 I7 SOURCES DE LA SEINE

NATURAL SITE

LOCATION: France

NOTES: Springs that were sacred to the Celts, where a number of wooden figurines have been found.

115 I7 CLUNY

A.D. 909

LOCATION: Burgundy, France

NOTES: One of the most important monasteries founded in France, it followed the strict Benedictine order of monastic life.

116 H7 CHAMELIERES

NATURAL SITE

LOCATION: France

NOTES: Sacred Celtic springs that also served as sanctuaries, where carved wooden offerings were deposited.

117 I7 LE-PUY-EN-VELAY

A.D. 962

LOCATION: Haute-Loire, France

NOTES: Town located in the bowl of a volcanic cone, with three landmark rock outcrops, each topped with a church or statue. The town became a large pilgrimage center in the tenth century. Pilgrims used to assemble at the Cathédrale de Notre Dame, which housed a sacred Black Madonna, and visited a druidic "fever stone," believed to have healing powers.

118 I8 MAISON CARREE

16 B.C.

LOCATION: Nîmes, France

NOTES: One of the best preserved Roman temples found outside Italy.

119 I8 MONTMAJOUR ABBEY

6TH CENTURY A.D.

LOCATION: Bouches-du-Rhône, France

NOTES: Important sixth-century church positioned on a pilgrimage route.

120 I8 NOVES

3RD CENTURY B.C.

LOCATION: Bouches-du-Rhône, France

NOTES: Celtic sanctuary site of the Monster of Noves, a stone statue with an erect phallus holding a half-eaten limb in its mouth. The Celts believed there was a close link between sacrifice and fertility.

121 I8 ENTREMONT

C. 200-100 B.C.

LOCATION: Aix-en-Provence, France

NOTES: Ancient Salyian capital where a long sacred way was once flanked with crouching figures. It is one of a number of sanctuaries to the dead and the divine that date from around this time.

122 I8 ROQUEPERTUSE

C. 300 B.C.

LOCATION: Gérin-Ricard, France

NOTES: Celtic sanctuary built on two levels. It had square pillars painted with animal motifs and carved sockets to display the skulls of conquered enemies. Lines of human or godlike figures were found inside the sanctuary.

123 H7 LASCAUX

C. 15,000 B.C.

LOCATION: France

NOTES: See pp.58-59.

124 H7 ROCAMADOUR

A.D. 650-1300

LOCATION: France

NOTES: Church complex that was one of the most important of the early Christian sites of medieval pilgrimage.

125 H8 NIAUX

C. 5000 B.C.

LOCATION: Pyrénées, France

NOTES: Prehistoric cave site with examples of prehistoric Magdelanian art linked to some form of hunting magic. Because of the size of the cave, it is likely that it was used for some form of large religious ceremony.

126 H8 LOURDES

A.D. 1858

LOCATION: Haute-Pyrénées, France

NOTES: Noted pilgrimage center. A local girl, Bernadette Soubirous, had visions of the Virgin Mary in a grotto at Lourdes, where a spring was declared to have miraculous qualities. Lourdes was legitimized by the Pope himself. A basilica was built on the site in 1876, and has become the focus of over three million pilgrimages a year.

127 H8 SAINT-SERNIN CHURCH

C. A.D. 1077

LOCATION: Toulouse, France

NOTES: One of the great pilgrimage churches during the Middle Ages.

128 H7 BOUGON

4700-3000 B.C.

LOCATION: Deux-Sèvres, France

NOTES: Necropolis and sanctuary of five monuments, whose structures were built by the Cous, pre-Chassey, and Chassey cultures and spread across an area of 6 mi (10 km).

129 H7 BAGNEUX

3500-3000 B.C.

LOCATION: Loire Valley, France

NOTES: The largest megalithic cavern in France, covered with stone slabs.

130 H7 COJOUX

4500-2500 B.C.

LOCATION: Ile-et-Vilaine, France

NOTES: An alignment of standing stones that were used as part of ceremonial functions over a long period of time. The first stones were laid around 4500 B.C., while other mounds and tombs were added at a later date. The function of one mound, crowned with a row of white stones, is still unexplained.

131 G7 ER-LANNIC

C. 4000-3000 B.C.

LOCATION: Arzon, Morbihan, France

NOTES: Two circles of standing stones aligned with a large monolith. The site has links with parts of the Chassey culture. It is likely that these were not funerary monuments, but instead some form of sacred enclosure.

132 G7 LE GRAND MENHIR BRISE

C. 3000 B.C.

LOCATION: Morbihan, France

NOTES: Site of megalithic tombs. The most famous is the Men-er-Hroeg – the Fairy Stone – now broken into four pieces. Many of its parts were used for the creation of other megalithic monuments. It may have been a site for astronomical observations and linked to the rituals that took place at Carnac (see pp.56-57).

133 G7 CARNAC

5TH MILLENNIUM B.C.

LOCATION: France

NOTES: See pp.56-57.

134 G6 CARN ISLAND

4160-4095 B.C.

LOCATION: Finistère, France

NOTES: A large barrow at this site contains three chambers and is over 6,000 years old. It is claimed to be the oldest stone building known anywhere.

135 G6 BARNENEZ

4700-4400 B.C.

LOCATION: Finistère, France

NOTES: A double tumulus, 230 ft (70 m) by 82 ft (25 m) that contains five gallery graves, each of which contained a number of grave offerings. Barnenez is thought to be one of the oldest prehistoric structures in France. A number of stone axes are carved on upright pillars and suggest beliefs in ancestral male power symbols. It is likely that worship continued at the site for over 2,000 years.

136 H6 LE MONT-SAINT-MICHEL

13TH CENTURY A.D.

LOCATION: Normandy, France

NOTES: Sacred island connected to the mainland by a tidal causeway. Believed to have been used by druids as a place of sun worship to the god Mithras and also used as a Celtic graveyard. However, Aubert, an eighth-century French bishop, made the site sacred to St. Michael, after which it became an important Christian pilgrimage center. La Merveille, a set of 13th-century Gothic religious buildings, dominates the island. It is still inhabited, despite its turbulent history.

137 I8 FILITOSA

5000-4000 B.C.

LOCATION: Corsica, France

NOTES: A group of megalithic chambers and standing stones with outlines of warriors and other figures on their surfaces. The site was no doubt used for religious purposes.

138 H8 MONTSERRAT

9TH CENTURY A.D.

LOCATION: Spain

NOTES: See p.55.

139 I8 ELS TUDONS

2ND MILLENNIUM B.C.

LOCATION: Minorca, Spain

NOTES: Stone-built chamber tomb site that has the oldest roofed building in Iberia and possibly in Europe. Remains of over 100 bodies were found here, together with mysteriously patterned discs.

140 I8 TREPUCO

C. 2000-1500 B.C.

LOCATION: Mahon, Minorca, Spain

NOTES: This is the main site of taula – large, religious, T-shaped stone tables that are exclusive to the island. It has been suggested that they were used in some form of bull worship.

141 I8 TORRE D'EN GAUMES

2000-1000 B.C.

LOCATION: Alayor, Minorca, Spain

NOTES: Prehistoric village site enclosing standing stones, taulas, and tombs. A statue of the Egyptian god Imhotep has been discovered here.

142 H9 SAN REAL

8TH-6TH CENTURY B.C.

LOCATION: Santa Margalida, Majorca, Spain

NOTES: Mass burial site on the coast, where the chambers are boat-shaped. Around 70 tombs have been excavated.

143 G8 BURGOS CATHEDRAL

A.D. 1221-1457

LOCATION: Spain

NOTES: One of the most important and beautiful Christian sites in the country, with its interior walls and altar decorated with Renaissance art.

144 G8 ALTAMIRA

17,000-10,000 B.C.

LOCATION: near Santander, Spain

NOTES: Ancient cave dwelling famous for its Paleolithic art, including drawings of bison. Strange symbols and images line the walls of the cave and imply that it was used in some form of magic hunting ceremony.

145 F8 SANTIAGO DE COMPOSTELA

A.D. 1078-1128

LOCATION: Spain

NOTES: See p.55.

146 G8 AVILA

12TH CENTURY A.D.

LOCATION: Spain

NOTES: Medieval Christian city, its major religious structures include a Gothic cathedral. The Convento de Santo Tomás includes the tomb of Tomás de Torquemada, the first Grand Inquisitor.

147 G8 CHRISTO DE LA LUZ

11TH CENTURY A.D.

LOCATION: Toledo, Spain

NOTES: In a city which was once home to Judaism, Christianity, and Islam, this church is one of the most impressive of its holy places. Once a synagogue, it was converted to a church in 1405.

148 G9 GREAT MOSQUE AT CORDOBA

8TH CENTURY A.D.

LOCATION: Spain

NOTES: The eighth-century mosque was the third largest Islamic structure in the world. Standing on ground sacred to three different religions – the Roman God Janus, the Christian Visigoths, and then Islam after the Moorish invasion – it was converted back to a Christian site in the 13th century. The cruciform cathedral was built in the 16th century in the middle of the mosque. Though this construction ruined its splendor, it still remains a site of sacred importance.

149 G9 ANTEQUERA

3500-3000 B.C.

LOCATION: Málaga, Spain

NOTES: A collection of megalithic monuments, including the Cueva de Menga, the Cueva de Viera, and the Cueva de Romeral, the latter being the most impressive; a double chamber lying under a 290-ft (90-m) long, 30-ft (9-m) high tumulus.

150 G9 LOS MILLARES

2500-1800 B.C.

LOCATION: Santa Fé de Mondújar, Spain

NOTES: Ancient settlement significant due to its cemetery of around 80 *tholos* tombs. Sometimes colored, these sites had ritual enclosures with cult pillars, while the grave goods, some engraved with eye goddess symbols, imply the existence of a mother goddess cult.

151 G8 ANTELAS

3500-3000 B.C.

LOCATION: Viseu, Portugal

NOTES: Megalithic site that includes stones painted with prehistoric art. One has "astral" shapes, while another shows the sun and moon in the center of some geometric motifs. The chamber itself is a classic dolmen.

152 F9 SAO PEDRO DO ESTORIL

C. 3000 B.C.

LOCATION: Tagus Estuary, Portugal

NOTES: Two Neolithic rock-cut graves constructed out of caves that were used as mass burial sites. At least 65 people were buried in the first cave, with a number of interesting burial goods.

153 F9 PALMELA

2000-1500 B.C.

LOCATION: near Setúbal, Portugal

NOTES: A grouping of hypogea – tombs replete with an antechamber – form this necropolis, whose grave goods are similar to the Late Neolithic finds at Almeria in Spain.

154 G9 ALMENDRAS

C. 4000-3000 B.C.

LOCATION: Guadalupe, Evora, Portugal

NOTES: See p.54.

155 G9 ANTA GRANDE DE ZAMBUJEIRO

C. 4500 B.C.

LOCATION: Portugal

NOTES: See p.54.

156 G9 ZAMBUJAL

C. 2000 B.C.

LOCATION: Portugal

NOTES: Site of a small fort that has been connected with a large megalithic tomb that dominated the countryside. It suggests the centralization of power around this time, and the offering of burial goods seem to have been part of the communities' rituals.

FORMER SOVIET UNION

The map for these listings is on pp.140-141.

● Site still in use

■ Site no longer in use

1 E5 HOUSE OF PERKUNAS
16TH CENTURY A.D.
LOCATION: Kaunas, Lithuania
NOTES: Built on site of a temple to the ancient Lithuanian thunder god Perkunas.

2 E5 THE GATE CHAPEL
18TH CENTURY A.D.
LOCATION: Vilnius, Lithuania
NOTES: Building that contains a miracle-working icon of the Virgin Mary.

3 E5 VILNIUS CATHEDRAL
15TH CENTURY A.D.
LOCATION: Vilnius, Lithuania
NOTES: Burial site for a number of Lithuanian princes containing the Chapel of St. Kazimeiras, named after a 15th-century prince. The cathedral was rebuilt at the end of the 18th century.

4 F6 CAVES MONASTERY
A.D. 1051
LOCATION: Kiev, Ukraine
NOTES: Russia's most important monastery, a cultural center for centuries has a collection of gold-domed churches and tomb-caves full of mummified monks.

5 F6 SANTA SOFIA
A.D. 548
LOCATION: Kiev, Ukraine
NOTES: Named after Santa Sophia in Istanbul, it was one of the greatest Christian churches for nearly 1,000 years. Most of the current buildings and frescoes date from the 11th century, and influenced many Russian Orthodox churches. The mosaic of Christ Prantocrator can be found inside, as can the coffin of its founder Yaroslav, carved with early Christian symbols.

6 F7 NEAPOLIS
3RD CENTURY A.D.
LOCATION: Simferopol, Ukraine
NOTES: Likely capital of the Scythian state until the fourth century A.D. It has various mounds with a stone reconstruction of a royal mausoleum, where 1,300 gold burial objects were discovered.

7 F3 SOLOVYETSKY MONASTERY
15TH CENTURY A.D.
LOCATION: White Sea, Russia
NOTES: See p.47.

8 F4 PETER AND PAUL CATHEDRAL
18TH CENTURY A.D.
LOCATION: St. Petersburg, Russia
NOTES: Part of the notorious Peter and Paul Fortress containing the tomb of Peter the Great and many other pre-revolutionary rulers.

9 F4 KAZAN CATHEDRAL
A.D. 1801-11
LOCATION: St. Petersburg, Russia
NOTES: Cathedral that once contained a miracle-working icon and houses the State Museum of the History of Religion.

10 F4 ST. ISAAC'S CATHEDRAL
A.D. 1818-58
LOCATION: St. Petersburg, Russia
NOTES: Built for Alexander I and finished by Nicolas I, it is one of the most lavish cathedrals in Russia.

11 F4 KIZHI ISLAND
12TH CENTURY A.D.
LOCATION: Kareliya, Russia
NOTES: The Church of the Transfiguration of 1714 with its 22 domes stands on the site of a 12th-century pagan ritual center. The 14th-century Church of the Resurrection is one of the oldest wooden buildings in the world.

12 E5 PECHORY MONASTERY
A.D. 1473
LOCATION: near Pskov, Russia
NOTES: Complex that includes St. Nicholas' Church, the Assumption Cathedral, and the Intercession Church. It is found in a ravine full of hermits' caves, which have tombs with over 10,000 bodies.

13 E5 TRINITY CATHEDRAL
A.D. 1699
LOCATION: Pskov, Russia
NOTES: One of Russia's most splendid sites with a colossal gilded central dome as high as a small skyscraper.

14 F5 ASSUMPTION CATHEDRAL
11TH CENTURY A.D.
LOCATION: Smolensk, Russia
NOTES: Built on the site of an earlier cathedral; it has a miracle-working icon of the Virgin Mary.

15 G5 BORIS AND GLEB MONASTERY
16TH CENTURY A.D.
LOCATION: Rostov region, Russia
NOTES: Complex that includes the Church of the Presentation. The first monastery was built here in the tenth century.

16 G5 IPATEVSKY MONASTERY
13TH CENTURY A.D.
LOCATION: Kostroma, Russia
NOTES: See p.46.

17 G5 ANNUNCIATION CATHEDRAL
A.D. 1562
LOCATION: Kazan, Russia
NOTES: In one of the oldest Russian cities, this cathedral is one of the prime examples of Tartar architecture. It is famous for its leaning black tower.

18 G5 TRINITY MONASTERY OF ST. SERGIUS
A.D. 1420
LOCATION: Zagorsk, Russia
NOTES: See p.46.

19 F5 CATHEDRAL OF THE RESURRECTION
A.D. 1656
LOCATION: Istra, near Moscow, Russia
NOTES: Founded by the patriarch Nikon with the intention of creating a City of God. Largely destroyed in World War II, it is now being slowly rebuilt.

20 F5 CHURCH OF THE TRINITY
A.D. 1650
LOCATION: Moscow, Russia
NOTES: Imposing church with onion domes. Among its many attractions are the realistic gospel frescoes by Simon Ushakove.

21 F5 CHURCH OF ST. ANTIPY-THE-CARRIAGE HOUSE
16TH CENTURY A.D.
LOCATION: Moscow, Russia
NOTES: Lopsided church commissioned by Malyuta Skarutov, head of Ivan the Terrible's secret police.

22 F5 ST. BASIL'S CATHEDRAL
A.D. 1555-61
LOCATION: Moscow, Russia
NOTES: See pp.48-49.

23 F5 DON MONASTERY
A.D. 1591
LOCATION: Moscow, Russia
NOTES: Founded to celebrate the Russian Army's defeat of the Tartars. Contains sacred icon of the Virgin Mary.

24 F5 DANILOV MONASTERY
LATE 13TH CENTURY A.D.
LOCATION: Moscow, Russia
NOTES: Headquarters of the Russian Orthodox Church, built by Danil, first Prince of Moscow and rebuilt by Ivan the Terrible. Turned into a factory and a prison after the 1917 revolution, it returned to its original use in 1983.

25 F5 NOVODEVICHY CONVENT
A.D. 1524
LOCATION: Moscow, Russia
NOTES: Burial place of various famous Russians, similar to the Kremlin wall, it includes the Smolensk Cathedral and a number of 16th-century frescoes.

26 F5 ASSUMPTION CATHEDRAL
A.D. 1475-79
LOCATION: Moscow, Russia
NOTES: Chief Russian Orthodox church, it contains tombs of many church leaders. Closed by the Communists in 1918, it was reopened in 1989.

27 G5 CATHEDRAL OF THE ASSUMPTION
A.D. 1158
LOCATION: Vladimir, Russia
NOTES: At one point the most important cathedral in Russia and model for many of Russia's cathedrals. Inside, it is lavishly illustrated with murals.

28 G7 MAIKOP
3RD MILLENNIUM A.D.
LOCATION: Caucasus Mountains, Russia
NOTES: Burial mound with three chambers, each containing human remains; one red ocher-covered skeleton was probably a prince.

29 G8 LYGYT VILLAGE
10TH CENTURY A.D.
LOCATION: Verkhny Chegem, Caucasus
NOTES: Site containing the remains of Muslim and Christian temples and tombs going back over 1,000 years.

30 G8 DARGAVS
14TH CENTURY A.D.
LOCATION: near Vladikavkaz, Caucasus
NOTES: Known as "the Village of the Dead," this huge cemetery with beehive tombs is believed to have been used by an ancient ancestor cult.

31 G8 VLADIKAVKAZ MOSQUE
A.D. 1906
LOCATION: north Ossetian ASSR, Russia
NOTES: Mosque with a blue dome, two towers, and 300 Qur'anic inscriptions.

32 G8 ABHKASIA
A.D. 2500-1500
LOCATION: Georgia
NOTES: Megalithic tombs – many with an antechamber, a slab-stone doorway, or cut out of a cliff – that were probably built by the Novisvobodnajan culture.

33 G8 TSMINDA SAMEBO
14TH CENTURY A.D.
LOCATION: Kazbegi, Georgia
NOTES: Holy Trinity Church reputedly built on the site of a cave monastery.

34 G8 GELATI MONASTERY
A.D. 1106
LOCATION: Georgia
NOTES: One of the finest, and once one of the richest, monasteries in Georgia, as well as its intellectual center.

35 G8 SVETI TSKHOVELI CATHEDRAL
15TH CENTURY A.D.
LOCATION: Mtskheta, Georgia
NOTES: Its name means "life-giving pillar" legend says that a Jew present at the Crucifixion brought back Christ's robe, causing an earthquake. The pillar was a cedar tree growing from where the robe fell. A wooden church, then a cathedral, sacked by Timur, was also built.

36 G8 ALAVERDI CATHEDRAL
11TH CENTURY A.D.
LOCATION: Georgia
NOTES: Large cathedral that has been compared to Chartres.

37 G8 ANCHISKHATI BASILICA
6TH CENTURY A.D.
LOCATION: Tbilisi, Georgia
NOTES: Stone church named after a sixth-century icon of Jesus. It is found next to the "holy mountain" Mtatsminda.

38 G8 SIONI CATHEDRAL
6TH CENTURY A.D.
LOCATION: Tbilisi, Georgia
NOTES: Center of the Georgian Orthodox Church containing its holiest relic – a cross of vine stems and hair woven by St. Nino, the woman who brought Christianity here in the fourth century.

39 G8 VARDZIA
12TH CENTURY A.D.
LOCATION: Georgia
NOTES: Large cave complex containing several churches. Mostly two-room residences; some were ceremonial, others monastic.

40 G8 AGARTSIN MONASTERY
10TH-13TH CENTURY A.D.
LOCATION: Armenia
NOTES: The most important religious and cultural center in Armenia during medieval times. The main building in the monastery is the Cathedral of the Virgin.

41 G8 ST GREGORY THE ILLUMINATOR
A.D. 303
LOCATION: near Yerevan, Armenia
NOTES: Once the site of a pagan shrine where St. Gregory had a vision of Christ descending to earth. Only parts of the seventh- and 17th-century buildings remain. Like the Geghard Monastery, it claims to hold the spearhead that pierced the side of Christ.

42 G8 GARNI
1ST CENTURY A.D.
LOCATION: near Yerevan, Armenia
NOTES: Remains of a Greek-style temple

dedicated to the god Mithras, who originated in Persia, and built by the Armenian king Tiridates I.

43 G8 GEGHARD MONASTERY
4TH CENTURY A.D.
LOCATION: near Garni, Armenia
NOTES: Named after the spear that pierced the side of Christ. The present churches date from the 13th century.

44 G8 ODZUN CHURCH
6TH CENTURY A.D.
LOCATION: Alaverdi, Armenia
NOTES: Early Christian church that contains some medieval cemeteries.

45 H8 KOBUSTAN CAVES
8TH MILLENNIUM A.D.
LOCATION: near Baku, Azerbaijan
NOTES: Caves covering a huge area that contain thousands of rock paintings, some dating back 10,000 years.

46 H8 SURAKHANY TEMPLE
18TH CENTURY A.D.
LOCATION: near Baku, Azerbaijan
NOTES: Built on a much older Parsee temple near natural gas vents, it is devoted to fire worship and was a place of pilgrimage for Parsees.

47 I8 KHIVA
10TH CENTURY A.D.
LOCATION: Uzbekistan
NOTES: Town full of mosques, mostly dating from medieval times. The Pakhlavan Makhmud Mausoleum, resting place of the town's patron saint is its main pilgrimage spot.

48 J8 KALYAN MOSQUE
16TH CENTURY A.D.
LOCATION: Bukhara, Uzbekistan
NOTES: At 154 ft (47 m), the Kalyan Minaret was once the tallest religious building in the world. It is now part of the 16th-century Kalyan Mosque.

49 J8 SAMARKAND
5TH CENTURY A.D.
LOCATION: Uzbekistan
NOTES: *See pp.126–127.*

50 J8 BEZEKLIK
8TH–9TH CENTURY A.D.
LOCATION: Kazakhstan
NOTES: Buddhist cave temple complex.

51 J8 MAUSOLEUM OF HODJA AKHMED YASAVI
14TH CENTURY A.D.
LOCATION: Chimkent, Kazakhstan
NOTES: Shrine of 12th-century Sufi poet Hodja Akhmed Yasavi, it has the largest dome in Asia.

52 M6 ABAKAN
3000–1000 B.C.
LOCATION: Siberia, Russia
NOTES: Site that contains burial mounds and stone idols.

53 O6 IVOLGINSK MONASTERY
A.D. 1946
LOCATION: Ulan-Ude, Siberia, Russia
NOTES: Center of Russian Buddhism. Rebuilt by Stalin in 1946 in return for help received from lamas during the war.

54 O6 KHAMAR-DABAN MONASTERY
A.D. 1972
LOCATION: Ivolginsk-Datsan, Siberia
NOTES: New Buddhist center containing a round shrine to Maitreya with a holy 108-volume Ganjur scripture, stupas, and a cutting from the original Bodhi tree.

UNITED KINGDOM & IRELAND

The map for these listings is on pp.142–143.

● Site still in use
■ Site no longer in use

1 G5 DEVENISH ISLAND
6TH CENTURY A.D.
LOCATION: Fermanagh, Northern Ireland
NOTES: Island where St. Molaise set up a religious community in the sixth century, it was important until the 17th century.

2 H5 NAVAN FORT
C. 100 B.C.
LOCATION: Armagh, Northern Ireland
NOTES: Royal seat of the kings of Ulster in early times. Within the enclosure is a high mound 190 ft (58 m) in diameter, probably the royal tumulus.

3 G5 CREVYKEEL
4000–3000 B.C.
LOCATION: Sligo, Ireland
NOTES: Impressive Neolithic cairn that includes a small passage grave.

4 G6 KNOCK
A.D. 1879
LOCATION: Mayo, Ireland
NOTES: Site where the Virgin Mary is said to have appeared to villagers in 1879. Subsequently a site of national pilgrimage famous for miraculous cures.

5 G6 CLONMACNOISE
6TH CENTURY A.D.
LOCATION: Offaly, Ireland
NOTES: Monastery founded by St. Ciaran, that became the greatest of the monastic schools. There are two 12th-century round towers, five high crosses – one elaborately carved – and nine churches, including the Romanesque Nun's Church.

6 H6 LOUGHCREW
C. 3000 B.C.
LOCATION: Meath, Ireland
NOTES: Passage grave cemetery known as Slieve na Caillighe, one of the chief groups of megalithic tombs in Ireland. There are about 30 passage graves, many of the distinctly Irish cruciform type.

7 H6 KNOWTH
C. 3000 B.C.
LOCATION: Meath, Ireland
NOTES: The greatest concentration of megalithic art in Europe. Knowth has two passage tombs and a number of finely carved curbstones.

8 H6 NEWGRANGE
C. 3000 B.C.
LOCATION: Meath, Ireland
NOTES: *See pp.72–73.*

9 H6 TARA
C. 3000 B.C.
LOCATION: Meath, Ireland
NOTES: *See p.73.*

10 H6 ST. PATRICK'S CATHEDRAL
A.D. 1192
LOCATION: Dublin, Ireland
NOTES: Founded next to a sacred well where St. Patrick baptized converts around A.D. 450, replacing a wooden chapel at the end of the 12th century. Today it is the national cathedral of the Protestant Church of Ireland.

11 H6 ST. BRIGID'S CATHEDRAL
C. A.D. 500
LOCATION: Kildare, Ireland
NOTES: A 13th-century cathedral in honor of the saint who founded a religious community here in about A.D. 500. There is evidence of pagan ritual here, including the burning of a perpetual fire that continued until the 16th century.

12 H7 ST. COLUMB'S HOUSE
A.D. 814
LOCATION: Meath, Ireland
NOTES: Possibly the stone church built by the monks of Iona (*see p.70*).

13 G7 GLENDALOUGH
6TH CENTURY A.D.
LOCATION: Wicklow, Ireland
NOTES: Remains of a monastery founded by St. Kevin. It was a center of pilgrimage for many centuries. Its remains include a roofless 12th-century cathedral, St. Kevin's Cross, and a tiny priest's house.

14 G7 ROCK OF CASHEL
12TH CENTURY A.D.
LOCATION: Tipperary, Ireland
NOTES: Since prehistoric times the seat of the Munster kings, given to the church in the 12th century. There is a round tower, Cormac's Chapel, a Romanesque church, ruins of a 13th-century cathedral, and the later Hall of Vicars' Choral.

15 G6 LOUGH GUR
C. 2000 B.C.
LOCATION: Limerick, Ireland
NOTES: A Stone Age settlement stood here as early as 3000 B.C., and there are a number of standing stones, burial mounds, and an impressive stone circle. The Giant's Grave here contained the remains of four children and eight adults.

16 G7 DRUMBEG
C. 14TH–15TH CENTURY B.C.
LOCATION: Cork, Ireland
NOTES: The finest of the west Cork stone circles. A pottery vessel containing cremated human bones has been excavated from a small central pit.

17 J1 MID HOWE
3000–2000 B.C.
LOCATION: Orkney, Scotland
NOTES: Huge cairn with a long gallery divided into "stalls" by pairs of upright slabs; bodies were laid in the walls on stone shelves.

18 J1 MAES HOWE
C. 3000 B.C.
LOCATION: Orkney, Scotland
NOTES: Chambered tomb in a huge cairn that forms one of the most impressive prehistoric monuments in Europe. The passageway is constructed of four slabs, while the central chamber is corbeled with smooth rectangular sandstone slabs.

19 J1 SKARA BRAE
C. 3000 B.C.
LOCATION: Orkney, Scotland
NOTES: Neolithic settlement, with some megalithic remains, likely to have housed astronomer-priests. The presence

of spiral motifs and geometric stone balls suggests links with the Boyne tombs of Ireland.

20 J1 RING OF BRODGAR
C. 2500 B.C.
LOCATION: Orkney, Scotland
NOTES: One of the largest stone circles in the British Isles set within a rock-cut ditch. Its diameter is almost identical to that of the inner circle at Avebury. It is linked to a larger complex used for seasonal ceremonies and burial rituals.

21 H2 CALLANISH
1800 B.C.
LOCATION: Western Isles, Scotland
NOTES: A long avenue leads to a central circle of tall standing stones, stone rows, and a chambered tomb. Believed to have been a lunar observatory site. Legend tells of a great priest-king who had the stones raised by black slaves.

22 H3 IONA
C. A.D. 600
LOCATION: Hebrides, Scotland
NOTES: *See p.70.*

23 I4 TEMPLE WOOD
C. 1750 B.C.
LOCATION: Kilmartin, Argyll, Scotland
NOTES: X-shaped alignments of five large cup-marked standing stones with a stone circle surrounding a large cist. The stones provided lunar sight lines using an observing "notch" on the skyline.

24 H4 BALLACHROY
C. 1800 B.C.
LOCATION: Kintyre, Scotland
NOTES: Astronomical site with burial cist and three standing stones.

25 I2 CLAVA CAIRN
C. 3000 B.C.
LOCATION: Inverness, Scotland
NOTES: Late Neolithic cemetery with two large passage graves. Between the graves are a ring cairn and a stone circle.

26 I3 FORTINGALL
2ND MILLENNIUM B.C.
LOCATION: Tayside, Scotland
NOTES: Three stone circles linked to the festival of Samhain that marked the beginning of the Celtic New Year. Bonfires called "Mounds of the Dead" were lit and people danced around them.

27 I3 CROFT MORAIG
C. 2850 B.C.
LOCATION: Perthshire, Scotland
NOTES: Stone circle surrounded by a shallow ditch that may have been roofed over to form a shrine. Posts were replaced by stones set in a horseshoe. Another circle of large stones was set up within the bank with a pair of outliers.

28 J3 SCONE
A.D. 843
LOCATION: Tayside, Scotland
NOTES: The Stone of Destiny was brought here in A.D. 843, on which all subsequent Scottish kings were crowned, until it was taken by the English. The stone was thought to be the one used by Jacob as a pillow when he dreamed of God.

29 J4 KINGSIDE HILL
C. 1500 B.C.
LOCATION: near Edinburgh, Scotland
NOTES: Ring of 30 stones 1,000 ft (300 m) in diameter. One entrance with a central mound may have been used for cremations.

30 J4 MELROSE ABBEY

A.D. 1136

LOCATION: Borders, Scotland

NOTES: Cistercian abbey founded by David I of Scotland. The heart of Robert the Bruce is said to be buried here in a silver casket.

31 I5 TOREHOUSEMUIR

2ND MILLENNIUM B.C.

LOCATION: Dumfries, Scotland

NOTES: Unusual circle of 19 stones, whose tops are hammered down, suggesting funerary rites rather than astronomical use. Some were excavated in the last century and reports of mysterious lights were made soon after this was done.

32 I6 BRYN CELLI DDU

C. 2000 B.C.

LOCATION: Gwynedd, Wales

NOTES: Mound with a fine chamber tomb that revealed human bones – some burned – and geometric carvings. The rituals enacted here have never been fully explained

33 J6 ST. WINIFRED'S WELL

7TH CENTURY A.D.

LOCATION: Clwyd, Wales

NOTES: Holy well said to have healing powers and to be the site of St. Winifred's martyrdom. Beheaded by a Welsh chieftain, water flowed from where her head fell, but she was restored to life by her guardian St. Bueno. The statue over the well depicts Winifred with a faint line around her neck. It has been the site of pilgrimages by invalids for centuries.

34 I6 DINAS EMRHYS

1ST-3RD CENTURY A.D.

LOCATION: Gwynedd, Wales

NOTES: Wooded hill associated with Merlin. There is an ancient fortress, of which some earthworks remain here. The fortress was said to be Merlin's and to contain his treasure. It was once known as Dinas Fforan – Fort of High Powers.

35 I7 ST. DAVID'S CATHEDRAL

A.D. 530

LOCATION: Dyfed, Wales

NOTES: See p.71.

36 I7 ST. GOVAN'S CHAPEL

5TH CENTURY A.D.

LOCATION: Dyfed, Wales

NOTES: Tiny rock-built chapel at the foot of limestone cliffs. Below it is a holy well that is said to have healing powers.

37 I7 GORS FAWR

3RD MILLENNIUM B.C.

LOCATION: Dyfed, Wales

NOTES: See p.71.

38 J7 THE FISH STONE

DATE UNKNOWN

LOCATION: Powys, Wales

NOTES: A 18-ft (5.5-m) high standing stone that tapers at the bottom, suggesting a piscine shape. Legend says that on Midsummer Eve the stone jumps into the nearby river and swims around.

39 J4 LINDISFARNE

A.D. 635

LOCATION: Northumberland, England

NOTES: Once known as Holy Island, its importance as a religious site began in A.D. 635, when its church and monastery were founded by St. Aidan. The Danish invasion in the ninth century forced the monks to flee to Durham, where they later founded its cathedral.

40 J5 COVENTINA'S WELL

C. 1ST CENTURY B.C.

LOCATION: Northumberland, England

NOTES: Celtic well site of votive offerings. Small bronze heads, a human skull, and an altar were found here. The head was a symbol of Celtic divinity.

41 J5 CASTELRIGG CIRCLE

C. 3000 B.C.

LOCATION: Cumbria, England

NOTES: Fine stone circle built within a bowl of the surrounding Lakeland fells. The relation of the position of stones in the circle to the surrounding mountains suggests an astronomical function.

42 J5 LONG MEG AND HER DAUGHTERS

C. 1700-1500 B.C.

LOCATION: Cumbria, England

NOTES: Stone circle where, legend has it, a witch and her daughters were turned to stone. Long Meg, weighing 28 tons, would have taken over 100 people to set up. Its carved spiral and concentric circles, possibly sun symbols, may relate to ceremonies of birth and death.

43 J5 DURHAM CATHEDRAL

A.D. 995

LOCATION: Durham, England

NOTES: Monks, driven from Lindisfarne and bearing the preserved body of St. Cuthbert, wandered for years before they founded a new monastery here. The later Norman cathedral contains the shrine of St. Cuthbert.

44 J5 PENDLE HILL

NATURAL SITE

LOCATION: Lancashire, England

NOTES: Long associated with witchcraft and home of Chattox and Demdike, witches who were put to death in 1612.

45 J5 ILKLEY MOOR

NATURAL SITE

LOCATION: West Yorkshire, England

NOTES: Prehistoric tumuli that include the Doublers Stones, a natural bowl-shaped rock formation with geometric marks linked to sun worship, and the Swastika Stone, possibly Celtic in origin.

46 K5 YORK MINSTER

A.D. 627

LOCATION: Yorkshire, England

NOTES: Built on the site of a small church where King Edwin of Northumberland, was baptized in A.D. 627. The present 12th-century building was the largest church in medieval England.

47 J6 ARBOR LOW

C. 2000 B.C.

LOCATION: Derbyshire, England

NOTES: Henge built by the Beaker people enclosed in a circle 250 ft (76 m) in diameter. Bronze Age barrows nearby suggest that it was probably an important religious site.

48 L6 WALSINGHAM

C. A.D. 1153

LOCATION: Norfolk, England

NOTES: Site of the shrine of Our Lady of Walsingham, where she saw a vision of the Virgin Mary in 1061. A famous pilgrimage center during the Middle Ages, it became so again in 1922 after another sighting of the Virgin.

49 K7 GRIMES GRAVES

3300-1650 B.C.

LOCATION: Norfolk, England

NOTES: Largest prehistoric flint mine in Europe. An altar of flints with antlers and a miner's lamp was erected to ensure continued fertility. A statuette of a pregnant mother goddess and chalk phallus were found in front of the altar.

50 K7 ELY CATHEDRAL

A.D. 1083

LOCATION: Cambridgeshire, England

NOTES: Queen Etheldreda founded a monastery here. Her buried body was found to be undecayed – the sign of a saint – and a church was built to house her relics. The interior walls of the present cathedral, built in 1083, have pagan carvings of the fabled Green Man.

51 J7 HEREFORD CATHEDRAL

C. 12TH CENTURY A.D.

LOCATION: Herefordshire, England

NOTES: Saxon church where the Christian king, Ethelbert of East Anglia, is buried. Miracles were attributed to him after his death, and the cathedral became an early place of pilgrimage. After Welsh and Irish raids, it was rebuilt about A.D. 1200.

52 J7 ROLLRIGHT STONES

C. 3000 B.C.

LOCATION: Oxfordshire, England

NOTES: Megalithic circle of 70 large stones and one tall megalith standing alone. A group of five megaliths stands nearby. Legend states that the monolith is the king, the five megaliths his knights, and the circle his men-at-arms, all turned to stone by a witch.

53 J7 WHITE HORSE

C. 1ST CENTURY B.C.

LOCATION: Oxfordshire, England

NOTES: Horse cut out of chalk that is 348 ft (106 m) long and 131 ft (40 m) high. Its stylized shape is distinctly Celtic, but may be older. It is said that St. George killed the dragon on this hill, but it is probably the emblem of the Atrobates, an Iron Age Celtic tribe who lived in the valley below.

54 J7 WAYLANDS SMITHY

C. 3500 B.C.

LOCATION: Oxfordshire, England

NOTES: Long barrow with six large stones marking the entrance, a central passage inside, and chambers for burials.

55 K7 ST. ALBAN'S CATHEDRAL

8TH CENTURY A.D.

LOCATION: Hertfordshire, England

NOTES: St. Alban, a Roman soldier, was beheaded here in A.D. 304 and became the first martyr in England. A church was built on the site; the abbey dates from the eighth century and was rebuilt after the Norman Conquest. It contains the still-venerated shrine of St. Alban.

56 K7 WESTMINSTER ABBEY

C. A.D. 1050

LOCATION: London, England

NOTES: Founded by Edward the Confessor on a previous Roman religious site, the abbey contains his shrine, which became a focus of pilgrimage in medieval times. William the Conqueror was crowned here, and it has been the setting for all coronations since, housing the Stone of Scone. Rebuilt in Gothic style in 1245, most English monarchs were buried here.

57 L8 CANTERBURY CATHEDRAL

A.D. 597

LOCATION: Kent, England

NOTES: St. Augustine, who brought Christianity to England, first preached on this spot, which became the site of the mother church of English Christianity.

Rebuilt after a fire in 1097 and again in the 12th century, it is where Thomas à Becket was martyred, and his shrine became the chief place of pilgrimage in medieval England. Since the Reformation, the cathedral has been the seat of the Archbishops of the Anglican Church.

58 K8 LONG MAN OF WILMINGTON

DATE UNKNOWN

LOCATION: Sussex, England

NOTES: Giant figure carved into a hill holding 230-ft (70-m) wands in his opened hands. When overgrown, it is also called the Green Man. Various unproven theories exist about its origin; suggestions include Roman soldiers, monks from Wilmington Priory, Saxons, and Celts, the latter being the most likely.

59 J8 AVEBURY

C. 2000 B.C.

LOCATION: Wiltshire, England

NOTES: See p.68.

60 J8 BUSH BARROW

C. 1500-1000 B.C.

LOCATION: Wiltshire, England

NOTES: Burial place of a rich Wiltshire chieftain containing a remarkable bone-mounted wand, which has affinities with finds in Mycenaean shaft graves.

61 J8 STONEHENGE

C. 3300 B.C.

LOCATION: Wiltshire, England

NOTES: See pp.68-69.

62 J8 SALISBURY CATHEDRAL

A.D. 1220

LOCATION: Wiltshire, England

NOTES: Completed in 1258, replacing an earlier cathedral in the abandoned town of Old Sarum, it is one of the finest Christian monuments in the world. The spire is the highest in England and is said to contain a piece of the Virgin Mary's robe preserved in a leaden casket.

63 J8 CHRISTCHURCH

11TH CENTURY A.D.

LOCATION: Dorset, England

NOTES: A mysterious carpenter who came to work on the site and then disappeared, giving rise to a belief that Christ himself had helped build the new church.

64 J8 CERNE GIANT

5TH CENTURY A.D.

LOCATION: Dorset, England

NOTES: Chalk hillside figure of a naked, club-wielding man, linked to fertility rites.

65 J7 STANTON DREW CIRCLES

2500-1250 B.C.

LOCATION: Avon, England

NOTES: Legend recounts that these stone circles were wedding guests, who danced to the Devil's fiddle on the Sabbath and were turned to stone.

66 J8 ROMAN BATHS

C. A.D. 70

LOCATION: Bath, Avon, England

NOTES: Hot springs, sacred to the ancient Britons, taken over by the Romans and turned into a temple complex called Aquae Sulis, dedicated to the goddess Sulis-Minerva. The site was still sacred as late as the tenth century, when King Edgar was crowned here.

67 J8 WOOKEY HOLE

A.D. 0-500

LOCATION: Somerset, England

NOTES: Celtic place of sacrifice where 14 skulls were discovered.

68 J8 WELLS CATHEDRAL
A.D. 1180
LOCATION: Somerset, England
NOTES: The first Gothic cathedral in England, its west facade displays the statues of nearly 400 saints, bishops, prophets, and kings once colorfully painted to attract pilgrims.

69 J8 GLASTONBURY
12TH CENTURY A.D.
LOCATION: Somerset, England
NOTES: *See p.69.*

70 I8 ALTARNUN CHURCH
1ST–5TH CENTURY A.D.
LOCATION: Cornwall, England
NOTES: The "Cathedral of the Moor," founded by St. Nonna, stands inside the enclosure of the first Celtic church here. To the east is her holy "bowsenning well," where madmen could be cured.

71 I8 TRETHEVY QUOIT
C. 3000 B.C.
LOCATION: Cornwall, England
NOTES: The only huge stones remain from a megalithic chambered tomb. One of the stones has a pecked porthole, perhaps providing for the exodus of the soul.

72 I8 HURLER'S STONE CIRCLE
1850 B.C.
LOCATION: Cornwall, England
NOTES: Three aligned stone circles once thought to have been men turned into stone for playing the Cornish game of hurling on a Sunday. The circles may have stellar and solar alignments.

73 H8 LANYON QUOIT
C. 4000 B.C.
LOCATION: Cornwall, England
NOTES: Burial site, a quoit – a Cornish "dolmen" – that is a four-sided rock enclosure with a large slab roof.

74 H8 BOSCAWEN-UN
5TH MILLENNIUM B.C.
LOCATION: Cornwall, England
NOTES: Thought to be the oldest circle in the British Isles. There are 18 upright granite stones and one block of almost pure quartz. It may have been used in the Dark Ages; it is mentioned in the Welsh triads as one of the three Gorsedds – bardic meeting places – of Britain.

75 H9 MERRY MAIDENS
C. 1500–1000 B.C.
LOCATION: Cornwall, England
NOTES: Stone circle with 19 symmetrical stones. Legend tells of maidens turned to stone while dancing on a Sunday.

76 H8 MADRON WELL
C. A.D. 500–1000
LOCATION: Cornwall, England
NOTES: Holy well, whose water runs to a nearby medieval baptistry. One of the oldest places of Christian worship in Cornwall and still a place of pilgrimage; those who seek healing hang rags off the bushes near the wells.

77 J9 LA HOUGUE BIE
C. 5000 B.C.
LOCATION: Jersey, Channel Islands
NOTES: Mound with a long passage grave underneath. A medieval chapel was built above and later replaced.

NORTH AMERICA

The map for these listings is on pp.144–145.

● Site still in use
■ Site no longer in use

1 I5 GITANMAKS VILLAGE
AFTER A.D. 1500
LOCATION: British Columbia, Canada
NOTES: *See p.81.*

2 I5 FRASER RIVER PETROGLYPHS
DATE UNKNOWN
LOCATION: British Columbia, Canada
NOTES: Carvings associated with shamanism made on large boulders by the Western Plateau culture.

3 I6 SPROAT LAKE
DATE UNKNOWN
LOCATION: Vancouver Island, Canada
NOTES: *See p.81.*

4 I6 OKANAGAN VALLEY
DATE UNKNOWN
LOCATION: British Columbia, Canada
NOTES: Rock paintings of humans, animals, and supernatural creatures. They were associated with ceremonies involving a search for a personal guardian spirit.

5 J6 CLUNY
A.D. 1872
LOCATION: Alberta, Canada
NOTES: Two cairns linked by a line of boulders, marking the spots where two warriors fought and fell.

6 J6 ROY RIVERS MEDICINE WHEEL
DATE UNKNOWN
LOCATION: Alberta, Canada
NOTES: Circle of boulders broken by two parallel pairs of lines of stones that lead to a central cairn. From this cairn, the sun appears to set directly over a figure built of smaller stones nearby.

7 J6 MAJORVILLE
2500 B.C.
LOCATION: Alberta, Canada
NOTES: Large ring of stones with a central cairn and radiating spokes that form the largest medicine wheel in the world, built by archaic hunters.

8 J6 MILK RIVER VALLEY
DATE UNKNOWN
LOCATION: Saskatchewan, Canada
NOTES: Prehistoric rock carvings cut in the valley bedrock.

9 K6 THE MINTON TURTLE
DATE UNKNOWN
LOCATION: Saskatchewan, Canada
NOTES: Medicine wheel with a central cairn in its center overlooking the Big Muddy River. It has the form of a turtle and is 130 ft (40 m) long.

10 K6 MOOSE MOUNTAIN
DATE UNKNOWN
LOCATION: Saskatchewan, Canada
NOTES: Medicine wheel with five spokes,

and cairns at the end of each. One spoke is aligned with the solstice. The central cairn is surrounded by a stone ring and was most probably for rituals. The site may well be over 2,000 years old.

11 L5 BANNOCK POINT
500 B.C.–A.D. 800
LOCATION: Manitoba, Canada
NOTES: Nine acres (three and a half hectares) of petroforms and mosaic animal outlines used for Ojibway initiations. The rocks are carved in the shapes of fish, snakes, birds, and other geometric forms.

12 M6 LAKE SUPERIOR
NATURAL SITE
LOCATION: Canada
NOTES: *See p.80.*

13 M6 DREAMER'S ROCK
NATURAL SITE
LOCATION: Ontario, Canada
NOTES: Quartzite rock rising 1,640 ft (500 m) above Lake Ontario. Sacred to the Ojibway, who worshipped the Great Spirit here. Young men used it as a guide in their search for a spirit.

14 N7 PETERBOROUGH PETROGLYPHS
C. A.D. 300
LOCATION: Rice Lake, Ontario, Canada
NOTES: *See p.80.*

15 N6 BON ECHO PROVINCIAL PARK
DATE UNKNOWN
LOCATION: Mazinaw Lake, Ontario, Canada
NOTES: Site of sacred Algonkian ochre rock paintings.

16 P6 PORT AU CHOIX
2000–1600 B.C.
LOCATION: Newfoundland, Canada
NOTES: Ancient mass burial site where the graves were deposited with red ochre and decorated Ramah chert stone tools.

17 P5 RATTLER'S BIGHT
2000–1600 B.C.
LOCATION: Labrador, Canada
NOTES: Ancient habitation site where the dead were buried in large cemeteries. Objects made of Ramah chert stone were "killed" to accompany the deceased.

18 P5 BISHOP'S MITRE
NATURAL SITE
LOCATION: Labrador, Canada
NOTES: Mountain home to an important Native American deity. Engraved pendants found in ancient burials around the area were shaped to resemble the mountain peaks.

19 N3 UNGARA
17TH–20TH CENTURY A.D.
LOCATION: Quebec, Canada
NOTES: Area of *inikshuits* and stone monuments built by the local Inuit.

20 N3 ENUKSO POINT
19TH–20TH CENTURY A.D.
LOCATION: Baffin Island, Canada
NOTES: An *inikshuit* is a cairn placed by the Inuit – it consists of life-size rock statues of men. Those of Enukso Point may have been intended to appease the spirits before dangerous water crossings.

21 F3 DENALI (MOUNT MCKINLEY)
NATURAL SITE
LOCATION: Alaska
NOTES: The tallest mountain in North America, once sacred to the Tena people.

22 I6 MOUNT BAKER
NATURAL SITE
LOCATION: Washington State
NOTES: Center of spiritual power for the Lummi and other local peoples.

23 I6 TAHOMA (MOUNT RAINIER)
NATURAL SITE
LOCATION: Washington State
NOTES: Many of this mountain's large stones, caves, and springs are ritual sites to the local Native Americans.

24 I6 MULTNOMAH FALLS
NATURAL SITE
LOCATION: Oregon
NOTES: Waterfalls on the Columbia River sacred to the Multnomah people. Legend tells of a chief's daughter who threw herself from the clifftop as a sacrifice to the Great Spirit to end an epidemic. The spirit created the falls in her memory.

25 I7 CRATER LAKE
NATURAL SITE
LOCATION: Oregon
NOTES: Lake created by the collapse of the Mount Mazama volcano 7,000 years ago, it was sacred to the Klamath, who regarded it as a place of great magical potency that could only be approached by experienced shamans.

26 I7 MOUNT SHASTA
NATURAL SITE
LOCATION: California
NOTES: Extinct volcano where Native Americans believe the power of the Earth Spirit is very strong. Several other nearby locations are used for purification rituals.

27 I7 BLUE LAKE
NATURAL SITE
LOCATION: California
NOTES: The Taos Puebla people make an annual pilgrimage to this spot, where they believe their tribe was created.

28 I7 SUNRISE ROCK ALTAR
DATE UNKNOWN
LOCATION: Greagle, California
NOTES: Ceremonial site with a flat stone altar, positioned by the Maidu people to receive the first sun rays of summer. Also the site of petroglyphs.

29 I7 MOUNT TAMALPAIS,
NATURAL SITE
LOCATION: California
NOTES: Found just to the north of the Golden Gate Bridge, it is sacred to local Native Americans.

30 I7 RING MOUNTAIN
NATURAL SITE
LOCATION: California
NOTES: Mountain sacred to the Miwok people, with a fertility stone as its peak that is seen as especially potent.

31 I7 TLAMCO (SAN FRANCISCO)
DATE UNKNOWN
LOCATION: California
NOTES: Before the present city was built, it was allegedly a temple site called Tlamco with seven hills that marked the orbits and diameters of the planet and formed a map of the Pleiades. Its Temple of the Sun is said to have stood on the present site of Haight and Shrader Streets.

32 I8 ESSELEN CREEK
NATURAL SITE
LOCATION: Big Sur River, California
NOTES: Site of great spiritual power and purification for native shamans.

Its warm mineral baths were used by the Esselen people for their religious purification rituals.

33 I8 POINT CONCEPTION
NATURAL SITE
LOCATION: California
NOTES: Chumash people see this as the western gate to the souls of the dead. They use nearby caves for vision quests.

34 J8 DESERT GEOGLYPHS
DATE UNKNOWN
LOCATION: Arizona & Nevada
NOTES: Giant sand figures similar to those found on the Nazca Plain, Peru.

35 J8 HAVASU FALLS
NATURAL SITE
LOCATION: Arizona
NOTES: Falls sacred to the Havasupai people who live in the canyon.

36 J8 WUPATKI
C. 11TH–13TH CENTURY A.D.
LOCATION: Arizona
NOTES: See p. 79.

37 J8 SUNSET CRATER
NATURAL SITE
LOCATION: Arizona
NOTES: See p. 78.

38 J8 METEOR CRATER
NATURAL SITE
LOCATION: Arizona
NOTES: See p. 78.

39 J8 MONTEZUMA'S CASTLE AND WELL
14TH CENTURY A.D.
LOCATION: near Sedona, Arizona
NOTES: "Castle" of five stories of adobe houses built into canyon walls by the Sinaguan people. The nearby well on Beaver Creek is called a *sipapu* – place of emergence – where ancestors came forth from the underworld.

40 J8 CAVE CREEK
NATURAL SITE
LOCATION: Arizona
NOTES: Site of hundreds of caves, many used as Hopewell ritual centers. Crystal Cave, accessible only on foot, has remarkable crystal-encrusted chambers.

41 J8 SNAKETOWN
A.D. 1000–1200
LOCATION: Arizona
NOTES: Hohokam site with remains of ritual ballcourts and platform mounds that suggest Mesoamerican influence.

42 J-K8 CHACO CANYON
C. A.D. 900–1300
LOCATION: Arizona
NOTES: See p. 78.

43 K8 MOUNT TAYLOR
NATURAL SITE
LOCATION: New Mexico
NOTES: Sacred Navajo site named after the spirit Tso-dzil that is believed to control it. The "Breathing Caves" near its base send out air rich in negative ions.

44 K8 BANDELIER NATIONAL MONUMENT
C. 4000 B.C.
LOCATION: New Mexico
NOTES: National park with thousands of archaeological sites, some as early as 8000 B.C. The rock shelters, probably used for ritual, date from 4000 B.C. Around A.D. 1100., the Anasazi came here and occupied the site for about 400 years.

45 K8 SANTUARIO DE CHIMAYO
19TH CENTURY A.D.
LOCATION: New Mexico
NOTES: Adobe church structure that has been called the "Lourdes of America." One of its founders claimed to see a burst of light here on Good Friday, and found a green crucifix while digging in the ground. Thousands of pilgrims converge here on Good Friday every year.

46 K8 THREE RIVERS PETROGLYPHS
A.D. 1000–1300
LOCATION: New Mexico
NOTES: Found on the sacred mountain of the Mescalero Apache, in the area populated by the Jornado branch of the Mogollon culture. There are many carvings of hands, faces, and animals.

47 K7 MANITOU SPRINGS
NATURAL SITE
LOCATION: Colorado
NOTES: Natural springs sacred to the Algonkian; the word manitou means "Great Spirit." The site has been worshipped by the Algonkian, Ute, Arapahoe, Sioux, Comanche, Shoshone, Kiowa, and Cheyenne.

48 K7 BIGHORN MEDICINE WHEEL
DATE UNKNOWN
LOCATION: Wyoming
NOTES: Called the "American Stonehenge," it lies on the shoulder of Medicine Mountain. Sacred to local Native Americans, it was used by them for rituals at sunrise and sunset.

49 K7 BEAR BUTTE
NATURAL SITE
LOCATION: South Dakota
NOTES: High ridge sacred to local Native Americans and used for vision quests – the individual search for spiritual power and self-knowledge. Around 4,000 Native Americans come to pray here every year.

50 K7 DEVIL'S TOWER
NATURAL SITE
LOCATION: South Dakota
NOTES: Sacred to the Sioux. One legend says it was formed after three young girls trying to escape a vicious bear, they were rescued by the Great God, who made the rock rise higher to save them.

51 K-L8 ENCHANTED ROCK
NATURAL SITE
LOCATION: Texas
NOTES: "Island mountain" sacred to the Kiowa, Apache, and Comanche people.

52 L8 SPIRO MOUNDS
C. A.D. 1000–1450
LOCATION: Texas
NOTES: One of the most important archaeological discoveries in North America. The 15 mounds were the sacred sites of a flourishing society that disappeared in the 15th century.

53 L8 HEAVENER RUNESTONE
A.D. 600–900
LOCATION: Oklahoma
NOTES: Eight small runic symbols are engraved on savanna sandstone; they consist of a series of crosses and other lines. It has been argued that the runes were carved by the first Norsemen who sailed to America long before Columbus.

54 L7 PIPESTONE QUARRY
NATURAL SITE
LOCATION: Minnesota
NOTES: Sacred red sandstone quarry used by Native Americans as a source of medicine-pipe bowls and stone for ritual use. Two nearby rocks are said to be spirit women who guard the quarry.

55 L7 POWERS FORT
13TH CENTURY A.D.
LOCATION: Missouri
NOTES: Small ceremonial center surrounded by fortified walls, with a central plaza and four adjacent mounds. The central one was the focal point for all the surrounding communities.

56 L8 TOLTEC
A.D. 900
LOCATION: Arkansas
NOTES: A complex settlement whose name derives from a misattribution to the Mexican people. Actually built by the Plum Bayou culture, it was an important religious center consisting of several burial and platform mounds.

57 L8 POVERTY POINT
C. 1200 B.C.
LOCATION: Mississippi
NOTES: Oldest mound complex in North America. It may have been built as an astronomical observatory, though it was probably also a major ritual and ceremonial center. It has an enormous mound in the center surrounded by six huge semicircular embankments.

58 L8 EMERALD MOUND
C. A.D. 1000–1500
LOCATION: Mississippi
NOTES: A natural hill flattened and modified into the shape of two pyramids of differing sizes. It belonged to the Natchez people, who were ruled by a chieftain known as the Great Sun. Its symbolism, like that of many Native American peoples, was linked to the sun.

59 M7 AZTALAN
C. A.D. 800–1200
LOCATION: Wisconsin
NOTES: Enclosure surrounded by three walls, each containing flat-topped earth pyramids surmounted by temples. Outside the walls a line of conical mounds were astronomically aligned. In one of these mounds the remains of a woman were found, wrapped in a robe of 1,200 polished shells – the so-called "beaded princess." There were once immense earth sculptures of birds, reptiles, and rabbits. The people may have been connected to the mound-builders of Cahokia. Nearby Lake Mills is said to contain a drowned cemetery.

60 M7 LIZARD MOUND
C. A.D. 1100–1300
LOCATION: Wisconsin
NOTES: Site of 30 effigy mounds sculpted from the earth, as well as pyramid-type structures. Some of the mounds also served as tombs.

61 L7 CAHOKIA MOUND
C. A.D. 1200
LOCATION: Illinois
NOTES: See p. 77.

62 M7 GORHAM PETROGLYPHS
DATE UNKNOWN
LOCATION: Illinois
NOTES: Rock-face with a series of sacred drawings of hands, circles, birds, crosses, and other images.

63 M8 TOWOSAGHY
10TH CENTURY A.D.
LOCATION: Tennessee
NOTES: Once a great ceremonial center, it was abandoned 600 years ago. The largest structure here was a ridge-topped pyramid. Another mound was surmounted with two temple buildings. It seems the culture here had the same beliefs as the great mound-builders to the east and worshipped a sun god.

64 M8 PINSON'S MOUNDS
A.D. 1000–1500
LOCATION: Tennessee
NOTES: Thirty mounds, some of them enormous, constructed by an unknown people. Covering 1,162 acres (470 hectares) the main site, known as Saul's Mound is 72 ft (22 m) high and the largest on the east coast.

65 M8 OLD STONE FORT
5TH CENTURY A.D.
LOCATION: Tennessee
NOTES: Erroneously assumed to be a fort by settlers in the 18th century, this is in fact a ritual site that was abandoned as early as the fifth century. It is an enclosure with stone walls along the edge of a steep slope. Nothing is known about the builders.

66 M8 MOUNDVILLE
13TH CENTURY A.D.
LOCATION: Alabama
NOTES: Site covering 297 acres (120 hectares) with 20 temple platforms. There are examples of hand-eye motifs, often symbolizing death, which are connected to the Southern Cult that was based throughout the Southeast.

67 M8 WICKCLIFFE MOUNDS
C. A.D. 900
LOCATION: Kentucky
NOTES: Mounds shaped like truncated pyramids that overlook the Ohio River and were inhabited for around 400 years. The top of the Great Mound is now surmounted by a wooden temple.

68 M7-8 ANGEL MOUNDS
C. A.D. 1100–1450
LOCATION: Kentucky
NOTES: It has been suggested that this site was built by the Mississippian people; the mounds have been aligned to the sun. The doorway of the main temple at Angel Mounds was oriented to the sunrise at the summer solstice.

69 M7 THE GREAT CIRCLE MOUND
C. 100 B.C.
LOCATION: Indiana
NOTES: Site of 11 earthworks near Indianapolis, maybe Hopewellian, dating back over 2,000 years. In the midst of an oak forest, the Circle Mound was 1,200 ft (366 m) across and about 10 ft (3 m) high, with an outer embankment surrounding the central mound. Other figures in the area include rectangles, ovals, and cones.

70 M7 NORTON MOUNDS
100 B.C.–A.D. 100
LOCATION: Norton, Michigan
NOTES: Hopewell mound burial site. Some of the mounds were lined with red ocher, and the bodies were often buried with lavish treasures for their journeys into the afterlife.

71 M6 SLEEPING BEAR DUNES
NATURAL SITE
LOCATION: Michigan
NOTES: A sand mountain sacred to the Ojibway, who consider it a giant mother bear waiting for her cubs, two offshore islands, to return to her.

72 M7 NEWARK MOUNDS
C. A.D. 100–200
LOCATION: Ohio
NOTES: The "greatest outdoor church in the world" is a vast complex of Hopewell mounds covering more than 200 acres (81 hectares). It includes the Great Circle, which is 1,200 ft (360 m) in diameter. The octagon enclosure to which it is connected is 11 times as large. The site is oriented to the rising of the moon and is believed to have been a vast observatory, designed for pinpointing solar and lunar eclipses, solstices, and the appearance of significant constellations.

73 M7 ADENA MOUND
10TH–6TH CENTURY B.C.
LOCATION: Ohio
NOTES: Site of the first of the Midwest cultures to use burial mounds to bury the elite. Built in two stages, the first level contained large log tombs with inhumations and burial remains, the second level contained simple burials.

74 M7 LIBERTY MOUND GROUP
100 B.C.–A.D. 100
LOCATION: Chillicothe, Ohio
NOTES: Group of 14 Hopewell mounds, geometrically arranged. Large buildings were found within the earth mounds, and probably housed the remains of important people in the community.

75 M7 MOUND CITY
100 B.C.–A.D. 600
LOCATION: Ohio
NOTES: A typical Hopewell burial site now protected as a National Monument. Copper images of birds of prey have been found here.

76 M7 FORT ANCIENT
A.D. 0–400
LOCATION: Ohio
NOTES: Gigantic sacred precinct capable of holding 12,000 people. The two main areas are connected by an ancient processional way. Extending from the enclosure are parallel earthworks leading to a single large mound.

77 M7 SERPENT MOUND
C. 100 B.C.
LOCATION: Ohio
NOTES: See p.76.

78 M8 ROCK EAGLE MOUND
A.D. 800–1500
LOCATION: Georgia
NOTES: Impressive mound attributed to the Middle Mississippian culture. Its center is the figure of an eagle.

79 M9 CRYSTAL RIVER MOUNDS
C. A.D. 400
LOCATION: Florida
NOTES: Sacred site believed to be connected in some way with the Maya of Central America. It has central pyramid mounds, burial earthworks, and a number of incised stelae.

80 M9 MADIRA BICKEL MOUND
200 B.C.–A.D. 1500
LOCATION: Terra Ceia Island, Florida
NOTES: Mound made almost entirely of sea shells constructed by the Timacuan people, symbolizing prosperity arising from the death of a previous generation.

81 M9 KEY MARCO
A.D. 1450
LOCATION: Florida
NOTES: A number of ritual artifacts have been found at this site. They have been attributed to the Calusa people, although this is by no means certain.

82 M8 PILOT MOUNTAIN
NATURAL SITE
LOCATION: North Carolina
NOTES: Sacred to the Cherokee Native Americans, who believe that the spirit of the mountain is called Jomeoki.

83 N8 DEVIL'S TRAMPLING GROUND
NATURAL SITE
LOCATION: North Carolina
NOTES: A sacred circle about 36 ft (11 m) across. According to centuries of Native American legend, certain malefic earth energies emanating from it prevent anyone spending a night here.

84 N7 ASSATEAGUE ISLAND
NATURAL SITE
LOCATION: Maryland
NOTES: Island lying off the coast of Maryland that was believed by Native Americans to be the Eastern Gate, by which souls entered and left the earth.

85 N7 INDIAN ECHO CAVERNS
NATURAL SITE
LOCATION: Pennsylvania
NOTES: Magnificent caverns sacred to the Susquehannock people, who claimed they were full of evil spirits.

86 N7 TRIPOD ROCK
DATE UNKNOWN
LOCATION: New Jersey
NOTES: A 130-ton rock balanced on three stones that resembles many of the megalithic remains in England. The site is aligned with the summer solstice.

87 N7 SLEEPING GIANT MOUNTAIN
NATURAL SITE
LOCATION: Hartford, Connecticut
NOTES: Over 2 mi (3.5 km) long, this site looks like a giant lying on his back. It was sacred to the original inhabitants, who called the giant "Hobbomock." Legend declares that the giant was the chief of a local tribe who ate too many oysters and fell into a deep sleep.

88 N7 NIAGARA FALLS
NATURAL SITE
LOCATION: New York State
NOTES: The Iroquois believe that Niagara is the home of the Great Spirit. Goat Island, which separates part of the falls, was an ancient Native American burial ground. Other islands were named according to the type of ritual performed there.

89 N7 MYSTERY HILL
DATE UNKNOWN
LOCATION: New Hampshire
NOTES: Group of underground passages and chambers often described as America's Stonehenge. It is one of many sites of stone chambers and arranged boulders throughout New England.

90 O6 MOUNT KATAHDIN
NATURAL SITE
LOCATION: Maine
NOTES: Sacred mountain of the Abenaki people, who believe that it is guarded by Pomola – a spirit with the head of a moose, the wings of an eagle, and a human body. It presides over weather and has a helper called the storm bird.

CENTRAL AMERICA

The map for these listings is on pp.146–147.

● Site still in use
■ Site no longer in use

1 F1 CASAS GRANDAS
A.D. 1000–1200
LOCATION: Mexico
NOTES: Site probably influenced by Toltec culture. Includes the remains of a number of pyramids and ball courts.

2 G5 IXTLAN DEL RIO
A.D. 300–450
LOCATION: Nayarit, Mexico
NOTES: Tomb site where figures, likely to be religious, have been found.

3 G5 CAPACHA
1500 B.C.
LOCATION: Colima, Mexico
NOTES: Ancient shaft tombs that held flat and hollow figurines; probably used for shamanistic purposes.

4 H5 EL OPENO
750–350 B.C.
LOCATION: Michoacán, Mexico
NOTES: Shaft and chamber tomb found at the site of a village.

5 H5 TZINTZUNTZAN
C. A.D. 1400
LOCATION: Central Highlands, Mexico
NOTES: Ancient capital of the Tarascans, dominated by a large ceremonial center.

6 I5 TULA
A.D. 900–1200
LOCATION: Hidalgo, Mexico
NOTES: Toltec capital ruled by the legendary god-king Quetzalcoatl. The site has several pyramids and a number of chacmools used as sacrificial stones.

7 I5 MALINALCO
A.D. 1472
LOCATION: near Mexico City, Mexico
NOTES: Aztec religious center. Site of a small circular temple with a serpent's mouth for an entrance; probably a penitential bloodletting chamber linked with the sinister goddess Malinzochitl.

8 I5 XOCHICALCO
6TH–10TH CENTURY A.D.
LOCATION: Morelos, Mexico
NOTES: Probably a retreat for the elite of Teotihuacán. The Temple of Quetzalcoatl was carved with feathered serpents. A nearby structure is carved with faces of gods and hieroglyphs, some calendrical. The hill also has underground passages.

9 I5 TLATILCO
1200 B.C.
LOCATION: near Mexico City, Mexico
NOTES: Lavish burial site with white Olmec-like figurines and "hollow babies." Tlatilcoans probably worshipped an earth goddess, placing great importance on the cultivation of corn.

10 I5 CUILCUILCO
10TH–4TH CENTURY B.C.
LOCATION: Mexico
NOTES: One of the earliest Mesoamerican temples, later covered by volcanic lava. The four-tiered pyramid was over 390 ft (120 m) wide. The circular temples were dedicated to Quetzalcoatl.

11 I5 TEOTIHUACAN
C. A.D. 250–650
LOCATION: Mexico
NOTES: See pp.84–85.

12 I5 TENOCHTITLAN
C. A.D. 1345
LOCATION: Mexico City, Mexico
NOTES: The Aztec capital named after its first ruler, the priest-king Tenoch, built on a marshy area ordained by the war god Huitzilopochtli. The holy precinct was dominated by the Great Temple and its shrines to the rain god Tlaloc and Huitzilopochtli. The Temple of Quetzalcoatl had a rack at its front to display the skulls of sacrificial victims.

13 I5 CHALCATZINCO
900–300 B.C.
LOCATION: Puebla, Mexico
NOTES: Olmec site with a number of monumental carved heads found in the center of three volcanic peaks.

14 I5 CHOLULA
C. A.D. 100–1200
LOCATION: Puebla, Mexico
NOTES: Major center dedicated to the god Quetzalcoatl; the main structure was a pyramid 177 ft (54 m) high. The Spaniards later built churches on top of the original temples, and it became a pilgrimage center once more.

15 I5 CACAXTLA
A.D. 750–900
LOCATION: Tlaxcala, Mexico
NOTES: Once the seat of an Olmec dynasty. It has a number of stelae similar to those found at Ceibal. Its buildings were painted with scenes of warfare, linked to a form of jaguar cult.

16 J5 EL TAJIN
7TH–11TH CENTURY A.D.
LOCATION: Veracruz, Mexico
NOTES: Religious center named after the Totonac rain god, whose practices were linked to Mayan underworld ideology. The Pyramid of the Niches has 365 niches to hold an idol for each day of the year.

17 J5 ZEMPOALA
15TH CENTURY A.D.
LOCATION: Veracruz, Mexico
NOTES: Totonac capital for 1,000 years, it became an Aztec outpost and was the place where Cortés landed. Site of the Templo Mayor, the Great Pyramid, and the Templo de las Chimenas.

18 J5 CERRO DE LAS MERAS
5TH–6TH CENTURY A.D.
LOCATION: Veracruz, Mexico
NOTES: Site of earth mounds and 15 stelae. It has evidence of Teotihuacános culture, especially in its rich burial goods.

19 J5-6 TRES ZAPOTES
400–100 B.C.
LOCATION: Veracruz, Mexico
NOTES: Veracruz center that retained a strong Olmec tradition, not least in the discovery of a huge Olmecoid head. Stela C is its main monument of interest and it has a jaguar mask carved in relief.

20 J6 SAN LORENZO
C. 1200-900 B.C.
LOCATION: Mexico
NOTES: See p.85.

21 I6 JUXTLAHUACA
900-700 B.C.
LOCATION: Guerrero, Mexico
NOTES: Olmec site with painted caves that combine human-animal motifs with rain fertility and origin-myth iconography. Linked to an underworld cult of the dead.

22 I6 OXTOTITLAN
C. 900 B.C.
LOCATION: Guerrero, Mexico
NOTES: Olmec cave site with sculptures of jaguar heads and a plumed serpent.

23 J6 MONTE ALBAN
500 B.C.-A.D. 750
LOCATION: Mexico
NOTES: Zapotec site with three central pyramids. The Temple of the Danzantes was encircled by 300 stone slabs carved with images of dying men, while another 140 were used in the temple itself.

24 J6 ZAACHILA
13TH-14TH CENTURY A.D.
LOCATION: Toaxaca, Mexico
NOTES: Zapotec capital where Mixtec pottery has been uncovered from tombs.

25 J6 DAINZU
450-300 B.C.
LOCATION: Oaxaca, Mexico
NOTES: Zapotec site with religious structures, about 50 stone slabs carved with masked human and animal heads, and a ritual ball court.

26 J6 MITLA
9TH-12TH CENTURY A.D.
LOCATION: Oaxaca, Mexico
NOTES: With the demise of Monte Albán, it became the residing place of a Zapotec high priest and a major religious center.

27 J6 YAGUAL
8TH-11TH CENTURY A.D.
LOCATION: Oaxaca, Mexico
NOTES: Mixtec center with ritual buildings, a ritual ball court, and cruciform tombs.

28 J6 LAS LIMAS
BEFORE 600 B.C.
LOCATION: Mexico
NOTES: Olmec site where a number of carved deities have been found.

29 K6 LA VENTA
C. 1000 B.C.
LOCATION: Mexico
NOTES: See p.85.

30 K6 PALENQUE
C. A.D. 500-900
LOCATION: Chiapas, Mexico
NOTES: Mayan ceremonial center with impressive temples, not least the Temple of the Inscriptions; reliefs here show the lineage of patron gods in glyphic form.

31 K6 TONINA
5TH CENTURY A.D.
LOCATION: Chiapas, Mexico
NOTES: Mayan site under excavation containing a pyramid mound, two ritual ball courts, temple ruins, and sculptures.

32 K6 BONAMPAK
C. A.D. 800
LOCATION: Chiapas, Mexico
NOTES: Mayan site with a number of frescoes depicting the underworld, sacrifices, and rituals.

33 K7 IZAPA
100 B.C.-A.D. 100
LOCATION: Chiapas, Mexico
NOTES: Ancient Izapan center with around 80 pyramidical mounds, large stelae, and toad-shaped altars.

34 L5 JAINA ISLAND
A.D. 600-900
LOCATION: Campeche, Mexico
NOTES: Island likely to have functioned as a necropolis for the Puuc élite. The Jaguar God of the underworld was worshipped among the deities, who were represented in figurines.

35 L5 EDZNA
7TH CENTURY A.D.
LOCATION: Campeche, Mexico
NOTES: Site of a ritual ball court and the Templo de los Cinco – a five-story step-pyramid used for habitation as well as ritual – almost unique in Mesoamerica.

36 L5 XPUHIL
10TH CENTURY A.D.
LOCATION: Mexico
NOTES: Site with three false facades, reminiscent of the temples at Tikal.

37 L6 RIO BEC
A.D. 600-900
LOCATION: Quintana Roo, Mexico
NOTES: Site of a pyramid-palace and other "temple" structures. They were probably funerary monuments.

38 L5 UXMAL
7TH-10TH CENTURY A.D.
LOCATION: Yucatán, Mexico
NOTES: Mayan site containing the famous Pyramid of the Magician. Its reliefs are made up from thousands of carved serpents and divine and human figures. The site also includes the Platform of the Stelae and the Great Pyramid.

39 L5 DZIBILCHALTUN
1000 B.C.-A.D. 1500
LOCATION: Yucatán, Mexico
NOTES: Occupied for 2,500 years, the site has remains of over 6,000 sacrificial offerings. The Temple of the Seven Dolls is named after figurines found inside.

40 L5 MAYAPAN
13TH CENTURY A.D.
LOCATION: Yucatán, Mexico
NOTES: City founded by the Itzá enclosing over 2,000 buildings. Excavation revealed many shrines and pottery in the form of gods. A castillo served as a ritual center – a virtual copy of that at Chichén Itzá.

41 L5 ZAYIL
6TH-9TH CENTURY A.D.
LOCATION: Yucatán, Mexico
NOTES: Classic Mayan pyramid site. Included within the complex are El Mirador and two other temples.

42 L5 LABNA
A.D. 600
LOCATION: Yucatán, Mexico
NOTES: Mayan site with a monumental archway leading to a ritual ball court, and many spectacular palaces.

43 L5 CHICHEN ITZA
C. 6TH CENTURY A.D.
LOCATION: Yucatán, Mexico
NOTES: See pp.86-87.

44 L5 COBA
A.D. 600-900
LOCATION: Quintana Roo, Mexico
NOTES: Very large Mayan site with temple-pyramids and a number of stelae. The most impressive of them is the Pyramid of Nocoh Mul.

45 L5 TULUM
11TH-12TH CENTURY A.D.
LOCATION: Quintana Roo, Mexico
NOTES: Site of elaborately painted and sculpted temples, including the Temples of the Frescoes and the Diving God.

46 L5 CERROS
100 B.C.-A.D. 850
LOCATION: Belize
NOTES: Mayan temple site with huge masks adorning its fronts, many of which depict the sun.

47 L6 LAMANAI
800 B.C.
LOCATION: Belize
NOTES: First inhabited around 1500 B.C., it soon became important as a ceremonial center. It reverted back to Mayan religious practices in the 17th century.

48 L6 ALTUN HA
A.D. 250-900
LOCATION: Belize
NOTES: Site of many tombs and temples, most important is the Temple of the Masonry Altars. A ruler was interred with a carved jade head in the Temple of the Green Tomb. A jade mask of the Mayan sun god, Kinich Ahau, was also found.

49 L6 XUNANTUNICH
800 B.C.-A.D. 850
LOCATION: Belize
NOTES: Ceremonial center destroyed by a volcanic eruption. Its main religious building was probably the Castillo.

50 L6 CARACOL
DATE UNKNOWN
LOCATION: Belize
NOTES: Large Mayan city currently under excavation, probably at its height during the Classic Mayan period (A.D. 300–900). It includes an acropolis, a ritual ball court, and the Temple of the Wooden Lintel that may be 2,000 years old.

51 L6 LUBANTUUM
C. 8TH CENTURY A.D.
LOCATION: near Punta Gorda, Belize
NOTES: Mayan religious site whose name means "fallen stones," with a number of temples, most still unexcavated.

52 K6 PIEDRAS NEGRAS
500 B.C.-A.D. 850
LOCATION: Guatemala
NOTES: Site that reached its zenith during the Late Classic Mayan period with many stelae. Its West Acropolis has a central palace flanked by two funerary pyramids.

53 K6 YAXCHILAN
6TH-8TH CENTURY A.D.
LOCATION: Usumacinta River, Guatemala
NOTES: Mayan center with many burial pyramids. Reliefs here portray violent acts and penitential rites of bloodletting.

54 L6 EL MIRADOR
A.D. 300-600
LOCATION: Petén, Guatemala
NOTES: Major ceremonial center with one of the largest temple-pyramids ever built. It remains mostly unexcavated.

55 L6 RIO AZUL
A.D. 300-850
LOCATION: Petén, Guatemala
NOTES: Site with a number of fourth-century tomb paintings, including some fourth-century text framed with Mayan deities. Watery symbols above the tombs portray the surface of the underworld.

56 L6 UAXACTUN
A.D. 250-850
LOCATION: El Petén, N. Guatemala
NOTES: Mayan site of ancestor worship with pyramids and temples and a rival to Tikal. Foundations date back 4,000 years.

57 L6 TIKAL
800 B.C.-A.D. 850
LOCATION: El Petén, Guatemala
NOTES: Huge Mayan ceremonial center with around 3,000 structures. Five large temple-pyramids dominate the site, some containing rich burials. The best known is the Temple of the Jaguar. The Great Plaza is lined with altars and stelae from the fourth to eighth centuries. Once the last mound is excavated, it will be the largest of the ancient Mayan pyramids.

58 L6 YAXHA
C. 5TH-7TH CENTURY A.D.
LOCATION: South of Tikal, Guatemala
NOTES: Site of pyramid complex, similar to Tikal in alignment. Each summit could be reached by one of four walkways. Located on a lake of the same name.

59 L6 CEIBAL
400 B.C.-A.D. 800
LOCATION: El Petén, Guatemala
NOTES: Mayan site with stelae and ceiba trees – the sacred tree of the ancient Maya. Round buildings discovered here were associated with Quetzalcoatl.

60 K6 ZACULEU
A.D. 1400-1500
LOCATION: Huehuetenango, Guatemala
NOTES: Late Mayan religious center with ball courts and temples.

61 K7 ABAJ TAKALIK
100 B.C.
LOCATION: Maya Highlands, Guatemala
NOTES: Site where a number of Olmec heads have been found.

62 K7 K'UMARCAAJ
14TH CENTURY A.D.
LOCATION: Western Guatemala
NOTES: Capital of the Quiché Maya people, it remains a ritual center today. Little has been excavated, but it is still a place of prayers and chicken sacrifices.

63 K7 IGLESIA DE SANTO TOMAS
A.D. 1540
LOCATION: Chichicastenango, Guatemala
NOTES: Simple colonial church, built atop a Postclassic Mayan temple, still heavily used for Mayan practices.

64 K7 IXIMCHE
A.D. 1200
LOCATION: Western Guatemala
NOTES: Capital city of the Cakchiquel Maya. It has four ceremonial plazas with temples and ritual ball courts.

65 L7 KAMINALJUYU
A.D. 400-600
LOCATION: Guatemala
NOTES: Mayan center consisting of over 200 mounds filled with log tombs; one contained over 340 objects. There are many mushroom stones in the area.

66 L7 CAHYUP
A.D. 1200-1300
LOCATION: Guatemala
NOTES: Site of a pyramid with four flights of stairs on its lower slopes. The twin

temples at the top have six more ramps, making it one of the most complex Mesoamerican structures.

67 K7 SANTA LUCIA COTZUMALHUAPA
C. A.D. 600
LOCATION: Guatemala
NOTES: Ceremonial center perhaps related to Teotihuacán. Reliefs depict ritual ball games between deities and humans.

68 K7 EL BAUL
C. 200 B.C.
LOCATION: Cotzumalhuapa, Guatemala
NOTES: Site with buildings and monuments in the Izapan style. Still an active place of pagan worship.

69 K7 MONTE ALTO
BEFORE 1000 B.C.
LOCATION: La Democracia, Guatemala
NOTES: Site of Olmec heads, reliefs, and a jade mask; all are said to predate the remains at San Lorenzo and La Venta.

70 L6 QUIRIGUA
A.D. 300-850
LOCATION: Guatemala
NOTES: Site of the largest Mayan stela; from the eighth century A.D., it shows the face of Mayan ruler Cauac Sky. A later ruler developed the zoomorph – a river boulder with carving of animal forms relating to Mayan gods – here.

71 L7 COPAN
4TH-9TH CENTURY A.D.
LOCATION: western Honduras
NOTES: Major site of structures dedicated to kingship rites. There are funerary pyramids, the great Hieroglyphic Stairway – a pyramid with 2,200 glyphs – stelae, ritual ball courts, and an acropolis.

72 M6 LA COLORADA
DATE UNKNOWN
LOCATION: Paseo Río Cangrejal, Honduras
NOTES: Unexcavated, but likely to be an important Mayan religious site.

73 L7 TAZUMAL
1200-200 B.C.
LOCATION: Halchuapa, El Salvador
NOTES: The name means "Pyramid where the victims were burned." It includes a restored pyramid, a ritual ball court, and the Estela de Tazumal basalt monolith.

74 L7 SAN ANDRES
DATE UNKNOWN
LOCATION: El Salvador
NOTES: Unexcavated pyramids with ritual courtyard and smaller mounds. An Olmec head was also found here. It has been inhabited by Aztecs, Pipils, and the Maya.

75 M8 VOLCAN MASAYA
NATURAL SITE
LOCATION: Nicaragua
NOTES: Active volcano that was the site of human sacrifices to the goddess of fire.

76 M8 ISLA DE OMOTEPE
DATE UNKNOWN
LOCATION: Lago de Nicaragua, Nicaragua
NOTES: Site of ancient stone statues and petroglyphs of the Chorotega people.

77 N8 LA BASILICA DE NUESTRA SENORA DE LOS ANGELES
A.D. 1635
LOCATION: Costa Rica
NOTES: A pilgrimage site, it is a Catholic church where a statue of the Virgin was found. A shrine was built on the spot, said to have miraculous healing powers.

PERU

The map for these listings is on p.148.

● Site still in use
■ Site no longer in use

1 E5 MACHU PICCHU
15TH CENTURY A.D.
LOCATION: Peru
NOTES: *See p.90.*

2 E6 CUZCO
11TH CENTURY A.D.
LOCATION: Peru
NOTES: *See p.91.*

3 D6 NAZCA LINES
200 B.C.–A.D. 400
LOCATION: Peru
NOTES: *See p.91.*

4 C5 ANCON
3RD MILLENNIUM B.C.
LOCATION: near Lima, Peru
NOTES: Artifacts found in pre-Incan burial sites here include pottery, textiles, and the oldest archer's bow in the continent.

5 C5 TEMPLE OF PACHACAMAC
A.D. 600-650
LOCATION: near Lima, Peru
NOTES: Major Incan religious site with earlier origins. Its name means "Earth's Creator." The god expressed his feelings through earthquake-like tremors. The Inca also built a sun temple here. Other temples include the Temple of the Moon and the Convent of the Sun Virgins.

6 C5 HUACA PUQUIANA
14TH CENTURY A.D.
LOCATION: Lima, Peru
NOTES: Huge pre-Incan mound with a hollow core named after a local chief. It may have been built in the shape of a frog – the symbol of a rain god who, it is believed, spoke to the priests through the large hollow. Possibly the oracle from which the Rimac Valley got its name.

7 C5 CHINCHA
14TH CENTURY A.D.
LOCATION: near Lima, Peru
NOTES: Site of the pre-Incan Huaca Centinela Temple.

8 D5 WARI-WILLKA
7TH-9TH CENTURY A.D.
LOCATION: Huancayo, Peru
NOTES: Sacred center of the pre-Incan Wari people.

9 E5 PISAC
15TH CENTURY A.D.
LOCATION: Cuzco Valley, Peru
NOTES: Incan ruins similar to Machu Picchu. A Temple of the Sun is built around an outcrop of rock. Like Machu Picchu, it has an *Intihuatana*, a "Hitching Post of the Sun," possibly used for predicting the position of the stars. A large area remains unexcavated and several burial sites remain hidden.

10 C5 VITCOS
A.D. 1438-63
LOCATION: Urubamba, Peru
NOTES: Plaza beyond Machu Picchu with ruins of an Incan temple. A white rock was the site of human sacrifice.

11 D5 ESPIRITU PAMPA
A.D. 1550-1600
LOCATION: Quillabamba, Peru
NOTES: The "Plain of the Spirits." The original buildings, built by Manco Capac's followers, predate the conquest.

12 D5 TRES CRUCES
6TH CENTURY A.D.
LOCATION: Sacred Valley, Peru
NOTES: Pre-Incan site of pilgrimage on the eastern edge of the Amazon forest. Late Nazcan pottery was found here.

13 E6 TIPON
A.D. 1450
LOCATION: Sacred Valley, Peru
NOTES: Incan site hidden on a natural shelf above the Huatanay Valley. A *huaca* has been built around a volcanic rock.

14 E6 VIRACOCHA
6TH-10TH CENTURY A.D.
LOCATION: Urcos, Peru
NOTES: Hill named after the creator-god whom local people believed lived there. A pre-Incan *huaca* was also built on the hill where he was worshipped.

15 E6 TEMPLE OF RAQCHI
15TH CENTURY A.D.
LOCATION: Urubamba, Peru
NOTES: Inca temple dedicated to the god Viracocha. An animated Raqchi festival still takes place here.

16 C6 CABEZA LARGAS
3RD MILLENNIUM B.C.
LOCATION: South Peru
NOTES: Ancient burial site. Up to 60 mummies were found in one burial.

17 D6 CAHUACHI
A.D. 200-300
LOCATION: near Nazca, South Peru
NOTES: Nazcan religious center. Citadel based around a small hill with six pyramid mounds, each with a courtyard.

18 C4 FORTRESS OF PARAMONGA
A.D. 1460
LOCATION: Ancash Coast, Peru
NOTES: Mainly a military base, but also a ritual center for the Chimú who may have built it on top of an ancient *huaca*.

19 C4 SECHIN RUINS
750 B.C.
LOCATION: Ancash Coast, Peru
NOTES: Site of around 90 monolithic slabs representing warriors, their trophy heads, and mutilated sacrificial victims.

20 C4 WILKAWAIN
7TH-10TH CENTURY A.D.
LOCATION: near Huaraz, Peru
NOTES: Two-story Wari temple.

21 C4 KOTOSH
2ND MILLENNIUM B.C.
LOCATION: Huánaco Valley, Peru
NOTES: Recently excavated temple ruins.

22 C4 TANTAMAYO
DATE UNKNOWN
LOCATION: north of Huánaco, Peru
NOTES: Architectural complex surrounded by watchtowers. Concentric circles of carved stone suggest a religious purpose.

23 B4 CHAN CHAN
A.D. 1100
LOCATION: Trujillo, Peru
NOTES: Capital of the Chimú Empire and one of the largest pre-Columbian cities.

24 B4 TEMPLES OF SUN AND MOON
A.D. 500
LOCATION: Trujillo, Peru
NOTES: The former is the largest adobe structure in America. The latter is smaller, but brilliantly frescoed. Built by the Mochica people, the Temple of the Sun rises 165 ft (50 m), topped by a ceremonial platform. The Temple of the Moon may have been a ruler's residence or the center of a sacrificial cult.

25 C3 CERRO SANTA APOLONIA
11TH CENTURY B.C.
LOCATION: near Cajamarca, Peru
NOTES: "The Inca's Throne," it has a sacrificial stone on the peak of a hill overlooking the town.

26 C3 EL CUMBEMAYO
300 B.C.
LOCATION: Cajamarca, Peru
NOTES: Water channel built at least 1,200 years before the Inca, probably used for rituals. It may have been connected with water worship.

27 C3 GRAN PAJATEN
DATE UNKNOWN
LOCATION: Cajabamba, Peru
NOTES: Recently uncovered ruins of a sacred city.

28 B3 EL PURGATORIO
8TH CENTURY A.D.
LOCATION: Chiclayo, Peru
NOTES: Major Sicán and Chimú city with adobe pyramids and platforms. *Curanderos* – folk doctors – still perform healing rituals at the site.

29 B3 SERRAN
A.D. 1450
LOCATION: Peru
NOTES: Site of impressive Incan buildings, including a sacred convent where 500 *mamaconas* – virgins of the sun – dedicated their lives to the Incan religion. There were two Incan sites in the area.

30 C4 CHAVIN DE HUANTAR
850-400 B.C.
LOCATION: Peru
NOTES: At its peak one of the largest religious centers in the world and probably also a center of pilgrimage. Carvings can be found in subterranean rooms together with a huge block of granite called the Lanzon. Three main gods were worshipped here: the Sun, the Moon, and a Jaguar creator-god.

31 F6 SILLUSTANI CHULLPA TOMBS
14TH-15TH CENTURY A.D.
LOCATION: Peru
NOTES: White stone burial towers that overlook Lake Titicaca. Some have fallen due to earthquakes and looting.

32 C4 PUNKURI
8TH CENTURY B.C.
LOCATION: Nepena Valley, Peru
NOTES: Terraced platform temple mound with Chavín decoration and a clay jaguar on one of its stairway landings.

33 C4 MOXEKE
9TH CENTURY A.D.
LOCATION: Casma Valley, Peru
NOTES: Site of an eight-terraced platform pyramid mound, similar to Punkuri.

SOUTH AMERICA

The map for these listings is on p.149.

● Site still in use

■ Site no longer in use

① K2 COCHASQUI

DATE UNKNOWN

LOCATION: near Quito, Ecuador

NOTES: Site of 15 pyramids built by the Cara people that are surrounded by 30 mounds. Judging by their alignments, most of the structures were built for ceremonial purposes.

② K2 INGAPIRCA

A.D. 1463-71

LOCATION: Ecuador

NOTES: One of the most important Incan sites. The main structure is probably a Temple of the Sun and has some of the best Incan stonework.

③ K2 LA PLATA ISLAND

500 B.C.-A.D. 500

LOCATION: Bahía de Caráquez, Ecuador

NOTES: Part of the Bahía phase, this site seems to have been a pilgrimage center. Several rectangular platform mounds have been found, some with rampways, others with unsculpted stones facing the structures.

④ K1 BURITACA

14TH CENTURY A.D.

LOCATION: Colombia

NOTES: Center for the Tairona people, who presided over one of the most impressive New World civilizations. Its structures include a ceremonial plaza.

⑤ K1-2 LAKE GUATAVITA

NATURAL SITE

LOCATION: near Bogotá, Colombia

NOTES: Sacred site of the Muisca people, where an elaborate sacred ceremony took place on the anointment of a new king. The new ruler was kept in a sacred cave for a period of time before journeying to the lake, where he was covered in gold dust and put on a raft covered in torches. He then set sail to the center of the lake to offer gold and emeralds to the water and mountain god.

⑥ K2 TIERRADENTRO

9TH CENTURY A.D.

LOCATION: Colombia

NOTES: A number of underground shaft tombs, many painted with figures in black, orange, and red paint. Artifacts found in these tombs are believed to have Amazonian origins.

⑦ K2 SAN AGUSTIN

1ST-5TH CENTURY A.D.

LOCATION: Magdalena Valley, Colombia

NOTES: Region in highland Columbia the site of megalithic mounds that cover an area of over 193 sq mi (500 sq km). San Agustín had previously been a place of habitation for over 1,000 years. Many sculptures and monumental figures have been found at the various sites, some of them depicting figures holding trophy heads.

⑧ L8 CUEVA DE LOS MANOS

BEFORE 1000 B.C.

LOCATION: Perito Moreno, Argentina

NOTES: "Cave of the Hands" was a sacred cave decorated by the Tehuelches people. The paintings are red, black, yellow, and white hand shapes that cover the whole cave. Also found here are various drawn animal and human figures.

⑨ L6 DIFUNTA CORREA SHRINE

19TH CENTURY A.D.

LOCATION: San Juan, Argentina

NOTES: Modern pilgrimage site attracting over 200,000 visitors a year. The saintly figure of Difunta worked and died here during the Civil War. Her spirit is believed to perform miracles.

⑩ N2 MARAJO ISLAND

DATE UNKNOWN

LOCATION: Brazil

NOTES: Site found in the depths of the Amazon where over 100 mounds have been found, several of which are tombs. At the moment the mounds that have been excavated have been dated to between A.D. 500 and A.D. 1500.

⑪ O4 CONGONHAS DE CAMPOS

18TH CENTURY A.D.

LOCATION: Brazil

NOTES: Church famous for its Christian sculptures and wood carvings. Also a site of pilgrimage.

⑫ O3 IGREJA DE BONFIM

17TH-18TH CENTURY A.D.

LOCATION: Bahia, Brazil

NOTES: Shrine famous for its curing powers. On entry to the church, a ribbon is tied around the wrist. The pilgrim then makes three wishes, which will come true by the time the ribbon naturally falls off the wrist.

⑬ O2-3 SETE CIDADES NATIONAL PARK

NATURAL SITE

LOCATION: Piauí, Brazil

NOTES: Two rock formations with strange scales on their surface. Another rock has red markings that are believed to be cryptic runes.

⑭ O4 SAO TOME DAS LETRAS

NATURAL SITE

LOCATION: near Minas, Brazil

NOTES: In an area full of mystery, myth, and superstition, its name refers to a large number of inscriptions found in caverns nearby. Legend speaks of extraterrestrials and other stories; there is also talk of a subterranean passageway leading to Machu Picchu.

⑮ L4 THE GIANT OF ATACAMA

BEFORE 1000 A.D.

LOCATION: near Iquique, Chile

NOTES: The Giant is, in fact, the largest prehistoric representation of a human figure found anywhere in the world. At 282 ft (86 m) long this stone figure is accompanied by another, possibly a monkey. Both are set among complex lines and circles, which hint that they were for ceremonial use.

⑯ L4 PINTADOS

DATE UNKNOWN

LOCATION: near Iquique, Chile

NOTES: A site where 400 prehistoric geoglyphs – geometric shapes or designs, as exemplified by the lines of Nazca – cover a hillside. Its size makes it one of the most complicated archaeological sites in the world. Among the figures carved are images of people, llamas, geometric shapes, and a gigantic arrow.

⑰ L6 VALLE DEL ENCANTO

2ND-7TH CENTURY A.D.

LOCATION: Ovalle, Chile

NOTES: Site of a number of sacred petroglyphs and pictographs attributed to the indigenous Molle people.

⑱ M1-2 MOUNT RORAIMA

NATURAL SITE

LOCATION: Guyana

NOTES: The highest point in the country, the Pedra de Macunaima hanging rock is sacred to the Maxuxi people.

⑲ L1 SORTE MOUNTAIN

NATURAL SITE

LOCATION: Venezuela

NOTES: Sacred mountain used as a healing center for the Maria Lionza religion, a recent shamanistic group. On arrival, the devotee is taken to a circle of mediums to be purified. In their midst, they enter a trance while a medium speaks in an ancient tongue, related to an ancient local religion whose followers used to worship the jaguar.

⑳ L4 WAKALLANI

A.D. 300-755

LOCATION: near Lake Titicaca, Bolivia

NOTES: Site containing the remains of three burial towers and two stelae brought from Lake Titicaca.

㉑ L4 LAKE TITICACA

NATURAL SITE

LOCATION: Bolivia

NOTES: See pp.88-89.

㉒ L4 TIAHUANACO

3RD-10TH CENTURY A.D.

LOCATION: Bolivia

NOTES: See pp.88-89.

㉓ L4 CHIRIPA

1300-500 B.C.

LOCATION: near Tambillo, Bolivia

NOTES: The Chiripa is one of the oldest cultures in the country, and this was one of its important ceremonial centers, whose artificial mound is likely to have been a temple platform. Nearby are a few burial towers.

THE PACIFIC & AUSTRALASIA

The map for these listings is on pp.150-151.

● Site still in use

■ Site no longer in use

① A7 NYUNGAR

NATURAL SITE

LOCATION: Western Australia, Australia

NOTES: The Nyungar people call this the "Island of the Dead."

② A7 BENNETTS BROOK

NATURAL SITE

LOCATION: Western Australia, Australia

NOTES: The Nyungar people consider this a place sacred to the Rainbow Snake.

③ A6 YARNDA THALU

NATURAL SITE

LOCATION: Western Australia, Australia

NOTES: Mound of stone placed across the ridge of a hill. It was used by elders of the Ngarluma people to regulate the temperatures of the local areas.

④ A6 KUNKUWARRA

NATURAL SITE

LOCATION: Western Australia, Australia

NOTES: Large granite rock containing a small hole in the top. Fires are lit in the hole so that the fertility of the honeybee is increased.

⑤ A-B6 WARMALANA ISLAND

NATURAL SITE

LOCATION: Western Australia, Australia

NOTES: Maralga, a leading Pilbara spirit man, created this island by flinging a huge rock into the sea. Its rocks and boulders are covered in carved figures.

⑥ B6 BARRALUMMA

NATURAL SITE

LOCATION: Western Australia, Australia

NOTES: The Bunuba elders declare that the Melatji Law Dogs swam across the Indian Ocean, touching all the main water sources on the journey. They then painted themselves on rocks here.

⑦ B6 NOONKANBAH

NATURAL SITE

LOCATION: Western Australia, Australia

NOTES: Ancestral beings are believed to enter and re-enter the ground here.

⑧ B6 UMPAMPURRU (PEA HILL)

NATURAL SITE

LOCATION: Western Australia, Australia

NOTES: Site where the hero Unyupu and two snakes went to earth. The area was later crossed by the pregnant Nangala and Looma the blue-tongued lizard woman. It is a powerful female place.

⑨ B5 WULLUNGGNARI

NATURAL SITE

LOCATION: Western Australia, Australia

NOTES: Sacred to the Kimberley peoples. An altar stands in front of a cave, as does a Walguna tree of wisdom, from which sacred objects are hung in times of ceremony. Wullunggnari represents the resting place of one of the local people's spirit ancestors.

10 C5 PUKAMANI BURIAL POLES
DATE UNKNOWN
LOCATION: Northern Territory, Australia
NOTES: Poles carved and painted with symbolic and mythological figures erected around the graves of the Tiwi people.

11 C5 MELVILLE ISLAND
NATURAL SITE
LOCATION: Northern Territory, Australia
NOTES: Along with Bathurst Island, it has a number of sacred places. Tokumbimi Tokumbimi lived here in the Dreamtime and ordered the Pukamani to make their sacred places on old campsites.

12 C5 BALAWURRU AND UBIRR
NATURAL SITE
LOCATION: Northern Territory, Australia
NOTES: Sites of numerous rock paintings in many different styles, and believed to be up to 20,000 years old.

13 C5 NOURLANGIE ROCK
NATURAL SITE
LOCATION: Northern Territory, Australia
NOTES: A long, red sandstone rock painted in areas with orange, white, and black stripes. Includes the Anbangbang shelter, a refuge from Namarrgon, the Lightning Man.

14 C5 YELANGBARA BEACH
NATURAL SITE
LOCATION: Northern Territory, Australia
NOTES: Landing place of Djanggawul and his sisters, the Dreamtime missionaries, who loaded a canoe with sacred objects and sailed to Australia. One rock is said to represent the canoe.

15 C5 KULALUK
NATURAL SITE
LOCATION: Northern Territory, Australia
NOTES: Site sacred to the Larrakia people.

16 C5 OOBARR
NATURAL SITE
LOCATION: Northern Territory, Australia
NOTES: Sacred to the King Brown Snake, allegedly the creator of the didgeridoo.

17 C5 INGELALADD
NATURAL SITE
LOCATION: Northern Territory, Australia
NOTES: Believed to be the point where the Lightning Brothers came into the earth. There are also many rock art images of ancestral beings.

18 C5 KULUNBAR (KATHERINE GORGE)
NATURAL SITE
LOCATION: Northern Territory, Australia
NOTES: Gorge said to have been made by the ancestor Koopoo, a red plains kangaroo, who became the Rainbow Snake after entering the gorge.

19 C6 DEVIL'S MARBLES
NATURAL SITE
LOCATION: Northern Territory, Australia
NOTES: Giant spherical boulders which, according to Aboriginal mythology, were laid by the Rainbow Snake.

20 C6 NGAMA CAVE
NATURAL SITE
LOCATION: Northern Territory, Australia
NOTES: Sacred place related to the Melatji dog men, tended by elders of the Walbiri.

21 C6 WINBARAKU
NATURAL SITE
LOCATION: Northern Territory, Australia
NOTES: Two peaks, the taller of the two summits represent the birthplace of the great snake Jarapiri. The lower peak represents Nabanunga women who came to take the snake to their camp but failed. The Melatji dogs, Hare-Wallaby, and other ancestors are also associated with the peaks.

22 C6 KATA TJUTA
NATURAL SITE
LOCATION: Northern Territory, Australia
NOTES: See p.97.

23 C6 ULURU
NATURAL SITE
LOCATION: Northern Territory, Australia
NOTES: See pp.96-97.

24 C6 N'DHALA GORGE AND EWANINGA
NATURAL SITE
LOCATION: Northern Territory, Australia
NOTES: Sites of ancient Aboriginal rock carvings that predate the current Aboriginal peoples in central Australia.

25 C6 ANTHWERRKE
NATURAL SITE
LOCATION: Northern Territory, Australia
NOTES: Also known as Emily Gap. A sacred place and origin of the caterpillar ancestors of Mpamtwe. These caterpillars created the local landscape, including the sacred ridge of Ntyarklkarle Tyaneme.

26 C6 NTARIPE
NATURAL SITE
LOCATION: Northern Territory, Australia
NOTES: Site dedicated to the dog ancestor Akngwelye, who fought a major battle and was later transformed into a boulder embedded in the ground.

27 C7 ARTA-WARARLPANHA
NATURAL SITE
LOCATION: South Australia, Australia
NOTES: Sacred Adnyamathanha site said to have been created by two snakes, whose heads are the two peaks of the mountain.

28 D8 FRANKLIN RIVER
NATURAL SITE
LOCATION: Tasmania, Australia
NOTES: Site of Aboriginal archaeological finds; it was apparently abandoned 20,000 years ago.

29 D8 OYSTER COVE
NATURAL SITE
LOCATION: Tasmania, Australia
NOTES: Site where many Tasmanian Aborigines died, now considered sacred by their descendants. Also a tribal revitalization area for local peoples.

30 D8 MUMBULLA MOUNTAIN
NATURAL SITE
LOCATION: New South Wales, Australia
NOTES: A mountain that is held sacred by the Mumbulla and Yuin peoples.

31 E7 KURING-GAI CHASE
NATURAL SITE
LOCATION: New South Wales, Australia
NOTES: Area rich in rock-art owned by local Aboriginal people, showing Baiame, great ancestor of the Kuring-gai people.

32 E7 RED HAND CAVE
NATURAL SITE
LOCATION: New South Wales, Australia
NOTES: Sacred Aboriginal shelter with hand stencils on the wall.

33 E7 TERANIA CREEK CAVE
NATURAL SITE
LOCATION: New South Wales, Australia
NOTES: Site held sacred by the Widbajal people. Younger men are brought for initiation ceremonies, to be tested for their perseverance and bush knowledge, and to make spiritual contact. A nearby waterfall is also considered sacred and inhabited by spirits.

34 E7 LENNOX HEAD
NATURAL SITE
LOCATION: New South Wales, Australia
NOTES: A bora ground (initiation site) of which only the larger ring remains. After each ceremony, any ground carvings or paintings were destroyed to preserve the ceremonial secrets.

35 E7 GOANNA HEADLAND
NATURAL SITE
LOCATION: New South Wales, Australia
NOTES: Once called Dirrawonga, this is a sacred goanna (lizard) site. In the Dreamtime the goanna chases a snake that attacked a bird. A fight ensues and the goanna is chased into the sea, where it becomes the promontory.

36 E7 WOOLOOL WOOLOOLNI
NATURAL SITE
LOCATION: New South Wales, Australia
NOTES: A place of granite tors held sacred for its association with the ancestral hero Woolool.

37 E7 BULL'S HEAD MOUNTAIN
NATURAL SITE
LOCATION: New South Wales, Australia
NOTES: Sacred to the Gidabal people. Important both as an energy place and also for the two mythological bulls' heads that are part of the mountain's contours.

38 E7 MOUNT BINGINGERRA
NATURAL SITE
LOCATION: New South Wales, Australia
NOTES: Large turtle from the Dreamtime whose body, according to the Yugunbir people, was turned into the mountain.

39 E7 WIDGEE MOUNTAIN
NATURAL SITE
LOCATION: Queensland, Australia
NOTES: Site related to the two dogs, whose remains were taken to the head of a nearby waterfall at the top of the creek where they turned to stone, one falling east and one west.

40 D6 CARNARVON GORGE
NATURAL SITE
LOCATION: Queensland, Australia
NOTES: Aboriginal rock shelters containing a wealth of art. The main caves are Baloon Cave, the Art Gallery, and Cathedral Cave.

41 E7 MOUNT TABLETOP
NATURAL SITE
LOCATION: Queensland, Australia
NOTES: Site formerly sacred to the Yuggera people, now no longer used as a place for ceremonial activity.

42 D5 LAURA
NATURAL SITE
LOCATION: Queensland, Australia
NOTES: The home of the Quinkan spirit-beings and an area rich in rock art.

43 G7 CAPE REINGA
NATURAL SITE
LOCATION: North Island, New Zealand
NOTES: Here, according to Maori legend, the spirits of the dead depart for Hawaiki.

44 G7-8 WAIMAMAKU VALLEY
18TH CENTURY A.D.
LOCATION: New Zealand
NOTES: Two small burial caves on the face of a precipitous cliff found packed with skeletons. Also inside were eight carved burial chests; six resembled tikis, images prominent in Maori mythology.

45 G8 MOKOIA ISLAND
9TH-11TH CENTURY A.D.
LOCATION: Lake Rotorua, New Zealand
NOTES: Early sacred place where Tua-Rotorua – one of the first Maoris – and his descendants worshipped.

46 G8 TAWHITINUI PA
AFTER A.D. 1500
LOCATION: near Opotiki, New Zealand
NOTES: Site where skeletons were found at the base of a building – the result of human sacrifice. Maori priests performed sacrifices when the eldest daughter of the high priest was to be tattooed. The ceremony only occured on the most important occasions.

47 G8 ONE TREE HILL
C. A.D. 1000–1500
LOCATION: North Island, New Zealand
NOTES: See p.99.

48 G8 MOUNT TONGARIRO
NATURAL SITE
LOCATION: North Island, New Zealand
NOTES: According to legend, a mountain once covered in snow, transformed into a volcano by the gods.

49 G8 RANGIATEA CHURCH
AFTER A.D. 1500
LOCATION: Otaki, New Zealand
NOTES: Maori church named after the sacred marae at Raiatea (see p.98).

50 G8 ARAHURA
NATURAL SITE
LOCATION: Westland, New Zealand
NOTES: The site where jade (considered sacred by the Maoris) was first found, allegedly brought by Ngahue.

51 F9 OTAGO AND CANTERBURY
NATURAL SITE
LOCATION: South Island, New Zealand
NOTES: Caves, overhangs, and rock shelters with paintings and carvings.

52 C3 NGERUTECHEI
DATE UNKNOWN
LOCATION: Palau
NOTES: Holy village where in ancient times, a group of gods, the Ruchel, used to meet on a stone pavement area known as Uchaladebong, meaning "origin point from which to go forth."

53 C3 IMEIONG
DATE UNKNOWN
LOCATION: Palau
NOTES: Similar to the holy village above, it is now considered the most sacred place on the island.

54 E3 WICHON FALLS
NATURAL SITE
LOCATION: Chuuk, Micronesia
NOTES: Waterfalls that are the site of ancient petroglyphs and play a major part in the island's legends. One story says a spirit took part of a nearby mountain and dropped it into the sea to form an atoll.

55 E3 NANDAUWAS
12TH CENTURY A.D.
LOCATION: Pohnpei, Micronesia
NOTES: See p.99.

56 F3 LELA RUINS

A.D. 1250–1400

LOCATION: Kosrae, Micronesia

NOTES: Remains of an ancient city with burial mounds and sacred compounds. Insru and Inoll are sacred areas that served as temporary burial places for the local kings. Female mourners kept watch until the body was decomposed. The bones were then taken in a ceremonial procession to a deep natural hole.

57 F3 UTWE

15TH–16TH CENTURY A.D.

LOCATION: Kosrae, Micronesia

NOTES: A basalt altar built to honor Sinlaka, the Kosraean goddess of famines, breadfruit harvests, and typhoons.

58 F6 MOMIES DE LA FATANOUE

19TH CENTURY A.D.

LOCATION: Koumac, New Caledonia

NOTES: Sacred burial ground for the chieftains of the Kanak people. The mummified remains are placed in the fetal position before being displayed.

59 F6 GROTTE DE KONG HULUP

NATURAL SITE

LOCATION: Ouvea, Loyalty Islands

NOTES: The path to this religious spot has several sacred articles. A banyan tree has a deep water-filled hole that is said to house the gods from the island of Canala, who arrived with Chief Wenegei. Its roots are said to connect with a tree on Canala.

60 G6 NAVATU ROCK

NATURAL SITE

LOCATION: Rakiraki, Fiji

NOTES: A steep cliff that has a number of legends attached to it. Excavations reveal it to be one of the first Fijian places of habitation. A small island nearby is said to be the departure point for the afterlife.

61 G6 KOROLAMALAMA

NATURAL SITE

LOCATION: Vatulele, Fiji

NOTES: Small cave considered sacred by the local people for its holy red prawns.

62 G5 LABASA

AFTER 15TH CENTURY A.D.

LOCATION: Vanua Levu, Fiji

NOTES: Small town surrounded by sacred sites. Nearby is the Floating Island, which has a number of legends associated with it. Also there is the Growing Stone, said to be constantly growing in size. It is beneath a Hindu temple, which attracts many pilgrims every year.

63 H6 HA'AMONGA-A-MAUI

C. A.D. 1200

LOCATION: Tongatapu, Tonga

NOTES: See p.98.

64 H6 PAEPAE'O TELE'A

16TH CENTURY A.D.

LOCATION: Tongatapu, Tonga

NOTES: The country's most important burial site, this pyramid-like stone structure was thought to have housed the remains of Tele'a, who reigned in the 16th century.

65 H6 NAMOALA

C. A.D. 1000–1500

LOCATION: Tonga

NOTES: A three-tiered pyramid with a stone burial vault on top.

66 H5 FALEALUPOTAI

NATURAL SITE

LOCATION: Savai'i, Western Samoa

NOTES: Village important in local legend.

To the Samoans it represents the gateway to the spirit underworld. One entrance is via a cave on a cape, the other is made by the sun's trail as it sets in the sea.

67 H5 PULEMELEI MOUND

A.D. 0–500

LOCATION: Savai'i, Western Samoa

NOTES: Largest ancient structure in Polynesia. A pyramid mound that is 200 x 164 ft (61 x 50 m), it rises over 40 ft (12 m). Smaller mounds can be found in the vicinity.

68 H5 CHIEFLY TOMBS

19TH–20TH CENTURY A.D.

LOCATION: Upolu, Western Samoa

NOTES: The resting places of the royal families of the Samoan Islands. At the end of the peninsula are the mausoleum of Tupua Tamesese and a seven-tiered tomb of the Tu'imaleali'ifano dynasty.

69 H5 MOUNT LATA

NATURAL SITE

LOCATION: Ta'u, American Samoa

NOTES: Highest point in the country, and sacred mountain of the Ta'u.

70 H5 'AOA

500–0 B.C.

LOCATION: Tutuila, American Samoa

NOTES: Ancient site that consists of 40 ancient "star" mounds – elevated stone platforms with stone protusions.

71 H5 PISAGA

NATURAL SITE

LOCATION: Tutuila, American Samoa

NOTES: An area just inside a volcano crater where spirits are believed to live. As a result, the locals keep quiet in its vicinity so as not to disturb them.

72 I2 WAILAU

A.D. 1200

LOCATION: Kauai, Hawaiian Islands

NOTES: Site of several heiau (Hawaiian stone temples). Hikini A Ka La Heiau (Rising of the Sun) was built around 1200. The remains of Aa Kukui Heiau are found here, along with petroglyphs. Holoholoku Heiau was once a place of human sacrifice, while Poliahu Heiau is named after the snow goddess.

73 I2 KAULU PAOA HEIAU

NATURAL SITE

LOCATION: Kauai, Hawaiian Islands

NOTES: Sacred hula dances were once enacted to impress Laka, the goddess of hula. Fern wreaths and other offerings are left in the crevices of the cliff face.

74 I2 KOKO CRATER

NATURAL SITE

LOCATION: Oahu, Hawaiian Islands

NOTES: Crater seen by the locals as an imprint left by the vagina of the goddess Kapo as she came to lure the pig-god Kamapua'a from her brother Pele.

75 I2 KAILAU

A.D. 1100–1450

LOCATION: Oahu, Hawaiian Islands

NOTES: The first chief of Oahu resided here. Once a giant, he turned himself into a mountain ridge. An open platform temple, Ulupo Heiau, over 30 ft (9 m) high is attributed to the Menehune – people said to have built some of the island's stone mounds.

76 I2 MAKAHA VALLEY

AFTER A.D. 1500

LOCATION: Oahu, Hawaiian Islands

NOTES: Kaneiki Heiau, a Lono temple.

dedicated to the god of agriculture, was used as a war temple until the early 19th century.

77 J2 BLACK ROCK

NATURAL SITE

LOCATION: Maui, Hawaiian Islands

NOTES: The westernmost point in Hawaii, believed to be the place where the spirits begin their journey to the ancestral home.

78 J2 HALEKII AND PIHANA HEIAUS

18TH CENTURY A.D.

LOCATION: Maui, Hawaiian Islands

NOTES: The two temples that overlook the whole island. The former is the house of an idol, the other a pyramid-style mound.

79 J2 HALEAKALA CRATER

NATURAL SITE

LOCATION: Hawaii, Hawaiian Islands

NOTES: Its Polynesian name means "House of the Sun." Legend has it that Maui tried to trap the sun so that it would give the mountain its full quota of sunlight. Hawaiians used to place propitiatory offerings on the crater.

80 J2 KAPUANONI

A.D. 1100–1450

LOCATION: Hawaii, Hawaiian Islands

NOTES: Location of several religious sites, including a fishing temple, the remains of a surfing temple, and a lava tongue with a number of petroglyphs.

81 J2 PU'UHONUA O HONAUNAU

A.D. 1650

LOCATION: Hawaii, Hawaiian Islands

NOTES: Local people came here to appease the gods when they broke the kapu, a sacred taboo. To reach the area, they had to swim shark-infested waters with strong currents. Hale O Keawe Heiau includes the bones of 23 chiefs.

82 J2 PU'UKOHOLA HEIAU

A.D. 1791

LOCATION: Hawaii, Hawaiian Islands

NOTES: Last of the major temples built in Hawaii by King Kamehameha to appease a war god. It was hoped that it would bring a victory over the whole island.

83 J2 MOOKINI HEIAU

A.D. 480

LOCATION: Hawaii, Hawaiian Islands

NOTES: One of the oldest temples on the island, built when human sacrifices were made to the war god Ku. Few locals visit the area as it had a kapu – a sacred taboo – placed on it until recently.

84 J2 KILAUEA

NATURAL SITE

LOCATION: Hawaii, Hawaiian Islands

NOTES: See p.79.

85 I6 MARAE ARAI-TE-TONGA

16TH CENTURY A.D.

LOCATION: Raratonga, Cook Islands

NOTES: Most sacred temple of the island, it was the area where the koutu – the priests – anointed the ariki – high chiefs.

86 I6 BLACK ROCK

NATURAL SITE

LOCATION: Rara, Cook Islands

NOTES: Standing alone in a coral lagoon, the rock marks the spot where spirits of the dead pass on their way back to the legendary homeland.

87 J5 VAIAHU

A.D. 800–1200

LOCATION: Maupiti, Society Islands

NOTES: The largest temple on the island,

it still contains the king's throne and ancient burials. Nearby is a sorcerer's rock. Local people believe if a fire is lit near it, they will be cursed and die.

88 J5 AEHAU-TAI

A.D. 1000–1500

LOCATION: Bora Bora, Society Islands

NOTES: Ancient temple near a marae that is a tall natural obelisk surrounded by several smaller stones.

89 J5 MARAE MAROTETINI

A.D. 1000–1500

LOCATION: Bora Bora, Society Islands

NOTES: Associated with Mount Otemanu, and considered the most important temple on the island. Myths surround the temple of those who disturbed the burial ground and the consequences that befell the hapless intruder.

90 J5 TEFANO

A.D. 1450–1700

LOCATION: Huahine, Society Islands

NOTES: Temple ruins that are covered by an immense banyan tree.

91 J5 MAITEREA HILL

A.D. 1450–1700

LOCATION: Huahine, Society Islands

NOTES: Site of 16 marae and ancestral shrines of local chiefs. The site is oriented toward the sacred mountain Moua Tapu. Maiterea-rahi is dedicated to Tane, the god of light.

92 J5 MANUNU

C. 19TH–20TH CENTURY A.D.

LOCATION: Huahine, Society Islands

NOTES: Site of a temple housing the grave of Raiti, the last great priest of Huahine. At the moment of his death, a great stone reputedly fell from the temple.

93 J5 ANINI

A.D. 1000–1500

LOCATION: Huahine, Society Islands

NOTES: Site of human sacrifice and religious petroglyphs. An ahu, a small temple platform, it was dedicated to the gods Oro and Hiro.

94 J6 MARAE MAHAIATEA

A.D. 1767

LOCATION: Papara, Society Islands

NOTES: Site of an 11-step pyramid, once the largest temple on the island. Now only a heap of stones, it was built on the orders of the chieftainess of Papara.

95 J6 MARAE ARAHURAHA

AFTER A.D. 1500

LOCATION: Paea, Society Islands

NOTES: A rectangular pyramid that is the only remaining pagan relic on the island. Its flat top has a wooden platform where human sacrifices took place.

96 J5 MOUNT TEMEHANI

NATURAL SITE

LOCATION: Raiatea, Society Islands

NOTES: Oro, the Polynesian god of war and peace, was born on this volcano.

97 J5 RAIATEA

NATURAL SITE

LOCATION: Raiatea, Society Islands

NOTES: See p.98.

98 N7 EASTER ISLAND

NATURAL SITE

LOCATION: Eastern Pacific

NOTES: See pp.94–95.

CHINA, JAPAN, & KOREA

The map for these listings is on pp.152-153.

● Site still in use

■ Site no longer in use

① G2 ERDENEZEU HIID
A.D. 1586
LOCATION: Hartorin, Mongolia
NOTES: Huge complex with 108 stupas and three temples in its courtyard; the first Buddhist center in the country.

② H1 GANDANTEGCHINLEN HIID
A.D. 1840
LOCATION: Ulan Bator, Mongolia
NOTES: One of the largest and most important complexes in Mongolia, containing four temples.

③ H1 THE FOUR HOLY PEAKS
NATURAL SITES
LOCATION: Mongolia
NOTES: The four sacred mountains – Tsetseegen, Songino Hairhan, Bayanzurh, and Chingelei – that surround Ulan Bator.

④ I2 GUNDGAVIRLAN HIID
A.D. 1660
LOCATION: Mongolia
NOTES: Temple, once home to over 1,000 monks until Stalin's reign of terror. It has recently reopened.

⑤ D4 KONQI SACRED CIRCLE
BEFORE 1000 B.C.
LOCATION: Sinkiang, China
NOTES: Remote site discovered less than 20 years ago, comprising ancient tombs and a stone circle. Stakes marking out the stones are positioned in the four cardinal points. Goddess figurines and wheat kernels suggest a belief system concerned with the afterlife.

⑥ B6 MOUNT KAILAS
NATURAL SITE
LOCATION: Tibet, China
NOTES: See p.119.

⑦ D7 SAKYA MONASTERY
A.D. 1073
LOCATION: Tibet, China
NOTES: Originally there were north and south monasteries, together forming a center for the Sakyapa order, but the north monastery was totally destroyed during the Cultural Revolution. The walls of the remaining building are lined with sacred Sakyapan relics. Inside the Hall of Silver Stupas are 11 silver-coated pagodas of previous Sakyapan leaders.

⑧ D7 TASHILHUNPO MONASTERY
A.D. 1447
LOCATION: Xigase, Tibet, China
NOTES: Built by the first Dalai Lama, the monastery once housed 4,000 monks. Includes a 86- ft (26-m) high statue of the Maitreya Buddha.

⑨ D7 LHASA
7TH CENTURY A.D.
LOCATION: Tibet, China
NOTES: See p.118.

⑩ E7 SAMYE MONASTERY
A.D. 770
LOCATION: Yarlung Valley, Tibet, China
NOTES: The main temple was said to correspond to the center of the cosmos. It is known as Mount Rirab, with the four cardinal points represented by four pagodas. Small temples represented the islands between the worlds. Two other temples represent the sun and the moon. The complex once consisted of 208 temples.

⑪ F7 SHANGRI MOUPO
NATURAL SITE
LOCATION: near Lijiang, Tibet, China
NOTES: Sacred mountain. On its slopes is a large white cliff where *dtombas* (Naxi shamans) once performed their rites.

⑫ G7-8 MOUNT JIZU
NATURAL SITE
LOCATION: Yunnan, China
NOTES: Sacred Buddhist mountain and pilgrimage site. During the Qing dynasty, there were 100 temples on the mountain and around 5,000 monks in residence.

⑬ F8 QIANXUN PAGODA
9TH CENTURY A.D.
LOCATION: Dali, Yunnan, China
NOTES: Qianxun Pagoda has 16 tiers that reach a height of 230 ft (70 m). There are two smaller pagodas nearby. All three stand on the side of the hill and are reflected in the lake below.

⑭ G8 YUANTONG TEMPLE
9TH-10TH CENTURY A.D.
LOCATION: Kunming, Yunnan, China
NOTES: A place of pilgrimage and the largest Buddhist complex in Kunming.

⑮ G8 MANFEILONG PAGODA
A.D. 1204
LOCATION: Damenlong, Yunnan, China
NOTES: Temple complex supposedly built on the spot of Sakyamuni's holy footprint.

⑯ G5 TA'ER LAMASERY
A.D. 1577
LOCATION: Huangzhong, Qinghai, China
NOTES: Birthplace of Tsong Khapa, founder of the Yellow Hat sect of Buddhism. There are six temples, a monastery, and eight stupas at the entrance to the complex.

⑰ E4 MOGAO CAVES
4TH-14TH CENTURY A.D.
LOCATION: Dunhuang, Gansu, China
NOTES: Dug in the fourth century A.D. and forgotten about until the 20th century, the caves contain the best preserved Buddhist cave art in China and the earliest printed book in existence.

⑱ G5 BINGLING SI CAVES
A.D. 618-907
LOCATION: Lanzhou, Gansu, China
NOTES: In a canyon near the Yellow River 183 Buddhist caves were carved from 197-ft (60-m) high cliffs containing frescoes and clay sculptures. Cave 169 is one of the oldest in China.

⑲ H5 LUOMEN
A.D. 386-534
LOCATION: Gansu, China
NOTES: Area that includes many sacred places: the Water Curtain Temple, the 102-ft (31-m) high rock-carved Buddha, and the Cave of the 10,000 Buddhas, which is now in quite a delapidated state.

⑳ H5 MAIJISHAN
NATURAL SITE
LOCATION: Gansu, China
NOTES: Mountain called the "Corn Rick" because of its shape. Famous for its cave temples and grottoes containing wall paintings, clay figurines, stone sculptures, and a statue of Buddha.

㉑ G5 GAO TEMPLE
15TH CENTURY A.D.
LOCATION: Zhongwei, Ningxia, China
NOTES: Temple rebuilt in the 18th century catering to Buddhism, Confucianism, and Taoism. There are statues of Buddha, the Jade Emperor, and the Holy Mother.

㉒ G7 EMEISHAN
NATURAL SITE
LOCATION: Sichuan, China
NOTES: See pp.114-115.

㉓ G6 MONASTERY OF DIVINE LIGHT
9TH CENTURY A.D.
LOCATION: Chengdu, Sichuan, China
NOTES: Buddhist temple with five halls and 16 courtyards, rebuilt in the 17th century. Houses a white jade Buddha and stone tablet engraved with 1,000 Buddhist figures (A.D. 540). The Arhat Hall contains 500 clay figurines of Buddhist saints and disciples.

㉔ G6 QINGCHENGSHAN
NATURAL SITE
LOCATION: Chengdu, Sichuan, China
NOTES: Holy Taoist mountain with around 100 monks living in various Taoist temples en route to the summit.

㉕ G7 THE GRAND BUDDHA
A.D. 713
LOCATION: Leshan, Sichuan, China
NOTES: Carved into a cliff-face overlooking a spot where the Min and Dadu rivers flow together, the influence of the Buddha was supposed to calm the raging waters. Possibly the largest of its type in the world: one of the ears alone measures 23 ft (7 m) across.

㉖ G6 WUYOU MONASTERY
A.D. 618-907
LOCATION: Leshan, Sichuan, China
NOTES: Monastery containing a hall of 1,000 terra-cotta monks, all with different facial expressions and posture.

㉗ H7 LUOHAN TEMPLE
10TH CENTURY A.D.
LOCATION: Chongqing, Sichuan, China
NOTES: Luohan means a person who has achieved the Buddhist ideal of non-attachment. Behind the altar is an Indian-style mural of Prince Siddartha cutting his hair in renunciation of the world. The temple also contains a golden Buddha.

㉘ I7 HENGSHAN
NATURAL SITE
LOCATION: Hunan, China
NOTES: The most southern of the Taoist holy mountains. In Chinese the pronunciation of the mountain differs from the northern Hengshan (see p.113).

㉙ I8 TEMPLE OF SIX BANYAN TREES
5TH CENTURY A.D.
LOCATION: Guangzhou, China
NOTES: The first temple here was built in the fifth century A.D. and rebuilt in the tenth. A poet celebrated the six banyan trees growing in the courtyard, hence the name. Within the compound is the 17-story octagonal Flower Pagoda. Bodhidharma, the Indian monk who founded Zen Buddhism, spent a night here and eliminated mosquitoes from the area once and forever.

㉚ H5 FAMEN TEMPLE
A.D. 300
LOCATION: Xi'an, Shaanxi, China
NOTES: In 1981, after rainstorms damaged the ancient brick structure, a secret crypt under the pagoda was discovered containing over 1,000 sacrificial objects.

㉛ H5 TOMB OF QIN SHI HUANGDI
C. 210 B.C.
LOCATION: near Xi'an, Shaanxi, China
NOTES: Tomb of the first emperor of a united China. The servants who worked on the tomb were buried alive in it to maintain secrecy. Nearby stands the famous army of terra-cotta warriors.

㉜ I4 YUNGANG BUDDHIST CAVES
A.D. 460-494
LOCATION: Datong, Shanxi, China
NOTES: Buddhist caves containing over 50,000 statues, where Northern Wei rulers came to pray for rain. These are some of the oldest examples of stone sculpture in China.

㉝ I4 HENGSHAN
NATURAL SITE
LOCATION: near Datong, Shanxi, China
NOTES: See p.113.

㉞ I4 WUTAISHAN MOUNTAIN
NATURAL SITE
LOCATION: Shanxi, China
NOTES: Sacred Buddhist mountain, site of over 15 temples. They include the Tayuan Temple with a bottle-shaped pagoda, the Longquan Temple, with its large statue of the Buddha, and the Luohou Temple, containing a rotating wooden lotus flower with eight petals opening to show carved Buddha statues on each.

㉟ I5 JINCI TEMPLE
10TH CENTURY A.D.
LOCATION: Taiyuan, Shanxi, China
NOTES: Temple with wall carvings of dragons and clay figures surrounding a statue of the Goddess Mother. In the grounds is the Forever Young Spring.

㊱ I5 LONGMEN CAVES
C. 5TH-7TH CENTURY A.D.
LOCATION: Henan, China
NOTES: Caves in the walls of the Yi River containing over 100,000 religious images. A colossal image of the Buddha Vairocana (Boundless Light) was intended to rival the large Buddha at Yungang in Cave 20.

㊲ I5 WHITE HORSE TEMPLE
1ST CENTURY A.D.
LOCATION: Luoyang, Henan, China
NOTES: Site of the first Buddhist temple in China. White Horse Temple was built to house Buddhist scriptures, brought there from India on a white horse.

㊳ I5 SHAOLIN MONASTERY
5TH CENTURY A.D.
LOCATION: Henan, China
NOTES: Monastery where martial arts began as a form of unarmed combat, founded by the Indian Chan Buddhist monk, Bodhidharma. Outside the temple is the Forest of Dagobas, where each tree commemorates a monk.

39 I-J5 **XIBEIGANG GRAVES**
14TH CENTURY B.C.
LOCATION: Anyang, Henan, China
NOTES: Site of late Shang Dynasty capital, where royal tombs and ruins of the palace were excavated. Local peasants have unearthed oracle inscriptions on fragments of polished bone and shell.

40 J4 **CHENGDE TEMPLES**
A.D. 1713–80
LOCATION: Hebei, China
NOTES: Once the site of at least 11 outer temples, now reduced to eight. The largest is the Putuozongsheng Temple, based on the Potala Palace in Tibet.

41 J4 **TOMB OF WANLI**
A.D. 1583–90
LOCATION: north of Beijing, China
NOTES: One of the most important tombs of a Ming emperor, with a tunnel leading to a small stela. The complex includes underground vaults and ritual buildings above the ground and contained lavish burial goods.

42 J4 **CONFUCIUS TEMPLE**
A.D. 1436
LOCATION: Tianjin, China
NOTES: The second largest Confucian temple in China. In the courtyard stelae are inscribed with names of scholars successful in Imperial Court exams.

43 J4 **FORBIDDEN CITY**
A.D. 1406–20
LOCATION: Beijing, China
NOTES: Vast palace, home of the divine Son of Heaven, the Chinese emperor. The best preserved collection of ancient buildings in China.

44 J4 **TEMPLE OF HEAVEN**
A.D. 1420
LOCATION: Beijing, China
NOTES: *See p.112.*

45 J4 **TANZHE TEMPLE**
3RD CENTURY A.D.
LOCATION: Beijing, China
NOTES: Largest of all Beijing temples. Early decorations of mythical animal sculptures and dragons are probably linked to the Dragon Pool nearby, where prayers were said to prevent drought.

46 J5 **FOUR GATE PAGODA**
6TH CENTURY A.D.
LOCATION: Ji'nan, Shandong, China
NOTES: Possibly the oldest Chinese pagoda.

47 J5 **TAISHAN**
NATURAL SITE
LOCATION: Shandong, China
NOTES: Most venerated of the five sacred mountains of China, revered by Taoists, Buddhists, Confucianists in turn. Imperial sacrifices were offered on its summit.

48 J5 **DAI TEMPLE**
11TH CENTURY A.D.
LOCATION: Tai'an, Shandong, China
NOTES: Resting place for emperors and other pilgrims. It has inscribed stelae, one dating from as far back as 2000 B.C.

49 J5 **TEMPLE OF CONFUCIUS**
478 B.C.
LOCATION: Qufu, Shandong, China
NOTES: Largest Confucian temple in China. The present buildings date from the Ming period, and include the Great Pavilion of the Constellation of Scholars, Dacheng Hall, and Shengjidan Hall. Also in the compound are stones engraved with the

life of Confucius, Confucius' Well, and Confucius Mansions, home of his descendants. Sacred Confucian texts were discovered in the Lu Wall in A.D. 220.

50 K5 **SHANG BURIAL SITE**
1800–1100 B.C.
LOCATION: Sufutun, Shangdong, China
NOTES: The largest of the Shang tombs found so far. The burial pit here had a cruciform burial chamber, and was once filled with rich burial goods, and remains of sacrificial dogs and humans.

51 J5 **DRAGONS IN THE CLOUD HILL**
NATURAL SITE
LOCATION: Xuzhou, Jiangsu, China
NOTES: Sacred hill with the Xinghua Temple at its summit and a grotto nearby containing a giant gilded head of the Sakyamuni Buddha.

52 J6 **QIXIA TEMPLE**
A.D. 479–502
LOCATION: Nanjing, Jiangsu, China
NOTES: Important monastery that was founded by the monk Shou Shezhai. A seventh-century pagoda stands behind the two main temple halls. Each of the pagoda's eight sides depicts the Sakyamuni Buddha.

53 K6 **LEANING TOWER PAGODA**
C. 6TH CENTURY A.D.
LOCATION: Suzhou, Jiangsu, China
NOTES: Shrine to the legendary Xia Dynasty of the 21st to 16th century B.C. Yu himself is seen as the great-grandfather of China.

54 K6 **SIX HARMONIES PAGODA**
C. 14TH CENTURY A.D.
LOCATION: Hangzhou, Zhejiang, China
NOTES: The temple, so named after the six codes of Buddhism, is said to have magical power to halt the tidal bore of the Qiantang River nearby.

55 K6 **TEMPLE OF INSPIRED SECLUSION**
A.D. 326
LOCATION: Hangzhou, Zhejiang, China
NOTES: Built and rebuilt many times. During the Cultural Revolution, Chou Enlai sent the monks to work in the fields, but gave orders to save the temple and nearby rock sculptures.

56 K6 **PUTUOSHAN**
NATURAL SITE
LOCATION: Zhejiang, China
NOTES: "The Buddhist kingdom at the end of the earth." The home of Guanyin (Avalokitesvara, the goddess of mercy) and the eastern Buddhist mountain.

57 J6 **JIUHUASHAN**
NATURAL SITE
LOCATION: Anhui, China
NOTES: One of the four Buddhist holy mountains. Taoists were the first to build temples on its slopes in the third century. Over 5,000 monks once worshipped here.

58 M3 **MOUNT PAEKTU**
NATURAL SITE
LOCATION: North Korea
NOTES: North Korea's highest mountain, the legendary origin of the Korean people. Hwanung (son of the lord of heaven) gave a bear and a tiger the chance to become human if they stayed in a cave and ate garlic for the whole winter. The tiger perished, but the bear succeeded and turned into a beautiful woman, mated with Hwanung, and produced the Korean race.

59 L4 **KUMGANGSAN**
NATURAL SITE
LOCATION: North Korea
NOTES: Mountain sacred to shamans, and a site of magical events and powerful Sanshins. Also important to Buddhists.

60 L5 **MANISAN**
NATURAL SITE
LOCATION: Kanghwa Island, South Korea
NOTES: Like Kumgangsan, a mountain sacred to shamans. It is also a major Tan'gun worship site.

61 M4 **WOLCHONGSA**
A.D. 654
LOCATION: Kangwon-do, South Korea
NOTES: Originally built by the Zen master Chajangyulsa to house the relics of the Sakyamuni Buddha, but destroyed by fire on three occasions, most recently in the Korean War. Some artifacts remain such as a kneeling bodhisattva, some stone stupas, and a nine-story pagoda.

62 M4 **PUSOKSA**
A.D. 676
LOCATION: Kyongsangbuk-do, South Korea
NOTES: Temple established by Uisang, a monk who returned from China with the teachings of Hwaom. It has been rebuilt three times and houses the oldest wooden construction in Korea and the oldest Buddhist wall paintings.

63 M5 **T'AEBAEKSAN**
NATURAL SITE
LOCATION: South Korea
NOTES: One of the three most sacred peaks in Korea. Site of the Ch'onjedan altar where religious ceremonies are performed. In the Tanngol Valley below is a shrine to the mythical progenitor of the Korean people, Tan'gun. It is a popular pilgrimage site.

64 L5 **CHIKCHISA**
5TH CENTURY A.D.
LOCATION: Kyongsangbuk-do, South Korea
NOTES: One of the first temples in the country, rebuilt in the seventh century. Destroyed completely in the 16th century, only 20 original buildings remain.

65 L5 **MAGOKSA**
A.D. 632–647
LOCATION: South Korea
NOTES: The Zen master Chajangyulsa built this temple and helped introduce Chinese Tang culture to Korea.

66 M5 **HAEIN-SA TEMPLE**
13TH CENTURY A.D.
LOCATION: Taegu, South Korea
NOTES: Temple containing 80,000 carved blocks inscribed with the *Tripitaka* (Buddhist scriptures).

67 M5 **SOKKURAM GROTTO**
8TH CENTURY A.D.
LOCATION: near Kyongju, South Korea
NOTES: An image of Sakyamuni overlooks the sea here. It is considered one of the greatest Buddhist works of art.

68 M5 **PAEKCHE TOMBS**
A.D. 475
LOCATION: Kongju, South Korea
NOTES: The tombs of this kingdom remain on a hillside just outside Kongju, though many were looted when excavations took place. The tomb of one of the last kings, King Muryong (501–523), is still intact.

69 M5 **T'ONGDOSA**
A.D. 646
LOCATION: Kyongsangnam-do, South Korea
NOTES: One of the largest Buddhist

temples in the country, with over 65 buildings. Founded by the Chinese Chajang, who reportedly brought back the ashes of Buddha, then enshrined them in the elaborate Sokka Sari-tap tomb, centerpiece of the complex.

70 L6 **HALLASAN**
NATURAL SITE
LOCATION: Cheju, South Korea
NOTES: Sacred mountain considered the counterpart to Mount Paektu in North Korea. Both have a lake in the center. The area has a rich history of shamanistic ritual.

71 L6 **SANBANGGULSA**
NATURAL SITE
LOCATION: Cheju-do, South Korea
NOTES: This natural cave inside a large volcanic cone became a temple during the Koryo period. The water that drips from the roof is said to be the tears of the goddess of the mountain, Sanbang-bok.

72 M6 **IBUSUKI SACRED WOOD**
NATURAL SITE
LOCATION: Ibusuki City, Kyushu, Japan
NOTES: Sacred woods in Japan have been places of veneration and evocation of the *kami* since early times. Found in trees, rocks, and streams, the shape of natural objects often have religious significance.

73 M6 **MOUNT KIRISHIMA**
NATURAL SITE
LOCATION: Kyushu, Japan
NOTES: Sacred Shinto mountain where legendary figure Ninigi no Mikoto allegedly "landed". There is a shrine here dedicated to him.

74 M6 **SAITOBARU**
5TH–6TH CENTURY A.D.
LOCATION: Kyushu, Japan
NOTES: Burial mound park covering several square miles. The mounds, some keyhole-shaped, range from insignificant bumps to larger hillocks.

75 M6 **AMA NO IWATO-JINJA SHRINE AND SACRED CAVES**
NATURAL SITE
LOCATION: Kyushu, Japan
NOTES: Shrine split into two by a river. On the east bank is a cave – the boulder door of heaven – where the sun goddess was lured out to bring sunlight back to the world. At another sacred cave nearby, visitors build cairns around the entrance.

76 N6 **SHIKOKU ISLAND**
A.D. 816
LOCATION: Japan
NOTES: Pilgrimage circuit of 88 Buddhist temples, first chosen by Kukai. At his death he became the saint Kobo Daishi. He is expected to return from the long meditation in his tomb in the company of Miroku, the buddha of the future.

77 M5 **ITSUKUSHIMA-JINJA SHRINE**
6TH CENTURY A.D.
LOCATION: Miyajima, Japan
NOTES: The island itself is holy and the shrine is a pierlike construction. Local people were not allowed to set foot on the island, and had to approach the shrine by boat. The shrine's unique "floating" *torii* dates to the 19th century.

78 M-N5 **IZUMO TAISHA SHRINE**
DATE UNKNOWN
LOCATION: Shimane Prefecture, Japan
NOTES: Oldest Shinto shrine in Japan dedicated to the god of marriage Okuninushi. Ranks with the Ise Shrine

in antiquity and importance. Rebuilt in 1744, it is on a site previously linked with sun worship.

79 N5 YAMATO CEMETERY
5TH CENTURY A.D.
LOCATION: Mozu, Japan
NOTES: Imperial cemetery, the site of keyhole-shaped tombs of Mozu nobles and courtiers; the largest is 1,591 ft (485 m) long and is attributed to the emperor Nintoku.

80 N5 MOUNT KOYA
NATURAL SITE
LOCATION: Japan
NOTES: Sacred mountain with a monastic complex on its summit. Founded in A.D. 816 by the priest Kukai, it is a center of Esoteric Buddhism. Its 120 temples have over 7,000 inhabitants and a famous red *torii*.

81 N6 NACHI NO TAKI WATERFALL
NATURAL SITE
LOCATION: Japan
NOTES: Japan's highest waterfall is regarded as a Shinto god. The Nachi Taisha Shrine, positioned next to the waterfall, and the Seiganto-ji Temple are popular pilgrimage sites.

82 N5 MOUNT OMINE
NATURAL SITE
LOCATION: Kinki District, Japan
NOTES: Sacred mountain pivotal to a Shugendo pilgrimage trail. Pilgrims had to undergo a number of rigorous rituals; those lacking faith were held over the cliff until they became enlightened.

83 N5 KUMANO HAYATAMA
14TH CENTURY A.D.
LOCATION: Yoshino Kumano, Japan
NOTES: The main festival here celebrates the arrival of the Kumano gods – Hayatama, Ketsu Miko, and Fusumi – from the Izumo province. The nearby Kannokura-jinja is where the gods arrived. Kumano Hongu is the largest of the shrines. It has been a sacred site since the first century B.C.

84 N5 ISE SHRINE
3RD CENTURY A.D.
LOCATION: Shima-hanto Peninsula, Japan
NOTES: *See p.108.*

85 N5 NARA
7TH CENTURY A.D.
LOCATION: Kinki District, Japan
NOTES: *See p.110.*

86 N5 ISHIYAMA-DERA TEMPLE
7TH CENTURY A.D.
LOCATION: Lake Biwa, Japan
NOTES: The temple has been important to the Tendai sect since the eighth century. Also nearby are the Omi Shrine and the Hiyoshi Taisha Shrine, containing the seven divine patronesses of Mount Hiei.

87 N5 ENRYAKU-JI TEMPLE
8TH CENTURY A.D.
LOCATION: Mount Hiei, Honshu, Japan
NOTES: Built by Emperor Kammu to ward off evil spirits from the north. The Tendai school was founded here. It dominated religious affairs for many centuries. At its peak, over 3,000 buildings stood on the site.

88 N5 KORYU-JI TEMPLE
7TH CENTURY A.D.
LOCATION: Kyoto, Japan
NOTES: Founded by Prince Shotoku, it houses sacred ninth-century statues.

89 N5 KIYOMIZU-DERA TEMPLE
8TH CENTURY A.D.
LOCATION: Kyoto, Japan
NOTES: Temple affiliated with the Hosso sect of Buddhism. The waters of the nearby Otowa waterfall are sacred and are believed to have medicinal qualities. Its Jishu Shrine also has qualities that are meant to improve the love life of Buddhist pilgrims.

90 N5 EIKAN-DO TEMPLE
A.D. 856
LOCATION: Kyoto, Japan
NOTES: Temple honoring the priest Eikan. At the south end of the complex stands the famous statue of Mikaeri Amida, in English called "Buddha Glancing Backward."

91 N5 FUSHIMI-INARI
9TH CENTURY A.D.
LOCATION: Kyoto, Japan
NOTES: Five shrines dedicated to Inari, the god of rice. Dozens of statues and red *torii* line the route on Mount Inari, where the complex is based.

92 N5 CHIKUBUSHIMA
NATURAL SITE
LOCATION: Lake Biwa, near Kyoto, Japan
NOTES: Rocky island in Lake Biwa sacred to Benzai-ten, goddess of fortune.

93 O5 MOUNT ONTAKE
NATURAL SITE
LOCATION: Nagano Prefecture, Japan
NOTES: Active volcano. A major pilgrimage site for centuries, sacred site of both a god and a goddess. The summit is called Jigokudani, the Valley of Hell, due to the volcanic vapor and the sense of fear that the mountain creates. There are five lakes on the mountain; holy water flows from two of them.

94 N5 EIHEI-JI
13TH CENTURY A.D.
LOCATION: Fukui, Japan
NOTES: Founded in 1244 by Dogen, it is one of the most important Zen Buddhist centers in the world. One of the two head temples for the Soto sect, the complex has over 70 buildings.

95 N5 MOUNT HAKU
NATURAL SITE
LOCATION: Kaga, Japan
NOTES: Sacred mountain with a small shrine at the summit of one of its peaks. Early center of mountain cult and later of the ascetic Shugendo Buddhism.

96 O5 MOUNT TATEYAMA
NATURAL SITE
LOCATION: Honshu, Japan
NOTES: Sacred mountain: a shrine was built on one of the peaks in A.D. 703.

97 O5 ZENKO-JI TEMPLE
7TH CENTURY A.D.
LOCATION: Nagano, Japan
NOTES: Pilgrimage center for millions. The temple is associated with the Tendai and Jodo sects of Buddhism, and there are about 60 other affiliated temples throughout Japan.

98 O5 MOUNT FUJI
NATURAL SITE
LOCATION: near Tokyo, Japan
NOTES: *See p.109.*

99 O5 THE BUDDHA OF KAMAKURA
A.D. 1252
LOCATION: near Tokyo, Japan
NOTES: *See p.111.*

100 O5 SENSO-JI TEMPLE
7TH CENTURY A.D.
LOCATION: Asakusa, Tokyo, Japan
NOTES: Temple built to house a golden image of Kannon that, according to legend, was fished out of the nearby Sumidagawa River. The image has remained in the same position since A.D. 628.

101 O5 NIKKO
A.D. 767
LOCATION: near Tokyo, Japan
NOTES: *See p.109.*

102 O4 OTAWA-IKE POND
NATURAL SITE
LOCATION: Niigata Prefecture, Japan
NOTES: Sacred to Takigamu, a dragon or snake god evoked here who first rose from the water when a beautiful female temple servant washed her apron stained with menstrual blood in the pond. She became the god's wife.

103 O4 DEWA SANZAN
NATURAL SITE
LOCATION: Northern Honshu, Japan
NOTES: Three sacred peaks – Haguro, Gas, and Yudono – worshipped for centuries by *yamabushi* – mountain priest – and pilgrims of the Shugendo sect. Each mountain has a number of shrines on its slopes.

104 O4 NONAKADO STONE CIRCLE
1ST MILLENNIUM B.C.
LOCATION: Oyu, Akita, Japan
NOTES: Ritual enclosure containing different–shaped stones in inner and outer circles. The sundial was reputedly used in sun worship, though it also has links with hunting and fishing rituals.

105 O3 MOUNT OSORE
NATURAL SITE
LOCATION: Aomori-ken, Japan
NOTES: Sacred volcano with a number of shrines, the most famous is the ninth-century Entsu-ji Temple. It is the mountain where dead souls allegedly go from every part of Japan.

SOUTHEAST ASIA

The map for these listings is on pp.154-155.

● Site still in use
■ Site no longer in use

1 F1 MINGUN PAGODA
A.D. 1795
LOCATION: near Mandalay, Burma
NOTES *See p.104.*

2 F1 KUTHODAW PAGODA
A.D. 1857
LOCATION: Mandalay, Burma
NOTES: Thirty five marble slabs around the pagoda are inscribed with the *Tripitaka*, the total canon of the southern schools of Buddhism, leading to the temple's fame as the "World's Largest Book."

3 F1-2 PAGAN
11TH-13TH CENTURY A.D.
LOCATION: Burma
NOTES: Religious city, once the center of the kingdoms of Pagan and site of hundreds of pagodas and temples.

4 F2 MOUNT POPA
NATURAL SITE
LOCATION: near Pagan, Burma
NOTES: Burma's religious mountain, center of the worship of *nats*, a group of spirits, objects of an extensive folk cult in Burma and Thailand. The *nats* are propitiated with offerings and perform harmful or protective actions, according to how they are treated.

5 F2 PEIKTHANO
1ST-5TH CENTURY A.D.
LOCATION: Burma
NOTES: A religious center, possibly Buddhist, with many earth mounds. Brick buildings were probably used for religious or ritual purposes, and a monastery was also found under one of the mounds.

6 F2 LAKE INLE
NATURAL SITE
LOCATION: Shan States, Burma
NOTES: Place of Buddhist pilgrimage, especially after a period of abstinence. The Intha (the sons of the lake) farm the lake with floating gardens, and worship and appease its spirits.

7 F2 SRI KSETRA
8TH CENTURY A.D.
LOCATION: Hmawza, Burma
NOTES: Old Chinese records speak of the capital of the Pyu people that once held over 100 monasteries. Three large Buddhist stupas survive.

8 F2-3 KYAIK PUN
A.D. 1476
LOCATION: near Pegu, Burma
NOTES: Four seated Buddhas positioned back to back. Four sisters were connected with the Buddhas, and it was alleged that the girls' marriage would lead to the collapse of the Buddhas. One of

the girls married and today only three out of the four of the Buddhas remain standing.

9 F3 SHWEDAGON
14TH CENTURY A.D.
LOCATION: Rangoon, Burma
NOTES: *See p.105.*

10 F2-3 SHWEMAWDAW PAGODA
9TH CENTURY A.D.
LOCATION: Pegu, Burma
NOTES: The Great Golden Pagoda enshrines two sacred hairs of the Buddha and two of his sacred teeth.

11 F2-3 KYAIKTIYO PAGODA
11TH CENTURY A.D.
LOCATION: North Kelasa Hills, Burma
NOTES: The Balancing Pagoda is only about 18 ft (5 m) high, it stands on a boulder covered in gold leaf, positioned precariously on the edge of a cliff. It is allegedly balanced by the placing of a hair of the Buddha within the temple.

12 G2 DOI SUTHEP
14TH CENTURY A.D.
LOCATION: Chiang Mai, Thailand
NOTES: Built to house a relic of the Buddha. To determine the site, a sacred white elephant was released, it made its way up the mountain, and where it rested, the new temple was built.

13 G2 WAT CHIANG MAN
A.D. 1296
LOCATION: Chiang Mai, Thailand
NOTES: The first of the city's Buddhist temples contains two important and ancient relics; a sila marble bas-relief Buddha said to be 2,500 years old, and a 1,800-year-old crystal Buddha.

14 G2 WAT PHRA THAT LAMPANG LUANG
A.D. 1476
LOCATION: Lampang Province, Thailand
NOTES: One of the most magnificent temples in northern Thailand and the oldest wooden building in the country.

15 G3 SUKHOTHAI TOWN
13TH–14TH CENTURY A.D.
LOCATION: Sukhothai Province, Thailand
NOTES: Thailand's first capital and once a vibrant religious center. The old town is the site of numerous temples.

16 G3 LOPBURI
7TH CENTURY A.D.
LOCATION: Lopburi Province, Thailand
NOTES: An important ceremonial center during the Mon and Khmer periods. It still contains the sacred Three-Spired Pagoda dating from this era.

17 G3 AYUTHAYA
A.D. 1350
LOCATION: Ayuthaya Province, Thailand
NOTES: The country's main historical site, and the capital for over 400 years. Within its palace compound stands Wat Phra Sri Sanphet and a number of other temples.

18 G3 BAN KAO CEMETERY
C. 8000 B.C.
LOCATION: Kanchanaburi Province, Thailand
NOTES: Major Neolithic burial site.

19 G3 PHRA PATHOM CHEDI
6TH–19TH CENTURY A.D.
LOCATION: Nakhon Pathom, Thailand
NOTES: The largest Buddhist monument in the world. First erected by the Theravada Buddhists of Dvaravati,

it was rebuilt by a conquering Khmer king in the 11th century. It was restored in 1860.

20 G3 WAT PHO
A.D. 1781
LOCATION: Bangkok, Thailand
NOTES: This is the city's oldest and grandest temple and contains the country's largest reclining Buddha 151 ft (46 m) long.

21 G3 LAK MUANG SHRINE
A.D. 1782
LOCATION: Bangkok, Thailand
NOTES: Shrine enclosing sacred pillar, erected to mark the founding of the new capital of Bangkok.

22 G3 WAT PHRA KAEW
A.D. 1782
LOCATION: Bangkok, Thailand
NOTES: Home of the Emerald Buddha, sacred image and the symbol of the Thai kingdom. The Buddha, first mentioned in the 15th century, is 29 in (75 cm) high and made of a type of jade. It has been repeatedly captured and fought over as the symbol of Thai sovereignty.

23 G5 WAT THAM SEUA
NATURAL SITE
LOCATION: near Krabi, southern Thailand
NOTES: Sacred area with the Tiger Cave Temple, a large forest monastery; monks' cells are built into the caves and cliffs.

24 G5 WAT PHRA MAHATHAT
8TH CENTURY A.D.
LOCATION: Ayuthaya, Thailand
NOTES: Site of an ancient Buddhist temple, reconstructed in the 13th century with a solid gold spire.

25 H3 PRASAT HIN PHIMAI
10TH–11TH CENTURY A.D.
LOCATION: Nakhon Ratchasima, Thailand
NOTES: Buddhist temple. The main shrine stands at the center of a cruciform structure, surrounded by other shrines. An important Khmer temple, comparable to Angkor Wat (*see pp.106-107*).

26 H3 PRASAT HIN KHAO PHANOM RUNG
10TH–13TH CENTURY A.D.
LOCATION: Buriram Province, Thailand
NOTES: The Stone Mountain, an extinct volcano core, site of Thailand's largest Khmer temple complex, and a place of Hindu worship. Perhaps its most impressive feature is the vast avenue leading up to the temple. The central shrine contains a phallic image of Shiva.

27 G-H2 PAK OU CAVES
NATURAL SITE
LOCATION: near Luang Phabang, Laos
NOTES: There are two caves; the lower one is entered from the river, and the upper cave opens off it. Both are crammed with Buddhist images.

28 H2 WAT SI MUANG
A.D. 1563
LOCATION: Vientiane Province, Laos
NOTES: The Buddhist temple grounds are the site of the city pillar, home of the guardian spirit of Vientiane. Selected as the site for a new city by a group of sages, it is allegedly placed over the sacrificed body of a pregnant woman.

29 H2 PHA THAT LUANG
AFTER A.D. 1500
LOCATION: Vientiane, Laos
NOTES: The Great Sacred Stupa, national symbol of Laos and the Buddhist religion. Four wats or temples were built around the stupa, one is the residence of the Supreme Patriarch of Lao Buddhism.

30 H3 WAT PHU
10TH–13TH CENTURY A.D.
LOCATION: Champasak Province, Laos
NOTES: Khmer temple later converted into a Buddhist temple. At the full moon in February, pilgrims visit the temple for the festival of Magha Puja.

31 H3 ANGKOR
9TH–13TH CENTURY A.D.
LOCATION: Cambodia
NOTES: *See pp.106-107.*

32 H4 PHNOM CHISOR
7TH–9TH CENTURY A.D.
LOCATION: near Phnom Penh, Cambodia
NOTES: Hilltop temple with inscriptions. Inside are a number of statues of Buddha.

33 H4 WAT PREAH KEO
A.D. 1892
LOCATION: Phnom Penh, Cambodia
NOTES: Wooden Khmer temple that includes an emerald Buddha made of green crystal and a gold Buddha set with 9,584 diamonds. The roof is covered with 5,000 tiles of solid silver, hence its name, the Silver Pagoda.

34 H4 WAT PHNOM
14TH CENTURY A.D.
LOCATION: Phnom Penh, Cambodia
NOTES: Large pagoda reputedly built to house four statues of the Buddha brought to the site by the nearby Mekong River and discovered by the woman Penh, who gave her name to the city. Later a center for Confucian, Buddhist, and Hindu worship. A site of pilgrimage.

35 H4 TA PROHM TEMPLE
A.D. 1181-1201
LOCATION: Tonlé Bati, Cambodia
NOTES: Temple built on the site of a sixth-century shrine, with a statue of the Hindu god Preah Noreay. Women who wish to have children come here to pray.

36 H4 SAM MOUNTAIN
NATURAL SITE
LOCATION: Mekong Delta, Vietnam
NOTES: Holy mountain surrounded by dozens of pagodas and temples.

37 I4 EMPEROR OF JADE PAGODA
A.D. 1909
LOCATION: Ho Chi Minh City, Vietnam
NOTES: Spectacular pagoda filled with unusual statues of various deities. Center for Buddhists and Taoists.

38 I4 TAM SON HOI QUAN PAGODA
19TH CENTURY A.D.
LOCATION: Ho Chi Minh City, Vietnam
NOTES: Ornate Chinese temple dedicated to a goddess of fertility. Pilgrimage site for couples seeking to have children.

39 I3 NGA HANH SON
NATURAL SITE
LOCATION: Da Nang, Vietnam
NOTES: Five stone hills each representing one of the five elements: Thuy Son (water), Moc Son (wood), Hoa Son (fire), Kim Son (metal or gold), and Tho Son (earth). The largest is Thuy Son: it has several caves with Buddhist sanctuaries.

40 I3 MY SON
4TH–13TH CENTURY A.D.
LOCATION: near Da Nang, Vietnam
NOTES: Vietnam's most important Cham

site, a religious center, and burial place of the Cham monarchs. Many of the 68 Hindu sites are aligned with cardinal points. The main sanctuary is called Bhadresvara, from Bharavarman, the king who started the complex and the suffix -*esvara*, meaning Shiva. Much was destroyed during the Vietnam War.

41 G5 GUNUNG JERAI
NATURAL SITE
LOCATION: north of Penang, Malaysia
NOTES: Mountain with a sixth-century Hindu shrine at its summit.

42 G6 IPOH CAVE TEMPLES
NATURAL SITE
LOCATION: Ipoh, Malaysia
NOTES: Perak Tong Temple is in a cave complex and is decorated with a number of figures of Buddha, including a picture of the goddess of mercy. Sam Poh Tong Temple is also built into the cliff and has a reclining Buddha statue.

43 G6 CHENG HOON TENG
A.D. 1646
LOCATION: Near Kuala Lumpur, Malaysia
NOTES: The oldest Chinese temple in Malaysia. Its name means "Temple of the Evergreen Clouds."

44 J6 NIAH CAVES
BEFORE 1ST MILLENNIUM B.C.
LOCATION: Sarawak, Eastern Malaysia
NOTES: Some of the largest caves in the world, which had been inhabited for around 40,000 years. They contain rock paintings associated with small canoe-like boats that were used as coffins.

45 H8 PASEMAH HIGHLANDS
BEFORE 1ST MILLENNIUM B.C.
LOCATION: Sumatra, Indonesia
NOTES: Site of megalithic statuary. Nearby are stone graves with paintings of warriors and buffaloes.

46 H8 PUGUNGRAHARJO
9TH CENTURY A.D.
LOCATION: Lampung, Sumatra, Indonesia
NOTES: Megalithic remains showing Buddhist and Hindu influences. Inhabited until the 16th century.

47 I9 BOROBUDUR
9TH CENTURY A.D.
LOCATION: Java, Indonesia
NOTES: *See pp.102-103.*

48 I8-9 DIENG PLATEAU
8TH–9TH CENTURY A.D.
LOCATION: Java, Indonesia
NOTES: The Abode of the Gods, a sacred priestly center with over 400 temples. The five main temples of the Arjuna complex are named after the heroes of the *Mahabharata* epic. Originally drained by canals, the deserted complex lay under water for many years.

49 J8 GEDUNG SONGO TEMPLES
8TH–9TH CENTURY A.D.
LOCATION: Java, Indonesia
NOTES: Complex of nine small Hindu temples. Nearby are hot sulphur springs, also considered holy.

50 I9 MENDUT
A.D. 850
LOCATION: Java, Indonesia
NOTES: Buddhist temple complex, restored at the beginning of the 20th century. Relief panels relate Buddhist folk tales. A shaft in the temple allows sun and moon rays to illuminate the central image of Buddha. Still a place of pilgrimage.

51 J9 MOUNT MERAPI
NATURAL SITE
LOCATION: Java, Indonesia
NOTES: Mythical residence of the god Indera (Indian god Indra) who resolves conflicts between heaven and earth.

52 J8-9 CANDI SUKUH
15TH CENTURY A.D.
LOCATION: near Solo, Java, Indonesia
NOTES: Large truncated pyramid associated with a fertility cult and site of a Hindu-Buddhist temple. Women were brought here to test their virginity before marriage, or their fidelity afterward.

53 J9 PRAMBANAN TEMPLE
9TH CENTURY A.D.
LOCATION: Java, Indonesia
NOTES: The largest temple complex in Java, comparable in size and age to Borobudur. The outer court contains the ruins of 224 temples, while the inner court contains eight large temples. The largest, the Shiva Temple, bears carvings from the Hindu *Ramayana*.

54 J9 KARANG TRETES CAVE
NATURAL SITE
LOCATION: Java, Indonesia
NOTES: Cave devoted to the Virgin Queen of the Southern Ocean, who lives in a splendid palace on the seabed surrounded by many spirits. The Javanese make elaborate sacrifices to her before venturing into the dangerous coastal area.

55 J9 GUNUNG PENANGGUNGAN
NATURAL SITE
LOCATION: East Java, Indonesia
NOTES: Sacred Hindu mountain, with over 81 temples, said to be the peak of the holy Mount Mahameru, which broke off and landed when the holy mountain was being transported from India to Indonesia. A major site of pilgrimage.

56 J9 MOUNT BROMO
NATURAL SITE
LOCATION: Java, Indonesia
NOTES: Active volcano where the god Bromo is said to reside.

57 K9 PURU SADA
14TH CENTURY A.D.
LOCATION: Badung, Bali, Indonesia
NOTES: Ancestral and royal temple of the Rajas of Mengwi, guarded by an ancient banyan tree, under which is a stone throne for the demons of the underworld.

58 K9 TANAHLOT SEA TEMPLE
AFTER A.D. 1500
LOCATION: Bali, Indonesia
NOTES: Temple of the gods of the sea. The large number of snakes living nearby are regarded as messengers of Basuki, the serpent and water god.

59 K9 PURU LUHUR ULU WATU
11TH CENTURY A.D.
LOCATION: Bukit Wadung, Bali, Indonesia
NOTES: The "Temple Atop the High Cliffs," dedicated to Dewi Danu, goddess of the sea. The temple is situated atop a sheer 660-ft (200-m) drop into the ocean; the cliff itself is said to represent the goddess' gown of stone. Along with eight other temples, it is thought to protect Bali.

60 K9 PURU TAMAN AYUN
A.D. 1634
LOCATION: Mengwi, Bali, Indonesia
NOTES: Built on a lotus-surrounded island, this temple is oriented in the direction of Lake Bratan (*see following*).

61 K9 LAKE BRATAN
NATURAL SITE
LOCATION: Bali, Indonesia
NOTES: Sacrifices are made here to Shiva, Vishnu, and the water goddess Dewi Danu. The lake is situated in an extinct volcano crater. There is also a pagoda containing five meditating Buddhas.

62 K9 PURA TEGEH KORIPAN
C. A.D. 500-1000
LOCATION: Batur, Bali, Indonesia
NOTES: One of the oldest temples in Bali. At nearby Pura Panarajon, 1,000-year-old symbols found on plinths are said to represent the female sexual organs. A number of sculptures can be found here of Vishnu, Lakshmi, and Ganesh.

63 K9 TAMPAK SIRING
10TH CENTURY A.D.
LOCATION: Bali, Indonesia
NOTES: Site of Gunung Kawi, a memorial cut into the rock-face. Also in the area is Tirta Empul, holy springs that bubble up into a temple. They were allegedly created by the god Indra, who pierced the earth to tap its elixir of immortality.

64 K9 GOA GAJAH
11TH CENTURY A.D.
LOCATION: Bedulu, Bali, Indonesia
NOTES: The Cave of the Elephant. A place of meditation since the 11th century. Hindus still place gifts before the images of Ganesh.

65 K9 BESIKAH TEMPLE
11TH CENTURY A.D.
LOCATION: Bali, Indonesia
NOTES: The holiest temple on the island, situated high up the side of the Agung Mountain. Founded as a shrine to Shiva, it became a Buddhist center of worship in the 11th century.

66 K9 THE DOUBLE TEMPLES
A.D. 1714
LOCATION: Lingsar, Lombok, Indonesia
NOTES: Two temples, one Hindu, the other to local deities, called Pura Gaduh and Kemaliq Lingsar respectively. The two outer shrines at Pura Gaduh face the sacred mountains (Bali's Gunung Anung and Lombok's Gunung Rinjani). The two inner shrines symbolize the bonding between the islands.

67 K9 SURANADI
DATE UNKNOWN
LOCATION: Lombok, Indonesia
NOTES: Site of the Temple of the Sacred Springs, bathing places decorated with reliefs and home to sacred eels.

68 K9 PURU MERU
A.D. 1720
LOCATION: Lombok, Indonesia
NOTES: The largest Hindu temple on the island. The second of its three courtyards is used for sacrificial offerings.

69 L9 WAIKABUBAK
19TH-20TH CENTURY A.D.
LOCATION: Sumba, Indonesia
NOTES: Site of many sacred tombs and of the annual Wula Podhu, a time of respect for the dead, when offerings are made.

70 L8 LEMO
19TH-20TH CENTURY A.D.
LOCATION: Sulawesi, Indonesia
NOTES: Impressive rock-face with a series of balconies for *tau tau* — wooden effigies of the dead. Locals here still have animist forms of belief and thus their burial areas are considered sacred.

INDIA & CENTRAL ASIA

The map for these listings is on pp.156-157.
● Site still in use
■ Site no longer in use

1 H2 MASJID-I JAMI
A.D. 1498
LOCATION: Herat, Afghanistan
NOTES: Impressive Friday Mosque. Religious buildings have stood on the site for over 1,000 years.

2 I3 MOSQUE OF THE SACRED CLOAK
18TH CENTURY A.D.
LOCATION: Kandahar, Afghanistan
NOTES: Mosque containing cloak allegedly worn by Muhammad and the tomb of Ahmad Shah Durrani, father of Afghanistan, who brought the cloak to the country.

3 I1 BLUE MOSQUE
15TH CENTURY A.D.
LOCATION: Mazar-i Sharif, Afghanistan
NOTES: The so-called grave of 'Ali, son-in-law of Muhammad, was discovered in 1480, and a shrine was erected. It is the holiest place in modern Afghanistan and the most important Shiite shrine.

4 I2 BAMIYAN
5TH CENTURY A.D.
LOCATION: Afghanistan
NOTES: Buddhist center including painted cave sanctuaries and two colossal figures of Buddha.

5 K1 SACRED ROCK OF HUNZA
1ST CENTURY A.D.
LOCATION: Hunza, Pakistan
NOTES: Rocks carved with pictures and inscriptions, the earliest dating from the first century A.D. The rocks include various interesting pilgrim inscriptions.

6 K1 SATPARA AND GILGIT BUDDHAS
7TH CENTURY A.D.
LOCATION: near Gilgit, Pakistan
NOTES: Sacred rock carvings including a large standing figure of the Buddha, high up on a cliff face. Nearby at Napur village are the ruins of a Buddhist monastery and stupa, and a cave where the Gilgit manuscripts – Buddhist birch-bark texts – were found in the 1930s.

7 J2 MOUNT ILAM
NATURAL SITE
LOCATION: near Saidu Sharif, Pakistan
NOTES: Mountain regarded as sacred by the ancient Greeks, Hindus, Buddhists, and even early Muslims.

8 J2 BUTKARA SHRINE
3RD CENTURY B.C.
LOCATION: near Saidu Sharif, Pakistan
NOTES: The shrine with enormous stupa was probably originally built by Emperor Ashoka, but it has been rebuilt five times since, each version enclosing the last. Rich pilgrims built over 200 stupas that at one time surrounded the main monument.

9 J2 COURT OF MANY STUPAS
1ST CENTURY A.D.
LOCATION: Takht-i bahi, Pakistan
NOTES: The ruins of a Buddhist monastery include a courtyard that once held as many as 35 stupas and 30 small chapels with Buddhist statues inside.

10 J2 KASHMIR SMATS
NATURAL SITE
LOCATION: Mardan, Pakistan
NOTES: Cave area sacred to Buddhists and Hindus. The Buddhists had a nearby monastery, a ritual bath, and stupas built here. Legend says a tunnel from the main cave leads to Kashmir.

11 J2 PANJA SAHIB
16TH CENTURY
LOCATION: Hasan Abdal, Punjab, Pakistan
NOTES: Site of a rock with a handprint said to be that of the Sikh founder Guru Nanak, who left this permanent mark after catching a rock bowled at him by a fellow holy man. A place of pilgrimage.

12 J2 TAXILA
100 B.C.-A.D. 500
LOCATION: Punjab, Pakistan
NOTES: Major trade center. Trade was often run by important Buddhists and there are important Buddhist sites – a number of stupas and monastery ruins, including the Shrine of the Double-Headed Eagle at Sirkap and the Jaulian Monastery, which contains a healing Buddha that allegedly cures pilgrims.

13 K3 TOMB OF JAHANGIR
17TH CENTURY A.D.
LOCATION: Lahore, Pakistan
NOTES: Emperor Jahangir was known as "Conqueror of the World." His elaborate mausoleum has the 99 attributes of Allah carved in Arabic calligraphy on the inlaid stone and marble walls.

14 K3 RANJIT SINGH
A.D. 1780
LOCATION: Lahore, Pakistan
NOTES: Cenotaph of Maharajah Ranjit Singh, founder of the short-lived Singh Empire. His ashes are kept in a lotus-shaped urn.

15 K3 BADSHAHI MOSQUE
A.D. 1673
LOCATION: Lahore, Pakistan
NOTES: Built for the Sultan Aurangzeb, it is one of the largest mosques in the world, with an open courtyard that holds up to 60,000 people. Relics, said to be hairs of Muhammad, are kept in a room over the gate.

16 K3 MAUSOLEUM OF DATA GANJ BAKHSH HAJVERI
11TH CENTURY A.D.
LOCATION: Lahore, Pakistan
NOTES: Shrine of the most important Sufi saint in Pakistan, the author of a celebrated book on mysticism famous for his generosity to the poor.

17 J3 SHRINE OF ST RUKN-UD-DIN ABUL FATAH
14TH CENTURY A.D.
LOCATION: Multan, Punjab, Pakistan
NOTES: Shrine to the Sufi scholar and saint. Regarded as the patron of Multan, his shrine is a center for devotees.

18 J3 UCH SHARIFF

13TH CENTURY A.D.

LOCATION: Punjab, Pakistan

NOTES: Once a major cultural and religious center, still a pilgrimage site famous for its numerous Sufi shrines. Sikhs revere the town as a place where relics of the Sikh founder Guru Nanak are kept.

19 I3 MEHRGAHR

C. 6000 B.C.

LOCATION: Baluchistan, Pakistan

NOTES: The earliest village discovered in central Asia, it contained a number of burials that included geometric microliths.

20 I4 MIR MASUM SHAH

A.D. 1614

LOCATION: Sukkur, Sind, Pakistan

NOTES: Once an important pilgrimage center, Sukkur contains the mausoleums of many Muslim saints. The most spectacular building is the minaret of Mir Masum Shah, 84 ft (26 m) high.

21 I4 MOHENJO-DARO

2500–1500 B.C.

LOCATION: Sind, Pakistan

NOTES: *See pp.124–125.*

22 I4 SEHWAN SHARIF

14TH CENTURY A.D.

LOCATION: Sind, Pakistan

NOTES: Shrine of Lal Qalandar Shah Baz, a Sufi saint. On the anniversary of the saint's death, a three-day festival is held in front of the blue-tiled mausoleum.

23 I4 MANGHOPIR

13TH CENTURY A.D.

LOCATION: Sind, Pakistan

NOTES: Shrine of the Muslim saint Mangho, guarded by crocodiles. Site of a healing sulphur spring.

24 I4 MONUMENT TO MIAN ABOUL HAKIM

AFTER A.D. 1500

LOCATION: Karachi, Sind, Pakistan

NOTES: A monument to this Sufi saint revered by followers throughout Pakistan. The green-domed building is built over a spring. A major pilgrimage site.

25 I5 MAKLI HILL

14TH CENTURY A.D.

LOCATION: near Thatta, Sind, Pakistan

NOTES: Necropolis covering 6 sq mi (15.5 sq km), thought to be the largest in the world.

26 I5 JAMI MASJID

A.D. 1644–47

LOCATION: Thatta, Sind, Pakistan

NOTES: Built by Shah Jahan, this huge mosque has a spectacular tiled interior.

27 I5 CHAUKUNDI

13TH–16TH CENTURY A.D.

LOCATION: near Karachi, Sind, Pakistan

NOTES: Ornate monumental tombs in a vast ancient cemetery.

28 M4 LUMBINI

3RD CENTURY B.C.

LOCATION: Western Tarai, Nepal

NOTES: One of the most important sites in the Buddhist world, the Sacred Garden is the birthplace of the Buddha himself. Its centerpiece is the Maya Devi Mandir. The Ashokan Pillar is the oldest monument in Nepal, dating to 294 B.C.

29 M4 LAKE TAUDAHA

NATURAL SITE

LOCATION: Kathmandu Valley, Nepal

NOTES: Sacred lake said to be the home of the serpent god Karkatoka. Legend says that when the valley was drained, it became a home for snakes, with the god coiled around a priceless treasure.

30 M4 SESH NARAYAN

17TH CENTURY A.D.

LOCATION: Kathmandu Valley, Nepal

NOTES: Holy to Buddhists and Hindus, it consists of four tranquil pools and a temple. Buddhists call it Yanglesho, the place where Guru Padma Sambhava wrestled a *naga*, a mythical snake, and turned it to stone. Padma Sambhava Cave, said to have the "footprints" of its namesake, is a major pilgrimage site for Tibetan Buddhists.

31 M4 KUMBESHWAR MAHADEV

A.D. 1392

LOCATION: Patan, Nepal

NOTES: The city's oldest temple, dedicated to Shiva. The pagoda's name comes from an incident when a pilgrim dropped a pot in the sacred lake of Gosainkund, near Kathmandu. The same pot later appeared at this site, prompting belief in an underground route to the lake.

32 M4 KUMARI CHOWK

A.D. 1757

LOCATION: Kathmandu, Nepal

NOTES: Site of the gilded cage of the "living goddess," Raj Kumari. Based around the cult of a girl worshipped as a living incarnation of Durga, the demon-slaying Hindu mother goddess. Candidates are placed in a dark room, surrounded by buffalo heads, while men dressed in demon masks dance around. The girl showing the least fear is then chosen as the next Kumari. When she reaches puberty, she is replaced.

33 M4 THE JAGANNATH AND TALEJU TEMPLES

16TH CENTURY A.D.

LOCATION: Kathmandu, Nepal

NOTES: The Jagannath Mandir contains a number of erotic carvings. The Taleju Mandir, dedicated to the goddess Taleju Bhawani, is Kathmandu's largest temple; a king decreed that no other building was to exceed it in height.

34 M4 SETO MACHHENDRANATH

17TH CENTURY A.D.

LOCATION: Kathmandu, Nepal

NOTES: One of the two main shrines to the protector god. Once a year his white mask is wheeled around the city.

35 M4 KATHESIMBHU STUPA

17TH CENTURY A.D.

LOCATION: Kathmandu, Nepal

NOTES: The city's largest stupa. Legend says it was built from leftover earth from the Swayambhu Stupa.

36 M4 SWAYAMBHU STUPA

C. 100–0 B.C.

LOCATION: Khatmandu, Nepal

NOTES: Hill previously used for animist rites, Now considered the major "power point" in the valley and one of the most important Tantric Buddhist sites. Buddhist statues can be found at the bottom of the stupa, correlating to the four elements. At the top of the stupa, a gilded cube has eyes representing the all-seeing Adi Buddha.

37 M4 BOUDHANATH

5TH CENTURY A.D.

LOCATION: Kathmandu Valley, Nepal

NOTES: Huge stupa, the most important Tibetan Buddhist monument outside Tibet. According to myth, when a daughter of Indra stole flowers from heaven, she was placed back on earth as a lowly daughter. She prospered by creating a stupa in honor of the Buddha of the Previous Age. Pilgrims flock here.

38 M4 PASHUPATINATH

17TH CENTURY A.D.

LOCATION: Kathmandu Valley, Nepal

NOTES: Holiest Hindu site in the country, based on the Bagmati River – most holy Hindu river in the country. Site of ritual bathing, where Shiva is represented in the form of Pashupati, Lord of the Animals.

39 M4 CHANGU NARAYAN

4TH CENTURY A.D.

LOCATION: Nepal

NOTES: Ancient Vaishnava temple complex, previously an animist shrine. The main temple is surrounded by other smaller ones.

40 M4 INDRESHWAR

A.D. 1294

LOCATION: Panauti, Nepal

NOTES: Dedicated to Shiva, the oldest surviving pagoda in Nepal. Its shrine area, the Khware, is considered a *tirtha* – a sacred power place. On January 14, pilgrims come here for ritual bathing.

41 M4 JANAKI MANDIR

10TH–3RD CENTURY B.C.

LOCATION: Janakpur, Nepal

NOTES: In Hindu mythology, the capital of the ancient kingdom of Mithila. It is here that Rama, the mortal form of Vishnu, strung a magic bow to win the hand of Sita. Sacred ponds here are used for ritual bathing.

42 O5 MAINIMATI RUINS

7TH–12TH CENTURY A.D.

LOCATION: Chittagong, Bangladesh

NOTES: Center of Buddhist culture for five centuries, including over 50 sites. At Koltila Mura three stupas represent Buddha, Dharma, and Sangha – the "Three Jewels of Buddhism." The plan of the central stupa is in the shape of a *dharma chakra*, the wheel of the law.

43 O5 DARGAH OF BAYAZID BISTAMI

10TH CENTURY A.D.

LOCATION: Chittagong, Bangladesh

NOTES: Muslim shrine with special pond full of turtles allegedly changed from bad spirits by the intervention of this saint.

44 N5 BAGERHAT

15TH CENTURY A.D.

LOCATION: Bangladesh

NOTES: Site of the mausoleum of Sufi mystic Khan Jahan Ali. There are also 360 mosques dedicated to him, scattered over the area surrounding Bagerhat.

45 N4 SOMAPURI VIHARA

8TH CENTURY A.D.

LOCATION: Paharpur, East Bengal, India

NOTES: Vast ruined Buddhist temple complex covering 27 ac (11 ha), occupied by Buddhists, Jains, and Hindus. Includes various stupas and a monastery. Over 170 monastic cells line the walls on the outside of the monastery, possibly the burial places of Buddhist saints.

46 N4 ADINA MOSQUE

14TH CENTURY A.D.

LOCATION: Pandua, West Bengal, India

NOTES: Impressive mosque, built on the site of a former Hindu shrine.

47 M4 NALANDA

7TH CENTURY A.D.

LOCATION: Bihar, India

NOTES: Until it was sacked by the Afghans in the 12th century A.D., Nalanda was one of the greatest universities in the world. The ruins include temples, monasteries, stupas, and images of the Buddha, venerated by modern pilgrims.

48 M4-5 BODH GAYA

7TH CENTURY A.D.

LOCATION: Bihar, India

NOTES: The most important site of Buddhist pilgrimage in the world. Within the grounds of the seventh-century Mahabodhi Temple is a bo-tree said to be directly descended from the original tree under which Buddha sat and meditated before finally reaching enlightenment. Beneath the present tree, a red sandstone slab known as the Diamond Throne marks the spot.

49 M4 AYODHYA

5TH CENTURY A.D.

LOCATION: Uttar Pradesh, India

NOTES: One of the seven holy Hindu cities and a major pilgrimage site revered for its mention in the *Ramayana* as the birthplace of Rama.

50 M4 SARNATH

C. 262 B.C.

LOCATION: Uttar Pradesh, India

NOTES: Site of Buddha's first sermon and one of the holiest cities in India. The great Buddhist emperor Ashoka erected magnificent stupas and monasteries here, as well as a lofty stone pillar.

51 M4 VARANASI

NATURAL SITE

LOCATION: Uttar Pradesh, India

NOTES: *See pp.120–121.*

52 M4 JAUNPUR

14TH CENTURY A.D.

LOCATION: Eastern Uttar Pradesh, India

NOTES: Founded in 1359 by Firuz Shih Tuhlug, Jaunpur became the capital of the independent Muslim Sharqi kingdom. Mosques were built on the ruins of earlier Hindu, Jain, and Buddhist temples, shrines, and monasteries.

53 L4 ALLAHABAD

C. 4TH CENTURY A.D.

LOCATION: Central Uttar Pradesh, India

NOTES: At the confluence of the river Ganges and the river Jamuna, site of one of the largest religious festivals in the world. Millions of Hindus come here to immerse themselves in the sacred waters. Allahabad stands on the site of an earlier Aryan holy city.

54 L3 HARIDWAR

NATURAL SITE

LOCATION: Northern Uttar Pradesh, India

NOTES: One of the seven sacred Hindu cities, positioned where the river Ganges leaves the Himalayas. Millions of pilgrims make the journey here every 12 years. The Har ki Pairi Ghat is placed where the Ganges changes and is sanctified by Vishnu's footprint.

55 K4 DARGAH MOSQUE

1570 A.D.

LOCATION: Uttar Pradesh, India

NOTES: Although the Mughal sultan, Akbar (1542–1605) was a Muslim, he was interested in a syncretistic religion that would unite all the other major religions and had this mosque built, reputed to be a copy of one at Mecca.

56 K4 MATHURA

C. A.D. 0-200
LOCATION: Uttar Pradesh, India
NOTES: One of the seven sacred Hindu cities and a major pilgrimage center. Amongst the thousands of temples here is the spot where Krishna was born.

57 K4 TAJ MAHAL

A.D. 1651-53
LOCATION: Agra, Uttar Pradesh, India
NOTES: Built by the Moghul emperor Shah Jehan in memory of his wife Mumtaz, and to house her tomb as well as his own. Regarded as one of the most beautiful buildings in the world.

58 L4 KHAJURAHO

A.D. 950-1050
LOCATION: Madhya Pradesh, India
NOTES: There were once 85 Hindu temples at this site, though only 20 of them survive. Most of these were dedicated to Vishnu and Shiva.

59 K3 GOLDEN TEMPLE

16TH CENTURY A.D.
LOCATION: Amritsar, Punjab, India
NOTES: Guru Arjun built the Golden Temple as a chief place of Sikh worship. It was rebuilt in 1764, entirely in white marble, decorated with copper-gilt filigree work. The holiest place for Sikhs.

60 K3 JAMI MASJID

A.D. 1648-50
LOCATION: Delhi, India
NOTES: This is the largest mosque in India. It was built by Shah Jahan.

61 L4 GWALIOR

9TH CENTURY A.D.
LOCATION: Madhya Pradesh, India
NOTES: Fortress town with several temples within its walls, including the Teli Ka Mandir. In the grounds of the Shah Jehan palace is a deep tank called the Jauhar Kund, where Rajput women committed mass suicide after the Raja was defeated in battle in 1232.

62 K5 GREAT STUPA OF SANCHI

3RD-1ST CENTURY B.C.
LOCATION: Sanchi, Madhya Pradesh, India
NOTES: On a hill are many Buddhist structures including stupas placed here by the emperor Ashoka after his conversion in the third century B.C. The Great Stupa is the main structure on the hill. It stands 52 ft (16 m) high.

63 K5 UJJAIN

13TH CENTURY A.D.
LOCATION: Madhya Pradesh, India
NOTES: One of the seven holy Hindu cities. The Mahakaleshwar Temple was one of the most sacred in India until it was destroyed in the 13th century.

64 J5 MOUNT ABU

NATURAL SITE
LOCATION: Rajasthan, India
NOTES: Sacred mountain, according to ancient mythology, created by the gods. On its summit, Jains built a large temple complex, which includes the 11th-century Vimala Sha Temple and the 13th-century Vastapula Temple.

65 J5 DEVNI MORI

2ND CENTURY A.D.
LOCATION: Gujarat, India
NOTES: Regarded as a holy place for several centuries. The stupa and monastery uncovered here are similar to Buddhist monuments found in Pakistan, and both show Gandharan influence.

66 J5 SIDI BASHIR MOSQUE

A.D. 1424
LOCATION: Ahmedabad, Gujarat, India
NOTES: Mosque renowned for its shaking minarets. When one is shaken, the other shakes in sympathy. It was built by the founder of the town, Ahmed Shah.

67 J5 GIRNAR HILL

12TH CENTURY A.D.
LOCATION: Junagadh, Gujarat, India
NOTES: Hill covered in temples, sacred to Jains. At its foot is the sacred tank of Damodar Kund, at the peak five Jain temples. The largest and oldest is the Temple of Neminath.

68 J6 NASIK

1ST CENTURY A.D.
LOCATION: Maharashtra, India
NOTES: An important religious center that attracts many Hindu pilgrims. Legendary home of Rama, the most important site is the Saivite Jyotirlinga Temple. Early Jain cave temples date to the first century A.D.

69 K6 ELLORA CAVES

6TH-8TH CENTURY A.D.
LOCATION: Maharashtra, India
NOTES: See p.123.

70 K6 AJANTA CAVES

200 B.C.
LOCATION: Maharashtra, India
NOTES: See p.123.

71 J6 ELEPHANTA ISLAND

A.D. 450-750
LOCATION: Bombay, Maharashtra, India
NOTES: Four temples have been carved out of the cliffs high up above the water. The main cave is devoted to Shiva.

72 J6 KARLA AND BHAJA CAVES

C. 80 AND 200 B.C.
LOCATION: Maharashtra, India
NOTES: Hinayana Buddhist cave-temple complex completed around 80 B.C. At Karla, a "sun window" allows light to fall on the stupa at the end of the long narrow cave. The nearby Bhaja Caves date from around 200 B.C.

73 J6 RATNAGIRI

C. 8TH CENTURY A.D.
LOCATION: Maharashtra, India
NOTES: Huge complex with a large star-shaped stupa and two monasteries, as well as shrines. The gate has images of the Mahayana Buddhist Tantric pantheon.

74 M6 JAGANNATHA TEMPLE

A.D. 1198
LOCATION: Puri, Orissa, India
NOTES: Great Temple of Jagannatha, Lord of the Universe, an incarnation of Vishnu. The eastern of the four Hindu sites associated with the cardinal points. No caste distinctions are enforced here; all Hindus are welcome before the Lord of the Universe. His image is carved from a tree-trunk, garlanded, and dressed for ceremonies throughout the year.

75 M6 BHUBANESWAR

8TH-13TH CENTURY A.D.
LOCATION: Orissa, India
NOTES: The temple town or cathedral city. The Lingaraj Temple is sacred to Tribhuvaneswar, Lord of the Three Worlds. His image is bathed in water, milk, and bhang daily. It is surrounded by around 50 smaller temples and shrines. Also here is the Bindu Sagar Tank, said to contain water from every holy water outlet in India, making it the most sacred in the country.

76 M6 THE SUN TEMPLE

13TH CENTURY A.D.
LOCATION: Konarak, Orissa, India
NOTES: Temple designed as a chariot for the sun god Surya. Around the base are 24 enormous carved stone wheels. Seven great stone horses haul at the temple, which is entirely covered with erotic sculptures and carvings.

77 L6 MECCA MASJID

A.D. 1614-1687
LOCATION: Hyderabad, India
NOTES: One of the largest mosques in the world. It holds up to 10,000 worshippers.

78 L7 NAGARJUNAKONDA

2ND CENTURY B.C.-3RD CENTURY A.D.
LOCATION: Andhra Pradesh, India
NOTES: Formerly one of the largest and most important Buddhist centers in south India, named after one of the most revered monks, Nagarjuna.

79 L7 ALAMPUR

7TH-8TH CENTURY A.D.
LOCATION: Andhra Pradesh, India
NOTES: Complex of nine Shiva temples, each dominated by a shikhara tower.

80 L7 TIRUMALA

NATURAL SITE
LOCATION: Tirupathu, India
NOTES: Holy hill, one of the largest pilgrimage sites in India, and site of the ancient Vaishnavaite Temple of Sri Balaji, a god whose eyes are covered in case they might scorch the world.

81 K7 SHRI SHANTADURGA

17TH-18TH CENTURY A.D.
LOCATION: Goa, India
NOTES: Temple dedicated to the goddess of peace.

82 K7 CHALUKYAN

6TH CENTURY A.D.
LOCATION: Karnataka, India
NOTES: At Badami, there are five caves in red sandstone cliffs connected by steps. Two are dedicated to Vishnu, one to Shiva, the fourth is a Jain temple, while the natural cave is a Buddhist temple. At Aihole, the Ladkhan Temple is surrounded by 70 sacred buildings.

83 K7 ACHYUTARAYA TEMPLE

14TH CENTURY A.D.
LOCATION: Hampi, Karnataka, India
NOTES: See p.122.

84 K7 VITTHALA TEMPLE

15TH CENTURY A.D.
LOCATION: Hampi, Karnataka, India
NOTES: See p.122.

85 K8 SRAVANA-BELGOLA

10TH CENTURY A.D.
LOCATION: Mysore, Karnataka, India
NOTES: One of the most famous Jain temple sites, it includes the 57-ft (17-m) high stone statue of Bahubali.

86 L8 KANCHIPURAM

C. A.D. 700-728
LOCATION: Tamil Nadu, India
NOTES: One of the seven sacred cities of India. The main temples are dedicated to Shiva, Vishnu, and the goddess Parvati.

87 L8 MAHABALIPURAM

7TH CENTURY A.D.
LOCATION: Tamil Nadu, India
NOTES: Seaport of the Pallava kings, the first Tamil dynasty who reigned between the fifth and eighth century A.D. It is famous for its Hindu shore temples.

88 L8 RAMESWARAM ISLAND

NATURAL SITE
LOCATION: southern Tamil Nadu
NOTES: Considered the Varanasi of the south. It is believed that Rama sanctified the spot after the battle of Sri Lanka.

89 L8 BRIHADESHWAR TEMPLE

10TH CENTURY A.D.
LOCATION: Thanjavur, India
NOTES: Temple with fortified walls and a moat. A crowning achievement of the Chola kings who ruled the area, it stands 267 ft (63 m) high, with a dome made out of a single piece of granite.

90 L8 SHRI MEENAKSHI TEMPLE

A.D. 1560
LOCATION: Madurai, India
NOTES: Named after the daughter of a Pandyan king who had three breasts. She was told the third would disappear when she met the man she was to marry. She met Shiva on Mount Kailas, who returned here and married her.

91 L9 ANURADHAPURA

C. 260-210 B.C.
LOCATION: Sri Lanka
NOTES: Sacred ancient city converted to Buddhism in the third century B.C. Excavations revealed palaces, temples, and monasteries. Many statues have been restored including one of a recumbent Buddha. There is a 2,000-year-old sacred bo-tree, the oldest in the world, where offerings are still placed.

92 L9 MIHINTALE MOUNTAIN

NATURAL SITE
LOCATION: Sri Lanka
NOTES: Site of the "couch of Mahinda," carved in the rock. Mahinda brought Buddhism to Sri Lanka from India. He was transported by air, and this mountain is the place where he landed.

93 L9 GOLDEN TEMPLE OF DAMBULLA

C. 1ST CENTURY B.C.
LOCATION: Sri Lanka
NOTES: Cave temple containing over 150 Buddhist images.

94 L9 POLONNARUWA

C. 12TH CENTURY A.D.
LOCATION: Sri Lanka
NOTES: After Anuradhapura, the second religious city. Includes a reclining Buddha over 360 ft (110 m) long, as well as Rankot Vihara, a huge domed Buddhist shrine.

95 L9 ALUVIHARA

C. 1ST CENTURY B.C.
LOCATION: Sri Lanka
NOTES: Rock-cut monastery containing frescoes and a reclining Buddha. Monks still worship here. One of the caves is a sort of horror chamber with a number of devil and sinner statues showing punishments in the afterlife.

96 L9 TEMPLE OF THE TOOTH

A.D. 313
LOCATION: Kandy, Sri Lanka
NOTES: Houses sacred relic of the Buddha's tooth. During an annual festival, the tooth is carried around the town in a torchlight procession with sacred elephants in jeweled cloths.

GLOSSARY

AHU
Polynesian stone temple platforms.

ANIMISM
Belief that supernatural beings control the world, and that animals and natural objects have their own souls.

BASILICA
Place of worship built in an oblong shape with a semicircular apse at one end, and sometimes double colonnades. Often of Roman or early Christian origin.

BHAGAVAD GITA, OR SONG OF GOD
Hindu scripture, part of the *Mahabharata,* consisting of a dialog between Prince Arjuna and Lord Krishna. Many Hindus regard it as the main expression of their religion.

BODHISATTVA
In keeping with the Mahayana Buddhist doctrine, it is one who can attain nirvana, but delays achieving it to help others.

BORA GROUND, OR BORA RING
Australian Aboriginal initiation site.

BUDDHISM
Religion founded in the fifth century B.C. by Gautama Buddha, the Enlightened One. It teaches that enlightenment is attained by freeing oneself of all desire to reach the condition known as nirvana.

CAIRN
Mound of stones, often one that covers a grave or burial chamber.

CHRISTIANITY
Religion based on the teachings of Jesus Christ (c. 6 B.C.–c. A.D. 30). Its doctrine was revolutionary in laying such emphasis on love as a redeeming force. Christians believe that through acceptance of Christ's death and resurrection, humans can reach salvation.

CIST
A "box" of stone, it is an ancient slab-lined grave set in the ground.

CONFUCIANISM
Religion and social philosophy founded by Confucius (551–479 B.C.), teaching that harmony between men is reached through *jen* – sympathetic understanding. Confucianism gradually acquired a religious element, with the ultimate "superior" Shang-ti, ruler of heaven.

COPTIC CHURCH
Christian tradition based in Egypt and the Sudan. It broke away from the Orthodox Church in A.D. 451.

CUP AND RING MARKS
Shallow depressions, spirals, and circles carved onto megaliths or stones, perhaps linked to astronomy or fertility rites.

DERVISH
Member of Sufi Muslim sect who vows to lead a life of poverty and moral severity.

DOLMEN
French term for a megalithic burial.

DREAMTIME, OR THE DREAMING
Aboriginal period contemporaneous to daily life, when the ancestors roam and create the world, shaping the landscape. It is intrinsic to existence past, present, and future. The spiritual energy of the Dreamtime can be evoked through ritual.

DRUIDISM
Religion of the Celts centered around sacred groves. Human sacrifices were sometimes carried out. Druidism was wiped out in England by the Romans, but survived in Ireland until the advent of Christianity.

EARTH MOTHER
Figure seen as the eternal source of all things, associated with fertility, creativity, and nourishment.

GALLERY GRAVE
Prehistoric burial with several stone chambers opening off a central passage.

GEOGLYPHS
Lines and geometric shapes carved on desert plains, like those at Nazca.

HAJJ
The Islamic pilgrimage to Mecca; one of the five pillars of Islam.

HEIAU
Hawaiian stone temple.

HENGE
Neolithic circle of standing or recumbent stones, surrounded by a bank of earth and pierced with entrances.

HINDUISM
The majority religion of India. Its many gods are regarded as manifold aspects of the one God, Brahma. The basic tenet of Hinduism is that Brahma is identical with the essence of the human soul, Atman. Vishnu and Shiva are also regarded as major deities.

HUACA
Indigenous Peruvian word for important religious sites, adopted by the Inca.

IMAM
Now a name of the leader of prayers in a mosque, it was once the title given to early Shiite leaders. After the 12th Imam disappeared, it was believed the final Imam would return as the savior, Mahdi.

INIKSHUIT
Cairn of the North American Inuit people.

ISLAM
The religion of Muslims. Revealed in the seventh century by Muhammad, it rests upon total obedience to the will of God (Allah), the creator of all things.

JAINISM
Religion that, like Buddhism, arose partly as a protest against the Hinduism of the sixth century B.C. It teaches that everything is eternal and individual souls are reincarnated. Nirvana is achieved through nine incarnations, though it can be achieved in 12 years by ascetic denial.

JUDAISM
The Jewish religion rests upon belief in one God, Jehovah; its sacred scripture is the *Torah,* the five books of Moses. The main emphasis of Judaism is on worship of God and on *halakah,* right behavior.

KAMI
Sacred powers and objects of worship revered by Shintoists.

LEY LINES
Lines joining two or more sacred sites.

MADRASAH
Islamic religious school.

MAHABHARATA
Sacred Hindu book that dates to the first millennium B.C.

MAHAYANA BUDDHISM
Practiced in China, Tibet, Nepal, Korea, Mongolia, and Japan, its main tenet is not to strive for personal perfection, but to help others to attain enlightenment.

MARAE
Polynesian temple site.

MAUSOLEUM
Magnificent burial place erected for royalty or people of eminent social or religious status.

MEGALITH
Large stone usually erected for ritual or funerary purposes. From the Greek *mega-lithos,* meaning "great stone."

MENHIR
Maen-hir (Celtic) meaning long stone, erected for funerary or ritual purposes.

MOAI
The imposing stone figures of Easter Island built to honor dead chiefs.

MOTHER GODDESS
Term used to describe an ancient female deity, often linked to fertility, who nourished and protected mankind. Not to be confused with the Earth Mother.

MYSTICISM
Found in nearly all religions, it centers on ultimate union of the believer with God or the absolute, a belief that all humans are capable of a wider range of spiritual experience.

NAT
In Burma, venerated spirits to whom offerings are made on ritual occasions.

NECROPOLIS
Ancient cemetery or burial place.

ORTHODOX CHURCH
Group of national churches that separated from Western Christianity in the 11th century, and recognized the Partriarch of Constantinople as its head.

OUTLIER
Megaliths in alignment with a nearby stone circle for astronomical or ritual uses.

PAGANISM
Beliefs and practices that do not adhere to monotheistic beliefs, especially not to those of the major world religions.

PAGODA
A many-tiered Buddhist building used as a place of worship, especially in China, Japan, Korea, and Southeast Asia.

PETROGLYPHS
Carvings on natural rocks depicting birds, animals, fish, or men, probably used for hunting rituals or shamanistic purposes.

RAMAYANA
Epic Sanskrit Hindu poem whose hero is Rama, a human form of Vishnu. The poem describes his exile. Probably composed between the second century B.C. and the second century A.D.

RUNE
Religious inscription used by the Viking, Germanic, and Anglo-Saxon peoples.

SHAMANISM
Religion based around the tribal priest, an intermediary with the spirit world. Shamans undergo long training to gain power to achieve the trance state.

SHIISM
One of the two main branches of Islam, it broke away after the death of Muhammad, accepting his cousin 'Ali as the rightful successor and developing its own systems of law and theology.

SHINTOISM
Indigenous Japanese religion based on worship of nature and its spirits, *kamis.*

STELAE
Carved or painted upright stone slabs erected for funerary or ritual purposes.

STUPA
Buddhist shrine in the form of a mound of a dome, often bell-shaped.

SUFISM
Islamic mystical movement originating in the ninth century A.D., whose goal is direct union with God.

SUNNI
The more common branch of Islam (80% of Muslims are Sunnis), it accepts the Sunna, the words of Muhammad, as the equal of those of the Qur'an.

TANTRIC BUDDHISM
Development of Mahayana Buddhism, mostly practiced in Tibet. It stresses the importance of everyday life rather than future nirvana. The "tantras" were mystical texts, developed by the 84 saints.

TAOISM
Based on the *Tao Te Ching* (The Way of Power) of Lao-Tzu (sixth century A.D.), Taoism teaches that there is an underlying universal harmony and individual enlightenment is reached through sensitivity to this harmony.

THERAVADA BUDDHISM
Conservative form of Buddhism practiced in Southeast Asia and Sri Lanka.

TRILITHON
Group of three megaliths, with two uprights and one stone resting on top.

TUMULUS
Earth burial mound or barrow.

VISION QUEST
Rite of passage for young Native American men, when ritual is rewarded with a vision of a personal guardian.

ZEN BUDDHISM
Founded by Bodhidharma, who brought it to China, Zen is a method of meditation that emphasizes simpleness of thought as a means of achieving enlightenment.

ZIGGURAT
Mesopotamian step towers that were surmounted by a temple.

ZOROASTRIANISM
Religion founded by the Persian prophet Zoroaster (c. 1000 B.C.), based on nature worship and purification rites.

BIBLIOGRAPHY

Amadio, Nadine *Pacifica, Myths, Magic and Traditional Wisdom from the South Sea Islands* Angus and Robertson, 1993

Ardagh, and Jones, Colin *Cultural Atlas of France* Time-Life, 1992

Bacon, Edward (ed.) *Vanished Civilizations* Thames and Hudson, 1963

Baines, John and Malek, Jaromir *Atlas of Ancient Egypt* Time-Life, 1992

Ballou, Robert O. (ed.) *The Bible of the World* Routledge, 1940

Bataille, Georges *Lascaux or the Birth of Art* Skira, 1952

Bauval, Robert, and Gilbert, Adrian *The Orion Mystery* Heinemann, 1994

Bauval, Robert, and Hancock, Graham *Keeper of Genesis* Heinemann, 1996

Bamm, Peter *The Kingdoms of Christ, The Story of the Early Church* Thames and Hudson, 1961

Bellwood, Peter *The Polynesians* Thames and Hudson, 1978

Bechert, Heinx, and Gombrich, Richard *The World of Buddhism* Thames and Hudson, 1984

Blendin, Caroline and Elvin, Mark *The Cultural Atlas of China* Phaidon, 1983

Brain, R. *Art and Society in Africa* Longman, 1980

Branigan, K. *The Atlas of Archaeology* Macdonald, 1982

Brooks, David *The Arrernte Landscape of Alice Springs* Institute for Aboriginal Development, 1991

Brown, Peter Lancaster *Megaliths, Myths, and Man* Blandford, 1976

Campbell, Joseph *The Way of Animal Powers* Times Books London, 1984

Chadwick, Henry and Evans, G.R. *Atlas of the Christian Church* Time-Life, 1987

Caine, Hall *The Life of Christ* Collins, 1938

Clarke, Peter (ed.) *The World's Religions: Understanding the World's Faiths* Reader's Digest, 1993

Collcut, Martin and Jansen, Marius and Kumakora, Isseo *Cultural Atlas of Japan* Time-Life, 1988

Colombo, John Robert *Mysterious Canada* Doubleday Canada, 1988

Conze, Edward (ed.) *Buddhist Scriptures* Penguin, 1959

Daniel, David *Thalu Sites of the West Pilbara* Department of Aboriginal Sites, Western Australian Museum, 1990

Davidson, Barry *A History of West Africa* Longman, 1965

Deussen, Paul *The Philosophy of the Upanishads* T and T Clark Edinburgh, 1906

Devereux, Paul *Secrets of Ancient and Sacred Places* Blandford, 1992

Evan-Wentz, W.Y. (trans.) *The Tibetan Book of the Dead* Oxford, 1927
Tibet's Great Yoga Milarepa Oxford, 1951
Tibetan Book of the Great Liberation Oxford, 1954

Eydoux, Henry-Paul *In Search of Lost Worlds* Hamlyn, 1971

Frith, Nigel *The Legend of Krishna* Abacus, 1959

Galwash, Ahmad A. *The Religion of Islam* Doha, 1973

Garlake, Peter S. *Great Zimbabwe: New Aspects of Antiquity* Thames and Hudson, 1973

Goddard, Dwight *A Buddhist Bible* E.P. Dutton, 1938

Goetz, Delia and Morley, Sylvanus G. *Popol Vuh, the Sacred Book of the Quiche Maya* Hodge and Co., 1951

Govinda, Lama Anagarika *The Way of the White Clouds* Rider and Co., 1980

Graham, Stephen *Ivan the Terrible* Ernest Benn, 1932
Boris Godunov Ernest Benn, 1933

Grimble, Sir Arthur *Pattern of Islands* John Murray, 1952

Gyatso, Geshe Kelsang (Norbu, trans.) *The Clear Light of Bliss: Mahamudra Vajrayana Buddhism* Wisdom Publications, 1982

Hancock, Graham *Fingerprints of the Gods* Heinemann, 1995

Hadingham, Evan *Circles and Standing Stones* Heinemann, 1975

Harpur, James *Atlas of Sacred Places* Cassell, 1994

Hawkes, Jacquetta *Atlas of Ancient Archaeology* Michael O' Mara Books Ltd., 1994

Isherwood, C. and Prabhavananda *The Bhagavad Gita* Phoenix House, London, 1947

James, John *Chartres, The Masons Who Built a Legend* Routledge, 1982

James, Joseph *The Way of Mysticism* Jonathan Cape, 1950

Jennings, Francis *The Founders of America* Norton, 1993

Johnson, Gordon A *Cultural Atlas of India* Time-Life, 1995

Joseph, Frank (ed.) *Sacred Sites* Llewellyn, 1992

Knappert, Jan *Pacific Mythology* HarperCollins, 1992

Lamb, F. Bruce *Wizard of the Upper Amazon* Houghton Mifflin, 1971

Laroche, Lucienne *The Middle East* Cassell, 1974

Lewis, Bernard (ed.) *The World of Islam* Thames and Hudson, 1976

Lillie, Arthur *Life of Buddha* Seema Publications, Delhi, 1974

Lundquist, John M. *The Temple, Meeting Place of Heaven and Earth* Thames and Hudson, 1993

McKenna, Stephen *Plotinus: The Enneads* Faber, 1956

Magill, Frank and McGreal, Ian (ed.) *Christian Spirituality* Harper and Row, 1988

Matthew, Donald *Atlas of Medieval Europe* Time-Life, 1989

Michell, John *A Little History of Astro-Archaeology* Thames and Hudson, 1977
Megalithomania Thames and Hudson, 1982

Miller, Mary Ellen *The Art of Mesoamerica* Thames and Hudson, 1986

Molyneaux, Brain Leigh *The Sacred Earth* ,Macmillan, 1995

Mohen, Jean-Pierre *The World of Megaliths* Cassell, 1971

Morgan, William N. *Prehistoric Architecture in Micronesia* University of Texas Press, 1988

Morrison, Tony *Pathways to the Gods* Book Club Associates London, 1978

Mudrooroo *Aboriginal Mythology* HarperCollins, 1994

Murray, Jocelyn *Cultural Atlas of Africa* Time-Life, 1986

Murray, Margaret *The Splendour That Was Egypt* Sidgwick and Jackson, 1951

Nayatuh, Jolanda and Finlay, Gail *Our Land, Our Spirit* North Coast Institute For Aboriginal Community Education

Nile, Richard and Clerk, Christian *Cultural Atlas of Australia, New Zealand, & the South Pacific* Time-Life, 1995

Pepper, Elizabeth and Wilcock, John *Magical and Mystical Sites: Europe and the British Isles* Harper and Row, 1976

Philippi, Donald L. *Kojiki* Princeton, 1969

Radakrishnan, J. *The 18 Principal Upanishads* Allen and Unwin, 1953

Rhys-Davids, T.W. (trans.) *The Question of King Milinda* Dover, 1963

Rimpoche, Lama Kunga and Cutillo, Brian *Drinking the Mountain Stream, Stories and Songs of Milarepa* Lotsawa, 1978

Rimpoche, Lama Kunga *The Miraculous Journey, Further Songs and Stories of Milarepa* Lotsawa, 1986

Roaf, Michael *Atlas of Mesopotamia and the Ancient Near East* Time-Life, 1990

Robins, Don *Circles of Silence* Souvenir Press, 1985

Robinson, Francis *Atlas of the Islamic World Since 1500* Time-Life, 1987

Rojas, Pedro *The Art and Architecture of Mexico* Hamlyn, 1968

Sharkey, John *Celtic Mysteries: The Ancient Religion* Thames and Hudson, 1975

Solzhenitsyn, Alexander *The Gulag Archipelago* Collins, 1975

Soothill, W.E. (trans.) *Analects of Confucius* World Classics, 1910

Speake, Graham *The Penguin Dictionary of Ancient History* Penguin, 1994

Streep, Peg *Sanctuaries of the Goddess* Little Brown, 1994

Suzuki, D.T. *Zen and Japanese Culture* Oxford, 1954

Swan, James A. *Sacred Places* Bear and Co. 1990

Thom, Alexander *Megalithic Sites in Britain* Oxford, 1967

Underhill, Evelyn *Mysticism* Methuen, 1911

Vastokas, Joan M. and Romas K. *Sacred Art of the Algonkians, A Study of the Peterborough Petroglyphs* Mansard Press, 1973

Waley, Arthur *The Way and its Power: the Tao Tse King* Unwin, 1934

Wallbank, T.W., Taylor, Alastair M. and Bailky, Nels (eds.) *Civilization, Past and Present* Scott Foresman and Co., 1962

Wilberforce-Clarke, H (trans.) *Hafiz: the Divan* Octagon Press, 1974

Woodward, F.L. (ed.) *Some Sayings of the Buddha from the Pali Canon* World Classics, 1939

Wright, Esmond (ed.) *A History of the World* 2 vols, Crown, 1982

Yutang, Lin (ed.) *The Wisdom of India* Random House, 1942
The Wisdom of China Random House, 1948

Zimmer, Heinrich *Philosophies of India* Routledge, 1951

INDEX

ACKNOWLEDGMENTS

I wish to thank Yuri Stolyanov for his generous help in finding information about Romanian and Russian sites, Nicholas Shakespeare for information on Peruvian sites, Ted Brown for providing invaluable books on Canada and the native Canadian people, Graham and Santha Hancock for help with African sites, particularly Lalibela, my wife Joy and my daughter Sally for their help with the gazetteer, and my editor Peter Jones and designer Mark Johnson Davies for their hard work and patience.

Dorling Kindersley would like to thank:
Dr. Marian Wenzel of the Bosnia-Herzegovina Heritage Rescue and Dr. Simon Stoddart of the University of Bristol.

Illustrated maps:
Peter Morter: Jacket, pp.66-67, 74-75, 82-83
Val Hill: pp.12-13, 92-93, 100-101
Richard Phipps: pp.34-35, 44-45, 116-117

Additional editorial assistance:
Caroline Hunt, Kirstie Hills

Additional design assistance:
Simon Murrell, Joanne Mitchell, Stephen Croucher

Index: Indexing Specialists

Dorling Kindersley would like to thank the following for their kind permission to reproduce the photographs:
AKG London: 30tl, 46tl, 58tl, 58-59b; American Museum of Natural History: 5bc, 75tr, 75br, 76bl, 77b, 78cl; Ancient Art & Architecture: Inside front flap, 37tl, 42bc, 55tr, 70tl /Mike Andrews 53tr, 53bl, Ronald Sheridan 42bl, 43bc, 52bl, 59tr, 61br, John P. Stevens / Ronald Sheridan 2; ASAP: Mike Ganor 128-129, 158-185 background image;

Ashmolean Museum, Oxford: 3, 53br, 67tl, 100tr, 118tl, 121br, 123tr; Bildhuset: Bruno Ehrs 45tl; Bord Failte: Brian Lynch 73br; Bosnia-Herzegovina Heritage Rescue / Marian Wenzel: 51bl, 51br; Bridgeman Art Library: Nationalmuseet, Copenhagen 49tr, National Museum of India, New Delhi 116bl, 120tl; British Museum: Back jacket tl, Front jacket tl, Front jacket tr, 12tr, 12bl, 13bl, 13br, 17tr, 17 far tr, 19tr, 21br, 25bc, 30cl, 30br, 31tr, 31br, 35tr, 35bl, 35bc, 37bl, 39tl, 43cr, 43br, 61bc, 99bc, 100bl, 117tr, 123tr, 127cl; CIRCA Photo Library: T. Halbertsma 113tr, 113bl, 113br; Bruce Coleman Collection Ltd: Allan G. Potts 70bl, Andy Price 91br; Colorific!: Tony Carr 20t; James Davis Travel Photography: Back jacket tr, Front jacket br, 17bl, 24b, 27b, 35br, 36b, 60br, 64tl, 64cr, 69tl, 69tr, 85tl, 88br, 95cr, 103tl, 103cr, 106 , 109tr, 110tl, 111br; Edinburgh University Library: 29cr; Robert Estall: 75cr, 76tl, 76cr, 80t; Eye Ubiquitous: L. Fordyke 79tr, L. Johnstone 79tl; Ffotograff: Charles Aithie 24tl, 71br, 97br; Werner Forman Archive: British Museum, London 21bl, N Saunders 88c, 66cr, 74tr, 81tr, 81bl, 98tr, 109tl; Fortean Picture Library: 67bl, 71tl, 71tr; FotoPacific: Ross Land 93bc; Sonia Halliday Photography: 9bl, 32cr, 60tl /FHC Birch 40b, 41bl, Laura Lushington 60c, Jane Taylor 26cr; Robert Harding Picture Library: Front jacket cr, Back jacket bl, 23br, 27tr, 31cl, 36tl, 37cr, 37bc, 45br, 64cl, 65tr, 68-69b, 73bl, 80b, 85tr, 102-103b, 104cr, 118br, 119br, 121tc, 124tl, 124-125b, 125tl /Martyn F. Chillmaid 55tl, Claye-Monique 98tl, Philip Craven 16tr, Niel Dyson 121bc, M. Leslie Evans 39b, Gascoigne 40t, Tony Gervis 42tl, Nigel Gomm 122tr, Ian Griffiths 22bl, 22br, Gavin Hellier 119tl, Paolo Koch 101tc, Adrian Neville 38c, J. Pate 23tl, Walter Rawlings 61tr, 78tl, Geoff Renner 20b, Ellen Rooney 48, 49br, Sassoon 19tl,

19b, James Strachan 126bl, Adina Tovy 84b, Adam Woolfitt 7tc, 34br, 38tl, 57cl, 57cc, 61bl, 68tr, 72tl, 72bl, 123br; Michael Holford: 1, 8bl, 82br, 83tr; Jim Holmes: 117tl; Hutchison Library: K Job 97bl, Michael Macintyre 99t, Isabella Tree 122cl; The Image Bank: Alberto Rossi 15tr; Images Colour Library: 55bl, 56b, 62, 63tl, 63c, 63b; CNCA - INAH - Mexico, reproduction authorized by the Instituto National de Antropologia e Historia: 82bl, 84tl, 85c, 87tc, 87tr; Link Picture Library: 108cr; MacQuitty International Collection: 125tr; Magnum Photos: Abbas 29tr, Fred Mayer 25tr; David Muench: 77cr; National Geographic Society: Otis Imboden 77tr; National Museum of Ireland: 4bl, 66bl, 73tc; National Museum of Scotland: Back jacket br, 89tr, 127bl; Office of Public Works: 72cr, 73tr; Orion Press: 108tl, 108bl, 110bl, 111tr, 111bl; Panos Pictures: Ian Cartwright 12cr, Marcus Ross 23cr, John Spaull 126tr, 22tl; Cindy A. Pavlinac - Sacred Land Photography: 57bc; Pictures Colour Library: 50cl, 104tl, 104b, 105b inset; Pitt Rivers Museum, Oxford: 92bl, 92-93t, 93cl, 97tr; Quest Picture Library: Andy Chadwick 18tr, 18b; José Rodrigues: 54cr, 54b; Roskilde Viking Ship Museum, Denmark: 44bl; Royal Museum of Scotland: 91bc; SCALA: 41br, 52tl; Scenix Photo Library: 98bl, 99br; Science Photo Library: Royal Observatory, Edinburgh 15tc; SCR Library: David Lund 46br, Val Whitchelo 46bl; Mick Sharp: Front jacket cl, 70cr, 70 far bl /Dave Longley 41t; South American Pictures: Robert Francis 87br, David Horwell 93tc, 95cl, Kimball Morrison 89tl, 89b, Tony Morrison 26bl, 83bl, 88l, 91bl, 91br; Statens Historiska Museum, Stockholm: 64bc; Dr. Simon Stoddart, Department of Archaeology, University of Bristol: 38bl; Tony Stone Images: Front jacket bl, 109bc /Jerry Alexander 107tl, 107c,

Doug Armand 14tl, 14-15b, 92cr, Dr. W. Bahnmuller 52c, James Balog 94tl, Paul Berger 74cl, Michael Braid 117cl, Paul Chesley 97tl, Cosmo Condina 86-87b, Joe Cornish 57t, D. E. Cox 10-11, Linny Cunningham 55br, C. M. Dixon 105tr, Laurence Dutton 33cr, Richard Ellliott 26bl, Rosemary Evans 50b, Mark Harris 8-9t, Gavin Hellier 46tl, Simeone Huber 33tl, Warren Jacobs 21tr, Geoff Johnson 127br, David Maisel 78br, Kevin Miller 107bc, John Moss 90br, Suzanne Murphy 85br, Murray & Associates 86tl, Dennis Oda 79br, Orion Press 6-7, 44tr, Richard Passmore 17tr, 56t, Peter Poulides 33br, 65bl, Herb Schmitz 102 tl, 112br, Hugh Sitton 15tl, Alan Smith 16br, Robin Smith 83br, 90c, A. M. Stone 42cr, Stephen Studd Back jacket cl, 16bl, David Sutherland 120-121, Tom Till 94-95b, Nabeel Turner 4cr, 28, Mike Vines 74br, 78bl, Jean C. Volpeliere 96tl, Jeremy Walker 13bc, Patrick Ward 96br, Peter Ward 92bc, Baron Wolman 25bl; Telegraph Colour Library: 9tr, 25tl, 32tl; Trinity College Library, Dublin: 67tr; Trip Photographic Library: Anil Adave 123tl, C C 103br, N Chesnokov 45tr, 47c, F. Good 114tl, 114-115b, 115tr, 115tl, W. Jacobs 21tl, 51tr, 91tl, 105b, N. M. Kelvalkar 122bl, I Macri 51tl, S. D. Manchekar 119cl, J. Moscrop 112bl, C. Rennie 127tr, O. Semenenko 47tr, 47br, I. Wellbelove 50tr; University Museum of Archaeology and Anthropology, Cambridge: 6tl, 59tl, 90tl; Viking Ship Museum, Oslo, Norway: 65tc; Wallace Collection, London: 5tr, 101br; ZEFA: 30bc, 112tl, 112tr /Hans Schmied 32br.

Every effort has been made to trace the copyright holders. Dorling Kindersley apologizes for any unintentional omissions and, in such cases, would be pleased to add an acknowledgment in future editions.